An Introduction to *Pragmatics*

Social Action for Language Teachers

Virginia LoCastro
Universidad de las Americas–Puebla

Michigan Teacher Training

The University of Michigan Press
Ann Arbor

Copyright © by the University of Michigan 2003
All rights reserved
Published in the United States of America by
The University of Michigan Press
Manufactured in the United States of America
♾ Printed on acid-free paper

2006   2005   2004   2003   4   3   2   1

No part of this publication may be reproduced, stored in a retrieval system, or transmitted in any form or by any means, electronic, mechanical, or otherwise, without the written permission of the publisher.

A CIP catalog record for this book is available from the British Library.

Library of Congress Cataloging-in-Publication Data

LoCastro, Virginia, 1945–
    An introduction to pragmatics : social action for language teachers / Virginia LoCastro.
      p.   cm.
    Includes bibliographical references and index.
    ISBN 0-472-08822-X (pbk. : alk. paper)
    1. Pragmatics.   2. Language and languages—Study and teaching.
3. Teacher-student relationships.   I. Title.
P99.4.P72 L6   2003
306.44—dc21   2002152247

To the late Joseph LoCastro (Che sia in pace) from whom I learned about cross-cultural pragmatics before the field existed.

Preface

This book presents an introduction to pragmatics, that is, the study of how speakers can mean more than they say and how listeners can understand them.

A: where's the *IHT*?
B: well, Dave's been around . . .

A wants to find the *International Herald Tribune,* which is not in its usual place in the teachers' lounge. B answers by commenting that a fellow teacher, Dave, has been seen in the school. B does not say, "Oh, maybe Dave has it, because he reads it every morning." Pragmatics is interested in explaining the reasons for B's indirect response and how A is able to construe it as appropriate. The conversation ends with A's stating:

A: oh, he is, is he! I bet it's in his office [*exits into the hallway*]

Pragmatics is a relatively new area of linguistics; it became a recognized field with the publication in 1983 of two seminal books, Leech's *Principles of Pragmatics* and Levinson's *Pragmatics.* Despite their important contributions, neither meets the needs of students or second language teachers who do not have a considerable background in linguistics.

This book is designed to meet those needs. It assumes only a rudimentary knowledge of linguistics (and motivation to learn more!). It may be used in introductory courses on pragmatics at both the undergraduate and the graduate levels, for students who are preparing to teach languages as well as for those with teaching experience who want to update their knowledge in an area of linguistics important for second language educators. As a result of the expanding interest in the cognitive and social dimensions of language use beyond single sentences, students majoring in linguistics, whether formal-theoretical or applied, cannot ignore pragmatics. This book is dedicated to helping them, starting from the basics and working toward a solid overview of the field. Students in related fields, such as communication and bilingual education, will find knowledge of pragmatics very helpful for their future careers.

For language educators, a solid knowledge of pragmatics is crucial in developing successful second and foreign language speakers and writers. As long as language education consisted mainly of learning the phonology, syntax, and vocabulary of the second or foreign language,[1] demands on the teachers were relatively limited and those on the learners potentially attainable. However, with the advent of more modern approaches, which reflect research in second language acquisition, classroom practitioners need to expand their knowledge about language and linguistics as well as their competencies as facilitators, in particular with the communicative language teaching approach. They now have to teach how to speak the second language (L2) and to train learners to use it in situationally appropriate ways.

Numerous studies in second language acquisition (SLA) proclaim that languages can only be learned in interactions where meaning is negotiated with native and nonnative speakers. Learners require opportunities to ask questions in the second or foreign language, seek clarification or confirmation of their understanding, and sort out misunderstandings. In effect, learners learn the second or foreign language by interacting with it. Since such activities entail knowing more than the correct pronunciation, grammar, and lexis of the L2, the model of language competence has to include more than linguistic knowledge. It is part of what has been labeled *communicative competence*. One such model is shown in the accompanying diagram. Knowing a language includes organizational and pragmatic competence, comprising both illocutionary and sociolinguistic competence. In other words, pragmatic ability means being able to use language to carry out everyday functions in culturally appropriate ways.

Clearly, an understanding of pragmatics will benefit teachers, particularly those teaching a language that is not their mother tongue or working with learners outside the target language community. Such

A framework for describing communicative language proficiency
(Bachman 1989, 253).

circumstances stretch teachers' roles in developing the pragmatic competence of learners. In second language contexts, with an acquisition-rich environment outside the classroom, teachers and learners can anticipate exposure that supports classroom activities. The foreign language environment explicitly raises the need for a comprehensive understanding of pragmatics and its importance in developing language proficiency. By considering the perspective of both ESL and EFL educators, this book will help them to

- Integrate the teaching of pragmatic competence in language programs and materials
- Understand the problems learners have with comprehension of messages requiring cognitive processing beyond that of the spoken or written word
- Provide insights into comprehension and production of pragmatic meaning
- Evaluate textbooks and other teaching materials as well as assessment procedures for language proficiency
- Assess the value of communicative language teaching practices
- Help learners develop strategies to handle misunderstandings and other communication problems
- Enhance awareness of spoken and written text in the mother tongue and second or foreign languages

Expand knowledge of how language is used in everyday situations, including classrooms

The book is divided into three parts. Part 1 comprises an orientation to pragmatics, introducing a broad definition of the term and the essential notions of the field. The first four chapters explain aspects of pragmatic meaning. Chapter 5 introduces research on the cognitive interpretation required to grasp pragmatic meaning. The following chapter takes up the role of social context, explaining why human beings go beyond the linguistic code itself to pragmatic meaning. All six chapters develop the readers' ability to understand how pragmatic meaning is created and comprehended. This first part provides the theoretical base for the later teaching-oriented chapters, addressing the following questions:

What is pragmatics? Where does it fit with other forms of language analysis? Where does it fit with regard to formal or theoretical linguistics?
What are the basic analytical notions for carrying out pragmatic analysis?
How do speakers convey pragmatic meaning?
How do listeners understand pragmatic meaning?

Part 2 introduces three major perspectives on the analysis of spoken or written texts: philosophical, sociolinguistic, and cognitive. Each seeks to account for pragmatic meaning in an inclusive framework. This part addresses such questions as the following:

What are speech acts? What are speech events?
What are the underlying principles of communication?
Why do speakers avoid saying or writing what they mean? What is politeness?
What is the role of preference structure in adjacency pairs?
What cognitive processes are involved in interpreting pragmatic meaning?

Part 3 explores the use of pragmatics in the everyday world, addressing the value of pragmatic analysis of extended uses of language. A series of topics, supported by studies using authentic data, illustrates how pragmatics can expand understanding of the sociocultural contexts of actions. The following questions are addressed:

> What role does the listener play in interactions?
> How do such features as stress and intonation affect comprehension of meaning?
> How can pragmatics inform studies of cross-cultural interactions and misunderstandings?
> What can pragmatics contribute to increased understanding of the interlanguage of second or foreign language learners?
> How can pragmatics be helpful in research on linguistic and nonlinguistic politeness?
> What is the role of the learner's self-identity in adapting to the L2 pragmatic norms?
> What can a knowledge of pragmatics contribute to research on classroom interactions?

The final chapter focuses on the acquisition of pragmatic ability in language classrooms. Taking into consideration the professional development of teachers of second or foreign languages, problems are raised and suggestions made toward informed practice in the learning and teaching of pragmatic competence.

Each chapter contains numerous examples, including instances of naturally occurring talk in English and other languages, collected in a variety of settings. At times, a constructed example is used to efficiently illustrate a concept. Discussion questions and tasks encourage readers to deepen their understanding of the concepts presented.

Note

1. English as a second language (ESL) and English as a foreign language (EFL) are different learning environments. Most often in this book the terms *ESL* and *EFL* are used as synonyms. In the same way, L2 (second language) includes both foreign and other languages (L3) learners may know. A distinction is made only when necessary.

Acknowledgments

I am grateful to students in my undergraduate Pragmatics courses at International Christian University, Mitaka, Japan, for providing the opportunity to write the first drafts of this book. I thank the Universidad de las Americas, Puebla, Mexico, for supplying me with some free time and some financial support for the revisions.

Grateful acknowledgment is made to the following organizations.

Cambridge University Press for material that originally appeared on pages 4 and 5 of *Using Language,* by Helen Astley and Eric Hawkins (Cambridge: Cambridge University Press, 1985). Copyright © 1985 by Cambridge University Press. Reprinted with the permission of Cambridge University Press.

Fondo al Museo Ampara for cover photograph of a piece of Mayan sculpture from the museum's collection in Puebla, Mexico (Registration No. 52 22 MA FA 57PJ 01372), "Altar Maya," photographed by Bob Schadlkwijk. Special thanks to the Senora Angel Espinoza Iglesias.

Every effort has been made to trace the ownership of all copyrighted material in this book and to obtain permission for its use.

Contents

List of Transcription Symbols   xvii

Part 1. Basic Concepts   1

    Chapter 1. What Is Pragmatics?   3
    Chapter 2. Meaning   36
    Chapter 3. Indexicality   61
    Chapter 4. Entailment and Presupposition   78
    Chapter 5. Information Structure   90
    Chapter 6. Face, Politeness, and Indirectness   108

Part 2. Analytical Perspectives:
    Theories of Pragmatic Meaning   131

    Chapter 7. A Philosophical Approach: Grice   135
    Chapter 8. Sociolinguistic Approaches   155
    Chapter 9. Cognitive Approaches   181

Part 3. Pragmatics in the Real World   203

    Chapter 10. Behavior of Listeners   205
    Chapter 11. Cross-Cultural Pragmatics   226
    Chapter 12. Interlanguage Pragmatics   250
    Chapter 13. Politeness Revisited   274
    Chapter 14. Learner Subjectivity   291
    Chapter 15. Pragmatics in the Classroom   312

References   337
Index   357

Transcription Symbols

The following transcription symbols are used in the dialogues that appear in this volume.

(*irrecoverable*)	speech that cannot be deciphered
. . . , –	very brief pauses
+, ++, +++	longer pauses
(0.1), (0.2), etc.	indicate pause length in tenths of seconds
?	rising intonation
[or // or =	overlap (between speakers)
[*silence*]	nonverbal behavior relevant to the conversation
(.)	indicates a pause of a length typical between two sentences

Part 1
Basic Concepts

Part 1 introduces the basic concepts of pragmatics, providing the tools needed to analyze language in use. The first chapter introduces an inclusive definition of *pragmatics,* which broadens the range of data and texts that can be appropriately studied by this approach to linguistic and language-related behavior. Chapters 2 through 6 take the reader through key terms, illustrating them with natural examples as much as possible, but adding created examples when necessary. The concepts and data are made as accessible as possible to those for whom English is not the first language.

Part 1 addresses prospective and experienced language teachers who wish to obtain a solid knowledge of pragmatics. It lays the groundwork for the later chapters, which introduce theoretical and practical issues in language education. The aim is to provide readers with the terminology and conceptual base for theories and applications of pragmatic analysis in everyday contexts, developed in parts 2 and 3.

Chapter 1
What Is Pragmatics?

This first chapter considers the problem of defining pragmatics. After a survey of different views and interpretations, a working definition is presented. This definition synthesizes different areas within pragmatics, focusing on two salient aspects—*action* and *context*. Both concepts are explained briefly here and developed more fully through the remainder of this volume.

Then the topic shifts to a controversial one, the place of pragmatics within linguistics, followed by a discussion of the limits of formal analysis in accounting for language usage. Finally, this chapter considers the place of pragmatics within an array of related fields—sociolinguistics, cognitive psychology and artificial intelligence, conversational analysis and discourse analysis, ethnography of speaking, interactional sociolinguistics, and ethnomethodology. The aim is to demonstrate that, despite some overlap, each area has its particular perspective, research questions, and areas of concentration. Even within the field of pragmatics, different issues draw the attention of different researchers and educators. However, all share the same aim: to understand human communication.

In research on pragmatics, the use of language to act in and on the world is most commonly called *linguistic action* (Kasper and Blum-Kulka 1993). However, this term, or the related term *linguistic act,* may limit analysis to linguistic forms in single utterances, specifically speech acts such as apologies, compliments, or requests. In this book, the subject of pragmatics is expanded to mean *social action,* a view derived from Clark's description of both speakers' and addressees' actions of language (1996, 17ff.). Because language requires a listener, it occurs within a social and cognitive context that includes both a speaker and a coparticipant, who may be present, on the telephone, or purely imaginary. To make explicit the importance of coparticipants, action, and context, the term *social action* appears in the subtitle of this survey.

Pragmatics explains how human beings create and understand meanings that can be derived only by going beyond the literal interpretation of signals. Linguistic forms are our most common signals—in fact, language is the primary semiotic resource available to human beings. To create and understand pragmatic meanings, the human mind uses inferencing, a cognitive process that underlies many human behaviors. Through inferencing, a listener can infer the speaker's meaning in such utterances as "Could you pass the salsa, please?" The question form here is, in its pragmatic meaning, a request for the listener to pass the needed condiment. It is what is known as a *conventional request;* that is, an expression generally recognized by speakers of English as a request not for information about the listener's capacity, but for the giving of the item mentioned.

Researchers in pragmatics are particularly interested in meanings inferred in nonconventional uses of language. Here is one example of what is called a *conversational implicature:*

A: have you heard the news?
B: I was so shocked . . . she didn't just die, she was snuffed out . . .

B uses inferencing in conjunction with shared background knowledge to infer the pragmatic meaning of A's question: A is introducing the topic of the recent death of Princess Diana. This example shows in a nutshell what pragmatics does—study the "extra" or implied meaning of language use in context.

Communicating and comprehending pragmatic meaning are as natural as sneezing when there is dust in the air. This chapter starts the trip up the garden path to a full understanding of pragmatics. Some of the questions to be answered are

What is pragmatics? What is pragmatic meaning?
How is pragmatic meaning produced by the speaker?
How is it comprehended by the listener?
Why is pragmatic meaning a commonplace feature of natural language use?

What kinds of meaning are there?
What kinds of data are used for research?

Linguistic Pragmatics

The term *pragmatics* was coined by a philosopher of language, Charles Morris, in 1938; however, his definition ("the science of the relation of signs to their interpreters" [1938, 30]) has since been developed. From Morris's location of pragmatics within philosophy of language (specifically semiotics), subsequent accounts of pragmatic meaning have focused on the signs or linguistic forms themselves. For example, Ferrara (1985, 138) defines pragmatics as "the systematic study of the relations between the linguistic properties of utterances and their properties as social action." Clark (1996, 391) labels the field "linguistic pragmatics" to exclude from consideration nonlinguistic elements.

One of the questions linguists ask is how users of a language employ linguistic forms to act in the world. For example, if a mother says to a child at home, "Someone forgot to shut the door," is the mother (1) asking the child to shut the door? (2) reprimanding the child for not closing the door? (3) reminding the child to shut it? Modes of description other than analysis of grammar and lexis are necessary to understand what the mother intends to convey. As this example shows, language is used to act, to achieve some aim, be it strategic or social, with other human beings in a variety of situations in our daily lives.

Ferrara (1985, 137) introduces pragmatics with the following scenario.

> (1) Suppose you and a friend are walking down the street in a foreign city, among people whose language you can neither speak nor understand. (2) A stranger comes up to you and very decidedly, but with a courteous tone of voice, utters a mercilessly obscure sentence. (3) You can wonder how the seemingly continuous stream of sounds is in reality made out of more basic, elementary sounds. (4) Or you could ask yourself how the sentence breaks down into words and how these words are related to one another. (5) In this case, you might even get into an argument with your friends over how you could possibly discover a pattern of relations within the sentence before you know the meaning of its elements. (6) And your friend

might convince you that the right thing to ask is what the conditions are under which what the stranger said would be true. (7) But maybe what you would really want to know is something else: What on earth does he want from me? (8) Well, this is pragmatics.

If the "continuous stream of sounds" (sentence 3) is of interest, then the researcher is studying the *phonology* of this unknown language. However, if "how these words are related to one another" (sentence 4) is a concern, then *syntax* and the structure of the language will be important. Researchers concerned with "the meaning of its elements" (sentence 5) are interested in *semantics,* while those who explore the conditions under which what the stranger said would be true (sentence 6) focus on questions addressed by philosophers of language. Pragmatics takes a different, but related, view of language, that is, the function of utterances in a specific context. If you and your friend ask the following types of questions, you are "doing" pragmatics (Ferrara 1985, 137).

> Is he warning me of some danger?
> Does he want some information?
> Does he want me to do something?
> Is he offering something?
> Is he pointing out something wrong that I have done?

All of these questions—and many more—are located in the field of pragmatics. All reflect an underlying interest in deriving the speaker's meaning or purpose from the linguistic forms used. However, limiting analysis of pragmatic meaning to the linguistic forms is not adequate.

Toward an Inclusive View of Pragmatics

Since Morris's original definition, there have been numerous attempts to explain pragmatics. The main problem is to determine what should be included in the term.

McCarthy (1991) defines pragmatics as the study of meaning in context, without specifying the nature of the context. According to Thomas (1995), context includes the speaker; the hearer; the linguistic forms, which provide the meaning potential; and the physical, social, and linguistic environment of the utterance. She emphasizes that meaning is created in the interaction between speaker and hearer, a dynamic process that is influenced by the linguistic forms and other features of the context.

Thomas's adoption of the hearer as a constitutive member acknowledges the important role of the users of language, both the speaker and the coparticipants. According to Crystal,

> Pragmatics is the study of language from the point of view of users, especially of the choices they make, the constraints they encounter in using language in social interaction and the effects their use of language has on other participants in the act of communication. (1985, 240)

Crystal broadens the original conception of pragmatics, noting the need to include the users and the addressee's linguistic and nonlinguistic response.

Clark wants to expand this perspective, arguing that linguistic utterances are composite signs in which words are accompanied by nonlinguistic signals. "Pragmatics generally includes the study of linguistic utterances in context," he points out, but "excludes nonlinguistic signals and phenomena of 'mere' performance" (1996, 391). For example, pragmatics has tended to limit its domain to analyses of speech acts (Blum-Kulka, House, and Kasper 1989), specifically to what the speaker does:

> *Customer:* I'd like a small cup of that new flavor of ice cream.
> *Clerk:* [*silence*]

Looking directly at the clerk, the customer may use gestures to point to the "small" cup and to "that" new flavor, so that the busy clerk will know quickly which size cup and what kind of ice cream. An addressee may signal purely nonverbally; in the example, the clerk without speaking may put the ice cream in the cup and hand it to the customer. This type of response has not often been of interest to pragmatics, except in discussions of cross-cultural differences. Yet gestures, eye contact, and other nonverbal responses are part and parcel of everyday language-related behavior. Leaving these features out of research impoverishes our understanding of language in use.

Consequently, this book adopts the stance that limiting the study of pragmatic meaning to individual speech acts or speech events is too narrow if our purpose is understanding how language is used by interactants. Clark maintains that all language use is "joint action," involving the speaker's meaning and the addressee's understanding. A useful analogy adopted by Clark compares these roles to those of jazz musicians improvising in an ensemble. Here is a related metaphor, taken from the program of a concert in Honolulu (from the program of the June 28, 1997, performance of the University of Hawaii Gamelan Ensemble, "Music and Dance of Java and Bali"):

> A gamelan is a unified instrumental ensemble, composed entirely of bronze percussion instruments. Gamelan ensembles do not rely on a visual conductor, but instead rely on audible drum signals to determine tempos and dynamics. In dance genres, dancers must adhere to the musical form, and at the same time, the musicians pay close attention to the initiative of the dancers. Thus there is a marvelous interplay among the performing artists which includes chance, predictability, and surprise.

The gamelan ensemble can serve as a metaphor for human communication. Clark claims that any account of "using language" must include more than an analysis of the linguistic forms. Pragmatics seeks to explain "chance, predictability, and surprise."

In fact, the phrase in the subtitle of this book, *social action,* reflects the need to consider the context of utterance. It connects directly with the term *pragmatics,* which originates in the Greek word *praktikos,* "actions, conditions for actions" (Partridge 1958, 519). *Social action* expresses that notion of "acting" in and on the world around us.

Another interpretation of pragmatics has been proposed by Duranti (1994), who drew on his experiences as a linguistic anthropologist in a Western Samoan village to call for more attention to sociocultural features of the nonlinguistic context. Although pragmatics may be defined as including analysis of contextual features, in practice, much more attention is given to linguistic forms and to a limited number of nonlinguistic aspects of the context, such as the speaker, hearer, social variables, and indexicals. Duranti suggests that pragmatics should be grounded in ethnography such that the analyst decides what to study in a verbal performance by examining what the local community considers to be important. An understanding of an insider's interpretation is needed. Duranti labels this approach "ethnopragmatics," which he describes as "a study of language use that relies on ethnography to illuminate the ways in which speech is both constituted by and constitutive of social interaction" (1994, 11). According to Duranti, pragmatic meaning can only be understood within socioculturally organized activities, that is, speech events (see also Hymes 1972), where speech is considered to be only one of the available semiotic codes or resources for signaling meaning and understanding it.

In the following lines spoken by a group of Japanese students studying English, it is possible to observe a cultural practice of Japanese group interactions. Each member is assigned a task, in this case, to act as discussion leader.

Mune: . . . discussion leader about question 1 to 4, er, 1 to 3.
Tomo: ok
Mune: and Toki is 4 to 7
Toki: ok
Mune: and Midori is 8 to 10
Midori: ok
Mune: hmm? ok, let's begin question 1

(LoCastro 1996)

In this discourse the learners are displaying orientation to the group context, transferring from what is commonly done in Japanese to their English lesson. An ethnographic study would show that this strategy avoids conflict; if everyone knows what role to play, then no conflicts should arise. In other words, an ethnographic approach enables the analyst to learn from the community members what is important to study from their point of view; more than linguistic forms are used in carrying out social action (Watanabe 1993).

More recently, the role of cognition in the processing of pragmatic meaning has drawn attention. Despite being labeled a code model of communication, pragmatics had always emphasized the underlying psycholinguistic base of inferencing as fundamental to comprehension of pragmatic meaning. In fact, all of pragmatics is based on an inferential model of human communication. However, there had been no attempts to explain what inferencing consists of from the perspective of processing pragmatic meaning. Sperber and Wilson (1986) set out to do just that. Their theory, called relevance theory, is described in more detail in chapter 9.

Given that formal linguistic analysis is inadequate to account for pragmatic meaning, a functional perspective toward language must be employed. This view looks at language as a semiotic resource, first of all, to communicate meaning.

Functional View of Language

Human beings are inherently *social* beings, and language is a social phenomenon, the primary means through which they act in the world to communicate with others, and the primary means through which they are acted on by others (Halliday 1978). Indeed, even in dream sequences, people recount arguing with others! This functional perspective seeks to describe how people engage in communication and interactions through language, starting first with communicative needs, not the forms.

According to Schiffrin (1994, 20–23), the functional view of language contrasts with the formalist perspective in the different assumptions made about the goals of linguistic analysis and theory, the methods for studying language, and the kind of data. First, while formal linguists (e.g., Chomsky) seek to develop a theory of language as a mental phenomenon, functionalists study it in relation to its social functions with the theoretical aim of describing universals of language use in society (see the work of Halliday, Hasan, and their colleagues).

These two major approaches to language analysis differ in methods of data analysis. Theoretical or formal linguistics starts with individual words or phonemes and stops with the sentence. Within the paradigm of functionalism, it is possible to begin an analysis of a piece of spoken or written text by first asking what purpose or aim the speaker or writer had in using language in the way observed in the text. The functional approach takes a different starting point from that of formal linguistics to understand the formal patterns or structures. It asks questions such as how speakers' meanings are realized by use of the linguistic elements. Here is an example:

> C: Can I have ten oranges and a kilo of bananas, please?
> V: Yes, anything else?
> C: No, thanks.
> V: That'll be dollar forty.
> C: Two dollars.
> V: Sixty, eighty, two dollars. Thank you.
>
> (Hasan 1985, 54)

The functional or communicative purpose, that is, the buying and selling of goods, in this service encounter is transparently realized through linguistic forms and turn-taking in this short piece of talk between a customer and a vendor. A functional analysis would notice ellipsis in the second and third lines. The ellipsis causes no problem of comprehension, as the context of situation enables the two interactants to understand the meanings each one is conveying. A formal analysis would label the second and third lines ungrammatical.

Finally, a functional approach analyzes extended texts of naturally occurring spoken or written language, that is, performance data. Constructed language samples are avoided.

Pragmatics is an inherently functional perspective on language: by asking how a speaker realizes an intended meaning through linguistic and nonlinguistic means, the question represents a functional point of view by looking *first* at what the speaker wants to do and *then* how it gets done via language. A full discussion of this perspective goes beyond the scope of this book; however, this is the paradigm that informs it.

Centrality of Action and Context

The notion that language is embedded within a context that largely influences the interpretation of meaning developed over time and reflects the thinking of not a small number of scholars, in particular sociologists, social psychologists, and anthropologists, who view language as only one resource among many. This section presents a brief overview of the development of the construct "social action."

In 1923, the British anthropologist Bronislaw Malinowski introduced the term *context of situation* to indicate that "the situation in which words are uttered can never be passed over as irrelevant to the linguistic expressions" (306). Language is embedded in a sociocultural framework and cannot be interpreted outside its local, instantial use. Further, language is a form of "practical action" more than a reflection of abstract thinking (Duranti and Goodwin 1992, 15). As an anthropologist, Malinowski claimed language should be studied in everyday, practical activities, such as fishing.

Another important contributor was Talcott Parsons, a major figure in twentieth-century American sociology, who, influenced by such scholars as Durkheim and Weber, developed a new "theory of action" (cited in Coulon 1995, 3). This theoretical approach considers everyday people as social actors who create and recreate with every encounter the social order, reproducing the internalized social order and being reconstructed themselves at the same time. This perspective emphasizes social actors, their processes of interpretation, motivations, and capacity to engage in actions to maintain a shared, relatively stable world. Thus, "the framework of social action results from a continuous construction, from a permanent creation of the norms of the actors themselves" (Coulon 1995, 31). In sum, social action theory regards the actor as acting, not only acted on by features of the social structure in the course of everyday activities.

The entry of linguistics into this framework was inevitable, as language is the primary resource for the construction of social life. The capacity to use language to represent thought and, more importantly here, to communicate attitudes, feelings, and wants to others—in other words, to create a social world—translates into the use of language to act in and on the social world. This new perspective on linguistic phenomena, in particular with ethnomethodologists and conversational analysts, followed with an explosion of research on "language in use," an expression synonymous with language as a form of social action. Pragmatics explores the conditions for action, that is, how utterances have meaning in the context of situation. The concept of context is critical in pragmatic inquiry, yet problematic to define. Indeed, attempts to clarify context may be more common than definitions of pragmatics.

Levinson (1983, x) employs a fairly narrow definition:

> Context . . . includes only some of the basic parameters of the context of utterance, including participants' identity, role and location, assumptions about what participants know or take for granted, the place of an utterance within a sequence of turns at talking and so on.

These dimensions, according to Levinson, constrain talk and the comprehension of pragmatic meaning.

Another view of context comes from Ochs (1979, 2–6, cited in Duranti and Goodwin 1992), a linguistic anthropologist. Her definition of context includes the following variables:

1. Setting: "the social and spatial framework within which encounters are situated" (1979, 6).
2. Behavioral environment: "the way that participants use their bodies and behavior as a resource for framing and organizing their talk" (7).
3. Language as context: this includes the notion of contextualization cues, that is, the way language itself provides a context for other language (7–8).
4. Extrasituational context: background knowledge, that is, social, cultural, historical, political frames within which local instances need to be interpreted (8).

Ochs's list reflects her anthropological background by including nonlinguistic elements.

From the philosophic tradition comes Wittgenstein's (1958) language games, the underlying notion being that people engage in action within recognizable natural activities that provide context. Levinson (1992) built on Wittgenstein's insight with his notion of activity types. An activity type—a bar mitzvah, a business meeting, a chat in a coffee shop, a classroom lesson—is the frame within which various features of the constituent talk can be interpreted and inferences calculated. The activity type is the organizing context that structures the talk as well as the permissible behaviors and roles of the participants.

However, as a result of recent contributions to pragmatics from related fields, a more dynamic view of context has been adopted, showing an interactive, mutually constitutive relationship between context and language. As a result, the definition of context has come to include sociocultural and cognitive dimensions. Throughout this book, the term *context* is to be regarded as the linguistic, social, and psychological world "in which the language user operates at any given time" (Ochs and Schieffelin 1979, 1). It includes linguistic and nonlinguistic features. *Co-text* is the term used to label the linguistic context; it includes any linguistic text prior to and subsequent to the utterance one is analyzing.

> *A:* she talked to someone today who made her feel better that, oh he might be looking at six months to a year (+) in jail, and that (0.2) would be a lot better than (+) she was thinking of seven years (+) Shawn would be grown up, going to college already or something
> *B:* laughter . . . [*simultaneous talk and laughter*]
> *A:* so now (0.2) it won't be that long (0.3) she hired this attorney today, so (+)
> *B:* is he expensive?
>
> (LoCastro 1990b)

In this example, a single utterance would not be sufficient to understand what A and B are talking about. The co-text, that is, the linguistic forms that occur before and after the word or part one wants to analyze, begins to provide more information; however, it is still not yet sufficient for the analyst to assign meaning to the referents for "she" and "he."

As for the nonlinguistic or situational variables, a general framework such as that of Brown and Fraser (1979) illustrates the possible contextual influences on language. Note that "social" can be an abbreviation for "sociocultural." A framework or model should not be regarded as listing all of the potential variables of the context, as there is no consensus as to what should be included in the construct of context. One thing that is clear is that both linguistic and situational variables affect the speaker's choice. Thus, a framework can only be a useful heuristic, providing a basis for investigations into the correlations between linguistic choices and contextual factors.

An Inclusive Definition of Pragmatics

Adopting elements from the definitions and approaches to pragmatics reviewed above, specifically those of Crystal, Clark, and Duranti, this book uses as a working definition that pragmatics is the study of speaker and hearer meaning created in their joint actions that include both linguistic and nonlinguistic signals in the context of socioculturally organized activities. As will be discussed below, formal linguistic and speech act analyses are necessary parts of pragmatics; however, it will become clear to the reader that limiting the study to linguistic forms does not enable the analyst to account for a greater range of instances of language in use.

Pragmatics and Its Place in Linguistics

Morris's (1938) definition of pragmatics placed the field within semiotics, the study of the relation of signs to the world. However, relocated into linguistics, pragmatics still did not have a home, as it was regarded as a kind of "rag bag" category, where anything that could not be explained by traditional linguistic analysis was dumped. Leech (1983, 6) discusses the question of whether or not pragmatics should be regarded as an "added" layer of linguistic description; he suggests a linear processing model (1983, 12; see the accompanying table). The three levels of the grammar, that is, phonology, morpho-syntax, and semantics, are "successive coding systems whereby 'sense' is converted into 'sound' for the purpose of encoding a message (PRODUCTION) or whereby 'sound' is converted into 'sense' for the purposes of decoding one (INTERPRETATION)" (1983, 12). Leech admits (1983, 13) that this linear model is inadequate to account for the high-pitched voice that signals a formal speech environment among Japanese women; in such instances, pragmatics interacts directly with phonology, not via semantics or morpho-syntax. According to Leech's model, pragmatics, like semantics, enters only once a formal linguistic analysis has been carried out. It is a linear, cognitive processing model that is believed by some researchers to reflect the way the human mind processes language input and encodes language output.

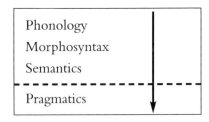

However, there is strong evidence that such a model is mistaken. In fact, both the decoding (comprehension) and the encoding (production) of language engage cognitive processes that utilize phonological, morphological, syntactic, lexical, semantic, and pragmatic aspects in an interactive, dynamic way, yet to be fully understood by researchers and documented with extensive experimental or empirical evidence. Intonation—a contour to signal tentativeness, for example—is not added at the end, so to speak. A speaker who wishes to signal tentativeness, a possible pragmatic meaning, in expressing an opinion must encode that meaning at the same time or simultaneously with the selection of other phonological and lexical-grammatical choices.

Both grammatical and semantic approaches conceive of language as rule-governed. Formal linguists seek to explicate the formal system: they are concerned with the content or the message of sentences. Pragmatics is governed by principles that can conflict, be applied in varying degrees, and are regulative; they can be infringed or broken, thereby creating a new or different meaning without taking the speaker outside the norms of the speech community, as would ungrammatical sentences. Further, pragmatics looks at how the speaker conveys attitudes toward the message or the addressee. In other words, pragmatics is concerned with interpersonal meaning, such as attitudes, and ideational or propositional meaning (Halliday 1985).

Interest in pragmatics has grown over the past two decades, in particular as a result of the realization that formal linguistic analytical procedures have limited application beyond single, analyst-constructed sentences. Once language in use is examined, that is, language as it is employed by everyone from supermarket clerks to academics giving lectures, the limitations of sentence-level analysis become apparent.

Pragmatics and Semantics

However, the search for appropriate methods continues. Semantics has attempted to reconstitute itself as pragmatics, without success, as it is not able to account for the vagaries of language use. For example, the following utterance illustrates several points. Two friends met in the evening and chatted about what they had done during the day.

A: well, it was kind of hot today . . . and we went to the beach . . .

A syntactic account of this sentence would indicate that it is well formed, and a dictionary lists the spelling and meaning of each of the lexical items. In a semantic analysis, "hot" would be given semantic features such as [+temperature] and "today" [+marker for sequence of days of a week], for example.

Semantics is also interested in the truth-conditions of the propositions expressed in sentences. A proposition typically corresponds to the literal meaning of an individual clause. In the example above, there are two propositions; within semantic theory, it can be argued that the propositional contents of the two assertions ("it was hot today" and "we went to the beach") are true if the speaker wishes to claim them to be so. In other types of assertions, such as "Hong Kong was returned to China on July 1, 1997," the truth of the assertion can be established on the basis of the facts of history.

In the context of truth-conditional semantics, sentences are regarded as logical constructions, and their propositions as descriptions of some state of affairs. Consequently, a test as to whether or not a sentence was a "real" one is the truthfulness of the propositional content. In a sense, meaning in semantics is limited to the truth-conditional content. The argument basically goes like this: the propositional content usually corresponds to the literal meaning of one clause. In logic, a proposition is expressed by letters such as x, y, and z.

It started raining and they took their umbrellas. : x & y

If x is true and y is true, then x & y is true. If either x or y is false, then x & y is necessarily false. According to Green (1989, 7), this semantic approach to language is based on the premise that "the meaning of an expression in . . . semantics represents a state of affairs that would have to hold if the sentence containing that expression is to be considered true." In other words, meaning in semantics is dependent on "conditions under which a sentence would be true (truth conditions)," such as being able to show the relation between the surface structure of a sentence and "the logical proposition it expresses" (Green 1989, 7).

However, Mey (1993, 14) notes that it is more interesting to ask *why* people say what they do, not just ask whether what they said was true or false. Further, again according to Mey, it was realized that people do all kinds of things with language that has little to do with its abstract, logical form. Whereas the test of truthfulness is appropriate for "statements," it is inadequate to account for a social action. Suppose that one adult says to another,

> You're not leaving!

Syntactically, this is a declarative. It appears to be a statement. However, its truth or falseness is irrelevant to speech act analysis. It is a command, and, because one adult does not under friendly conditions order another to stay put, one possible meaning, inferred by the listener, is that the speaker is angry. The sentence is an expression of attitude.

Clearly, truth-conditional semantics is a restricted area of linguistics. It serves a useful function within the context of the research of philosophers of language. However, pragmatics seeks to develop a theory of meaning in interaction and entails rejection of forms of analysis concerned with a theory of sentence meaning. In the case of checking the truthfulness or falsity of the beach example above, the identity of the speaker needs to be clarified. Once that question is posed, however, details about the context become important. Consequently, pragmatics already has a role. The analysis of the literal meaning of the propositions results in an assertion that the extent to which the content faithfully reflects the state of affairs depends on the speaker.

Still another indication of the limits of semantic analysis comes once the "little" words (function words) of a language are examined. For example, the word *and* in a semantic analysis is neutral; that is, it has no semantic content that signals a temporal dimension. If that were true, it would be possible to reverse the order of the two propositions and leave the meaning of the utterance unchanged.

We went to the beach, and, well, it was kind of hot today.

Reversing the clauses changes the meaning of the utterance. Only with a pragmatic analysis can we understand that when two friends chat about what they did during the day, *and* tends to mean "and then," indicating the sequence of events. Thus, pragmatics is needed to flesh out semantics.

Additional evidence of the limitations of linguistic theory in accounting for meaning is apparent in an attempt to analyze "well" and "kind of" in the example. Neither of these little words adds to the literal, basic meaning of the propositions. Rather, both have something to do with signaling the speaker's attitudes toward the propositional content or the addressee. *Well* commonly functions as a hesitation marker at the start of an answer to a question. It may also be a cue that the answer is contrary to what the speaker thinks the asker of the question expects. "Kind of" is a phrase similar to "sort of." It signals hesitation and can make the speaker seem less confident. It can be used by a speaker who wants to appear to lack confidence, in offering weather conditions as an appropriate excuse for not working in the library and going to the beach instead. The linguistic forms provide only the base for the interpretation of the speaker's pragmatic meaning, and we must also take into consideration the linguistic context (for example, the preceding utterance in a conversation) as well as the relationship of the two conversational partners.

Consequently, this one example leads to the conclusion that language can only be understood with recourse to contextual features, that is, by attending to pragmatics in an analysis of language in use. In talking about the beach, for example, facial expressions may help the interactants comprehend meanings, both ideational and interpersonal. Comprehension of pragmatic meaning must go beyond consideration of linguistic forms only.

Although the intention to communicate is a minimum requirement, the speaker must also intend to have an effect on the addressee. A strict cost-benefit analysis or an excessive concern for the rational, strategic goals of the speaker may be misplaced (see Leech 1983); however, to ignore the possible effect of the speaker's utterance on the addressee is unhelpful. Linguistic pragmatics has tended to exclude the effect on the addressee, which may not be manifested in verbal form and is unpredictable. Recall the example of the ice cream vendor; a verbal response may not be given or may be abbreviated. Rather than excluding attention to the effect on the addressee, however, this book stresses the need to incorporate the listener in assessing pragmatic meaning. The analysis of the perceived effect on the addressee signals understanding of the speaker's intended meaning.

There is a danger, admittedly, in enlarging the scope of pragmatics, such that the analyses may appear to be arbitrary and the analysts unable to account for their explanations. Nevertheless, a theory of pragmatics needs to be related to the study of communication and of the variety of semiotic resources used in interaction to carry out social actions. Limiting pragmatics to the study of linguistic action only is an unfortunate reminder of traditional linguistic approaches.

Pragmatics and Related Fields

Stepping out of the traditional areas of linguistics, the reader meets a sometimes confusing array of possible approaches to studying language as it is used beyond individual sentences. The purpose of this section is to explain briefly several fields related to pragmatics so that distinctions become apparent and decisions can be made about the best form of analysis for the kind of data and purposes of a research project. The descriptions that follow introduce the main perspectives.

Sociolinguistics

One field that grew out of calls for an alternative perspective on language, specifically as it is utilized in social life, is sociolinguistics. It developed out of anthropology and sociology, emphasizing in particular variation in use as the result of social conditioning. Sociolinguistics studies the differences in the use of a language or a set of languages (i.e., bilingualism) by different social groups in a community, from a small village to an entire nation state. A classic example from Labov's (1972) studies of New York vernacular, the everyday talk of people living in New York City, is the dropping of the postvocalic /r/. Labov found that the /r/ phoneme tended to be deleted most often in the postvocalic position, as seen in such phrases as "It's on the fouth floo" (It's on the fourth floor), by speakers from lower socioeconomic groups.

Sociolinguists seek generalizations that can be made at a societal level, correlating social groups with variations in speech. A dropped /r/ distinguishes lower socioeconomic groups from others. In a similar way, "don't" instead of "doesn't" with third-person singular subjects may be a means for members of certain ethnic groups in New York to signal their group membership: "He don't know what he's doing."

In contrast to sociolinguistics, pragmatics examines the choices made by an individual speaker on a particular occasion to signal meanings such as relative differences in role, status, age, social distance, and so on. One native speaker of French uses the informal *tu* to address the supervisor of the French department, while another uses *vous*. The supervisor uses *tu* to talk with both of them. It is more a pragmatic question to interpret the language use of the three women rather than a sociolinguistic one. In another example, the researcher could study how individuals avoid explicitly marking social status in greetings. In Mexico, it is common to hear "¿Qué tal?" or "¿Comó estamos?"—expressions that avoid *tu* and *usted*. Pragmatics would focus on the language use of individuals in this context whereas sociolinguistics would study this avoidance of social markings as a society-wide phenomenon.

Pragmatics studies individual instances in a specific context to signal a meaning that cannot be assigned to the utterances without bringing in the common knowledge shared by the interactants. For example, if a professor uses a dialectical or nonstandard, informal form, *wakaranee* ("I don't understand" in Japanese), instead of the standard, and more situationally appropriate *wakarimasen,* at a faculty meeting, the professor is communicating more than simply an assertion of noncomprehension. The faculty member is signaling also his less than positive attitude toward the subject being discussed.

Cognitive Pragmatics and Artificial Intelligence

Two other related fields are cognitive psychology and artificial intelligence (AI), which seek to understand cognitive processes of comprehension and production. Cognitive pragmatics (Kasher 1994) limits its field of study to linguistic forms within the framework of cognitive sciences. The major objective is an understanding of the human mind and brain, specifically the neural evidence of psycholinguistic operations of linguistic activity. Cognitive pragmatics aims to describe a systematic relationship between language use and cognitive processes utilized to work out pragmatic meaning and ultimately a linguistic theory to explain pragmatics. Relevance theory (see Sperber and Wilson 1986) is one such attempt. Much of the work in cognitive pragmatics has used as its model a information-processing metaphor (Mey and Talbot 1988).

AI researchers aim to understand cognitive processing to develop both hardware and software so that computers can produce and comprehend natural speech. This endeavor, however, involves more than language itself. Brown and Yule (1983a) argue that, among a variety of features involved in the cognitive processing of information, knowledge of the world or conventional sociocultural knowledge is indispensable in arriving at an interpretation of a speaker's meaning. At a poolside in Hong Kong, an Australian comments to an American that it is time for a "sundowner." The American responds that a sundowner would be nice, calculating that, since it was sundown, adults often have a cocktail before having dinner and, because there was a poolside bar right nearby, the Australian probably meant that it was time for a drink called a "sundowner." The American's world knowledge enabled the person to make a good guess; the Australian in fact meant it was time for a drink, although not any particular drink.

The role of such background knowledge in the production and comprehension of language has been prioritized in cognitive pragmatics and AI; the issue involves programming computers to do what human beings can do, that is, provide the background knowledge. Both fields view language primarily as a means to represent thought, although it is claimed that this focus is a temporary narrowing of the field in order to examine that aspect in depth before addressing the effect of social dimensions.

Consequently, although much progress has been made in the case of natural speech processing, its successful applications have been limited to, for example, machine translation of technical or scientific texts or voice-activation systems in restricted domains.

Conversational Analysis and Discourse Analysis

Two areas that more directly overlap with pragmatics are conversational analysis (CA) and discourse analysis (DA). CA can be described as an approach within DA. The aim is to carry out microanalysis of extended samples of naturally occurring talk to achieve insights into the enactment of everyday social action in conversational interactions. In particular, CA is interested in the structure of talk and its subsystems. For example, analysis of turn-taking in a variety of types of language texts or genres increases understanding of turn-taking as a subsystem. Conversational analysis, which began as a field within sociology that emerged from the work of ethnomethodologists (see Sacks, Schegloff, and Jefferson 1978), has tended to abstract away from most social features of the context of utterance, including the goals of the interactants, to concentrate on describing observable, immanent principles that are constitutive of everyday conversation. The aim is to write a grammar of the system and the subsystems such as turn-taking, repair, and selection of the next speaker.

As for DA, researchers in this field tend to focus on overall text issues, beyond individual utterances or sentences, such as the macrostructures of texts (for example, problem-solution, cause-effect, the structure of narratives [McCarthy 1991]) as well as microanalysis of characteristics of spoken versus written texts, and of the linguistic forms characteristic of different registers. The paragraph that follows is an essay written by a speaker of Mexican Spanish studying English an example of learner data that could be analyzed for a variety of discourse features. The learner is reacting to an essay prompt that asked for the writer's opinion about whether or not the desire to become a member of the target language community was the "best" kind of motivation.

> It is true, that if you want to learn a certain language, you must have the desire to fit into a language community. The very best way to learn the idiom is to be part, be member of that community. In that way you attempt

to speak like a native speaker. You must venture in your quest of speaking that language. In finding the true meaning of the language, you'll find the true meaning of the culture. You'll see the complexity of that culture, exemplify by its language. You'll see how this particular language community sees the world in that particular way. (LoCastro 2000b)

A discourse analysis of this text would, first of all, comment on the organization of the paragraph. From the beginning of the paragraph, the writer directly states agreement with the content of the essay prompt. The writer develops the point about learning to speak the language, connecting it to learning about the culture and supports the argument with evidence. In addition, the writer chose to use *you* as an indefinite pronoun. In this text, *you* is not being used to address the reader directly. In effect, it is a synonym for the inclusive *we* in this context; it includes the writer and any potential readers. This briefly is the kind of analysis that is expected in studying discourse.

Discourse analysis is both a product and a process. As a product, it is the analysis of situated speaker-hearer interactions and accomplishments. The term is also frequently used as a synonym for extended text. For example, doctor-patient talk is one kind of discourse. As a process, it is more than an examination of linguistic forms across clausal and sentential boundaries; it is the study of the choices made by the speakers and hearers and the patterns observed in their choices within the context of utterance. DA is retrospective and engages in thick or grounded description of the circumstances of the context to enlighten the analyst about the patterns of interaction.

A particular approach to discourse analysis in the last decades examines the connections between language use and relations of social power. It is called *critical discourse analysis. Critical,* in this case, designates the aim to make transparent the connections between unequal power relations and language, connections that often remain hidden. Fairclough, for example (1989), studies the exercise of power through language use. He focuses on the control through language over access to goods and services as well as local instances of individuals in positions of power using language to constrain the behavior of those with less power. For example, speakers of a nonstandard variety of English in the United Kingdom may find it difficult to find employment, enter university, and become a full member of a community, while a doctor or university professor is free to use language to control subordinates, mirroring the unequal social status and thus power of the individuals involved.

Ethnography of Speaking

Derived from Hymes's SPEAKING model (1972), this approach to natural data takes as the basic unit of analysis the speech event. The speech event—a classroom, a court trial, a psychoanalytic consultation—is the frame within which interpretation of meaning occurs. The ethnographer studies the speech event and carries out a linguistic analysis based on the local, socioculturally defined categories. In other words, the ethnographer does not start with hypothesis-driven categories, influenced by the researcher's own cultural and personal background. Rather, the analyst attempts to view the speech event through the eyes of the actual people engaged in the event.

Pragmatic analysis plays a role in interpreting a speaker's meaning in the context of a culture's specific norms and expectations. For example, Nwoye (Saville-Troike 1982) studied greetings in Igbo, a language of Nigeria, and found the belief that greetings affected one's fortunes for the rest of the day. Consequently, people in a village avoided greeting others they thought were unlucky. In China, anecdotal evidence suggests that in the past it was considered unwise to talk about a newborn children, especially in a positive way, as the evil spirits might be attracted, with unpleasant consequences for child. In both cases, local knowledge is indispensable for the ethnographer in making sense of interactants' meaning.

Interactional Sociolinguistics

According to Schiffrin (1994, 97–106), interactional sociolinguistics grew out of concern for how culture, society, and language come together, from anthropology, sociology, and linguistics. Goffman, an American sociologist, sought to describe the role of language in everyday circumstances, how it reflects and creates meaning and structure in such institutions as mental hospitals (1963). Goffman, in particular, is well known for having introduced the notion of frames, the lens through which people view and interpret their and others' experiences. Frames are "socially situated," that is, they are derived from the social context—a coffee shop or a board meeting, for example—and constrain the rights and obligations of the participants and permissible topics. For example, within the frame of a language classroom, teachers have certain rights, such as the right to reprimand a late student, and obligations, for example, to explain a grammar point in a language lesson. The rights and obligations are enacted in the language used by the teacher.

The anthropologist John Gumperz introduced the concept of contextualization cues (1982a), which are features of verbal and nonverbal behavior, such as intonation contours, pausing, facial expressions, and head nods, which correlate with a particular sociocultural context. They are cues that trigger interpretation of pragmatic meaning. In a well-known analysis of context, Gumperz studied a British female job counselor's interview with a male Indian speaker who was seeking employment. Examining the verbal and nonverbal cues, Gumperz showed that the two interactants had divergent interpretations of the socioculturally constituted event of a job counseling interview. The cues in the counselor's talk were not understood by the job seeker and vice versa, resulting in miscommunication.

Both Goffman and Gumperz share the following perspective on language, culture, and society, as summarized by Schiffrin (1994, 99):

> Cognition and language, then, are affected by social and cultural forces: the way we behave and express ourselves in relation to a linguistic code and the underlying categories of the code itself are open to external influence.

In taking an interactional sociolinguistics perspective to carry out an analysis of natural speech data, pragmatics is the tool that enables the analyst to infer the speaker's intended meaning from the contextualization cues. The following example from Gumperz (1982a, 133) illustrates the phenomenon.

> The graduate student has been sent to interview a black housewife in a low income, inner city neighborhood. The contact has been made over the phone by someone in the office. The student arrives, rings the bell, and is met by the husband, who opens the door, smiles, and steps towards him:

>   *Husband:* So y're gonna check out ma ol lady, hah?
>   *Interviewer:* Ah, no, I only came to get some information. They called from the office.
>   [Husband, dropping his smile, disappears without a word and calls his wife.]

The husband's question was, according to Gumperz, a formulaic expression used in the black community to "check out" strangers under such circumstances. The interviewer was black himself, but did not recognize the husband's pragmatic meaning. Had the student responded in kind, he would have communicated membership in the community and thus that he was a "member of the same social group," not a representative of the social welfare bureaucracy. The cues in this instance are the formulaic expression and undoubtedly the prosodic features, although Gumperz does not comment on them.

Ethnomethodology

Ethnomethodology (a research perspective rather than a method, despite its name) seeks to discover the processes underlying conversational interaction that enable the participants to produce and interpret communicative events (Garfinkel 1984). An example of an ethnomethodological perspective in research is Abou (1978), who studied Lebanese immigrants to Latin American countries and employed concepts from Freud and Marx to interpret the traumas individuals experienced in adjusting to life in their adopted countries.

Ethnomethodology grew out of the work of a group of sociologists who took an antipositivist, phenomenological stance and who were dissatisfied with the mainstream, quantitative, hypothesis-driven approach. They sought to understand how the social order and social organization are constituted by the social actors, that is, laypeople, as they live their everyday lives, not as the researchers viewed their lives and their world. One specific question was how shared background is established in discourse, as ethnomethodologists assumed that shared knowledge is necessary for any extended communication. Owing to the location of this field within sociology, the concern has always been for communication and not for grammar or linguistic forms, and thus ethnomethodologists have used from the start performance data.

Summary

The accompanying table serves as a heuristic aid to keep track of the different approaches to the study of meaning. There are two kinds of data: *(a)* sentences, often constructed by the analyst, and *(b)* text or discourse of any kind of language use, specifically naturally occurring performance data, with all the messiness of human beings using language. A focus on sentences limits the number of analytical perspectives, which are widely practiced within the field of formal or theoretical linguistics.

Different but overlapping approaches can be taken to the analysis of natural discourse. If one wants to limit pragmatics to speech acts, it can be practiced as a form of linguistic analysis. However, if the text analyzed is more than a single utterance, another approach will be required to account for contextual features. Thus, it is within the framework of one of the approaches to analysis discussed above—textual features (DA), culturally constructed social action (ethnography of speaking), conversational sequences (CA), construction of common ground (ethnomethodology), cognitive processes and constraints (cognitive pragmatics and AI), social class markers (sociolinguistics)—that pragmatic meanings are interpreted.

Type of Data	Type of Analysis
1. Sentences: abstracted from social variables	Grammar: phonetics Phonology Morphosyntax Semantics
2. Discourse: spoken or written, including linguistic and nonlinguistic context	Discourse analysis Ethnography of speaking Conversational analysis Ethnomethodology Cognitive pragmatics Artificial intelligence Sociolinguistics Pragmatics

Role of Pragmatics

Nevertheless, pragmatics can be separated from these other, related fields, despite the fuzzy boundaries. It is useful to imagine trying to do close-up photography with a single lens reflex camera: if one zooms in on one petal of a flower, the rest of the flower goes out of focus. Adopting this metaphor, one can see all these fields as part of the fuzzy, out-of-focus background, while narrowing down to one approach will enable the analyst to study with relative clarity one view of how language is used. The researcher's choice of analytic perspective is basically constrained by the purpose of the study; put simply, it depends on what the analyst wants to understand. For example, if it is the structure of conversation, then CA will drive the analyst's work. However, at the micro level, the researcher is "doing" pragmatics. Specifically, pragmatics is characterized by the following distinguishing features:

Meaning is created in interaction with speakers and hearers.
Context includes both linguistic (co-text) and nonlinguistic aspects.
Choices made by the users of language are an important concern.
Constraints in using language in social action (who can say what to whom) are significant.
The effects of choices on coparticipants are analyzed.

Here is an illustration of pragmatic analysis. A teacher who wants a student to lower the temperature of an overheated classroom might say one of the following sentences:

It's warm in here!
Please open the window.
Is it all right if I open the window?
We're wasting electricity!

Pragmatics analyzes the differences among these utterances and asks why they are more likely than, "I want the heat turned down or, failing that, a window opened!" What circumstances make it possible for the students to understand the teacher's meaning? The context includes the nonlinguistic environment (the students, the overheated room). The teacher's choices are constrained by her social distance from the students. (She could be direct in her request with close friends, family members, or clear subordinates.) Had she commanded them to open the window, students would have been offended ("Who does she think she is, ordering us around!").

To "do" pragmatics we must consider the formal features of the instance of language. Yet the analysis does not end there. Because an extended text, that is, more than a single utterance, constitutes the data, a discourse analysis is required, which means consideration of contextual features. To unravel pragmatic meanings, created in the interaction of speaker and hearer, the analyst may use an understanding of conversational analysis, ethnography of speaking, or sociolinguistics, to inform a microanalysis of the local occurrences in the talk or written text.

Language Data

One distinguishing characteristic of research in pragmatics is the use of naturally occurring, extended samples of language as data. In other words, the data are not constructed by the analyst, and further, are composed of more than one decontextualized sentence. Often, the samples of language are from everyday situations: dinner table talk, business negotiations, or arguments between a landlord and a drunken tenant.

What may seem commonplace today was not so until recently, and may still be regarded as unacceptable for proper linguistic research in some circles. Spoken language, even more so than written texts, is viewed as "performance" data, thus riddled with all kinds of "errors," such as slips of the tongue, hesitations and false starts, grammatical sloppiness, and a fragmented, on-line processing quality. Discourse markers and connectors tend to be limited in variety ("so," "and," "but," and "then"), and clauses are conjoined into compound rather than complex sentences. Written texts are more structured and believed to reflect more closely the innate competence of the language users, and consequently are of greater interest to sentence grammarians whose goal is to describe that innate capacity. There may also be in some cultures the belief that spoken language data is "dirty," perhaps embarrassing as it does include performance errors, in the same way clothing regarded as socially inappropriate at a formal event may be said to reflect badly on the individual who has worn it. In fact, no clear-cut border divides spoken from written texts; there is a gradation from academic and scientific texts to informal chat with friends, with a whole variety of text forms or genres between. A new one has been added relatively recently: e-mail messages, which are closer in form to casual talk than to careful writing.

(A short note about the word *text:* It will be used throughout this book to denote any piece of language, spoken or written, from a single word or phrase, to a multiparagraph example or a sequence of lines from a conversation, to the entire book. It is used as a synonym of *discourse,* discourse as a product; both text and discourse are regarded as productions of human beings, and the terms will be used interchangeably in this book).

Sentence grammarians have considered everyday empirical data unacceptable. Yet just that type of data is needed to understand language as action. All the disciplines influenced by Parson's theory of action as well as those within the functionalist paradigm broke with previous research methodologies to draw data directly from everyday activities, for it is in those contexts precisely where the researcher can learn how laypeople use language to construct their worlds.

Usage and Use

Pragmatics can be a study of both language usage and language use. In keeping with the definition of Widdowson (1978), *usage* refers to the inclusion of features of the context of an utterance that are encoded in the language itself. Usage—what usually occurs—is concerned with a linguistic item as a part of the linguistic system. An example of usage is that features of participants, such as their social status, age, and gender, are grammaticalized in languages such as Japanese, where it is not possible to speak or write the language without signaling the relative social position of the speaker by using sentence final particles, lexical items, or address forms. The absence of such linguistic forms is noticeable and breaks with the norms of the usage rules of Japanese.

Use, which denotes linguistic action that may not conform to the norms of a language and its users, refers to the ways people actually speak and write. It refers to how linguistic forms function for the purpose of communication in specific instances. In Quebeçois French, for example, native speakers tend to use *tu* with any other French speaker as a solidarity marker. Grammaticality, appropriateness, and performance errors are not matters of interest to pragmaticists who are exclusively interested in how the semiotic resources of languages are employed to make meanings.

In effect, usage and use are not a dichotomy; rather, they lie on a continuum, with "rule-influenced" behavior or regularities on one end and creative use of language on the other. Pragmatics is concerned with explaining the regularities as well as creative, norm-ignoring uses of language in everyday life, and all the gradations between the two poles.

Usage ←——————→ Use
[Rule-influenced regularities]   [Norm-ignoring creative language use]

Conclusion

Pragmatics tends to be limited to analysis of speakers' meaning in context, focusing in particular on such features of the context as the linguistic or co-text and social elements such as the age, social status, and social distance of the interactants.

With the basic premises of pragmatics having been clarified, the next chapters examine a number of pragmatic phenomena to show how language is used to convey more than propositional content.

Discussion Tasks

1. Pragmatics is, put simply, about communication. Yet how do we define "communication"? Here are some examples of the word *communication* in advertisements, in English, in Tokyo.
   Bath Communication
   Aluminication
   Workout: creates comfortable sweat, communication and
     mutual understanding

Security communication
Communication happens only once or twice a lifetime.
Computers, communications, and microelectronics

What do you suggest the word means in each case? Can you write one definition for *communication* that includes all these uses? If you are working in a group, share answers with students from a different cultural background.

2. Can there be different definitions of *communication?* A bilingual Japanese-English dictionary gives "communication" as the translation of *dentatsu,* which means the transmission of a superior's order to a subordinate. Do you know words in other languages that imply a different view of communication? Might different interpretations of what communication is about influence interactions in language classrooms?

3. A basic concept of pragmatics is that human beings act in and on the world through language. Give some examples that illustrate this concept.

4. Make a list of social factors that influence how you interact with other people. Have you ever noticed that you may have offended your conversational partner? What might be some reasons for causing offense? Discuss.

5. From a functional perspective, how do you realize age differences in any language(s) you speak? How do second language learners realize through language the beliefs that their L1 culture has about interacting with teachers, usually older and with higher status than the learners?

6. List some characteristics of spoken and written language use. How do they differ? How are they similar? Does it matter what language it is? For example, some languages, like Arabic, have one written form with many spoken dialects.

7. Give examples of language that, although spoken, resemble written texts. Give examples of language that, although written, resemble spoken language.

8. Eight related research areas have been explained. State briefly the main goals of each area, distinguishing it from pragmatics.

9. Can you predict how pragmatics will be important in language classrooms?

Text Analysis

Directions: Use the dialogue transcript that follows to answer these questions:

1. Who's speaking? How many people are speaking? Who are they, based on the information in the data?
2. What is the physical situation?
3. What is the context: social, cultural?
4. What is the topic—main and related topics?
5. What type of speech event or genre is this?
6. What is the purpose of this event?
7. What is being communicated about?
8. Can you say anything about the act sequence, that is, the ordering of the communicative acts?
9. What rules of interaction are being practiced in this event?
10. What kind of shared background knowledge is being used by the participants?

1. *A:* she talked to someone today who made her feel better that, oh he might be looking at six months to a year (+) in jail and (0.2) that would be a lot better than (+) she was thinking of seven years (+) Shawn would be grown up, going to college already or something
2. *B:* laughter . . . [*simultaneous talk and laughter*]
3. *A:* so now (0.2) it won't be that long (0.3) she hired this attorney today, so (+)
4. *B:* is he expensive?
5. *A:* umh (0.2) I don't know (+) I think they all are (+) but she didn't want to take her chances with a public attorney
6. *B:* really? (0.3) sometimes though (+) those public defenders (+) really you know are for their clients (+) . . . [*overlap*] you know (+) so

7. *A:* yeah, it depends (+) it's like ugh the roll of the dice (+) you don't know who you're gonna get
8. *B:* yeah, um sure [*overlap*] you might get somebody who could care less
9. *A:* (*irrecoverable*) Glen's lawyer was (+) really bad
10. *B:* the public defenders?
11. *A:* um hm (+) because they'd only come in, like, maybe half an hour before court is when Glen could see them (+) and they already had this deal kinda worked up in their mind and then that's when they run it past Glen so they really didn't talk to Glen or get his ideas or anything (+) and so
12. *B:* (0.15) huh
13. *A:* she thought a criminal lawyer might be different [*irrecoverable*]
14. *B:* yeah, it might be better (+) I just hope it doesn't break them (+) they're already broke
15. *A:* [*Overlapping*] they're already broke (0.3) she's ugh looking at taking her car to the to a school to get it fixed [*rising pitch, confirmation seeking*]
16. *C:* that might be a good idea
17. *B:* like the high school's that [*irrecoverable*]
18. *A:* yeah
19. *C:* yeah
20. *B:* but isn't it cheaper (+) all they have to pay for is parts I hear
21. *A:* yeah
22. *C:* [*irrecoverable*] [*overlapping talk, then only one talks, but soft, irrecoverable*] but still she'll have to car pool Sunday

(LoCastro 1990b)

Suggested Readings

Leech, G. N. 1983. *Principles of pragmatics.* London: Longman.

Levinson, S. C. 1983. *Pragmatics.* Cambridge: Cambridge University Press.

Mey, J. L. 1993. *Pragmatics: An introduction.* Oxford: Blackwell.

Stilwell Peccei, J. 1999. *Pragmatics.* London: Routledge.

Thomas, J. 1995. *Meaning in interaction: An introduction to pragmatics.* London: Longman.

Yule, G. 1996. *Pragmatics.* Oxford: Oxford University Press.

Chapter 2
Meaning

Meaning is a key problem within the field of pragmatics. Understanding what a speaker intends to communicate, as we do without apparent effort in our daily use of language, becomes a less transparent process once we ponder it. Exactly how is the speaker-intended meaning in a stream of sounds understood? One way to study this process is to observe the difficulties interactants have using a second language, as in this conversation between a Japanese undergraduate and a teacher who is a native speaker of English.

> T: Please tell me, what is the topic of your paper?
> S: em I . . . my topic is m . . . current education should change . . . should change
> T: current, you mean education the way it is now? the way people are educated now in Japan should be changed?
> S: yes
> T: so current education
> S: current?
> T: current . . . world is happening now current education should=
> S: =   oh, I see
> T: = be changed the (method of) current education should be changed ok all right?
>
> (Mori 1996, 56)

The teacher and student are clearly having some difficulties in understanding each other. The main problem seems to center around the word *current*, which might lead the reader to conclude it is only a matter of vocabulary. However, pragmatics is also involved. It is possible the student's cultural background (Japanese) is getting in the way of asking questions of the teacher; cultural practices in Japan discourage students from asking direct questions of someone with higher status. The student's hesitations may signal discomfort. This pragmatic meaning is inferred by the listener. Still another point that can be made here is the student's final comment, "oh I see." Depending on the prosodic features of that phrase, the student may in fact "see," that is, understand. However, it is also possible that the student is merely saying that so as not to appear to be ignorant once again of what the word *current* means. Clearly, aspects in the conversation have to do with meanings that go beyond the meanings of the words themselves.

The purpose of this chapter is to explore the notion of meaning by, first of all, proposing a general framework for analysis. The bulk of what follows introduces the types of meanings that must minimally be processed and understood at the first level of analysis. These meanings are generally derived from the microfeatures of the discourse. The second and third levels are also discussed briefly, and examples are given to provide a full, coherent view of the concept of meaning within pragmatics.

Framework for Analysis

In chapter 1, the importance of adopting the perspective that human beings perform actions, social actions, within both a linguistic and nonlinguistic context was emphasized. Just what the relationship *is* between language use and the sociocultural context is a source of controversy.

There have been several attempts to build a theory or model of pragmatic meaning that incorporates the linguistic and nonlinguistic contributions to processing meaning. The controversy still remains of the extent to which the cognitive-social context influences and constrains language use and, consequently, the meanings that are derived in interactions. At the extreme, some researchers maintain that the social structure of societies is replicated in interactions. Cicourel's (1980) framework of three levels of information is a useful guide in an analysis of language use.

As Cicourel states, a central issue in discourse analysis is the listener's ability to use various sources of information to derive the speaker's meaning. Cicourel's model includes sources that are linguistic elements as well as shared background knowledge, which goes beyond the language code. These information sources can be categorized as follows (Cicourel 1980):

1. Low-level predicates: linguistic and paralinguistic features, such as prosodic features (for example, stress and intonation)
   CO-TEXT

2. Expansion level: rights and obligations and personal biographies of the participants, the history of the relationships among the participants
   CONTEXT

3. Higher-order predicates: normative rules and dominant values that come from the structure or organization of the society; sociocultural knowledge that is taken for granted
   CONTEXT

The first category consists of microphenomena of language in use, while the third includes the macro notions of the society. This framework is not linear; that is, analysis does not necessarily start at level 1 and continue though level 3. Rather, the levels are separated out for the purposes of discussion. In natural language use it is difficult to isolate one level because of the complex, interactive nature of human communication. This framework serves a heuristic purpose, as it enables the analyst to focus on the sources of information used by the listener to establish meaning in the context of social interactions.

In this chapter, the different types of meaning that a sentence or an utterance can have will be considered and explained. Pragmatic meanings can potentially be assigned to any instance of spoken or written language. In the course of a conversation, the coparticipants move quickly to find the meaning that applies in the context of utterance, and resort to figuring out word meanings only when something in the context requires or precipitates closer assessment of the meaning of individual words. The principle of economy of effort avoids unneeded cognitive processing.

The principle of economy of effort is well known from research in psychology. Human beings usually do not listen to every item, for example, in a news report on the radio. They only listen closely to what interests them, such as reports of traffic jams if they commute by car from home to office, or who won the World Cup if they are soccer enthusiasts!

Basic Units of Meaning

All approaches to analyzing text define minimal units of analysis, depending on such factors as whether the researcher is working with written or spoken language samples or what the purpose of the analysis is.

Sentences and Utterances

First of all, a distinction needs to be made between "sentence" and "utterance." In natural language, a *sentence* is an artifact of the written language, created by human beings to represent speech. In English, it starts with a capital letter and ends with some form of punctuation: a period, an exclamation mark, or a question mark. All codified languages will follow standardization in their written form. In modern linguistics, *sentence* refers to the unit of analysis used by grammarians, specifically structural linguists. A technical definition is "the largest unit of grammatical organization within which parts of speech and grammatical classes are said to function. In English, a sentence typically contains one independent clause with a finite or conjugated verb" (Richards, Platt, and Platt 1992, 330). In the following sentences, the verbal elements are italicized:

1. A new president *has been elected* in Mexico.
2. *Walking* down the street, Susana *spotted* her lost cat.
3. Carlos *was* happy *to be going* to the U.K. for a year to study economics.

The first sentence has a finite verb. The second has two verbal elements, a participial and a finite verb. The third has a finite verb ("was") and a nonfinite verb ("to be going").

An *utterance* is a sample of spoken language, whether a single word or many, in use. It denotes instances of spoken or written language, and grammaticality is not in question. As pragmatics is concerned with language as used in everyday life, the word *utterance* will figure prominently in this book.

Sentence Meaning

In assigning meaning to a speaker's language, the first step is to establish the abstract meaning of the words and phrases, which give the potential meaning of each element, typically found in a dictionary. Sentence meaning, that is, the linguistic meaning, addresses the questions "What does X mean?"—X being a word, a phrase, a verb and any attached morpheme. This type of meaning is studied within semantics, the field of formal linguistics that involves purely linguistic knowledge. From all the possible meanings of a word, sense is assigned to each content word; *sense* refers to the meaning the speaker intends a word to have in a particular instance of use (Thomas 1995, 2–5).

    A: you look smart—that color suits you
    B: oh, thank you

"Smart" is an example of lexical ambiguity; it is polysemous. As a consequence of a word having more than one meaning, it can be ambiguous when it is used unless the context of the sentence enables the addressee to disambiguate it. The addressee of A's compliment would be confused: is A commenting on B's clothes or intelligence? Without the added phrase "that color suits you," the addressee cannot disambiguate the speaker's meaning. The co-text helps to narrow down the word meaning.

As is clear from the example, processing sentence meaning within the framework of semantics does entail use of context. However, the context is limited to the co-text of the individual sentence. Establishing pragmatic meaning of an utterance requires in addition consideration of the physical and sociocultural context as well as the co-text.

Context

Within the framework of pragmatics, at the first level of Circouel's model, context comprises the linguistic co-text and paralinguistic variables. Prosodic features, such as intonation and stress patterns, are the paralinguistic features most commonly included. Paralinguistic elements accompany linguistic items; they do not occur alone, but are important in clarifying or adding meaning. In fact, it is rather difficult to speak even the simplest utterance (from "oh" to something much longer) in any language and not communicate extra meaning through stress and intonation. Frequently, those meanings convey the speaker's attitudinal stance. Try saying "Well . . . " when a friend has just asked to borrow a large sum of money from you.

Contextual Meaning

Contextual meaning refers to what may also be labeled "utterance" meaning (Thomas 1995). Rarely in pragmatics is an utterance studied outside its context. Clearly, it is important to decide which of the potential meanings is likely to be the meaning the speaker intends. At this stage, contextual factors are considered. They narrow all the potential, abstract meanings down to the intended message.

> B: really? (0.3) sometimes though (+) **those** public defenders (+) really you know are for their clients (+) [overlap] you know (+) so
> A: yeah, it depends (+) it's like ugh the roll of the dice (+) you don't know who you're gonna get
>
> (LoCastro 1990b)

The literal meaning of "public defenders" lets the analyst know that the attorney in question is the kind assigned by the legal system to a client unable to pay for a private lawyer. The shared background knowledge is required to interpret A's utterance: it is a matter of luck with such attorneys, just as certain gambling games involve rolling the dice. The speaker is making an analogy to express her point of view on the matter of public defenders. The listener knows that the discussion is not about literal gambling.

Reference

In addition to using background knowledge to narrow down the meaning of an utterance, reference must also be assigned to understand who or what is being referred to in the context of the utterance. In the example above, the listener may wonder if B is referring to some specific public defender by using the word "those," or if B is expressing a dismissive, cynical attitude toward the abilities of such lawyers.

Reference and Context

The traditional semantic view of reference studies the relationship between words and their referents. Words are said to refer to things, places, and people in the world, and indeed all language may be regarded as referential in nature. Within the field of pragmatics, the construct considers that people use words to refer; that is, referring is an action on the part of the speaker or writer to enable the hearer or reader to identify a person, place, or thing mentioned in the linguistic text. Common referring expressions in English are proper nouns (Mount Fuji, China, Montreal), noun phrases that are definite (the book, the ocean, the trees) or indefinite (an Italian restaurant, a tall mountain), and pronouns (he, she, it, them). The choice of referring expression is made by the speaker on the basis of the speaker's assumption of how much help the addressee needs to comprehend the speaker's utterance.

1. My neighbor told me not to park my car in front of her house.
2. You know my unfriendly neighbor? She told me not to park my car in front of her house.

In number 2 the speaker assumes the addressee needs information to understand that the neighbor in question is the one who has in the past been presented as unfriendly and complaining. If the speaker assumes that a conversational partner does not need help in assigning reference, the talk can become almost incomprehensible to a third person.

> *A:* um hm (+) because **they'**d only come in like maybe half an hour before court is when Glen could see **them** (+) and **they**

already had **this** deal kinda worked up in **their** mind and
then that's when **they** run **it** past Glen so **they** really didn't
talk to Glen or get **his** ideas or anything (+) and so
B: (0.15) huh
A: **she** thought a criminal lawyer might be different [*irrecoverable*]
(LoCastro 1990b)

As this example demonstrates, it is not always possible to disentangle the who or what. Without a context for these three turns at talk, it is not possible to assign reference to most of the words that appear in bold. The need for knowledge shared by A and B becomes clear.

It is important to note that the category of referring expressions is not a closed class. That is, reference involves more than the usual pronouns. In fact, a great deal of creativity can be seen in referring expressions. The only limit is the hearer's ability to infer the speaker's meaning. An interesting example is when one faculty member speaking to another uses a nickname to refer to the head of the department: "His royal highness has got his trainers on today." In the context of the academic department, the two colleagues in face-to-face talk easily understand to whom they are referring, while an outsider would not understand, lacking an insider's information.

Types of Reference

There are two main categories of reference: exophoric and endophoric. *Exophoric* reference denotes linguistic items in a text that signal that some entity outside the text (*exo,* "outside") must be considered to understand the meaning of the utterance. A transparent example is "She's pregnant." This constructed example suggests that, if the front page of the *Japan Times* were to print the phrase as the headline on the lead article one day, most people in Japan would undoubtedly process "she" as representing the crown princess, whose long-awaited pregnancy would allay concerns about the imperial line in Japan. Another example involves the headline in a Mexican newspaper: "Oh, la, la!" It appeared the day after the World Cup final on the front page of the sports section and, through a stereotypical French phrase, communicated to insiders (who knew that France and Italy were the two contenders) that France had won. In other words, exophoric reference often requires knowledge of the sociocultural context in which the text is found.

The second main category of reference, *endophoric* (*endo,* "inside"), refers to linguistic elements that are present in the linguistic text itself. The most common form of endophoric reference in English is *anaphora,* where the analyst has to go "backward" in the text.

> *A:* so now (0.2) it won't be that long (0.3) she hired **this attorney** today, so (+)
> *B:* is **he** expensive?
>
> (LoCastro 1990b)

Most of us are familiar with anaphora; textbooks are full of exercises that ask students to find the antecedent for a pronoun.

The second type of endophoric reference is *cataphora,* which comprises reference requiring that one go "forward" to find the referent.

> It's going down quickly, the sun. (Brown and Yule 1983a, 193)

The "it" at the start of the utterance is used to refer to "the sun," which follows it in the linear text. Cataphoric reference is typically found in newspaper articles or other narratives where the writer wants to engage the readers' curiosity.

> *The* trip would hardly have been noteworthy, except for *the* man who made it. In mid-July a powerful American financier flew to Mexico City for a series of talks with high-level government officials, including President Miguel de la Madrid and his finance minister, Gustavo Petricioli. (*Newsweek,* September 21, 1987, 44, quoted in McCarthy 1991, 42)

The passage describes "the" trip in the second sentence; however, the referent for "the man" is not made clear until later. The purpose of cataphoric reference is to entice the readers into continuing to read the article in *Newsweek.*

The third type of endophoric reference is *zero anaphora,* which denotes instances where the referent is ellipted. In "I was waiting for the bus, but he drove by without stopping" (Yule 1996a, 131), the reader does not learn explicitly who "he" refers to; the assumption is that the pronoun can only refer to the bus driver. Zero anaphor is less common than anaphoric or cataphoric reference and tends to be found in spoken discourse.

In sum, reference is an important feature of language use. It is collaborative in nature: it depends on the shared knowledge between the speaker and addressee and influences the listener's ability to infer the speaker's intended meaning. Production and comprehension of reference is one feature of the joint actions carried out by the coparticipants in talk.

Ambiguity, Intentionality, and Force

In addition to the concepts referred to above, that is, sense, sentence and contextual meaning, co-text, context, and reference, others are involved in assigning pragmatic meaning.

Ambiguity

In addition to assigning sense to words, which as noted may be polysemous, and references to words, which may have unclear referents, understanding requires resolving structural ambiguities. Most introductory textbooks of linguistics list such examples as the following:

> Flying planes can be dangerous.
> The man saw his neighbor with the binoculars.

In most instances, the context of utterance resolves any difficulty, and the hearer can disambiguate the speaker's meaning. Although recourse to the context generally resolves the ambiguity, in some cases the hearer may be unable to decide with confidence the speaker's meaning.

> Puisqu'il parle toutes les langues indifférémment.
> (Thomas 1997, 3)

Like English *indifferently,* "indifféremment" in this context may have two opposite meanings: the "he" referred to speaks all languages equally well or equally badly. If the hearer does not know the person mentioned, the speaker's meaning is difficult to discern. The hearer may have to ask for clarification or be left unable to sort out what the speaker intends to communicate.

Intentionality

When assigning sense, reference, and contextual meaning, intentionality has to be considered. The underlying assumption is that the only grounds for communication with another social being is that the speaker, consciously or unconsciously, has something to say of some value to the hearer. It may be a transfer of information ("Try the telephone directory for the number of the restaurant"), an acknowledgment of the copresence of a fellow human being ("Hi there, been busy lately?"), or an assertion of power over someone ("You will need to serve tea to the guests when they arrive"). In one sense, pragmatics is a study of how intentionality is carried out in language use. For example, what do speakers signal by their choice from these possible ways of asking for the salt?

> I think this dish needs some salt.
> Would you mind passing the salt?
> Could I ask you to pass the salt?
> Could you pass the salt, please?
> I need the salt.
> Pass the salt!

As we move down the list of possibilities, the degree of directness increases. In the first sentence, the speaker appears to be expressing an opinion but doesn't ask for salt. The last example is a direct request. The basic meaning may be the same: the speaker wants to add salt to the food. However, in the first sentence the speaker conveys the meaning indirectly, probably to avoid making the cook feel bad. The curt final sentence may show that the relationship between the speaker and addressee allows such directness or that the speaker intends to signal dominance over the addressee.

Force

Sorting out the speaker's intent in communicative actions requires attention to the force of an utterance. *Force* is the term used to denote the speaker's communicative intention (Thomas 1995, 18). If a policeman stops you, asking, "Is that your bicycle over there?" just after you locked your bike to a fencepost, you are liable to begin to feel a bit nervous. You know that "your bicycle" is used by the policeman to refer to your possession, and that "over there," especially if the words are accompanied by a pointing gesture, means at a distance from both of you, but still within sight. However, unless you are particularly good at understanding intonation cues, you may be at a loss to assign force to the utterance. Is he about to reprimand you for locking it to the fencepost? Or is he going to warn you that it may be stolen? Figuring out the speaker's intended meaning entails assigning the most likely force for the situation. (Chapter 8, "Sociolinguistic Approaches," discusses in more detail this aspect of pragmatics.)

As with the policeman, it is possible to understand an utterance in context, yet not be able to work out the intended meaning or force of the utterance. Intentionality is key in assigning meaning in context. In the next sections, the focus is on the importance of considering the speaker and the addressee in the context of an interaction.

Interactional Context

Speakers usually do not talk in a vacuum. Even though some university lecturers may appear to go on and on without consideration of their audience, their discourse does reflect in subtle ways awareness of the perceived audience's expectations. A salient word here is "perceived." In second language teaching contexts, teachers may experience a mismatch between their lecture style and those of their second language learners. The audience effect becomes apparent in cross-cultural environments. For example, the lack of direct eye contact with one's students in a lecture setting may be unnerving to a teacher who is from a culture where eye contact is expected. Whether in speaking or writing, there is always at least an imagined audience that constrains how the speaker or writer uses language. The real or imagined interactional context influences potential meaning.

The Speaker's Meaning

Some scholars of pragmatics view the field as essentially about a speaker's meaning. Imagine a skier in the middle of rapidly descending a steep slope, who suddenly hears someone yelling "Watch out!" In this instance, the hearer is most critically interested in what the speaker of that phrase means: is there a tree, a person, a snowmobile, a sharp drop-off ahead? The analyst focusing on the speaker's meaning asks, "What does the speaker mean by saying X?" In the case of the skier, it is possible to comprehend what someone in such a situation wants to know. Here is an example in which it is not clear:

> *A:* oh, have you lost some weight recently?
> *B:* no, why do you ask?

In this case, B may have no clue as to what A's intended meaning is and so responds to the surface meaning. It is only later in the day that B suddenly remembers the conversation with A and realizes that it was an indirect message, concerning the baggy pair of trousers B had put on hurriedly that morning. Even having achieved that level of awareness of A's probable intended meaning, B still did not know if A was suggesting that he not wear that pair of trousers again or that B was criticizing him for his poor taste and sloppy habits!

Meaning in Interaction

The view that pragmatics focuses on speakers' meanings obscures the fact that the interpretation of the speaker's meaning is only one of the necessary requirements for a conversation to continue successfully. The addressee or hearer must take up, that is, understand, the speaker's intended meaning. In order for that to happen, the speaker must take into consideration the addressee to assure that the intended meaning has been conveyed. In the case of the baggy trousers example above, A may have intended that her message be ambiguous.

According to Clark, "Language use is really a form of *joint action*. . . . Doing things with language is likewise different from the sum of the speaker speaking and a listener listening" (1996, 3). Clark maintains that a product approach to language use, which grew out of the formal linguistic study of words and sentences, emphasizes the products, the utterances, and their meanings. The product view is similar to the code model of communication, by which interactions are regarded as having an encoder and a decoder. The participants exchange utterances as if they were playing a game of tennis. In contrast, the "action tradition" (Clark 1996, 56), which views language as inherently interactive in nature, investigates how speakers and hearers jointly engage in social actions. From this perspective, context is not something that is consulted only after the other cognitive processing has been carried out. Joint activity is the basic domain of analysis. Clark's view is that "in language use, a central problem is coordinating what speakers mean. And what their addressees understand them to mean" (1996, 73).

An example of how language is constructed to attend to the need for coordination can be observed in certain conventional expressions. Such expressions, recognized by all members of a speech community, are especially useful as coordination devices, that is, signals that enable the participants to engage smoothly in joint action. Greetings are an example of conventional behavior that may not be as likely to precipitate interactional problems between two or more interactants, in comparison to, for example, the potential problems asking for a favor might entail. Another conventional use of language involves presequences, as in the following example:

A: are you free tonight?
B: well, I was planning on getting home early
A: oh, okay—well, see you bright and early tomorrow

A's first utterance is a preinvitation, a testing of the waters, so to speak, to avoid A's being too disappointed if B refuses. A, in fact, decides not to continue with the actual invitation ("I was just wondering if you wanted to catch a bite to eat first") after hearing B's response.

In addition to the coordination problem, subsequent to the recognition of the speaker's intentions, the hearer needs to engage in uptake, that is, to attend to the speaker's contribution to the joint action, showing understanding, in effect (Clark 1996, 200). Shows of understanding can be linguistic:

> *Stone:* I'll be right there
> *Clark:* okay
>
> (Clark 1996, 51)

and/or nonlinguistic:

> *A1:* so you don't have the space here?
> *J2:* no, space itself is . . . already available, but not yet *dana* (1) no walls [*laughter*]
> *A1:* no walls
> *J2:* no walls [*simultaneous talk*]
> *J1:* we should have the walls by, by July
> *J3:* [*laughter*]
> *J2:* July?
> *J1:* sure
> *A1:* chairs [*simultaneous talk and laughter*]
> *J2:* it's one big room at this moment
> *J1:* we may not have chairs [*laughter*]
> *A2:* *zabutons*
> [*simultaneous laughter*]
>
> (LoCastro 1990b)

Note: Dana = a hesitation marker meaning "isn't that true?" *zabutons* = cushions one uses to sit on the floor in temples, and so on, in Japan.

Clark emphasizes that, within any discussion of language use, all forms of signaling, such as voice, head nods, gaze, posture, and laughter can be used by speakers and hearers to communicate intentions, recognition, and uptake.

Put simply, without the recognition and the uptake by the hearer, the speaker's attempts at initiating a joint activity are for naught. Further, it can be shown that a speaker orients the talk to obtain the necessary cooperation—or recognition—from the addressee. In this way, the hearer or audience influences the meaning potential available to the speaker in the course of carrying out the joint action; the speaker engages in audience design of utterance production. (This notion of recognition, uptake, and the narrowing of the meaning potential will be developed further in chapter 8.)

The following summarizes the elements that contribute to understanding the meaning of an utterance.

	Joint Activity
Cognitive processing:	Abstract meaning
	Contextual meaning
	Speaker meaning
	Addressee recognition
Enactments:	By speaker and addressee, and
	By means of signaling systems,
	Both linguistic and nonlinguistic

Pragmatic Meaning

A speaker's meaning may be problematic to establish for reasons already alluded to in the preceding pages. The addressee must assign the most relevant meaning to the speaker's utterance by considering contextual factors. Once the listener begins to seek out the implied meaning—the implicature—then it is the pragmatic meaning that is being processed by the listener. As has been pointed out, what is meant can only be derived from what is said by means of the cognitive process of inferring the implied meaning.

A basic distinction between conventional and conversational implicatures needs to be made. Prefabricated or conventional routines abound in everyday talk. Most of them are conventionalized to the extent that the interactants do not take them at their literal, face meaning, but rather react and respond to them as if the routinized, socially accepted meaning were the only one conveyed. Thus, in English, someone may greet another person by saying,

Hi, how are you? (American English)
Are you all right? (Northern British)

The conventional meaning of greeting, not an inquiry into the person's health, is interpreted by the listener, and the response will not be a rundown of the person's recent state of health. In a similar way, in Japanese, the phrases to excuse oneself, that is, *sumimasen, gomen nasai,* and *shitsurei shimasu,* are not translated to make apparent their literal meanings of apologies. The use of these phrases to make excuses is conventionalized. Indeed, where an actual apology is called for, the phrasing is more elaborate. The linguistic forms have, in essence, lost their original meanings and have taken on the conventional, generalized meaning assigned by the speech community.

An example of conventional implicatures in Spanish can be observed in the use of the imperfect tense to soften the assertiveness of the proposition.

> Venía a preguntar por los billetes a Mallorca. [I was coming to ask about tickets to Mallorca.]
> Queríamos ver las ofretas para el mes de julio. [We wanted to see the specials for the month of July.]
>
> (Chodorowska-Pilch 2000, 30)

The use of the simple present tense would be viewed as too direct in service types of encounters such as visiting a travel agency to inquire about tickets and package vacation trips.

As for conversational implicatures, the implied meaning, which must be inferred by the addressee, can only be discovered in the context of a particular utterance, in the interaction between speaker and addressee, with consideration of the relevant linguistic and nonlinguistic contextual features. Here is an example (Yule 1996a, 40):

> *Charlene:* I hope you brought the bread and cheese
> *Dexter:*   Well, ah, I brought the bread . . .

Dexter does not state that he forgot to bring the cheese along with the bread; nevertheless, Charlene can work out his implicature, that he forgot to bring cheese.

Pragmatic meaning thus refers to the inferred, intended message that becomes salient or ostensive in the context of the speaker-hearer joint action. Conventionalized implicatures abound in everyday life; inferences communicated through conversational interaction are the real stuff of joint activities.

Expansion Level

The next two sections briefly elaborate on the second and third levels of Cicourel's model. These two subcategories of context reflect the discussion above: communication is composed of joint activities in which the speaker and audience have equally constitutive roles. In levels 2 and 3 of Cicourel's framework, some of the important constituent features of the speaker and addressee are considered. Cicourel's second level of information sources comprises factors that are related to the participants: the rights and obligations, the biographies of the interactants, and the history of the relationship between and among them.

Rights and Obligations

In any interaction, each and every participant has rights and obligations. In a chat at a café, for example, the rights include the chance to contribute to the ongoing conversation by introducing a topic, giving an opinion, or telling a joke. An obvious obligation is to share the floor, allowing others to contribute to the chat. Another obligation requires that one speak loudly enough to be heard.

Now, clearly, this is a description of an ideal environment where equality seems to reign. In the real world, the situation is more complex, and rights and obligations of individuals with more power and social status, such as judges or lawyers, are reflected in their use of language. In the following example the defendant's lawyer is questioning the plaintiff in a rape case (Levinson 1992, 82).

> *L:* Your aim that evening then was to go to the discotheque?
> *P:* Yes
> *L:* Presumably you had dressed up for that, had you?
> *P:* Yes
> *L:* And you were wearing make-up?

P: Yes
L: Eye-shadow?
P: Yes

It is clear who can ask the questions and who has to answer in monosyllables.

Biographies and Histories

Participants in interactions have a history of experiences, including interacting with the others in talk. Cicourel points out that each individual has a unique conversational style that reflects who they are as a human being. In addition, coparticipants interact differently depending on how well they know each other. Moreover, Wolfson (1986) found that, even if interactants do not know each other, they react differently according to their expectations of the possibility of a future relationship. Wolfson called this "bulge theory." This metaphor reflects how the results of her study would appear if one were to plot them on a chart or graph. The "bulge," or high frequencies of linguistic signals of elaboration and negotiation in language use, always occurred when the conversational partners were known to each other, but "non intimates, status-equal friends, co-workers, and acquaintances" (Wolfson 1986, 694). This unexpected use of language contrasted with less elaboration and negotiation of social distance signals when the coparticipants were "status unequals" or complete strangers—in other words, when the social situation was clear. Where the social situation is not clear, then more work with language to establish a relationship—now or in the future—is noticeable. Wolfson's research particularly focused on compliments as used by middle-class Americans.

A: Hi Marianne, how are you?
B: // Fine
A: // *What a beautiful scarf*
B: Oh thanks, it is, isn't it? I'm so embarrassed—Keiko gave it to me'n you know these aren't cheap
A: Oh I know
B: mm so how have you been?

(Hatch 1992, 136–37)

The compliment is being used as part of the greeting, the opener of the conversation. It functions as a "bonding" signal between the two Americans, most likely two women who are colleagues, and although they may work together everyday, they are not likely to be intimate friends. While the compliment may seem insincere to observers from different cultural backgrounds, the important point is that it would be an example of language use, functioning to maintain and perhaps build the relationship. The compliment may not be authentic, but it softens any potential face threat. In contrast, for coparticipants who already have an ongoing relationship, directness, laughter, and even direct challenges are not sources of discomfort in an interaction. Lots of elaboration and negotiation through language—that is, "bulge" behavior—is not necessary. The shared background knowledge and the expectation that the relationship will continue facilitates the processing of pragmatic meaning.

Higher-Order Predicates

The third level of Cicourel's model of information sources is composed of the higher-order notions of a society. The normative rules and dominant values of a society are enacted in the sociocultural context. They are generally taken for granted and unexamined; rarely are most coparticipants aware of the extent to which their beliefs and values are involved in their everyday activities or conversations. This component of Cicourel's model directly emphasizes the importance of beliefs and values in interpreting pragmatic meaning. Both how discourse is produced and how it is comprehended are influenced by the values each participant holds.

The conversation in the accompanying table is a well-known example. What is a friendly question to one person may seem to be an invasion of privacy to another. The machine-gun questioning style (Tannen 1984, 64–65) reflects the speaker's sociocultural background, in this case, New York Jewish (Tannen 1981), which includes values such as high involvement with her conversational partners. The pace of the talk is fast with considerable overlap of talk. Each time Deborah speaks, the focus of the conversation shifts, as if she were putting Steve and Peter on the spot. A close analysis of the text indicates that Steve may have felt ill at

1.	*Steve:*	I think it's basically done . . . damage to children. That what good it's done is . . . outweighed by . . . the damage.
2.	*Deborah:*	Did you two grow up with television?
3.	*Peter:*	Very little. We had a TV in the Quonset.
4.	*Deborah:*	How old were you when your parents got it?
5.	*Steve:*	We had a TV but we didn't watch it all the time. . . . We were very young. I was four when my parents got a TV.
6.	*Deborah:*	You were four?
7.	*Peter:*	I even remember that. . . . I don't remember
8.	*Steve:*	I remember they got a TV before we moved out of the Quonset huts. In nineteen fifty four.
9.	*Peter:*	I remember we got it in the Quonset huts.
10.	*Deborah:*	[*Chuckles*] You lived in Quonset huts? When you were how old?
11.	*Steve:*	Y'know my father's a dentist said to him what's a Quonset hut?

Source: Tannen 1984, 64–65.

ease, presumably because he did not share her background or conversational style. He undoubtedly assigned a different pragmatic meaning to her utterances than she intended. Her friendliness might have been interpreted as her being too nosey about him and his brother.

Conclusion

The next chapter adds to the reader's growing knowledge of pragmatics by considering more deeply the concept of reference, specifically indexicality. Indexicals compose an indispensable language resource as they are prototypical instances of the interaction between context and linguistic forms.

Comprehension Questions

1. What is a central issue in pragmatics? Why is it so?
2. How do the information sources in Cicourel's framework contribute to establishing pragmatic meaning? Give examples.
3. Do interactants in talk always go through all the steps to assign a speaker's meaning, as described in this chapter? Why/why not?
4. Explain and illustrate the distinction between *sentence* and *utterance*.
5. Explain and give examples of the following terms: abstract meaning, sense, contextual (utterance) meaning.
6. What is reference? Who or what refers?
7. Find an example of each type of reference.
8. How can lexical and structural ambiguities be resolved?
9. Why is intentionality important?
10. Explain what the force of an utterance is. Give examples.
11. What is speaker meaning? How does it differ from utterance meaning?
12. Explain Clark's contribution to establishing meaning in interactional contexts. What is the main point he is making?
13. What is pragmatic meaning? What are the two types introduced in this chapter? How do they differ from each other? Give examples.

Tasks

1. For each of the following headlines, write at least two interpretations and comment on what caused the ambiguity. Which interpretation is more likely? Why?
   Drunks Get Nine Months in Violin Case
   Iraqi Head Seeks Arms
   Teacher Strikes Idle Kids
   Clinton Wins Budget; More Lies Ahead
   Juvenile Court to Try Shooting Defendant

Stolen Painting Found by Tree
Include Your Children When Baking Cookies
Local High School Dropouts Cut in Half

2. The accompanying table is an example of Japanese learner of English and native English speaker teacher data. What kinds of meanings can you find in the data? Are there any instances of problems of communication due to the participants' messages?

1.	T:	Hajime, my point is that however you support it remember you need specific examples to support if you don't have a specific example about curiosity then maybe its a bad topic ok? so look at one of your other choices so which one of these ideas do you think you have good examples?
2.	S:	mm . . . m . . . mm . . . hm hm? this one?
3.	T:	but . . .
4.	S:	huhum?
5.	T:	should it be that way?
6.	S:	mm
7.	T:	you say high school is thought of as a means of preparation for university or college is this right? is it wrong? do you agree with this?
8.	S:	oh
9.	T:	I I don't know what your opinion is

Source: Mori 1996, 72.

3. Consider the concepts introduced in this chapter. Where are second language learners likely to have problems producing and understanding pragmatic meaning?

Text Analysis

Answer these questions for the transcript presented in the table.

1. What kind of information do you need to understand what is happening in the conversation?

1.	<S01>	And erm so we thought we'd have someone to dinner and have a
2.		party you know a dinner party over this coming weekend but they're
3.		not going to be here so
4.	<S02>	Well that would be boring
5.	<S01>	Don't . . . not quite sure when they thought we were going to do it
6.		but there we are
7.	<S02>	But she's saying that erm loads of people that they're meant to be
8.		staying with can't remember [*laughs*]. Apparently erm someone's
9.		moving well to a new job and someone else has got relatives coming
10.		to stay. So they can't
11.	<S01>	Oh up in Suffolk?
12.	<S02>	Mm. Don't know. But anyway
13.	<S01>	Oh. But they're not. I mean they knew we were away for that whole
14.		week cos I wrote and told them.
15.	<S02>	What week? Easter week?
16.	<S01>	Yes
17.	<S02>	Mm
18.	<S01>	And they they'd already made their plans for various visits before
19.		they arrived. It's called a hoof.
20.	<S02>	What is that? [*laughs*] Is it rubber?
21.	<S01>	Yes. I think it's probably quite old and rather
22.	<S02>	Where'd you get it?
23.	<S01>	inflexible
24.	<S02>	Where's it from?
25.	<S01>	A chemist. Erm do you know the chemist which is now Boots in
26.		Petswood?
27.	<S02>	Yeah
28.	<S01>	That's where I got it. I mean they [*laughs*] . . . you use it like this.
29.	<S02>	[*Laughs*]
30.	<S01>	Push back the cuticle.
31.	<S02>	Mm
32.	<S01>	And when I had a manicure free of charge.
33.	<S02>	When did you have a manicure?
34.	<S01>	They were doing them free in the Army and Navy when I went to a
35.		special shopping evening.
36.	<S02>	Were they?
37.	<S01>	Yes. So I had one.
38.	<S02>	Mm Mm

Source: Carter and McCarthy 1997, 71.
Note: <S01> female; <S02> female; <S01> and <S02> are mother and daughter. In this recording, the two speakers are at home.

2. Find a word or phrase in the text with an abstract meaning that differs considerably from the sense the word has in this conversation.
3. For line 9, give the contextual meaning.
4. What is the speaker's meaning in line 12?
5. For lines 10–13, explain how the meaning in interaction between the mother and daughter is created.
6. Find examples of different types of reference in the talk.
7. In line 4, what is the speaker's intended meaning?
8. What is the force of line 30?
9. What is the conventional implicature of line 6?
10. What is the conversational implicature of line 17?

Suggested Readings

Cicourel, A. V. 1980. Three models of discourse analysis: The role of social structure. *Discourse Processes* 3:101–32.

Chodorowska-Pilch, M. 2000. The imperfect of politeness in Spanish. *Southwest Journal of Linguistics* 19, no. 1: 29–44.

Hatch, E. 1992. *Discourse and language education.* Cambridge: Cambridge University Press.

McCarthy, M. 1991. *Discourse analysis for language teachers.* Cambridge: Cambridge University Press.

Wolfson, N. 1986. Research methodology and the question of validity. *TESOL Quarterly* 20, no. 4: 689–700.

Chapter 3
Indexicality

The previous chapter drew attention to the importance of assigning reference to words and phrases in an utterance. The listener has to be able to determine who or what the speaker is referring to in the context of the utterance.

> A: The part that broke is a little plastic thing, sort of like a wing that turns all the way round
> B: Do we have any more of those wings?
>
> (Yule 1997, 11)

This two-part sequence from a conversation about fixing things in the house is uninterpretable if A and B assume that "wings" is referring to those of birds or airplanes. If so, then reference cannot be assigned.

Reference is an action by which a speaker or writer uses linguistic forms to enable a listener or reader to identify something or someone in the context of utterance. Reference is a philosophical and theoretical issue within linguistics (Mey 1993, 90), beyond the scope of this book. Nevertheless, it is also a pragmatic problem in that meaning cannot be established if words such as "I" and "you," prototypical examples of undetermined referential expressions, remain ambiguous. In this chapter, one category of words, a particular kind of referential expression, which functions in a more obvious way to denote the relationship between language and context, will be discussed. These linguistic forms are called *indexicals*. Indexicality itself is a phenomenon of language, indispensable in assigning reference to linguistic forms in an utterance.

Indexicality is not a new word; in linguistics, it refers to "all the contextual determinations that are implicitly attached to a word . . . although a word has a transsituational signification, it also has a distinct significance in each particular situation in which it is used" (Coulon 1995, 17). For example, "I'm here now" has meaning, yet takes on a particular contextual meaning in each situation in which it is used. If a friend telephones from Grand Central Station in New York City, with the message "I'm here now," the caller and the person on the end of the telephone line must have agreed on what "here" and "now" mean, that is, at the information booth in the main hall at 7:00 P.M., or they may never find each other in the large train station.

Indexicals are prototype instances of signals of how interaction between context and linguistic forms are inseparable. Words such as "I," "you," "here," and "now" demonstrate how the incompleteness or indeterminacy of language is explicitly manifested in the indexical expressions found in all natural languages. The characteristic of indeterminacy enables a linguistic form to be used in many contexts, as the form has no clear meaning outside an instance of use. When one son returns home without the other son, the mother might say, "Where's Tony?" She might receive the response, "He fell down" (Green 1989, 8, 12). The indeterminacy of the words in the response leaves the mother to assign sense and reference to the utterance: where? what were the circumstances? is he seriously hurt? In an actual context of situation, such words as *he* and *fell down* are "indexed," compared against elements in the local context so that their "value" or meaning is determined; that is, they are given an "index" or label. Here is another example:

B2: so **this other** lady who was on the phone wouldn't know
A1: what colour hair did **the** girl—**the** lady **with the telephone** + did she have
B1: long brown hair
A1: brownish **sort of**

(G. Brown 1995, 136)

This piece of talk indicates how commonplace the indeterminacy of everyday language is, specifically with demonstratives and the definite article. This chapter now considers categories of indexicals in more detail; examples of indexicals, more commonly called *deictic markers,* are present in most instances of language in use.

Deixis

The following example comes from a map-drawing task, where A has to tell B how to get from one place on a map to another. Both have the same map, but they are sitting on opposite sides of a divided table and can only use verbal signals to communicate with each other; no pointing with hands is permitted.

> *A:* go – up towards between the mountains and across *the bridge* on the big river
> *B:* what *bridge* on the big river?
> *A:* the river on the –
> *B:* och aye
> *A:* and you go + round towards *the wood* + but you cut off between + the top of the – river and *the woods* ++ and then up towards the castle
>
> (G. Brown 1995, 79)

As this example shows, it is impossible to describe to someone how to get from point X on a map to point Z without using several "little" words to point via language to items, persons, and places in the context of the utterance. In fact, *deixis* comes from the Greek term meaning "pointing," and such words as *that, now, the, you,* and *here* are considered deictic forms. In English, demonstrative pronouns and adjectives, first- and second-person pronouns, and some time and place adverbs can perform the function of pointing—or more correctly, can be used by speakers to point. Comprising a closed class of words, they are employed to indicate something in the context of the utterance. This capacity thereby assumes that the speaker and the hearer share the same context, or at least knowledge of the same context. The importance of common knowledge can be clearly illustrated. In large cities of the world with extensive underground systems, such as in Tokyo or Paris, both speaker and hearer must share the same contextual knowledge about the subway system when they are negotiating a meeting over the telephone: "front end of the train, on the platform," requires they know which platform, which train line, and from which direction the train is traveling. In the example, the italicized words are those that can cause some difficulty for the listener unless both the speaker and listener are looking at the same place on the same map.

The most basic distinction made by deixis seems to be "near the speaker" and "away from the speaker." Thus, there are proximal terms—*this, here*—and distal terms—*that, those, there.* As with following directions on a map, both speakers and addressees have to know where the deictic center is located, for example, the You Are Here marker on the map. Typically, the deictic center in face-to-face conversation is the speaker's location. If a friend flies from London to Chicago on a business trip and leaves on your answering machine the message, "Just wanted you to know I'm here . . . Talk with you later," you can only assume that "here" means Chicago and "later" means after the day's business, or that evening, Chicago time.

Some languages have a three-part deictic system: in Japanese, it is possible to distinguish near the speaker ("here," *kore*), near the addressee ("there," *sore*), and away from both ("over there," *are*). The Spanish of Spain also has three: *aquí* (here*), ahí* (there) and *allí* (over there). Outside Spain it is also possible to hear *acá* (here) and *allá* (there). Of course, it is possible to say "over there" in English; however, it is not with a single word as in Spanish and Japanese. The main point about deixis is that it is not possible to interpret the speaker's use of deictic forms without knowledge of the context of occurrence. There are several kinds of deictic expressions: person, spatial, temporal, social, and discourse deixis.

Person Deixis

Many languages have a three-part set of linguistic forms: in English, first person *(I)*, second person *(you),* and third person *(he, she, it,* and *they).* The speaker uses "I" to refer to him- or herself, refers to the addressee as "you," both when the hearer is one or more persons, and employs "he," "she," "it," "they" to signal other persons in the context of the utterance. In face-to-face conversation, the persons to whom "I" and "you" refer are constantly changing, as the speaker and hearer exchange roles in the course of the talk. If the speaker wants to include the addressee with the speaker explicitly in the talk, "we" can serve that function, as "we" can be inclusive or exclusive, depending on the speaker's intention in a specific context of use. Here is a part from a speech given by President Reagan in 1984 (Lakoff 1990, 189).

> By beginning to rebuild our defenses, **we** have restored credible deterrence and can confidently seek a secure and lasting peace, as well as a reduction of arms. As I said Wednesday night, America is back and standing tall. **We**'ve begun to restore great American values: the dignity of work, the warmth of family, the strength of neighborhood and the nourishment of human freedom. But **our** work is not finished.

It is not clear about whom Reagan is talking when he uses "we" and "our:" the government of the United States, the people, or both. The strategy is a subtle means to bring the people into believing they are the U.S. government, reinforcing nationalistic beliefs and values through use (or his speech writers' use!) of language.

Note that not all uses of *you* in English or *vous* in French are deictic. When *you* is deictic, it should be possible to point out the referent, commonly the addressee. However, in other cases, such as "You never know what's going to happen," the pronoun has no specific referent and may include the speaker and any copresent participants. Here is an example from an essay written by a Mexican learner of English.

> I think that if **you** are really convinced about **your** goals **you** don't need to be socially accepted, but if it occurs that **you** can't reach that desire, **you** could get frustrated. **You** only have to look for the biggest goal, not for other factors that **you** can attain on the way to reaching the biggest one. (LoCastro 2000b)

In this case, "you" does not directly refer to the addressee or reader of the essay. An interesting example where "you" is arguably nondeictic—that is, not being used to address someone in particular—can be observed when a speaker refers to members of the audience, in effect, overhearers of television interview programs. A politician may be perceived to be answering the interviewer's questions, while, in fact, he or she is employing "you" to refer as well to the listening audience, the mass of voters. The speaker may be well aware of the ambiguity, using it to create a kind of slippage from appearing to address the interviewer's question while at the same time talking to the voters in the audience.

Spatial Deixis

The second category of deixis concerns space and movement. The most obvious deictic expressions in this category of spatial deixis in English are *here* and *there*. However, these adverbs are only two of many possible linguistic forms. Rather than take a static view of spatial deixis, it is preferable to consider movement toward or away from the speaker with the deictic center located with the current speaker. The verbs *come* and *go* illustrate this distinction well.

> Come home! (movement toward the speaker)
> Go home! (movement away from the speaker)

Note that the English distinction may not hold for all languages. A pair of verbs that can be confusing for second language learners of English is *borrow* and *loan:* A loans a book to B and B borrows the book from A. However, in Latin American Spanish, the verb *prestar* can mean both "to borrow" and "to loan." The direction of the verbal action, from A to B or B to A, is kept separate in English, but not always in other languages.

Another important point about spatial deixis is that distance from the speaker or addressee may be psychological and not simply physical; it is dependent on the speaker's affective stance. For example, psychological distance can be communicated by the speaker uttering, "I don't like that," referring to behavior of a child standing right in front of the speaker. The speaker uses "that" to convey an attitude of displeasure, even anger, toward the child's behavior.

Temporal Deixis

This category of deictic markers includes forms used to refer to such meanings as the time of a speaker's utterance, "now," in comparison to "before," which can signal an event that happened prior to the present moment of speaking.

> Now, I have a wonderful new car. Before, I was always driving a junky, secondhand car.

In other words, the point here is that deixis is concerned with the time of an event relative to the actual time of speaking about it. It can be complicated, as in the following example.

> I can give you a lift home *then*. (A few minutes from now)
> I was able to swim five hundred meters *then*. (When I was a child)
> I will meet you at noon. See you *then*. (Tomorrow, over the weekend)

Interpretation of these utterances depends on knowing the utterance time, that is, when the speaker is doing the talking, as with expressions such as "the day before yesterday" (see the accompanying table). If a teacher leaves a note on his or her office door that reads, "I'll be back in an hour. Gone to the library," students coming to visit the teacher for help cannot know when the hour is up unless they know the time the message was put on the board. Confusion may also result in deciding the meaning of "last" versus "this" or "next week." If today is Sunday, and the speaker is talking about activities of "this week," for example, is the speaker including Sunday in the entity of the six days before the Sunday or in the entity of the six days following the Sunday? Both can be possible interpretations of "this week." This can be a difficult point for speakers of other languages if the system of their first language, in a sense, cuts the pie in a different way than that of the second language.

There is another type of temporal deixis that can help the listener understand a speaker's meaning. In English, the present and past verb tenses can signal proximal and distal deictic meanings. The distal form, in particular, can communicate distance from the current moment as well as distance from current reality.

the day before yesterday	yesterday	today	tomorrow	the day after tomorrow

Current moment: I teach in Mexico (now).
Distance from current moment: I lived in Paris (in the late 1960s).
Distance from reality: If I could live anywhere in the world . . .
   [but I don't have such choice]

The tense system signals the event time, which may be simultaneous with the utterance time or with the time reported in the utterance (see the next table).

To these categories can be added social deixis and discourse deixis. The study of naturally occurring talk has demonstrated that traditional approaches to deixis cannot account for the full range of this phenomenon.

Social Deixis

Some languages encode social status differences as constraints on the speaker's choice of person deictic expressions. This is called social deixis; it can be observed in the *tu/vous* distinction in French. *Tu* is used with friends and intimates; it also expresses solidarity in Quebeçois French. *Vous,* however, is employed with all nonfamiliars in continental French. The same distinctions can be found in many European languages, such as German *(du/Sie)*. Spanish and Italian have more complex systems. Two forms are used with familiars, *tu* (taking Italian as our example) for second-person singular, and *voi* for second-person plural. However, to signal social distance, *lei* is polite second-person singular and *loro* second-person plural. Peninsular Spanish has four forms as well: *tu/vosotros, usted*

Congruent	It's raining now.	Utterance time same as event time
Incongruent	By the time you read this, I will have arrived in Paris.	Time of intended receipt of the message and event time later than utterance time
Incongruent	Zakia will be back on Wednesday.	Event time later than utterance time

Indexicality • 69

Subject pronoun	Singular/Plural	Informal/Formal
Tu	Singular	Informal
Usted	Singular	Formal
Ustedes	Singular and Plural	Informal and Formal

and *ustedes*. There are also regional variations; in Mexican Spanish, only *tu, usted,* and *ustedes* are used (see the next table).

Still other languages, such as Japanese, avoid use of personal pronouns despite their existence ("I," -*watakushi,* "you," -*anata,* "he" -*kare,* "she" -*kaoejo* with the plurals formed by adding a suffix, *tachi,* to the base forms). When they are used, in addition to the literal meanings, social and attitudinal meanings are present that are not related to the pointing function. The following example signals that the speaker has a negative attitude toward the person *(kanojo)* or her habit of being late.

Kanojo wa, itsumo osoi n desu. [Her, she's always late.]

To avoid expressing an attitudinal stance, titles, address forms and/or family names are used with an honorific marker: Yamamoto + *san* (standard form)/*sama* (more formal) *gakucho, sensei* (sir/madam, dean, teacher). The choice of the situationally appropriate deictic form made by the speaker is therefore dependent on social and other contextual considerations.

Social deixis allows the speaker to express degrees of closeness or involvement and of distance or independence from the addressee. Levinson (1983, 63) defines social deixis as "the encoding of social distinctions that are relative to participant-roles." Javanese in Indonesia has six levels that encode the social status of the speakers and listeners. The question "Did you take that much rice?" can be said in six different ways (see the accompanying table, in which the levels are listed in order of decreasing status). The speaker shifts from one level to another, depending on contextual variables.

In a language such as Japanese, the honorific system is the codification or grammaticalization of social deixis, as a speaker of Japanese

Question Marker	You	Take	Rice	That much	
Menapa	*nandalem*	*mundhut*	*sekul*	*semanten?*	3a High
Manapa	*panjenengan*	*mendhet*	*sekul*	*semanten?*	3
Napa	*sampeyan*	*mendhet*	*sekul*	*semonten?*	2
Napa	*sampeyan*	*nyupuk*	*sega*	*semonten?*	1a
Apa	*sliramu*	*mundhut*	*sega*	*semono?*	1b
Apa	*kowe*	*njupuk*	*sega*	*semono?*	1 Low

Source: Holmes 1992, 273.

must encode relative social distance in each utterance. Indeed, one way of looking at deixis is to view it as an example of the grammaticalization of contextual features. Person deictic expressions (*tu/vous,* for example), which are used to show differences in social status, encode sociocultural features of the context in language. Of the two sentences below, the first one expresses the greatest degree of deference; the speaker signals more humbleness toward the professor than in the second one.

> Sensei wa moo okaeri ni narimashita-ga. [The professor has already gone home.]
> Sensei wa moo kaeraremashita-ga. [The professor has already left.]
> (Maynard 1990, 278–79)

It is important to note that the encoding of social deixis even in Japanese does not necessarily reflect any permanent relationship between the speaker and addressee. The social status of conversational partners is relative in a particular instance of talk. In one context, a listener may be addressed with forms signaling higher status than the listener, such as in a teacher-student relationship at school or at the university. Shopping in a department store with family members, the same person will not necessarily be addressed as *sensei*. Further, speakers can use the forms of social deixis in different situations to signal, proactively, lesser or greater social distance or involvement with the addressee. In other words, speakers can indicate that they wish to shorten the social distance between themselves and their conversational partners by using the less formal markers. In any language that makes the *tu/vous* distinction, a switch to *tu* from *vous* in conversational interactions carries that meaning.

> A: ¿hola, cómo estás? [Hi, how are you?]
> B: muy bien, y tú? [Very well, and you?]

But if B responds by saying "¿Que tál?" A is left not knowing where the relationship stands. "Qué tal" can be a way to avoid signaling social distance.

Here is an example of how Japanese works.

> (1a) John *ga* Mary *to*   *dekake* +*masu*. [*masu* form]
>   SUB   with   go out
>   "John goes out with Mary."
>
> (1b) John *ga* Mary   *to* *dekake* +*ru*. [plain form]
>   SUB   with   go out
>   "John goes out with Mary."

(Cook 1997)

Cook (1997) suggests that, although the referential meanings of the two sentences are the same, the social meanings differ as a result of the verb endings. The linguistic view has been that the *masu* form is polite, formal style, while the "plain" form is for informal, insider relationships. Cook challenges this interpretation, arguing that, according to her data, interpersonal and intrapersonal distances are indexed by the choice of the verb ending. That is, the choice is not static, but rather open to personal choice in many contexts. She gives the example of a mother using the plain form to mark proximity with her child, and then in the same conversation using the distancing *masu* form when she disciplines her child.

> A: otoofu no omisoshiru ga sukoshi nokot**te imasu** yo [masu]
>   [there's some tofu left in your soup bowl.]
> B: iranai (plain) [I don't want it]

It is possible to signal such meanings in English:

Somebody didn't clear up *her* room.
We clean up after *ourselves* around here.

Even though the addressee is present, the third-person singular or the exclusive "we" performs the function of social deixis, distancing the speaker from the "her" and the person who did not clean up who is not included in the "we."

Hatch (1992) suggests that deictic expressions such as "across the tracks" reflect the social organization of a speech community. It implies that the people who live "across the tracks" or "on the wrong side of the tracks" are of a lower social class than those who live elsewhere in the town, at least in the folklore of towns in the United States.

Social deixis or social indexicality is readily observed indexing degrees of social involvement and distance. In some languages, it is more codified or grammaticalized than in others. Nevertheless, it is pervasive in all languages; it is just done differently in different languages. Where one language signals social status through choice of words, in another language status may be communicated through intonation or stress.

Discourse Deixis

According to Levinson, discourse deixis has to do with "the encoding of reference to portions of the unfolding discourse in which the utterance (which includes the text-referring expression) is located" (1983, 62). Here is an example.

> For two years, I will have to interact with a new system, being part of it. *This* is a dilemma: on one side, I have to be prepared for a different life; on the other, I am not inclined to forget all values and tastes that I had before. The trade-off between *those* two opposite tendencies showed me that, at least, my home should reflect my personality. (Hatch 1992, 219)

A more typical example is the following:

> *This* chapter will *first* define speech acts and provide a brief overview of how this field of discourse has been applied to second language acquisition

(SLA). *Next,* research methodologies used in studying speech acts will be examined, and selected empirical studies that have appeared in recent years will be considered. *Finally,* the available studies on the teaching of speech act behavior to nonnative speakers will be reviewed, and the pedagogical implications of the findings to date will be described. (Cohen 1996, 383)

In both examples, the italicized words enable the writer to refer to other parts of the text. Discourse deixis provides signposts for the reader to follow the speaker or writer's train of thought and intended meaning.

Reported Speech

All of the complexity of deixis comes together in considering reported speech, which seems to add a layer of abstraction or of distance.

> **Is** it okay if **I** ring **you this** evening? (Direct)
> **She asked if** it **was** okay for **her** to ring in **the** evening. (Reported)

The present tense, personal pronouns, demonstrative, and articles are changed, and the necessary introductory phrase in the past tense is added. All the proximal forms commonly change to distal forms in Standard English. Nevertheless, exceptions abound in everyday talk with reported speech and, as any change from the normal pattern can signal some "extra" meaning, the exceptions can illustrate pragmatic meaning. For example, a person recounting a recent experience might say, "So she asks if she can call me at home." Talking about a past event in the present tense typically makes the telling more dramatic. The speaker's voice may rise in pitch and sound more emphatic. Here is another example:

> A: Not all that long since, perhaps ten years ago, this friend of mine, her son was in hospital, and he'd had a serious accident and he was unconscious for a long time . . . anyway, she went to see him one day and she said "Has anybody been to see you?" and **he says** "no, but a right nice young lady came to see me," he said, "she was lovely, she stood at the foot of my bed, you know, she . . . had a little word with me." Well, eventually he

came home, and they'd a lot of the family in the house, and Emma, this friend of mine, brought these photographs out, of the family through the years, and passing them round, and **he's looking at them** and he said "Oh, that's that young lady that came to see me when I was in bed." She'd died when he was born . . . so.
B: Good God.
A: He'd never seen her.
B: No . . . heavens.

(McCarthy 1991, 61)

This sudden switch to the present ("he says," "he's looking at them"), called the historic present, signals the "extra" pragmatic meaning of emphasis: the really good part of the story is coming!

Conclusion

A further development on indexicality was precipitated by Garfinkel (see Coulon 1995, 18), who has claimed that all natural language is indexical, as it is only in the particular context of use that a local interpretation of daily language can be assigned more determinate meaning. A full discussion of the expansion of what constitutes indexicality is beyond the scope of this book (for a discussion, see Ochs 1992, 335–58); nevertheless, a short example will illustrate an integration of a theory of language socialization and indexicality. Ochs regards indexicality as "a property of speech through which . . . social identities (e.g. gender) . . . are constructed" (1992, 335). Tag questions, for example, can be viewed as indexing uncertainty or hesitation in making as assertion on the part of the speaker; this contextual feature may in turn index or create female gender identity.

You were missing last week, weren't you?
Were you missing last week?

By using the tag form of the question, women and others in subordinate roles are said to reinforce their weak positions in society. Although other researchers (Cameron, McAlinden, and O'Leary 1988) have provided evidence that tag questions can also be used to communicate dominance, the main point is still true that indexicals do construct social identities.

Discussion Questions

1. What is indexicality? What is deixis? Give examples.
2. Can you think of any examples in languages other than English to illustrate the five categories of deixis?
3. Why is deixis important in the study of pragmatic meaning? Give an example to support your statements.

Task

A good task for intermediate learners of English is a map-drawing exercise in which they practice giving directions and using them to draw a route on a map. Teachers of English need to be able to predict where their students may have problems with vocabulary and deictic markers. Using the map on page 76, make a list of potential problems in giving directions or understanding them.

Example: "You Are Here. How will one of the learners tell the other one where to start?"

Text Analysis

Examine the deictic markers in this piece of everyday talk and provide an analysis.

1. *B:* I gather [*unrecoverable*] was really upset about the fact that she didn't get to to have any input of when Barb's last day would be
2. *C:* huh? I knew it
3. *B:* she said she had no idea whatsoever that this was going on and she thought that was really unfair

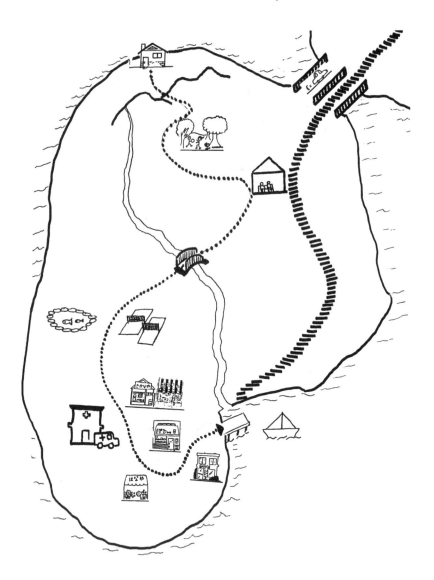

4. *C:* that's a lie
5. *B:* oh, yes cause she knew about it
6. *C:* right
7. *B:* and then she said about um what's she gonna do with the committee now and more help she needs her to attend those meetings so Barb said that she would go to to this last meeting which is Wednesday, the 15th

8. *C:* the 15th
9. *B:* and then she would go to the Board of Health meeting and that's it . . . I said Barb you know what she's gonna make you do too
10. *C:* [*unrecoverable*]
11. *B:* she's gonna do the minutes and everything and she goes no way
12. *C:* yeah
13. *B:* I said you shoulda just told her no let her handle it and she said no and I said you didn't volunteer for it did you and she said no she actually told me I should

(LoCastro 1990b)

Suggested Readings

Brown, G. 1995. *Speakers, listeners, and communication: Explorations in discourse analysis.* Cambridge: Cambridge University Press.

Cohen, A. 1996. Speech acts. In *Sociolinguistics and language teaching,* ed. S. L. Mackay and N. H. Hornberger. Cambridge: Cambridge University Press.

Coulon, A. 1995. *Ethnomethodology.* Qualitative Research Methods Series 36. Thousand Oaks, Calif.: Sage.

Holmes, J. 1992. *An introduction to sociolinguistics.* London: Longman.

Lakoff, R. T. 1990. *Talking power: The politics of language.* New York: HarperCollins.

Yule, G. 1997. *Referential communication tasks.* Mahwah, N.J.: Lawrence Erlbaum.

Chapter 4
Entailment and Presupposition

This chapter introduces a pair of terms that figure in discussions about pragmatic meaning, *entailment* and *presupposition*. Both are forms of inferencing and therefore are considered together. Entailments are not of great concern within the field of pragmatics, however, and once the concept is defined and examples given, the chapter will focus on presupposition, which plays a more important role in understanding pragmatic meaning.

Entailment

An entailment, also called a logical consequence, is derived from approaches to pragmatic meaning within the philosophy of language and semantics. An entailment has to do with "understood" information derived solely from the words or sentences. For example, if a fan of the New York Yankees states, "They won," the entailment associated with the word "won" is that the Yankees scored more runs than the opposing team. Thus, a semantic inference, essentially the same as the dictionary definition, is always assigned to the word *won,* irrespective of the context. Semanticists also claim that an entailment is canceled if denied. Grundy provides this example (1995, 43):

1. We have a child.
2. We have a child, in fact, we have none.

The first sentence entails that the speaker has at least one child. The second cancels its own entailment.

Entailments are usually not stated. The statement "Henry VIII had six wives" entails that he had two wives, but not that he had *only* two wives (Stubbs 1983, 208). If a desk clerk in a Japanese inn announces, "The bath is ready" to guests checking in for the night, the statement entails bathwater that is at least warm because it must be so for the bath to be "ready" (Levinson 1983, 138).

Note that this technical use of the word *entail* differs from the ordinary meaning as given in a dictionary. There *entail* means "to cause or involve by necessity or as a consequence: 'a loss entailing no regret'" (*Random House College Dictionary,* 1984). The basic meaning, that is, that an entailment is a logical consequence, is still present; however, the logic used in everyday usage of the term is not strictly associated with the meaning of the words, but rather a situation that is described.

> The road construction around Chicago *entails* our having to change our route to the airport, or we'll be late for the departure.

In this example, a synonym of "entails" could be "means."

Both entailments and presuppositions are inferences that can be drawn from utterances, but it is important to distinguish them. The remainder of the chapter is devoted to presuppositions, as they involve speakers and addressees and language in context. Entailments is a purely semantic concept, having to do with sentence meaning, not speaker-listener meaning, the proper domain of pragmatics.

Presupposition

In contrast to entailments, which logically follow from what is asserted by the linguistic forms in a proposition, presuppositions, although also part of the taken-for-granted "invisible" information, are assumed by the speaker to be part of the background, unstated assumptions of the interactant. In a sense, presuppositions are forms of embedded information that inform human communication outside awareness. Within the category of presuppositions is included knowledge of the world, which can come from multiple sources, such as books and experience with the world in general. Presuppositions are part of what is communicated, but *not* part of what is said. Speaker and hearer share them as assumptions; note that speakers "have" presuppositions, whereas entailments "belong" to or are properties of sentences. The speaker designs an utterance on the basis of assumptions about what the hearer is likely to "know." In most circumstances, when a speaker makes an assertion, the speaker is treating the proposition as noncontroversial. That is, the speaker takes it for granted the addressee can infer the unstated presuppositions. If someone asks you at a party: "Did you buy this awful wine?" the person is presupposing (1) you also think the wine is awful, (2) you have better taste than to buy it, (3) the speaker can tease you, and (4) someone else at the party has bad taste in wine.

A humorous example of a presupposition is that most human beings operate always as if the sun will rise tomorrow. The fact that that may not always be so is encoded in interactions in Arabic, or when native speakers of Arabic insert *insha'allah* (God willing) into their conversations in English. According to their religious and cultural practices, it is only with "the grace of God" that we will be around tomorrow.

An example of graffiti on a notice board during final exam week at an American university communicates about such presuppositions:

> Tomorrow has been canceled due to circumstances beyond our control.
>
> —God

Some of the presuppositions are

> There is a God.
> God controls the universe.
> It is possible that "tomorrow" is an optional event.
> God makes mistakes too.
> Students during final exams fantasize that "tomorrow" will not come, especially if they have a particularly difficult exam on that day.

In fact, to understand the humor of the graffiti, the addressee must activate the presuppositions held by the addressee him- or herself and people in general. Once they are listed, the humor dissipates. The addressee processes the content of the unstated presuppositions, as relevant to the context of utterance, without concern for truthfulness or falsity. Here is a diagram of the process, both cognitive and linguistic.

			Types of meaning Hearer (Addressee)
Presuppositions			*can process*
Existing knowledge, presumed or assumed	→ Speaker Production of utterances	↔ Hearer	→ Entailments Conventional and conversational implicatures

This process takes place in milliseconds in the human brain; the parts of the process are separated here so as to analyze what happens. The shared assumptions or presuppositions are usually not stated, due to the principle of economy; speakers package what they want to say to make it appropriate for the addressees, but they say only what they have to say, not more, unless there are reasons to do otherwise. For example, it is a common strategy to ask questions as a means to find out about a new conversational partner. However, that strategy, by in effect stating presuppositions, may be perceived as insulting.

> *A:* oh, do you know that there is a town, not too far away from London, where you can go watch Shakespearean plays?
> *B:* [*silence*]

Although B was from the United States, B had, like students all over the world, studied Shakespeare in high school, and Stratford-upon-Avon was well known at least from books to B. Presuppositions, explicitly stated, communicate the speaker's assumptions about the addressee's background knowledge. In this case, A's comment was perceived as insulting by B, a possible interpretation when presuppositions are stated in many conversational interactions.

Conventional and Pragmatic Presuppositions

There can be two types of presuppositions: conventional and pragmatic presuppositions. Note, however, that the differences between the two types is a matter of degree, along a line or scale of dependence on the context of utterance. Conventional ones are not as context-dependent and are more closely linked to linguistic forms, such as proper names and a class of elements that includes such words as *some* and *any*. They should not be confused with entailments for, with presuppositions, speakers have an element of choice; entailments logically follow from a sentence irrespective of the speaker's implied, pragmatic meaning. For example, if A asks B:

Would you like *some* coffee?

The word *some* presupposes existence, that is, the coffee is already prepared; one can smell it brewing. Compare:

Would you like *any* coffee?

This question is neutral with regard to existence; there may or may not be any coffee, perhaps some left from the morning. The presupposition communicated by *some* enables the speaker to imply that the addressee is welcome in a way that *any* does not. With *any*, the addressee may feel the speaker will have to go through some extra trouble to make a pot of coffee.

Pragmatic presuppositions are very much more context-dependent, and speakers may choose which ones to activate for emphasis. Here is an ad in the classified section of an American publication about meeting unattached people:

> CONCERNED SINGLES NEWSLETTER links singles concerned about environment, peace, social justice, gender equity, personal growth. Nation-wide, all ages, Since 1984. Free sample: Box . . . (*Utne Reader,* May–June 1997, 110)

Now, there are many singles newsletters, as evidenced in classifieds in publications in many parts of the world. The main concern on the part of potential members revolves around finding someone who shares one's values and interests. This ad addresses that issue by articulating a characteristic that a certain subsection of the population would want a group of this sort to have, to be composed of "concerned" people. The ad writer follows up that catch phrase with a display of what "concerned" means. The presuppositions are made explicit by stating that the newsletter and the organization that publishes it is "concerned about environment, peace, etc." Consequently, it is clear that, although presuppositions are part of the background assumptions, they are tied to linguistic forms (Levinson 1983, 179–80).

According to Mey (1993), pragmatic presuppositions are not only context-dependent; they also invoke with what is frequently labeled "common" or "shared" knowledge. The speaker's assumption about the addressee's knowledge will influence the decision as to what presuppositions need to be made explicit.

A: where is your new apartment? how far away is it from the airport?

This question and its answer presuppose knowledge shared by the questioner and the responder about the city, that is, Honolulu, and the tendency for relatively new residents to orient themselves from the deictic center of the airport. If the addressee is uncertain, the next contribution to the conversation might be to ask another question to assess how well the original speaker knows Honolulu.

B: do you know where Makiki is?
A: well, yeah, but it's a big area
B: well, that's true . . . close to the university . . .

In this instance, the interactants are working out how much each knows about Honolulu and what can be left as unstated presuppositions and how much knowledge has to be articulated.

Background knowledge, in Mey's interpretation, includes attitudes, wants, and fears. For instance, the comment, "I'll be back in Madison August 1st (yuk! yuk! yuk!)" on a postcard from a friend in England shows how a speaker may make partially explicit the knowledge the addressee needs to arrive at a pragmatic presupposition, that the speaker is dreading having to return to Madison on the first of August. Understanding requires that the speaker and addressee share considerable knowledge about each other's attitudes toward events and places.

Presuppositions can be flouted. That is to say, a speaker can make a comment that contradicts the presupposed knowledge the speaker believes the hearer holds and, as a result, makes the assumed knowledge more apparent.

A: would madame care to dine at the local Chinese takeout?

Presuppositions set up by the phrase "would madame care to dine" create an image of an elegantly dressed couple off to a posh French restaurant in a BMW. However, those presuppositions are turned around by the second half of the sentence.

Presuppositions also become transparent in answers to questions as the responder focuses on part of the question.

A: did you take out the garbage?
B: uh, yeah, I did . . . I put out the nonburnable 'cause it's Friday.

In this case, the presuppositions are that there are two categories of trash, burnable and nonburnable, which must be put out on different days of the week. B provides "new" information by indicating one presupposition: Friday is nonburnable-garbage day.

Presuppositions and Prosody

Presuppositions can also be triggered by prosodic features, specifically the stress patterns and intonation contours of an utterance. Prosodic features convey pragmatic meaning and can trigger presuppositions that the speaker assumes the addressee will process in disambiguating a particular utterance. Grundy cites two useful examples (1995, 75). The first is from Shakespeare's *Twelfth Night:*

If music be the food of love, play on.

Depending on how much stress is put on "if," either of two presuppositions is possible:

1. Music is not the food of love (counterfactual conditional)
2. Music may or may not be the food of love (real conditional)

The second example comes from Lakoff (1971, 333; cited by Grundy 1995, 75): "John called Mary a Republican, and then *she* insulted *him*." This comment presupposes that calling someone a Republican is an insult.

Presuppositions and Implicatures

It is generally accepted that presuppositions are processed cognitively before any implicatures are worked out. For example, if a faculty member leaves with a colleague for lunch on campus and tells the secretary, "Tell Ken we've gone to the Ritz for lunch," the secretary is assumed to presuppose that (1) there is no Ritz on campus, (2) Ken also knows there is no such place on campus, and (3) Ken is likely to be late to join them for lunch, but will be coming soon. Consequently, the secretary can recognize the intended meaning: when Ken arrives, she should tell him to find the others in the common room, which is not the Ritz, but is the *best* place on campus! Presuppositions 1 through 3 must be processed before the intended implicature can be understood.

Presuppositions and Pragmatic Meaning

Presuppositions thus form part of the background knowledge that speaker and hearer must share for communication to occur. Unless they hold some knowledge in common, speakers and addressees find it difficult to even begin a conversation. Evidence of this is transparent at social events of all sorts where introductions are expected, by a host or hostess for example, to enable interactions to proceed smoothly.

As explained earlier in this chapter, the presuppositions held by a speaker are not articulated unless there are reasons to do so. They remain a vital part, nevertheless, of the existing knowledge that, along with the addressee's knowledge of the world and any entailments, enables the addressee to recognize the implied meaning of the speaker. The following example illustrates this phenomenon:

A: the movie is rated R
B: I guess I better get a babysitter

Presupposition: A assumes that B does not want her children to see an R-rated movie.

Knowledge of the world:
1. There is a rating system for movies.
2. R-rated movies have scenes with sex and violence.

Entailment: The movie will have explicit sex and violent scenes if it has a R rating.

Implicature: A is suggesting that B may not wish her children to see the movie and so should consider getting a babysitter for the evening.

Conclusion

As entailment is a concern of semantics, involving logical consequences of meaning derived from the linguistic forms in an utterance, it is not useful to debate its role in pragmatics beyond establishing the difference between entailment and presupposition. It should be clear, however, that presuppositions contribute to the addressee's ability to sort out the implicature or pragmatic meaning intended by the speaker.

The claim here is that only a difference of degree distinguishes conventional from pragmatic presuppositions. Presuppositions comprise an indispensable source of information and play a vital supporting role in the creation of meaning in interaction.

Discussion Questions

1. What are the (conventional) presuppositions of each of the following?

    a. The Taiwanese president happened to be in the lobby of the UN headquarters when Deng Zhou Ping arrived to give his speech at the General Assembly.
    b. *Mother:* did you eat all the food?
    c. *Policeman:* okay, how fast were you going when you ran the red light?
    d. *Doctor:* when did you stop smoking?

2. What are the (pragmatic) presuppositions of each of the following:

    a. *Visitor:* excuse me, could you tell me how to get to the Imperial Hotel?
    b. The present president has been living in exile.
    c. Whenever you get the chance, come over to Brooklyn and I'll show you the Promenade.
    d. You're late.
    e. I went to the Monet exhibit.

3. What kind of background knowledge would one need to understand this passage?

    B: I'm sorry it's heavy for you to carry
    A: oh no problem
    B: and—did you have any problems?
    A: ahh not a big problem but ah—some students smoked—in the toilet
    B: in the plane?
    A: in the toilet—ah of the restaurant
    B: yeah and and?
    A: and the Australian lady noticed this
    B: what, a customer?
    A: yeah,

B: yeah?
A: mm
B: and what happened?

(Sakuma 1996)

4. Explain the presuppositions flouted in this instance (data from a travel agency in the United Kingdom).

   A: can you help me I have to go to Edinburgh (.) somebody told me it was cheaper to go by plane than by train (.) is that right
   B: (1.5) well we're not British Rail agents so I don't know the difference

   (Grundy 1995, 108)

5. In your own words, summarize the role of presuppositions in establishing pragmatic meaning. Is it possible to have interaction between two human beings and not have presuppositions? Give examples.

6. Research in SLA has indicated that, for some learners, negative question forms in English may take longer to acquire. It can be assumed that figuring out the inferences from possible entailments and presuppositions would also be problematic. Here are some questions that may occur in a conversation with native speakers and learners. Generate inferences that derive from entailments and presuppositions and then discuss in groups.

   a. Aren't you going to Jim's party?
   b. Don't birds have beaks?
   c. Don't you think she should wear different colors?
   d. No te gusta los gusanos? [Don't you like eating worms?]

Text Analysis

A mother and a daughter are discussing what the daughter should do about her roommates.

Entailment and Presupposition • 89

> *D:* you want me to just say "YOU clean it"?
> *M:* yeah! if they say "No," just say "Why?
> *D:* you can't – it's not like somebody you really know you can't just say – you can't say "YOU do this and you do that"
> *M:* go ahead and just ask them
> *D:* well, they're not really dirty +++ but they're not really clean it's not like with someone you really know
>
> (Hatch 1992, 273)

What unstated but assumed knowledge are both mother and daughter using? How do the presuppositions they hold result in a disagreement between the two? Comment as well on any implicatures important to the understanding of each other's talk.

Suggested Readings

Grundy, P. 1995. *Doing pragmatics.* London: Edward Arnold.

Levinson, S. C. 1983. *Pragmatics.* Cambridge: Cambridge University Press.

Stilwell Peccei, J. 1999. *Pragmatics.* London: Routledge.

Stubbs, M. 1983. *Discourse analysis: The sociolinguistic analysis of natural language.* Oxford: Blackwell.

Chapter 5
Information Structure

So far the focus in this book has been on linguistic pragmatics, meaning related to actual linguistic forms. Specifically, chapters 1 through 4 explain the concepts indispensable for an understanding of the field, when analysis involves describing and explaining instances of language use. Now, concepts that derive from efforts to relate what is known about cognitive processes and linguistic phenomena are introduced. This is not to claim that the first four chapters have nothing to do with how the human mind works. On the contrary, the linguistic notions are regarded as reflecting internal, psycholinguistic entities and processes. It is in this chapter, nevertheless, that more direct input from cognitive research is introduced to build readers' knowledge of pragmatics.

Cognitive Explanations

If scientists are to develop computers that can process natural language discourse, that is, comprehend and produce texts without a human interface, the machines must be able to handle meaning that goes beyond the actual linguistic forms, that is, what is said. This is problematic at all levels, starting with the need to narrow down from the literal, abstract meaning of words to their sense in the context of utterance. Conversational implicatures are particularly demanding for computer scientists and artificial intelligence (AI) researchers. Comprehension of implicatures requires that one "read between the lines." Some progress has been made; the next section reviews models proposed to account for the organization of speech events, specifically the structuring of the events and the flow of information in them.

Metaphors for Human Memory

A start has been made to account for conventional or stereotypical representations of the shared background knowledge necessary to interpret texts and the events of which the texts or discourse are constitutive. The representation of that knowledge available for coparticipants in a particular speech event is viewed as composed of default elements, that is, features of the event always present whenever it occurs (Brown and Yule 1983a). Examples often given are visits to a dentist and ordering food at a restaurant. The language used in one of these speech events is constrained by the event, forming an organizing frame within which all linguistic behavior is realized.

Here is an example of a restaurant script (Greene 1986, 38):

Name: Restaurant
Props: Tables   *Roles:* Customer
        Menu   Waiter/waitress
        Food   Cook
        Bill   Cashier
        Money   Owner
        Tip

Entry conditions: Customer is hungry   *Results:* Customer has less money
                    Customer has money   Owner has more money
                                                     Customer is not hungry

Scene 1: *Entering*
         Customer enters restaurant
         Customer looks for table
         Customer decides where to sit
         Customer goes to table
         Customer sits down

Scene 2: *Ordering*
         Waitress brings menu
         Customer reads menu
         Customer decides on food
         Customer orders food

             Waitress gives food order to cook
             Cook prepares food

Scene 3:   *Eating*
             Cook gives food to waitress
             Waitress brings food to customer
             Customer eats food

Scene 4:   *Exiting*
             Customer asks for bill
             Waitress gives bill to customer
             Customer gives tip to waitress
             Customer goes to cashier
             Customer gives money to cashier
             Customer leaves restaurant.

 Brown and Yule distinguish five different but overlapping models that account for this knowledge. These they label metaphors "for how knowledge of the world is organized in human memory" (1983a, 238). These metaphors are in effect miniature theories of what happens in the brain when language is used. Research has shown that the brain and its functions are organized in some way, and these metaphors seek to capture the likely organizing principles.

 The first two metaphors, from AI research, are frames and scripts. Frames are regarded as structures in memory composed of static elements, for example, a House, and changing or optional elements, such as a Carport, Rec Room, and Study of House. This example indicates that a house exists and that it may have a carport, recreation room, and study, all optional spaces within the concept of House in the United States.

 Scripts, such as the restaurant example above, are descriptions of event sequences, such as the schedule of steps in registering for a term of study at a university. Scripts are conceptual in that they are not directly manifested in the linguistic forms of text and are derived from expectations of how an event is commonly enacted.

 From psychology come three other metaphors: scenarios, schemata, and mental models. Scenarios are situation-specific, frequently used to designate preexisting knowledge representations to account for expectations of the roles of participants in the event. The written text of a play is a good example of a scenario.

Schemata (sing. *schema*) are more general knowledge representations that are considered to reside at a subconscious level in each individual for a variety of contexts, including everyday speech events, the narrative structure for a mystery novel, or the rhetorical style for an academic paper. They are called "structures of expectation" (Brown and Yule 1983a, 248); in other words, they are brought by a participant into a situation and reflect the individual's cultural, ethnic, gender, and personal history. Indeed, it is impossible for human beings to function in everyday life without their schemata being activated. This phenomenon is one explanation of the existence of stereotypes about ethnic groups.

The schemata then interact with the discourse and the features of the context of situation, forming part of what a listener utilizes to interpret pragmatic meanings signaled by the participants in their talk. Although regarded as "conventional or habitual knowledge structures" (Brown and Yule 1983a, 247), schemata can be modified, usually as a result of experiences of the participants. For example, before the changes in the late 1980s and early 1990s in Eastern Europe, the former Soviet Union, and China, there existed schemata for "left" and "right" to describe political parties and governments in the world. However, it is no longer possible to use those words to describe the governments in many parts of the world.

Finally, mental models (see the accompanying figure) are created by participants by drawing more directly on the linguistic forms of a text, event, or conceptual space. This model does not assume stereotypical knowledge, nor are maps necessarily held in common by coparticipants. One person's mental map of New York will differ from that of another person. The term can be utilized to denote a kind of outline for an academic paper.

Now the discussion of cognitive dimensions continues, narrowing down the area of concern to discourse itself, to sentences and utterances; knowledge structures exist at this level as well, in the form of information structures.

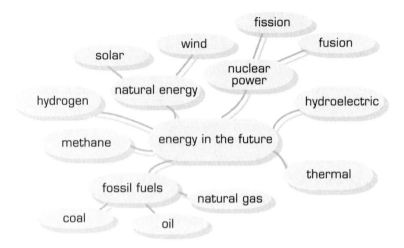

Presentation of Information

A feature of discourse that needs to be considered in any analysis of pragmatic meaning is how information is presented by the interactants. Not only what is said, but also in what order, may be of importance in the interpretation of meaning. Due to physiological constraints, language is produced in a linear stream of speech sounds, and it is tempting to consider that the structure as manifested in the linguistic forms mirrors the information structure or the cognitive ordering of events (Brown and Yule 1983a). However, it is rather more appropriate to examine how the information in a text is given some status or salience so that the addressee can distinguish what is important or new from the rest of the propositional content of the text.

In the next section, the discussion revolves around the topic of the structure of information, first, focusing on the co-text or formal linguistic context. Then attention will be drawn to the role of prosody in marking off the information of a proposition. Finally, the topic–comment pattern of information structure is introduced. This chapter draws heavily on the work of Brown and Yule (1983a). Although their perspective is explicitly linguistic and cognitive, it is a well-articulated view on the subject of information structure. As one purpose of this book is to introduce its readers to the variety of analytical approaches and concepts within pragmatics, it seems appropriate to include a look at a cognitive view of the subject.

Linearization and Staging

The linearization problem, mentioned above, refers to the fact that the co-text (i.e., what comes before a particular linguistic element and what follows it) constrains all subsequent language use. In effect, the human mind can only process speech linearly in real time. One consequence is that implicatures are set up due to the sequential organization of the flow of speech. Here is an example (Brown and Yule 1983a, 125) that illustrates the point:

> *A:* I can't stand Sally Binns. She's tall and thin and walks like a crane.
> *B:* I do admire Sally Binns. She's tall and thin and walks like a crane.

Whether the listener is led to conclude that the speaker considers "tall," "thin," and "walks like a crane" as positive or negative attributes depends entirely on the first utterance.

Nevertheless, speakers and writers can, in effect, overcome the linearization problem by setting up the information structure of a sentence or utterance to communicate what is to be regarded as salient by the speaker by staging the information. Staging is not a technical term; rather it is a metaphor from theater vocabulary that connotes an arrangement of the information so that one element stands out prominently. This can be done through choice of the syntactic arrangement of linguistic elements.

A clause consists of *(a)* the theme, the leftmost constituent just to the verb, and *(b)* the rheme, which is everything that follows. According to Halliday (1985, 39), the theme is "the starting-point for the message; it is what the clause is going to be about." It typically contains the given information, already mentioned in the text or recoverable from the context. The italicized part in each of the following sentences is the theme (Eggins 1994, 275):

> *The compelling sound of an infant's cry* makes it an effective distress signal. *However, cries* are discomforting.

> *Many reasons for crying* are obvious, like hunger and discomfort due to heat, cold, illness, and lying position.
> *These reasons,* however, account for a relatively small percentage of infant crying and are usually recognized quickly and alleviated.
> *In the absence of a discernible reason for the behavior,* crying often stops when the infant is held.
> *In most infants,* there are frequent episodes of crying with no apparent cause.
> *Infants* cry and fuss for a mean of 1¾ hr/day at age 2 wk, 2¾ hr/day at age 6 wk, and 1 hr/day at 12 wk.

The general rule of thumb is that the theme includes everything up to the finite or conjugated verb. The unmarked case is that the theme is the same as the grammatical subject.

If the default or unmarked theme consists of the grammatical subject, then all deviations or marked cases presumably are likely to lead to implicatures, which the addressee must process to recognize the speaker's intended meaning. In choosing to have a marked theme element in an utterance, the speaker is making a judgment as to what is needed to signal to the addressee what the speaker seeks to communicate. Indeed in spoken language, it is possible to observe a speaker start, stop, and restart a turn at talk, reorganizing the utterance to use a different thematic structure. It is often to produce one of the following kinds of patterns that a speaker will do this, creating an almost visible, ongoing readjusting of the information flow.

> It is only recently that I learned about the leaky roof in the house I bought only a month ago!
> This is where I met my husband.
> What he's done is move the whole wall and put in a window.

Thus, by careful choice of the theme element, the speaker can stage the information of the utterance to make some aspect of it more prominent. There is psycholinguistic evidence for this process, as studies have shown that what is made prominent is more likely to be recalled, and staging affects what will be interpreted by the listener. In sum, the constituent that is thematized, made into the theme, is what the speaker wants most to talk about.

> Thematic organization appears to be exploited by speakers/writers to provide a structural framework for their discourse, which relates back to their main intention and provides a perspective on what follows. (Brown and Yule 1983a, 143)

Speakers decide to stage the presentation of the information they want to convey for several reasons. One is to link the current utterance with what has come before to provide coherence.

> *Europe* after 1500, entered a time of far-reaching and scientific discovery and development. *Inland Africa,* by contrast, did not. *Inland peoples* continued with the steady but slow development of their own civilization. (Bloor and Bloor 1995, 73)

A second is to signal a new point of departure: "By the way, you know that new Japanese film *Shall We Dance?*"

The underlying purpose, however, comparing cognitive evidence and performance data, is the speaker's adjustments of the thematic structure based on the speaker's assumptions about the addressee's knowledge and presuppositions. The speaker attempts to give prominence to that information which the addressee needs to recognize and then take up the speaker's meaning. One way to become aware of thematizing salient information is to study an example with too many marked structures in a paragraph.

> As for the Santa Clara Fire Department, it evacuated two apartment buildings at the corner of Country Club Drive and 5th Avenue at 3 A.M. last Sunday. There was someone who had discovered a furnace in the basement of one of the buildings from which oil was leaking. What was sprayed by firemen over the oil for several hours was chemical foam. It was by 8 A.M. that the situation was under control. What someone had averted was any danger of explosion or fire, and as for the leaky furnace, it was sealed. What the residents of the two apartment buildings were given in the Country

Club High School gymnasium was temporary shelter. Possession of their apartments was regained by them at 5 P.M. (Finegan 1994, 197)

It seems the wrong information is thematized! Moreover, marked structures occur in every sentence.

The next important step in understanding the organization of information in text is to consider just how it is done. Thematization is one strategy, but there are others.

Prosody and Information Structure

Adopting the Prague School's perspective on information structure in conversational discourse, Halliday (1967) and Brazil (1985) have suggested the importance of prosodic resources to give prominence or salience to elements of talk. Specifically, Halliday adopted the given/new dichotomy, whereby "given" information is that regarded by the speaker as known to the addressee, while the "new" is viewed as unknown to the addressee. Note that it is the belief of the speaker about the addressee's background knowledge and shared assumptions that result in the choice by the speaker to mark some information as old or given, and other as new.

One way of marking the new versus given information is through the thematic structure as described above. Generally, the theme element is regarded as including the given information, with the exception of the first sentence or utterance of a text, where the new information will be in the rheme element. Halliday and Brazil examined the role of prosody, specifically intonation, in marking information as given or new by the speaker. Intonation functions as a means to realize the information structure of a clause, the basic grammatical unit in Hallidayan work. (A clause in Halliday's approach is the same as a single sentence with subject-verb-complement in traditional grammatical analysis.)

Intonation Units

To explain how information structure is realized by intonation, some basic concepts must be introduced, the most important being the intonation unit. A stream of speech has to be broken up into units that can be processed by the interactants. The units may be smaller than a clause, but are larger than individual sounds or syllables, generally. There are cognitive and physiological reasons for this phenomenon; there are limits to the length of a unit that can be processed and then held in short-term memory so that a response can be made by the listener (Chafe 1994). In the following example, the symbol // marks the boundaries of each unit. All nonprominent syllables are in lowercase letters.

> // AND // MOST OFten // when they GET these decisions WRONG // it's beCAUSE // they HAVEn't had the opporTUNity // of TALKing // FACE to FACE // WITH the CLAIMant // and REALly FINDing // the FACTS // (Brazil 1985, 27)

The information unit can also be called a phonemic clause, on the basis of characteristic prosodic features. The phonemic or information unit tends to be coextensive with a syntactic constituent, in other words, with a clause or phrase with a distinctive intonation contour. Further, not infrequently, pauses in the stream of speech occur after each unit, sometimes so short in duration that even a computer analysis cannot distinguish them in the stream of speech. Chafe (1994) claims that cues occur in clusters of features: syntactic, prosodic, and propositional content as well as nonverbal cues. The listener uses syntactic cues along with prosodic cues to predict the ends and beginnings of information units in the stream of speech.

Within the phonemic clause or intonation unit, one syllable, the tonic syllable, receives the maximum pitch, according to Halliday and Brazil. More recent work indicates that clauses may include both primary and secondary stresses (Chafe 1994). The speaker increases the pitch and loudness of one or possibly two syllables to mark new or salient information. In the following example, a man is taking a picture of his girlfriend in front of a church in England and he is trying to give her instructions so that he can take a good photo of her.

> TURN slightly towards me . . . your HEAD slightly towards me . . . only SLIGHTLY towards me . . . JUST a bit further to the RIGHT . . . I mean to MY right . . . LIKE THAT . . . NOT QUITE like that . . . HOW about a SMILE . . . CAN you make it a more NATural smile? (Bradford 1988, 7)

All the words or parts of words in capital letters are made prominent by means of a higher pitch from that used with the others in the co-text. The man also uses a slightly louder voice. As this example demonstrates, the prominence given the tonic syllables by means of a higher pitch and louder voice signals a general "watch this" cue, to get the addressee to pay particular attention to the presumably "new" information. In the case of the photography session in the example above, it is clear that what is marked as "new" is what the speaker wants the hearer to take in as salient, important, that is, to be attended to. Thus, while the given can be taken as "what the listener is expected to know already" (Chafe 1976, 30), the "new" may be interpreted as what the speaker wants to emphasize or contrast with the given.

Topic-Comment Structure

Still another means to organize the information flow in speech is the topic-comment structure. The preferred subject-predicate (SVO) word order of English, indeed of many European languages, when analyzed from a theme/rheme perspective, leads to the theme element being the grammatical subject while the rheme is composed of the verb and complement. In contrast, many Asian languages have as a basic sentence/utterance type the topic-comment structure, the topic in effect comprising the theme and the comment, the rheme element. Here is an example from Chinese.

Huang	*se*	*de*	*tu-di*	*dafeu*	*zui*	*heshi*
yellow	color	rel. clause marker	soil	manure	most	suitable

The yellow soil [topic], manure is most suitable.

(Li and Thompson 1976, 479, cited by Young 1982, 73)

The topic element sets the scene, so to speak, by introducing what the utterance will be "about," carrying the old information, with the comment element comprising the new (Young 1982). Note that a topic-comment structure is certainly possible in spoken English:

Hey, you know my father, he's decided to remarry.
Speaking of Tom, he's just sold a painting.

In everyday talk in English, such utterances are not uncommon, despite the fact that the first statement would not be regarded as grammatical.

In fact, the topic-comment structure reflects more efficiently the basic concept of the theme/rheme approach; that is, the theme segment, even in English, is ideally analyzed as functioning to signal "hey, watch this," while the rheme element is expected to provide the new information. In fact, the English structure does not lend itself as effectively as the Asian language structure to this kind of analysis. For example, Japanese marks the topic element with the particle *wa:* "Suzuki-san wa, mada kaerimasendishita" [As for Mr. Suzuki, he has not come back yet].

The topic-comment pattern representing an old/new information structure can be observed in data collected by Young (1982, 75–76) from Chinese businessmen. The new or significant information comes at the end of the turn at talk (italicized section):

> As you know, I have spent five hundred and seventy thousand pounds last year to on the machinery and components and ah if ah Mr. ah Lincoln would like to increase the ah production in ah through the coming year, I think we have to make our budget ten percent on top of the amount five hundred and five hundred and seventy thousand pounds because there will be a ten percent on uh increase in price on average. And, uh, *in other words, I need another sixty thousand pounds to buy the same material and quality.*

This delay of the significant information until the end, which contrasts with the tendency to do the exact opposite in English, carries with it certain pragmatic implicatures. The Chinese way of structuring information seeks to clarify the reasons for a request, for example, preparing the terrain, before actually making the request at the end, a discourse pattern that reflects the Asian value of avoiding conflict that might arise with a direct initial statement of a request.

The point is that information is structured in a variety of ways; the patterns mirror cognitive processing constraints both in comprehension and production. Pragmatic meaning is conveyed by the speaker's choice of which of several possible structures are available. Cultural practices or preferences will constrain the speaker's or writer's choice as well.

Conclusion

The purpose of this chapter has been to provide a brief introduction to the field of cognitive pragmatics and artificial intelligence, particularly with reference to the structuring of the flow of information presented in spoken and written language. The choice of how information is presented reflects both cognitive processing constraints and the speaker's assessment of the help the listener may need to disambiguate the intended meaning.

Tasks

1. You went to an Italian restaurant in New York and left a small tip because the food was poorly prepared and the service slow. First, change the slots in the restaurant script given at the beginning of this chapter to account for your story, and, second, explain what inference you wanted to convey to the waiter by your behavior (adapted from Greene 1986, 39).

2. Here is a partially completed scenario (Greene 1986, 41); complete it by adding actions in the empty slots based on your own experiences.

Attending a Lecture

ENTER ROOM
Look for friends
_____

SIT DOWN
Settle belongings
TAKE OUT NOTEBOOK
Look at other students
_____

Look at professor
LISTEN TO PROFESSOR

CHECK TIME
Ask questions
Change position in seat

Look at other students
Take more notes

Gather belongings

Talk
LEAVE

3. Study this schema for a cat from research on prototype theory. Then fill in the empty spaces with appropriate information.

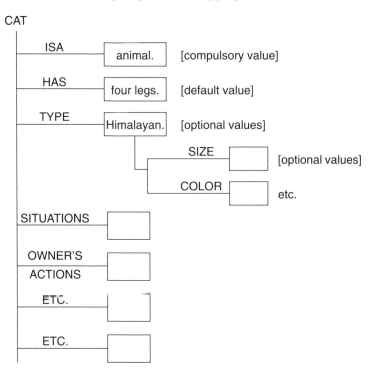

4. The following sentences are equivalent in many ways, but they are not interchangeable. Explain the differences between them (Eggins 1994, 283).
   1. Last week in the city Diana donated blood.
   2. Last week Diana donated blood in the city.
   3. Last week blood was donated by Diana in the city.
   4. Diana last week donated blood in the city.
   5. In the city last week Diana donated blood.
   6. Blood was donated last week in the city by Diana.
   7. Donated last week was blood by Diana in the city.

5. In the following example of naturally occurring talk, decide which syllables would get the primary stress and which the secondary stress, if there is one. Does each intonation unit have a syllable that is made prominent by the speaker? (Chafe 1994, 61–62).
   A: Have the . . . animals,
      ever attacked anyone in a car?
   B: Well I
      well I heard of an elephant,
      that sat down on a VW one time
      There's a gir
      Did you ever hear that?
   C: No,
   B: Some elephants and these
      they
      there
      these gals were in a Volkswagen
      and uh,
      they uh kept honkin' the horn,
      hootin' the hooter,
      and uh,
      and the . . . elephant was in front of em
      so=he just proceeded to sit down on the VW
      But they . . . had . . . managed to get out first

6. In this example a Chinese businessman in Hong Kong is speaking in English. Analyze this talk for the topic-comment structure.

I have also one thing to say. Because the personnel manager, he mentioned a few days ago that uh there are some difficulties in the equipping more new workers and ask the existing workers to work overtime by paying them some extra money, and therefore I think that we have no alternative but to buy a new machine or otherwise incur a lot of cost by using the existing one. (Young 1982, 78)

Text Analysis

In the following discussion, what are the students using language to do? What function is being enacted in their language use? Which of the metaphors given above could be used in this case? (Watanabe 1993, 183–84).

1. *Suwako:* ja onegai shimasu
   then ask
2. *Yasuo:* eeto, yappari ano ichioo junban-o funde
   well as you see uhm number-OP following
3. *Keiko:* soodesune, ichiban, niban, sanban to
   right number one number two number three
4. *Fumiko:* h-h-h-h
5. *Yasuo:* hn. hairi-yasuidesu-ne
   hm enter-easy-FP
6. *Keiko:* soodesu-ne. jaa. maa u-
   right -FP then uhm
   ichiban ue-wa hitori hitori hanasu
   number one top-TP one one talk
   shika nai kashira
   only NEG wonder
7. *Fumiko:* soo-ne.
   right
8. *Yasuo:* soodesu-ne. junban kara. doo-shimasu-ka . . .
   right-FP turn from how-do -QP
9. *Ikuo:* redii faasuto
   lady first
10. *Fumiko:* doozo
   please

11. *Yasuo:*   *aa   iidesu-ne,   sore-wa*
              oh   good–FP   that–TP
12. *Fumiko:*   [*Laugh*]
13. *Keiko:*   [*Laugh*]
14. *Keiko:*   *ja*   *wakai   kata   kara* [*laugh*]
               then   young   person   from
15. *Fumiko:*   *doozo*   [*laugh*]
                        please
16. *Fumiko:*   *iya   iya   oneesama* [*laugh*]
                no   no   big sister
17. *Keiko:*   *ee::?*
                What
18. *Ikuo:*   *dotchidemo   ii-ja   nai   desu-ka*
                either one   okay   NEG   -QP
19. *Keiko:*   *yappashi* [*Keiko takes turn*].
                As you see

Translation:

1. *Suwako:*   Then, please
2. *Yasuo:*   Let's see, as you see, uhm, basically we'll follow the number.
3. *Keiko:*   [That's right. Number one, number →
4. *Fumiko:*   [H-h-h-h.
                two, and number three.
5. *Yasuo:*   Hm. It's easy to get in.
6. *Keiko:*   That's right. Then
                Well, the top one, each one of us has to talk in turn, I wonder.
7. *Fumiko:*   That is so.
8. *Yasuo:*   That's right . . .
                following numbers, how are we going to do . . .
9. *Ikuo:*   Ladies first.
10. *Fumiko:*   Please.
11. *Yasuo:*   Oh, that sounds good.
12. *Fumiko:*   [*Laugh*]
13. *Keiko:*   [*Laugh*]

14. *Keiko:*   Then, from ⎡the younger one. ⎡[*laugh*]
15. *Fumiko:*   ⎣Please   ⎣[*laugh*]
16. *Fumiko:*   No, no. Big sister [*laugh*]
17. *Keiko:*   What?
18. *Ikuo:*   It doesn't matter, does it.
19. *Keiko:*   As you see [*Keiko takes turn*].

Suggested Readings

Bloor, T., and M. Bloor. 1995. *The functional analysis of English: A Hallidayan approach.* London: Arnold.

Brazil, D. 1985. *The communicative value of intonation in English.* Birmingham: University of Birmingham.

Brown, G., and G. Yule. 1983. *Discourse analysis.* Cambridge: Cambridge University Press.

Eggins, S. 1994. *An introduction to systemic functional linguistics.* London: Pinter.

Finegan, E. 1994. *Language, its structure and use.* 2d ed. New York: Harcourt Brace.

Halliday, M. A. K. 1994. *An introduction to functional grammar.* 2d ed. London: Edward Arnold.

Lock, G. 1996. *Functional English grammar: An introduction for second language teachers.* Cambridge: Cambridge University Press.

Chapter 6
Face, Politeness, and Indirectness

In all interaction a speaker and addressee must coordinate their linguistic activities to communicate their meanings. The speaker uses linguistic and other signals to engage the addressee, and the addressee takes up the perceived message and responds. The linguistic forms and patterns of information flow reflect the cognitive processing constraints of the human mind and the interactants' mutual orientation to each other as social actors.

1. *C:* wouldn't it be good if you could go
2. *B:* yeah, a part of a business trip
3. *C:* that'll be great
4. *A:* but . . . unfortunately we don't have a lot of money to do that, so . . .
5. *B:* hmm, no budget?
6. *A:* it's not in the budget
7. *B:* yeah . . . too bad . . .

(Sasaki 1995)

The three participants co-construct the talk, each one building on the previous speaker's contribution. A has apparently made a comment in the turn prior to the first line in the example about wanting to make a trip somewhere. C picks up the topic and B then seamlessly agrees and adds that if it were a business trip, perhaps A could go at the expense of the company. C adds a confirmatory move in line 3. Then in lines 4 through 7, A and B continue, as if they were doing a dance, not just moving back and forth, but adding to and further developing the topic. They orient to each other, and linearly and jointly build the interaction.

Clark (1996, 127) proposes a frame for explaining this communication of meaning:

> By presenting *s* to A, S meant for A that *p*.

S is the agent of the action, the speaker or writer; A is the audience; *s* is the deliberate human action or signal, such as the production of the utterance; and *p* is the proposition or content of the utterance. In Clark's model, the claim made is that each speaker in the discussion above of a possible business trip must enact this process of presentation to engage a member of the audience, in this case composed of the two other participants.

Indeed, this complex undertaking is made even more so due to the fact that the social relationships of speakers and hearers influence not only what they say to each other, but also how they do it. Instead of being friends, suppose A, B, and C are colleagues at work. Perhaps they would not even discuss the topic of how A could use company money to make a combined business-tourism trip. Even if they did, it is likely that the language used would be different; C might say something like this:

> Perhaps you could add an extra day to a business trip so that you could at least visit the Eiffel Tower?

Furthermore, *social factors* can also act as constraints on the interpretation of an utterance. If someone unknown to an addressee suddenly calls her by her nickname, the speaker's effort to show friendliness may be rebuffed. The addressee is used to hearing her nickname only from family members or close friends. The sudden decrease in the social distance between the speaker and the addressee, which is communicated by the nickname, may be viewed as an example of rude behavior. Societal expectations about nicknames or terms of endearment signal friendliness and intimacy, influencing the interpretation by the participants and other participants in an interaction. Interpretations are also influenced by the local culture. For example, in Thailand, most people use nicknames even in formal contexts. In Britain, university professors prefer to be called "Geoff" or "Mick." However, women in many parts of the world may be sensitive to nicknames or diminutives, particularly in the work environment, as they may view such use as a signal of lack of respect.

Various social factors may be considered in making sense of interactions. As the previous examples indicate, they influence the degree of social distance or closeness between interactants. Some are *external* and involve the participants in the interaction, whether they are addressees or overhearers; this category includes relative status, based on social standing, age, gender, and power. Others are largely *internal;* they typically concern such aspects as the weight of imposition, the degree of friendliness, and attitudes of the speaker and hearer. While the external ones tend to be more static, the internal factors are open to change in the course of an interaction.

To account for uses of language that show attention to social factors, and to explain the strong reactions provoked by failure to pay attention to them, the concept of *face* is commonly offered. It is possible to view human communication as potentially fraught with difficulties such that even a greeting may be viewed as an imposition, entailing the obligation on the part of the addressee to respond. Goffman (1963) studied interactions between people at mental institutions and in public places and found that, once a person acted in a way that was contrary to expectations, others immediately felt uncomfortable. Not responding to a greeting seems to put the individual into the category of not being mutually cooperative with other human beings. The concern for face needs reflects what may be a human universal.

Face

Face is a technical term to denote the public self-image all human beings wish to maintain. It includes emotional and social aspects, such as that one is honest, well-behaved, clean, and a member of particular groups and institutions in society. A person expects others to recognize and acknowledge their face needs. Although this definition may be an adequate one, some researchers prefer a two-part definition that is found in some cultures, specifically the Chinese treatments of face.

There are two aspects to the Chinese view of face *(mianzi)*. The first, *mien-tsu,* is what can be labeled "acquired face," conveying the notion that it has been acquired or earned through social behavior in daily life. The other, *lien,* is "ascribed face," referring to what every individual is entitled to receive as a human being. *Mien-tsu* is earned by demonstrating trustworthiness, expertise, and competence, and includes the notion of moral conduct; further, it can apparently be acquired by being born into a family with high acquired face. *Lien* is not something one can gain; it is given to one, connoting general confidence in the person's social performance by society (see Ho 1976).

The two-part view of face can be useful to explain some instances of cross-cultural misunderstandings that arise when one participant is from a culture with the one-part view of face and the other, from a culture that holds the two-part view. In Britain, for example, graduate studies secretaries are important people despite their title of "secretary" in the administration of the university and, consequently, expect to be treated with respect and deference. They seek to have their public self-image or face needs acknowledged. However, an overseas research student, whose home culture requires that respect be shown to individuals with high acquired social status, such as presidents, vice chancellors, and professors, rather than to those who, with job titles as secretaries, are perceived as having a lower social status, may not be well regarded by the graduate studies secretary. Tensions may arise due to the expectations held by both parties about how face is shown and to whom.

Nevertheless, in this book, face refers only to the general, one-part interpretation *(lien),* as that is the definition used in the most influential theory of face and politeness, that of Brown and Levinson (1987).

Face and Politeness

It is generally believed that, in everyday social interactions, people act in such a way as to show respect for the face wants or needs of their conversational partners. It is a story, simply, of "you respect my public self-image and I'll respect yours." The use of language to carry out social actions where mutual face wants are respected, can be labeled linguistic politeness. Yule (1996a, 60) defines politeness as follows:

> Politeness, in an interaction, can then be defined as the means employed to show awareness of another person's face.

It is important to realize that Yule and others are only concerned with *linguistic* politeness, the use of language per se to communicate the attention to the face needs of coparticipants. This view of politeness contrasts with the notion that politeness is also concerned with nonverbal behavior, usually called etiquette, which involves learning how to use the right fork for formal dinner parties, among other behaviors. Chapter 8 takes a more inclusive view in order to examine the connection between verbal and nonverbal behavior in some cultures. The field of ethnopragmatics, discussed in the introductory chapter, contends that linguistic politeness cannot be separated from other semiotic means to signal attention to mutual face needs.

Face Needs

The existence of another person's face needs becomes transparent when a speaker says something that may threaten the addressee's public self-image. A salient example would be a nurse having to ask the medical doctor she works for to sign an insurance claim, something he forgot to do. Her perceived lower status, gender, and possibly age are social factors that may result in the doctor's feeling imposed on as he may consider his public self-image or face to be threatened by being reminded of something he had not done by a subordinate. The act that the nurse needs to carry out—a request—is called a face-threatening act (FTA). In order for the nurse to carry out this FTA and to avoid showing too much disrespect for the doctor's face needs, she uses language in a way to soften or mitigate the threat. She might say the following:

> I know you are very busy, and I'm sorry I have to bother you, but could I get your signature . . . right here?

The nurse is using linguistic politeness to mitigate the face threat. With "I know you are very busy," she takes responsibility, and she uses a common conventional excuse for the doctor's not doing something. The nurse makes it clear the doctor need not offer any excuse. Then, she apologizes, "I'm sorry," and implies that it is not her own will, but some external force that is causing her to interrupt him ("sorry I have to bother you") By uttering "could I get your signature," she is asking permission, employing "could," a modal form typically used to signal politeness, indicating that the doctor has an option, that is, that he could refuse her request. The final phrase, "right here," suggests she is standing, pen in one hand, ready to give it to the doctor, and pointing with the other hand to the exact line on which he needs to write his signature. He does not have to do any extra work to comply with her request. Finally, an interrogative form also signals that the doctor may respond to the question negatively, should he wish to do so.

This is just one of many examples that can be found in everyday life of attention to the face of conversational partners by means of the linguistic enactment of politeness. In their theory of politeness, Brown and Levinson elaborate a framework to describe and explain the different ways of performing politeness linguistically.

Positive and Negative Face

It is considered a truism about human beings that, while people want to be independent and to function unimpeded by others, at the same time, they want to be approved of by their fellow beings, to be viewed in a positive light, and to be members of the same group as their conversational partners. Humans want to be independent and yet involved with others, a constant push and pull that can explain some of our behavior. Consequently, in interactions, speakers, in attending to the addressees' face, need to pay attention to their negative face needs, the desire not to be imposed on by others, and their positive face, that is, the need to be connected with others. According to Brown and Levinson's theory, strategies in language use that seek, for example, to apologize for or mitigate any imposition on the addressee's time are labeled negative strategies. Those that show solidarity and make the addressee feel their wants are important are categorized as showing positive politeness. Some strategies can do both. Showing deference, a negative politeness strategy, can also perform the function of flattering the person, which signals positive politeness. A famous professor may not want to be disturbed at a conference by overly attentive junior professors or graduate students; however, he would be highly insulted if they did not at least acknowledge his existence! Thus a simple greeting will meet his face needs to be acknowledged and not to be disturbed.

Positive and Negative Politeness Strategies

Before discussing the specific strategies to signal positive or negative politeness, the overall framework of Brown and Levinson must be explained. Brown and Levinson claim that speakers enacting an FTA use three superordinate or macro strategies:

1. Do the act on-record, *(a)* baldly or *(b)* with redressive action.
2. Do the act off-record.
3. Don't do the act.

The choice of strategy is dependent on the speaker's estimate of the threat to the addressee's face. If the threat is great, then strategy 3 is used, whereas strategy 1 will be chosen if the estimate is that the face threat is weak. Here is an example of the strategies applied to dealing with a smoker.

1. A says to C, the smoker: *(a)* "You can't smoke here." *(b)* "Would you mind not smoking here?"
2. A says to B, a companion, about C, the smoker: "I wonder if there is a smoking section" (said aloud to B so that C overhears).
3. No linguistic action; A and B move away.

By "on-record," or "baldly," Brown and Levinson mean speaking directly without an effort to save the face of the addressee. Redressive action is an effort to soften the force of the speech act. "Off record" would be characterized by hints or indirect suggestions. "Don't do the act" indicates the speaker decides to refrain from saying anything because the risk too great.

Within the category of "redressive action," involving some form of modification, there are two other strategies: Do the act on-record with positive politeness redress, and do the act on-record with negative politeness redress. "On-record" denotes that the speaker does do the act. The redressive action is a means to "give face" to the addressee to counteract the potential face threat or damage of the FTA.

This modification or addition takes one of two forms: positive redressive action or negative redressive action. In the smoking example, in the case of positive politeness, A might say to C: "You know, they do have a section for smokers over there. Let's go find it so you can have a cigarette." Or for negative politeness, A could say: "Would you mind our asking you to smoke in the nonsmoking section?" Negative politeness does not mean that the speaker is being impolite. Rather it reflects a greater degree of social distance between the speaker and the hearer or the desire to convey it, signaling the intended meaning that the speaker wishes to disturb the addressee as little as possible.

Here is another example that illustrates the five categories of strategies. If your neighbor in the apartment above yours has, for the third time, let the water from her washing machine run onto the floor rather than into the sink and, consequently, the water has come through the ceiling into your apartment, you have several choices as to what you can say and do.

Baldly, on record:	Do *not* let the water from your washing machine run onto the floor ever again!
On-record, negative politeness:	I'm sorry to have to ask you, but I wonder if you could be a bit more careful with the hose on your washing machine? It must need repair as it apparently comes unhooked and then the water seeps down into my apartment.
On-record, positive politeness:	Well, I guess you must have been busy with something else, because I got some water in my place again the other day from your washing machine. How about my helping you fix it or finding a repairman who can do it for us?
Off-record:	Do you need a hand with your washing machine? Perhaps you aren't used to the kind of machine we have here in Japan.

If you select "Don't do it at all," the landlord or manager of the apartment building might be asked to act as a go-between to settle the problem. This is a strategy that would be less threatening to your upstairs neighbor's face than your speaking directly with the neighbor.

The important point here is that the speaker's choice of which face-saving strategy to use is constrained by contextual factors, involving the speaker's perception of degrees of intimacy, power, and weight of the imposition. Distance, specifically social distance, considers the relationship between the interactants; a family member or good friend can ask a sister or friend for help by using bald, on-record strategies. Power also refers to the relationship; a doctor is much more likely to give orders without redress to subordinates than a nurse can to a peer or the doctor.

The concern with imposition is the weight of seriousness attached to a linguistic action by the speaker. An illustration may help. In a situation where the speaker wishes to make a request, the imposition is on the addressee, whereas the benefit, that is, having the request accepted, rests with the speaker. The imposition on the addressee threatens his or her wants not to be impeded. Every speech act presupposes a cost-benefit analysis. Sometimes, the speaker benefits, other times the addressee does, and in some cases, both do. Thanking someone or promising benefits the addressee; a compliment may make the speaker feel good for acknowledging the other person and, at least in the United States, usually the person complimented has face needs met as well. Thus, both benefit.

In addition to figuring out who benefits, we need to ask how weighty an FTA is. In the case of a request to borrow an addressee's pen, the weight of the imposition of loaning a pen is not very costly to the addressee, whereas a request to borrow her car or a large sum of money is likely to be so.

The fact that it is not always the speaker who benefits and the addressee who experiences the imposition may vary cross culturally. It depends on the linguistic or speech act. In the United States, for example, thanking functions as a social lubricant and does not place any heavy imposition on the person doing the thanking or on the person being thanked. It shows attention to the positive face needs of the thanked person and at the same time displays the speaker's wish to be positively regarded by the coparticipants. Both benefit. However, in some cultures, the speech act of thanking incurs future obligations. Thanking can entail a *nonreciprocal relationship* and may consequently threaten the speaker's negative face wants, especially if the person has a relatively higher social status vis-à-vis the person being thanked (Hinkel 1994, 73). Apologizing is another speech act that can be problematic in some cultures, as higher-status people do not normally apologize to others. Apologies involve humbling oneself.

Brown and Levinson consider that a calculation of these three factors—distance, power, and imposition—results in the degree of face-threat that needs to be compensated for by appropriate linguistic strategies. It is important to select a politeness strategy that balances distance, power, and the weight of the imposition. It is as if, first of all, the speaker decides on the amount of potential face threat a specific linguistic action might incur. Then, second, the speaker decides which of the five strategies is most appropriate. Third, if the speaker has selected either type of on-record with redressive strategies, there are several possible strategies within each of the macro categories. The following is a partial list from Brown and Levinson with examples (1987, 131, 102).

Negative Politeness Strategies

1. Be conventionally indirect.	Could you please pass the salt?
2. Question, hedge.	I don't suppose you could pass the salt.
3. Be pessimistic.	You don't have any envelopes, do you?
4. Minimize the imposition.	I just dropped by for a second to ask . . .
5. Give deference.	We very much look forward to your dining with us.
6. Apologize.	I am sorry to bother you, but . . .
7. Impersonalize S and H.	It appears that we may have to . . .
8. State the FTA as a general rule.	Passengers will refrain from . . .
9. Nominalize.	I am surprised at your failure to reply.
10. Go on record as incurring debt or as not indebting H.	I'd be eternally grateful if you could . . .

Positive Politeness Strategies

1. Notice, attend to H (interests, wants, needs, approval).	You must be hungry . . .
2. Use in-group identity markers	Tu t'es bien amusé à la plage? [Did you have a good time at the beach?]
3. Seek agreement and avoid disagreement.	Yes, the weather is wonderful today, isn't it?
4. Presuppose or assert common ground.	Help me with this bag, luv?
5. Joke.	How about lending me a few fivers?
6. Offer, promise.	I'll drop by sometime next week.
7. Be optimistic.	I'm sure you won't mind if I . . .
8. Include both S and H in the activity.	Let's have a drink next week . . .
9. Give or ask for reasons.	Why not go to the seashore?
10. Give gifts (sympathy) to H.	I'm really sorry to hear about your cat.

The rest of the chapter will focus on one of the negative strategies, the use of indirectness (strategy 1: be conventionally indirect), for three reasons: (1) indirectness is ubiquitous in language use; (2) some pragmaticists do not believe indirectness is a politeness strategy; and (3) differences in the use of indirectness become transparent with learners when using their second language.

Politeness and Indirectness

This section considers the relationship between politeness and indirectness. One fact of human communication is that more often than not interactants do not say directly what they intend to mean. Some researchers consider indirectness and politeness to be closely related, while others argue that they are rather different.

A range of linguistic resources is used to enact indirectness. This section will first explore what some of the strategies are. Second, the reasons for indirectness are considered. If it is so pervasive, there must be communicative advantages in its use.

Indirectness Strategies

Indirectness is realized linguistically in a number of ways. The first one that comes to mind involves sentence form or modality. As directness tends to be associated with the imperative form in many languages, an interrogative is employed in place of the imperative to avoid directness: "Why don't you talk to the manager?" or "Would you mind lending me a couple of dollars for lunch?" These phrases are preferred to "Talk to the manager" or "Lend me some money!" "Why don't you . . . " is a conventional use of language to make a suggestion, while "Would you mind . . . " conventionally signals a request.

When such an indirect relationship between structure and function occurs, we have an *indirect speech act*. A direct speech act constitutes a matching of structure (e.g., a declarative) and of a communicative function (an assertion). With an indirect speech act, structure and speech act are not matched. In the accompanying table, the indirect speech act conventionally suggests that A should dress warmly.

In addition to conventional indirectness, the other main category of means to signal indirectness is conversational implicature. In other words, the speaker's indirectness occurs in one particular instance of use, and the addressee must use background knowledge and the context of utterance to comprehend the intended or pragmatic meaning. Here is an example from Blum-Kulka's data on family interactions in Israel (1989, 39; translated from Hebrew):

Mother: Danny, do you have any homework?
Danny: I've already finished it.
Yael: Danny didn't answer Mommy's question.
Yuval: He did, he did.

Direct speech act	Declarative/ assertion	It's going to snow tonight. Take your warm coat along.
Indirect speech act	Interrogative/ suggestion	It's cold outside! It's going to snow tonight. *Why not take your warm coat?*

This piece of dinner table talk provides an example of pragmatic indirectness. One common question of parents in such a context is to inquire about the kind of homework the children have. However, the implied meaning, which the son, Danny, takes up, is that the mother is actually asking if he has completed it. The son responds to the pragmatic meaning, but the daughter, Yael, only recognizes the conventional meaning of the question, that is, mother is asking for information. It may just be sibling rivalry in action here; however, second language learners may only be able to process the conventional meaning and respond in what they think is an appropriate way. In the north of England, for example, a common greeting is "Are you all right?" It means the same as "Hi, how are you?" in American English or "¿Hola, qué tal?" in Spanish. However, the foreigner or student of British English may mistake the greeting as a sincere question about his or her state of health, mental or physical!

Important Features of Indirectness

Undoubtedly a universal feature of human interaction, indirectness is believed to be a motivated strategy used with all languages. Indirectness is intentional, and a speaker has some communicative purpose in using it, for it has risks and costs. The distinction between directness and indirectness is not absolute, but a matter of degree (Thomas 1995, 119).

Intentionality. It is important to consider only intended indirectness; perceived indirectness that results from linguistic inadequacy or a performance error is not a concern of pragmatics. Despite beliefs to the contrary, yawning during a lecture may not always communicate boredom!

Risks and Costs. Indirectness may require more cognitive processing. The addressee will normally assume some meaning is intended and will search for it. Psycholinguistically, this results in more time spent by the addressee; a passive sentence in English takes more cognitive processing time than does an active sentence, for example. In addition, it is risky, as the hearer may misunderstand. An example from Thomas (1995, 121) illustrates the potential hazard: when a visitor, after some long meetings, was asked on arrival at a colleague's home what she wanted to drink, she responded,

Well, I've been on whisky all day . . .

The woman wanted to say that, as she had been drinking whisky, she would continue with it on the assumption that it is better not to mix drinks or kinds of alcohol. However, her host assumed she meant that she had had enough whisky and wanted some tea instead. Indirectness rather than a direct response ("I think I should stay with whisky") led to a misunderstanding of the pragmatic meaning of the speaker.

Directness and Indirectness Scale. Once the speaker decides to use indirectness, a number of parameters are involved in the calculation of indirectness: relative power between speaker and hearer, social distance, weight of imposition, rights and obligations, and the degree of involvement in the interaction by the participants. Note that all of these parameters are relative and negotiated in the course of the interaction. The choice made by the speaker is manifested in the linguistic code (address forms, honorifics, indirect speech acts, passives, formulaic language, and forms of mitigation) and paralinguistic means, specifically through prosody.

An example will suggest how far one speech act can vary in directness. Consider the sentence "Go to Ivan's party." This is an imperative, and the force is that of an order. The hearer has no choice, and the sentence implies a power difference between the speaker and the hearer. A parent may say to a child in the family, "I want you to go to Ivan's party." This is a direct statement of information of the speaker's feelings or wants and the force of the utterance is clear, bald, and on-record. It is difficult to respond interactively, as the hearer will have to negotiate with the speaker to arrive at some mutual understanding about attending Ivan's party. However, negotiations are likely only if the speaker and hearer are intimates, which allows for the direct expression of wants and needs. There are other means to talk about going to Ivan's party.

Why don't you go to Ivan's party?
I heard Ivan's having a party.

In the first example, the question form is used to make a suggestion. The hearer has a choice and may simply give a reason for not attending the party. The force (suggestion) is clear; however, the conventional indirectness allows options. In the second instance, one interpretation is that the speaker is hinting that s/he and the addressee might want to attend the party together. Optionality is also present, although hinting is not a conventional means to convey it.

These examples, from more direct to less direct, illustrate that indirectness is a matter of degree; the amount of inferencing that the hearer has to engage in to derive the force from the sense varies, depending on the linguistic forms, the context of utterance, and any social and cultural norms concerning indirectness.

Purposes of Indirectness

Despite its costs in cognitive processing and the risk of being misunderstood, speakers still use indirectness. Why? Six purposes, which are not mutually exclusive, may be mentioned.

First, speakers' goals may clash, and, as a consequence, interactants may wish to avoid direct assertions. Directness may appear insensitive to the feelings of the hearer. The preferred strategy may be hinting at the truth or obfuscating. If B comes to work one day with an article of clothing that A considers in poor taste, she may avoid hurting B's feelings by telling a small lie.

> *A:* is that a new sweater? that's a lovely color on you
> *B:* well, my mother bought it for me and well, you know how it goes . . . I have to wear it

Second, if indirectness has worked in the past, there is no impetus for change. On the basis of instrumental rationality, whether or not it be an individual's conversational style or a preferred style of interaction in a particular culture, indirectness may be utilized at an unexamined level in achieving communicative goals. If the communicative goal is to cheer her listener up, A may say,

> That new hairstyle makes you look as if you were ready for summer vacation.

Third, indirectness leaves the speaker a way out if challenged by the addressee. Indirectness provides a means to deny perceived intentions, avoid conflict, and escape from responsibility for an utterance. A husband and wife might have the following conversation while watching television:

A: are you enjoying the game?
B: well, why do you ask? do you want to watch something else?

Attribution may be difficult to ascribe: it is not clear whether A wants to watch something else.

As a result of her studies of requestive hints, that is, speech acts of request that are not stated directly, Weizman (1989) suggests that indirectness allows denial by the speaker. If a man states, "I've missed the bus" to a coworker at the end of the day, he can, if necessary, deny that he was hinting at a ride home. The coworker may not recognize the intended meaning, or may recognize it but pretend not to. Or the coworker may offer a lift (Weizman 1989, 93–94). Indirectness thus allows the speaker to avoid responsibility for a direct request.

Fourth, indirectness is frequently regarded as polite, although researchers differ on this topic. Thomas (1995, 119–22) regards indirectness, both conventional and conversational, as a strategy to achieve communicative goals, face-saving being one. Brown and Levinson (1987) state that the degree of indirectness is inversely proportional to the degree of face threat. Consequently, the greater the face threat, the greater the need to use linguistic politeness, and the more indirectness is used.

Blum-Kulka (1987, 131–46) separates indirectness from politeness. If a speaker is too direct, the addressee's face needs may be violated, and thus the speaker has been impolite. However, too much indirectness may have the same result, as a perceived lack of clarity is a marker of impoliteness as well. On the basis of research carried out with native speakers of Hebrew and English, Blum-Kulka states that the preferred strategies are conventionally indirect ones, that is, on-record indirectness. Here are two examples of conventional indirectness.

The kitchen's a mess.
Would you give me hand?

Both convey indirectly the intended meaning: "Let's clean up the kitchen," and "I need your help with this heavy package." With non-conventional indirectness, however, Blum-Kulka's (1987) informants regarded the illocutionary force as lacking transparency. Although studies of other cultures might have different results, Blum-Kulka suggests her findings are universal because they reflect cognitive processing constraints. "Real" indirectness, that is, nonconventional indirectness, requires more processing to reach the intended meaning, and this cognitive burden would tend to cause an imbalance in the interaction, a state that would be impolite.

Thus, indirectness is not the same thing as linguistic politeness. However, Brown and Levinson regard it as a negative politeness strategy to mitigate an FTA.

Still another reason for speaking indirectly is the fun of it. It can be creative and playful. It may at the same time allow the speaker to assess how well the addressee can understand the intended meaning, thus *joining* the speaker as a member of a select group.

1. *A:* [*to a new student*] macroeconomics is a fascinating subject
   B: oh really?
2. *A:* [*to a new student*] macroeconomics is a fascinating subject
   B: oh, yes, I agree, I think so too

If A's intended meaning is to communicate sarcasm or irony, and if B interprets A's comment in that way (example 1), then B, in a sense, has shown, from A's point of view, proper thinking for a student and can be A's friend. If B takes A's comment seriously (example 2), then B is likely to be left out. In this instance, the speaker is testing out the common ground shared by the speaker and addressee; it can be a strategy to bring the addressee into the same community.

Finally, a related purpose for using indirectness is as a strategy to gain or maintain power over others. It can exclude from an interaction any participant who is not able to disambiguate the speaker's meaning.

> *Doctor:* and might you not make one examination of the head almost at square one, before you begin
>
> (Fairclough 1989, 45)

Face, Politeness, and Indirectness • 125

In this case, a medical doctor in a hospital training session with new interns makes this comment, interrupting one of the interns who is demonstrating to the others a procedure. The indirectness conveyed conventionally by "And might you not make . . . " may be interpreted by the medical students, despite the indirectness, as a strong reprimand that the intern has not carried out the demonstration as the doctor wishes.

Cross-Cultural and Interlanguage Differences

Blum-Kulka's study of indirectness introduces the reader to the importance of differences in cross-cultural expectations about production and comprehension in indirectness and its interpretation. Learners may transfer the norms regarding indirectness from their L1 into interactions in the L2. Here is one example from a university office in Japan with a clerk making a comment in English, her second language, to a visiting professor from the United States.

Clerk: oh, you look like you're ready to go to the beach . . .

The faculty member was unable to interpret the pragmatic meaning. Some possibilities are

A compliment about the dress and sandals she was wearing
A criticism for wearing such clothing to an office
An icebreaker, showing her desire to be friendly in a way the clerk thought she should

What made the utterance even more difficult to interpret was the social distance between the two: a clerk, especially one virtually unknown to the professor, would not be expected to make such a comment in an English-speaking environment. Moreover, the visiting professor knew that the general practice in Japan is to deny or avoid compliments (Saito and Beecken 1997). It is also known that questions are used as hints in Japan as disguised criticisms. Logically, the professor would assume then that the clerk was criticizing her attire. Yet, in the professor's culture, office clerks do not criticize people in higher-status positions. A "correct" interpretation of the pragmatic meaning is impossible to arrive at due to the mixture of cultural norms, expectations, and learner language.

Examples of this sort recur frequently in our daily lives in intercultural contexts and can result in misunderstandings and the reinforcement of stereotypes about an ethnic group. In the following section, the focus is on a case study of indirectness in African American English.

African American Indirectness

African American interaction is characterized by indirectness; according to Morgan (1996), it is used in multiple everyday activities by young children, adolescents, and, in particular, adult women. The text that follows is a segment of a conversation where African American women are using indirectness in what is called "signifying" (Morgan 1996, 405). Signifying is described by Mitchell-Keenan (1972, 317–18) as "the recognition and attribution of some implicit content or function which is obscured by the surface content or function."

According to Morgan, two forms of indirectness are used in signifying. The first is pointed indirectness, where a speaker makes a statement to an addressee, whose content or message is actually meant to be recognized by an overhearer, the "real" addressee. The second form is called baited indirectness; the speaker claims that a coparticipant has a particular feature, which is untrue or which the speaker knows the addressee does not consider to be true. Pointed directness has a "mock receiver," the presumed addressee, although hearers who share the same background knowledge will recognize a conversational strategy masking the real, "addressed target." Neither the mock target nor the actual target will respond, as to do so would indicate agreement with the speaker's comment. If the mock target does respond, the result is embarrassment—a signal that the individual is not a member of the group.

Baited indirectness involves negative assessment of an unspecified but present target. In other words, the designated target is within hearing distance, but is not named or cued via eye contact. Any response from such an overhearer would signal that the content of the signifying was true. Note that the two kinds of indirectness are not mutually exclusive; they can co-occur.

Teenage Days

1.	MM:	What—what—I MEAN—what was teena—being a
2.		teenager like I mean what was::
3.	JM:	O;h I was; gor [geous
4.	BR:	{OH well by that time HO:NEY? her hea; d was SO:
5.		big
6.	R:	{O:H my GO:D O:H my GO:D
7.		(.)
8.	MM:	This is the Coca-Cola pha:se?
9.	BR:	O::H BABY The whole works
10.		(.)
11.		She was the only one
12.		(.)
13.		She ran in the Miss black WHAT ((high pitch)) EV?: ER thing
14.		they was RUNNING in those da:ys=
15.	R:	= Sure di:d

Source: Morgan 1996, 405–34.
Note: MM = Marcyliena, JM = Judy, BR = Baby Ruby, R = Ruby.

In the accompanying table, all of the participants are relatives and all grew up together. Judy, sixty-three years old, and Ruby, seventy-eight years old, are sisters, and Baby Ruby, who is also sixty-three, is their niece. Marcyliena is one of Judy's daughters. The taping takes place in a dining room, and they are surrounded by their grandchildren and other family members. The episode is labeled "Teenage Days," as the topic of the talk is that period of shared adolescence. Marcyliena establishes the topic. Judy takes up the topic and immediately gives a focus to the talk by making a comment about herself. Baby Ruby and Ruby then start signifying with line 4, using both pointed and baited indirectness. Marcyliena is the mock receiver, while the baited indirectness is enacted in the form of negative attributes assigned to Judy. Marcyliena adds to the baiting by recalling that Judy used to describe her body as resembling the shape of a Coca-Cola bottle, which Marcyliena calls the "Coca-Cola phase" in line 8. It is noticeable that Judy remains silent. She can only wait until the topic changes. Morgan explains that the signifying mode is further enacted through the mixture of American English and African American English lexical items ("honey," "baby," "god," "whatever") and the prosodic cues such as the elongated vowels and high pitch and loudness.

Thus, rather than mocking or making fun directly of how Judy fashioned her behavior as a teenager, indirectness is performed through the conversational act of signifying. Morgan notes that signifying is always done with an audience and with the person who is baited present.

Conclusion

It has been established in research studies in pragmatics that face is the concept underlying the linguistic enactment of politeness, such that mutual respect of each other's positive and negative face needs motivate interactants to adjust their language use to attend to their coparticipants. Brown and Levinson's theory of face and politeness is not without its critics; nevertheless, it remains the theory against which all others are compared, the deictic center, so to speak, of discussions of linguistic politeness.

Indirectness is apparent in many instances of language use and is frequently analyzed as a form of politeness, as it enables the speaker to show consideration for an interlocutor's face needs, among other purposes. More than one reason may prevail; avoidance of attribution and the desire to establish mutual ground with a new acquaintance may occur. If the effort goes wrong by using indirectness, then the speaker can retreat without any loss of face by either party.

Discussion Questions

1. Analyze the markers of linguistic politeness in the first dialogue in this chapter. What is the social relationship of the participants? How does the relationship influence their linguistic choices? What is the evidence for your analysis?
2. Explain how social factors internal to the interactants can change during an interaction. Give an example.

Face, Politeness, and Indirectness • 129

3. Which definition of face do you feel is most appropriate for your own first-language culture? Why?
4. Give the strategy from Brown and Levinson enacted by the following utterances (most are adapted from Brown and Levinson 1987).
   Look, the point is this: Chirac has got to go.
   What a fantastic garden you have!
   You must be famished. It's been a long time since breakfast.
   I'm looking for a comb.
   Open other end.
   Could you find me a computer so I can check my e-mail?
   Are you by any chance able to post this letter for me?
   Mind if I smoke?
   Take a seat.
   Help me with this bag, will you, luv?
   As is well known, you can't buy a plane ticket at British Rail.
   I'll be eternally grateful if you could . . .
   How was I to know that the ticket agent would be closed today?
5. Here is a dialogue example in Mexican Spanish. A student asks a language coordinator for help. All of the verbs in boldface are in the imperfect. Using politeness theory, can you explain the reason the present tense is not used?
   S: El coordinador? [Are you the coordinator?]
   C: Si [Yes.]
   S: **Quería** ver si me **podía** cambiar de horario. [I was wondering if I could change the schedule of my English class.]
   C: Dejame ver . . . [looks at the computer information] **Estabas** con el profesor Texcucano. [Let me see. You have been with Professor Texcucano.]
   S: Si [Yes.]
   C: Dale esto al profesor [giving a memo to the student] [Okay, give this to him.]

   (Garrido 2001)
6. In what ways can indirectness be considered to be synonymous with politeness? In other words, when and how do they co-occur? Give examples.

Text Analysis

The accompanying table is an example of transactional talk, that is, where some business is being conducted. Is it an example of negative politeness or positive politeness? Why? Identify in the text evidence to support your answer.

1.	S01:	Can I have a second class stamp please Les?
2.	S02:	You can . . . there we are
3.	S01:	Thank you
4.	S02:	And one penny thank you
5.	S01:	That's for me to spend is it?
6.	S02:	That's right
7.	S01:	I bought a new book of ten first class when I was in
8.		town today and I've left them at home in me shopping bag
9.	S02:	Have you?
10.	S01:	And I've got one left
11.	S02:	Oh dear [*laughs*]
12.	S01:	Bye
13.	S02:	Bye

Source: Carter and McCarthy 1997, 92.
Note: S01 = customer, female; S02 = assistant, female

Suggested Readings

Blum-Kulka, S., J. House, and G. Kasper, eds. 1989. *Cross-cultural pragmatics: Requests and apologies.* Norwood, N.J.: Ablex.

Brown, P., and S. C. Levinson. 1987. *Politeness: Some universals in language usage.* Cambridge: Cambridge University Press.

Goffman, E. 1963. *Behavior in public places: Notes on the social organization of gatherings.* New York: Free Press.

Morgan, M. 1996. Conversational signifying: Grammar and indirectness among African American women. In *Interaction and Grammar,* ed. E. Ochs, E. A. Schegloff, and S. A. Thompson. Cambridge: Cambridge University Press.

Saito, H., and M. Beecken. 1997. An approach to instruction of pragmatic aspects: Implications of pragmatic transfer by American learners of Japanese. *Modern Language Journal* 81, no. 3: 363–77.

Part 2
Analytical Perspectives: Theories of Pragmatic Meaning

The basic notions explained in the first part of this book provide a background for the second part, designed to develop an understanding of three approaches to analyzing naturally occurring talk, approaches that attempt a deeper understanding of pragmatics. These three provide tools that enable the researcher and student to do pragmatics. One level up from the basic concepts are analytical approaches, all of them widely recognized theoretical frameworks for explaining systematically how the coparticipants in interactions derive what is meant from what is said. These frameworks also address the role of the contextual variables, from the points of view of both speaker and the listener. All of them seek to explain the relationship of meaning and use and to enable the calculation of pragmatic implicatures generated in both spoken and written texts.

The first approach is the philosophical. Grice, a philosopher of language, claims that there are underlying principles of human behavior of cooperativeness and mutual, reciprocal attention to the needs and wants of others that provide a base against which language use is studied and compared. The principles and maxims are part of the presupposed knowledge shared by speaker and hearer. Implicatures, which are created as a result of language behavior that seems to be breaking the norms or maxims, can then be understood against the background of cooperativeness.

The second perspective on pragmatic meaning concerns the role of sociolinguistic aspects such as expected response patterns in conversation, the function of utterance force in interactions, and nonverbal accompaniments of verbal communication. Two frameworks are explained: preference organization and speech act theory. Preference organization introduces the notion of coherence in discourse. The main point is that the calculation of implicatures is possible by taking into consideration the structure of talk, in particular pairs of utterances called adjacency pairs, which pushes the listener to seek to understand the speaker's pragmatic meaning. Speech act theory focuses on the force of utterances, specifically when the function or illocutionary force does not match the linguistic form, thereby generating implicatures that the listener must recognize. This mismatch of form and function is particularly apparent in the use of indirectness. Further, it is argued that speech act theory must be expanded to include the analysis of utterances in the context of larger speech events or activity types, both of which influence and constrain the language use.

The third chapter in this part of the book, chapter 9, takes up cognitive or psycholinguistic perspectives on pragmatic meaning. Two are considered in some detail. The first is relevance theory, which maintains that the maxim of relevance is the only one necessary to account for a speaker's intended meaning. The theory purports to account for the cognitive processes that underlie the disambiguation of a speaker's intended meaning on the basis of the construct, optimal relevance. Then, second, the action approach, reviews the psycholinguistic analysis of interaction developed by Clark. While Clark includes the sociocultural factors that influence human communication, he is primarily interested in describing what happens in the mind during interactions.

These approaches or theories suggest different means to arrive at the calculation of implicatures, or pragmatic meaning. The aim is to understand how human beings are able not only to recognize implied meaning, but also produce it.

Here a second language acquisition perspective can be introduced. All of the theoretical approaches to pragmatic meaning involve universals of human behavior such as, for example, preference organization in talk. Second language learners, presumably, will transfer skills and strategies from their L1 production and comprehension. The problems for L2 learners arise, in the first instance, because of inadequate L2 proficiency, particularly in efficient, automatic cognitive processing. However, even

Analytical Perspectives • 133

for more advanced learners, important issues can arise from lack of a common sociocultural background not only with regard to content of an utterance, but also general preferences of a culture for specific speech acts, enactments of politeness, and levels of indirectness. The chapters in part 2 continue to build the base for the role of pragmatics in the context of second language acquisition.

Chapter 7
A Philosophical Approach: Grice

H. S. Grice is a philosopher of language and, consequently, did not base his thinking on empirical data. Yet the importance of his contribution to pragmatics cannot be overestimated. His is an inferential model of communication that rests on the notion of intention. Specifically, Grice argued that a listener can work out the inferences in a speaker's utterances only if the listener assumes that the speaker intends to communicate something. Communication has the two characteristics of deliberateness and intention. (By contrast, yawning may not be an act of communication, just as looking at one's watch may be just a nervous habit.) For communication to occur, the speaker must intend to communicate and the listener must recognize that intention.

Grice regarded conversations as rational, cooperative activities. Once the listener recognizes the speaker's intention to communicate, the meaning of an instance of talk can be worked out. An example will illustrate Grice's approach. Two friends are about to pay the bill for lunch.

A: oh no, I'm out of cash . . . I forgot to go to the bank . . .
B: oh, don't worry . . . I've got a credit card . . . you can pay me back

A, looking at her wallet, may be making a metacomment on her own behavior, but by talking aloud, she is offering an excuse and asking for help at the same time. Assuming A intended those meanings, B quickly works out the inferences and offers to pay for lunch ("Oh, don't worry. I have a credit card") and suggests a solution to the debt ("You can pay me back"). Note that B's knowledge of cultural contexts involving cash, banks, and sharing the cost of meals is instrumental.

Grice's Concept of Meaning

To account for pragmatic meaning, Grice claimed that there is a particular type of meaning, created by human beings, that is intended:

> It's the taste.
> (From an advertisement, cited in Grundy 1995, 36)

This message cannot be disambiguated without a context: it could be an ad for a brand of tea, and the implicature would be that the tea tastes good. It could be the reason a student does not want to eat in the university canteen: the taste is not good! Such meaning is not as closely associated with the linguistic form and it varies with the context. Consequently, intentional meaning comprises the nonconventional meaning. In sum, Grice theorized that meaning is the intended effect a speaker wishes to produce in a hearer by getting the hearer to recognize the intention.

The Cooperative Principle

Communication requires not just recognition of intention but also the assumption that the speaker and hearer operate rationally. That is, they are presumed to observe certain rational principles of communication. The underlying principle, according to Grice, is cooperativeness; he called it the Cooperative Principle (CP):

> Make your conversational contribution such as is required, at the stage at which it occurs, by the accepted purpose or direction of the talk exchange in which you are engaged. (Grice 1967)

Although admonishment was Grice's choice of rhetorical style, he had no moral intention. He was making a general statement of human behavior to explain how participants act in order for addressees to arrive at speakers' intended meaning.

The CP is regarded as the underlying principle in all cases of interaction. Sometimes, people speak directly and say what they mean.

A: I'm going to be late for work . . . could you take care of washing up the breakfast dishes for me?
B: sure, I'll take care of them for you

In this case, B does not have to infer what A's intended message is. However, in cases where indirectness is used—a more common occurrence—it is on the basis of the assumption of cooperativeness and intentionality that relevant meaning can be inferred as the implicatures are worked out. In the second example, A gets up from the breakfast table, while B remains seated, drinking coffee and reading a newspaper.

A: I have to go or I'm going to be late for work . . . I know it's my turn [*looking over at the unwashed breakfast dishes*]
B: oh, I'll do them for you

Within this context of utterance, B infers, although A did not state so directly, A's intended meaning that A cannot wash up the breakfast dishes due to the risk of her being late for work. B assumes A is following the CP, that is, making an effort, out of awareness in most cases, to interact with B cooperatively, and therefore must have intended some meaning B will be able to recognize and work out through inferencing. In this case, the implicature is A would like B to take care of the washing up for that morning.

Grice (1967) argued that in calculating implicatures, the hearer must do the following:

1. Process and arrive at the literal meaning of the utterance
2. Check the literal meaning against the CP (and see the maxims below)
3. Check the context of utterance
4. Check background information
5. Assume that numbers 1–4 are part of the mutual knowledge shared by the speaker and hearer
6. Calculate any implicatures

Conventional and Conversational Implicatures

There are in fact two types of implicatures, as was pointed out earlier. The first type, conventional implicatures, is associated with the linguistic forms, specifically the meanings of particular words. The same implicature or inference is always conveyed, regardless of the context.

Sentential connectors are usually cited as the most transparent in conveying conventional implicatures. One such example of a word that always functions to implicate conventionally a meaning of contrast is *but*. Note that semantic analysis regards *but* as an alternative to *and;* that is, they are interchangeable. A pragmatic analysis of meaning reaches a different conclusion.

1. Sasha, Amid, and John came to the barbecue, **but** Suzanne couldn't.
2. Suzanne couldn't, **but** Sasha, Amid, and John came to the barbecue.
3. Sasha, Amid, and John came to the barbecue, **and** Suzanne couldn't.
4. Suzanne couldn't, **and** Sasha, Amid, and John came to the barbecue.

It is possible to accept number 2 as having the same meaning as number 1. However, both 3 and 4 have different meanings from the original one, and thus it is not possible to accept that *and* and *but* are interchangeable. Sentential connectors are considered within semantics to join two sentences without regard to the meaning of each individual proposition in the context of use.

Well, commonly found at the beginnings of utterances, can conventionally implicate that the following proposition is not what the addressee is hoping to hear.

A: let's go to a movie
B: *well*, I'd rather get some fresh air; it's such a lovely evening . . .

Another example can be seen with *anyway,* which can implicate that the speaker wants to return to the main topic.

> *A:* what about Hawaii-kai?
> *B:* yeah, there are reasonable places there too, but, well, *anyway,* shall we go see that place in Kailua tomorrow morning?

B's use of *anyway* signals to A that she wants to return to the original topic, location of a house. The reference marker *that* in the phrase "that place" conveys prior mention in this instance.

Other words that commonly implicate meaning beyond what is said are *honestly* ("really," "speaking truthfully"), *actually* ("although it is difficult to verify"), and *even* ("what comes after *even* is a proposition at the end of a scale of probability").

> Even Steffi Graf can't win them all.

> As good as Graf was at tennis, she could not win every match.

The second type of implicature is conversational implicature, which can only be understood in the context of the particular utterance. It is possible to separate this main category into two subcategories. Generalized conversational implicatures are calculable without reference to one particular instance of occurrence; yet the context is important.

> *A* boy came to deliver the paper.
> *The* boy came to deliver the paper.

Unlike the first statement, the second implies that the same boy comes every morning, or that he is known to the people who subscribe to the newspaper.

Particularized conversational implicatures require local interpretation. This category constitutes the prototypical type that requires inferencing to recognize the speaker's meaning.

> *A:* I finished writing all the Christmas cards
> *B:* the stamps are in the drawer

A could be expressing great relief or even pleasure with having finished this annual task. Then B provides useful information about the stamps, possibly signaling that A can stick them on the envelopes and conveying B's desire not to do it.

> *A:* there's a towel in the closet
> *B:* I didn't think it was going to rain today

B has just arrived in a pouring rain at A's home without an umbrella. Before B can say anything, the host has volunteered information on where B can find something with which to dry off. Without their contexts, these pairs of utterances (or *adjacency pairs;* see chapter 8) would be processed only with difficulty.

The Maxims

To the CP Grice added four more principles of human communication to explain more precisely the range of behavior observable all around us. These maxims, in addition to the CP, provide the backdrop against which the implicatures of both types are understood. Without the assumption that speakers are following some basic principles, hearers cannot presume rational behavior and follow the intention behind what may appear to be obscure instances of talk.

> Quantity
> 1. Make your contribution as informative as is required (for the purposes of the exchange).
> 2. Do not make your contribution more informative than is required.
>
> Quality. Try to make your contribution one that is true.
> 1. Do not say what you believe to be false.
> 2. Do not say that for which you lack adequate evidence.
>
> Relation. Be relevant.
>
> Manner. Be perspicuous.
> 1. Avoid obscurity of expression.
> 2. Avoid ambiguity.

3. Be brief (avoid unnecessary prolixity).
4. Be orderly.

The maxim of quantity is internal to a particular text; the appropriate amount of information is what is required, not more and not less. The maxim of quality, that is, the truth or falsity of the speaker's utterance, is concerned with the real world. The maxim of manner involves the text itself, the actual linguistic features, and consequently the way in which the information is provided in the text. As for the maxim of relevance, it has been claimed to be of a different order. It is the one maxim that appears to be present in all instances and the one most frequently flouted. In the following conversation, the role of the maxims can be assessed.

1. *C:* um, I was in a smaller town, outside Tokyo, and I was there, I guess, '91 to '92
2. *B:* really?
3. *C:* yeah, so, I guess a little bit after you guys were there.
4. *B:* the suburb?
5. *C:* yeah, yeah, suburb, it was between Tokyo and Chichibu I told Mona how I loved the location
6. *B:* really?
7. *C:* 'Cause, 'cause I could go kind of either way to Tokyo, for city, and the other way to Chichibu, for the mountains
8. *A:* that's great!
9. *B:* the best of both worlds.

(Sasaki 1995)

In line 1, C provides information about her stay in Japan, to which B reacts with "Really," implying some surprise. In fact, B's response is not clear in isolation; it is in line 3 that the analyst can understand how B understood line 1, that is, with surprise, perhaps delight. B was not questioning the truth of C's statement, but rather recognizing that C had been in Japan after both B and A had been living there. The maxim of quality is respected. B enters again in line 4 with another comment. Notice that in line 5, C assumes shared knowledge and does not give too much detail, only enough for B and A to have a general idea of where

C lived. Thus, the maxim of quantity is also in operation. As regards the maxim of manner, in line 7, C again gives enough information, her contribution being brief, orderly, without ambiguity or obscurity of expression. Because all three lived near Tokyo, they shared the knowledge that the area in which C lived does indeed allow one to go either direction (on the train lines, literally, either to Tokyo or the lovely mountains). Finally, the maxim of relevance has been adhered to as well. Even the final comments of B and A at the end of this segment of the data are relevant to C's account of her living environment in Japan in the early 1990s.

Flouting the Maxims

Now the focus shifts to examining what happens when speakers flout one or more of Grice's maxims. That is, they appear to be violating not only the CP by not stating directly what they mean, but they also break or flout one or more of the maxims. The hearer still has to assume, according to Grice, cooperativeness and intentionality, as speakers theoretically obey the maxims. In other words, the basic principles of the CP and of the maxims are the baseline against which any deviation is compared, leading the listener to assume the speaker has a reason to violate one or more of the maxims or of the CP. There is still an intended meaning for the listener to recognize.

The flouting of the maxims or the CP has the same effect as the breaking of any norms: human beings attribute relevance and coherence to human activities and, when the conventions are broken, we assume there is some reason. The listener or reader assumes coherence and seeks to find the regularities within the irregularities, to paraphrase a Popperian comment. This is a universal of human behavior: the effort to find meaning and coherence.

Further, note that not all of the maxims have equal weight. The maxim of relevance is probably the most important. Any one of the three maxims of quantity, quality, and manner may vary cross-culturally, whereas the establishment of relevance of a speaker's utterance is a minimum requirement of any interaction.

Grice's CP and the four maxims provide a baseline that enables the listener to interpret, in contrast, what types of meaning are conveyed when a speaker flouts one or more of the maxims or the CP. That type of meaning is also regarded as conversational implicature. Here is an example.

> *A:* what time is it, honey?
> *B:* well, the paper's arrived . . .

If A is a harried husband at breakfast and B is his wife, it is possible to calculate the conversational implicature that B is conveying by her utterance: if both A and B share the same knowledge that the morning newspaper always arrives by 6:30 A.M., then the time must be later than that. There is no reason to believe that B is not being cooperative. Yet she is flouting two maxims:

> The maxim of relevance: B's response does not at first appear to answer A's question. However, A assumes his wife is cooperating and consequently that her response is relevant.
> The maxim of quantity: B does not seem to be providing enough information. She could have added, "so that means it must be past 6:30."

Clearly, some knowledge of this particular family's daily routine and associated events is needed in this example of conversational implicature triggered by the flouting of, in this case, two of Grice's maxims.

A particularly interesting example of the flouting of the maxim of relevance is the so-called pope question. Assume that B is a lover of ice cream and is asked the following question one hot summer evening:

> *A:* I don't suppose you'd like to go out for a walk to get some ice cream . . .
> *B:* is the pope Catholic?

What appears to be a totally irrelevant answer is in fact completely relevant. The answer to B's question is "Yes, of course the pope is Catholic." Since it is obvious that the pope is Catholic, it should also be obvious that B will go with A to get some ice cream because A knows that B likes ice cream! And that is precisely B's answer to A's indirect question; in fact, B could add, "as you ought to know . . . "

To sum up, implicatures are pragmatic meanings that one must work out by using the following sources of information:

> Conventional or literal meanings, reference, deictic markers, and so on
> Specific linguistic and nonlinguistic context features shared by the speaker and hearer
> The recognition by both speaker and hearer of the CP and the maxims
> Background knowledge

It is also necessary to keep in mind that when analysts study a speaker's intended meaning, they have limited knowledge of what the speaker wanted to say. Analysts usually are limited to studying possible interpretations of the speaker's utterances. In fact, the hearer is also in a similar position—human beings have limited access to what is occurring in the mind of another person. However, the hearer is in a better position than the analyst, being copresent in the actual situation and able to attend to any nonlinguistic cues that may be significant in disambiguating a speaker's meaning. The analyst is limited to working with the text.

Hedges

Without going so far as to flout the maxims, speakers may want to signal less than full adherence to them by using expressions called hedges. These are signals of caution, indicating that the speakers are aware of the maxims and that normally they do adhere to them as cooperative interactants. Nevertheless, at times speakers use hedges to signal that they are not fully adhering to a maxim.

With regard to the maxim of quality, a hedge such as *as far as I know* signals that the speaker has limited certainty about the truthfulness of information.

> *A:* when is she due to arrive?
> *B:* *as far as I know,* next Tuesday . . .

Other expressions used to hedge this maxim are "I'm not sure, but I heard . . . ," "I may be mistaken, but . . . ," and "I guess."

Hedging the maxim of quantity tells the hearer that the speaker may not wish to present all of the information possessed by the speaker.

A: how was your trip?
B: well, *to make a long story short,* we were disappointed with the service at the hotel, but the scenery was gorgeous . . .

Similar expressions are "as you probably know," "I won't bore you with the details," and "they say."

Concerning the maxim of relevance, hedges such as "oh, by the way," "anyway," or "well, anyway" are signals that the speaker has digressed from the main topic, as the speaker understands it, and wishes to return to it.

A: not to change the topic, but have you seen Joe recently?
B: no, *come to think of it,* not recently . . . why?

In this instance, both A and B are using hedges to make metacomments on their having strayed from a topic that might have occupied them in a conversation earlier. Now they desire to return to it.

Finally, the maxim of manner can also be hedged.

A: I may be a bit confused, but I think the best route is over the mountains . . .

When A expresses the possibility that she may not be able to express herself clearly, due to some fuzziness in her thinking, she is signaling some caution with regard to taking what she is saying at face value. Other expressions are "if you see what I mean," "I don't know if this is clear, but . . . ," and "I'm not sure this makes any sense, but . . . "

Note that hedges can function as both minimizers and maximizers (sometimes called intensifiers) of the maxims. As metalingual comments, they do not contribute to the content of the talk, but rather are indications of the speaker's attitudes toward the level of informativeness, truthfulness, and relevance of the utterances. They function as signals that the speaker is adhering to a maxim, yet, in the case of hedges, without strictness. The examples above are of hedges used as minimizers, that is, to signal less than 100 percent adherence to a particular maxim. With maximizers, the speaker is indicating that adherence is definite, at more than a 100 percent level. Here is an example of a maximizer:

> *A:* okay, first you put in the sautéed onions, *then* you add the eggs and cheese . . .

In addition to such linguistic items as "then," which intensifies relevance, "in the final analysis" maximizes manner, "it is true to say that . . . " maximizes quality, and "at this stage" maximizes quantity.

Using hedges and flouting the maxims signal to the addressee that something "special" is going on, thus triggering extra cognitive work to calculate the appropriate implicature. While flouts break the CP or the maxims, hedges in fact signal the existence of these principles of communication by commenting on them, indicating the speaker is either adhering to a particular maxim less than would be expected or doing so even more directly than the norms require.

Limitations of the CP and the Maxims

One criticism of Grice's CP and the maxims concerns the meaning of the word *information*. One reading of Grice is that he is focused on transactional information, that is, the content only of propositions and not on interpersonal aspects of talk, where an interaction may not be about anything other than establishing or acknowledging the copresence of another human being. The interpretation that Grice is concerned only with information, narrowly defined, relates to his position as a philosopher of language and the fact that his theory draws on human beings as rational, using means-ends reasoning. A prototypical example of transactional language is buying and selling of stocks via telephone, fax, or e-mail. In such an exchange, the buyer and seller are exclusively interested in the minimal amount of information needed to transact or carry out the business at hand. However, most pragmatists argue that "information" includes interpersonal information, and, consequently, formulaic routines to inquire about another person's well-being would be included within Gricean pragmatics.

The example in the accompanying table illustrates the role of interpersonal factors in the speech event of complimenting in Japanese. Japanese informants will say that such language is used today only by elderly people, in particular women. Nevertheless, the point can still be made that A is using language to show deference and to flatter B about her garden. Undoubtedly, A is the younger woman who is making positive comments on B's garden using very formal language. B may be a neighbor or perhaps the wife of someone with whom A needs to stay on good terms. The information being exchanged in the talk is not the

A:	maa, go-rippa na o-niwa de gozaamasu wa nee, shibafu ga hirobiro to shite ite, kekkoo de gozaamasu wa nee.	[My, what a splendid garden you have here—the lawn is so nice and big, it's certainly wonderful, isn't it!]
B:	iie, nan desu ka, chitto mo teire ga yukitodokimasen mono de gozaimasu kara, moo, nakanaka itsumo kirei ni shite oku wake ni wa mairiamasen no de gozaamasu yo.	[Oh no, not at all. We don't take care of it at all any more, so it simply doesn't always look as nice as we would like it to.]
A:	aa, sai de gozaimashoo nee. kore dake o-hiroin de gozaamasu kara, hitotoori o-teire asobasu no ni datte taihen de gozaimashoo nee. demo maa, sore de mo, itsumo yoku o-teire ga yukitodoite irasshaimasu wa. itsumo honto ni o-kirei de kekkoo de gozaamasu wa.	[Oh, no, I don't think so at all—but since it's such a big garden, of course, it must be quite a tremendous task to take care of it all by yourself; but even so, you certainly do manage to make it look nice all the time; it certainly is nice and pretty any time one sees it.]
B:	iie, chitoo mo sonna koto gazaamasen wa.	[No, I'm afraid not, not at all.]

Source: Miller 1967, 290, cited in Leech 1983, 136–37.

kind that traders on the floor of the New York Stock Exchange use! With a more inclusive interpretation of information, or of being informative, it becomes transparent that the CP and the maxims may be regularly flouted out of concern for the face needs of the interlocutors in the context of use.

A second criticism of Grice's approach to pragmatic meaning notes limitations due to activity-specific inferences and cultural differences in the realization of the CP and the maxims. In a television interview, for example, maxims may be suspended, according to Weizman and Blum-Kulka (1996). In an effort to extract an answer to a question, a newscaster interviewing a politician will not hesitate to pursue the interviewee in a hard-hitting manner. Such directness would not be tolerated, or at least would not be the norm, in other contexts. Thus, the CP and the maxims can be suspended in particular contexts or settings to allow for the pursuit of the purpose of, in this case, an interview: to obtain genuine answers to questions of great interest to the viewing public, that is, the voters. In the accompanying interview, specific inferences can be observed. All of the interviewer's statements or questions push the interviewee to give an explanation, flouting the CP and the maxims—as if the interviewer were being rude. Yet within the context of a political interview, this linguistic behavior may be tolerated, perhaps even welcomed, depending on the cultural expectations of the audience.

With regard to cultural differences, taking first the maxim of quantity, what constitutes the appropriate amount of information may vary, depending on one's culturally constructed point of view. Is it preferable to give bad news, that is, that the Thai restaurant has no more coconut ice cream, at the beginning of the meal or only at the end, when the desserts are about to be brought to the table? Here is another example:

A: can I get a bus ticket for Prague here, at this agency?
B: no, we only sell train tickets

B has answered the question, providing the information asked for by A; however, B offers no suggestions to A as to where a bus ticket can be purchased. These example may indicate different views regarding what is "enough" information.

Interviewer:	How do you explain this uh collapse of the road system (?) Roads that merely underwent a few days of rain look like ruins
Interviewee:	First of all I would like to refer to inter city roads only [. . .] and I would like to explain this . . .
Interviewer:	Uh I am sorry before you explain doesn't it sound a bit strange? Uh only uh a week even less of rain and it couldn't do what's expected of it. It didn't rain like it does in Switzerland not even the US!
Interviewee:	No, let me explain [. . .]
Interviewer:	I'm sorry I must ask you again on this point, it's not]
Interviewee:	[Please do
Interviewer:	A certain capacity which is too small for three days of rain?
Interviewee:	Uh I would like to explain three days of rain [. . .]
Interviewer:	Is our system designed for drought, uh 360 days a year?
Interviewee:	Our system [. . .]

Source: Weizman and Blum-Kulka 1996.

Concerning the maxim of quality, regarding the truthfulness of the speaker's contribution, cultural practices such as not displaying one's knowledge publicly and avoiding giving "bad" news may be much stronger influences on a speaker than the admonishment of making one's contribution truthful. Rather than admitting that a computer part is not available, a small company may even accept a payment for it, only to return the money later when it has become apparent that the company cannot provide the wanted part.

Although relevance in talk is undoubtedly a universal characteristic, a "relevant" remark may only be worked out within a particular culture's worldview. If two neighbors meet on the street in the morning in their neighborhood in Japan, one may say to the other *Doko e?* [Where are you going?] In China, a person greeting another may ask, "Have you eaten?" without seeking to know if the addressee has in fact eaten. The remark is relevant as a greeting in context.

With regard to the maxim of manner, ambiguity, obscurity, and prolixity may sometimes be valued within a culture's worldview. Jokes and puns, for example, depend on flouting the maxim of manner.

> Did you hear about the Buddhist who refused his dentist's Novocain during root canal work? He wanted to transcend dental medication.

Lakoff (1990, 188–89) presents a speech by former President Reagan to demonstrate his mastery of ambiguity.

> It has been nearly three years since I first spoke to **you** from this room. Together, **we**'ve faced many difficult problems and I've come to feel a bond of kinship with each one of **you**. . . . But worst of all, **we** were on the brink of economic collapse . . . I had to report that **we** were "in the worst economic mess since the Great Depression." While **you** tightened **your** belt, the federal government tightened its grip. But **our** work is not finished. **We** have more to do in creating jobs.

In this passage *we* has more than one meaning. Reagan sometimes uses it to include the public, but the last instance is the exclusive *we*. The effect is the perception that he is paying attention to each member of the audience, attending to their emotional needs, including their need for a president who is in charge.

Still other limitations in Grice's framework of pragmatic inference call for an extension beyond speech act analysis, the original purview of his work. Further, some researchers argue that the maxim of relevance is the only one needed. This alternative to the CP and the four maxims will be discussed in chapter 9.

Conclusion

Despite their limitations, Grice's concepts are of considerable value in explaining pragmatic meaning. They capture basic characteristics of human interaction, particularly norms and expectations. The following two chapters on sociolinguistic and cognitive perspectives take the discussion further by including other factors that influence the production and interpretation of meaning.

Tasks

1. Advertisements in magazines and newspapers, on television, and on billboards flout maxims regularly. First, collect several examples—three to five is a good number—and then analyze them to see what maxims are being flouted. Second, explain why advertising companies write such ads. For example, an English ad around Tokyo several summers ago proclaimed, "I feel Coke!" (the accompanying picture was of a young person in stylish summer clothing). An ad in Mexican Spanish reads "Disfruta Coca-Cola!" [Enjoy Coca-Cola!].

2. What maxims are flouted in the following?
   A: I'd like a coffee
   B: black? white? with or without?

3. Study the accompanying table. What is the topic of the conversation? Are any maxims flouted? Has relevance been violated?

1. *Gary:*		well, I got pictures tomorrow night-boy, I I love that that State Theatre
2. *Pauline:*		Oh, isn't it beautiful
3. *Gary:*		//yeah
4. *Bronwyn:*		//yeah
5. *Gary:*		//yeah
6. *Pauline:*		//I really love it—my favorite
7. *Pat:*		I've never been there
8. *Bronwyn:*		//oh, it's beautiful
9. *Pauline:*		//oh, it's beautiful—it's got chandeliers and things
10. *Pat:*		I've been to the one in Wollongong
11. *Bronwyn:*		//oh no—look nothing beats the State really it's beautiful
12. *Pauline:*		I've always loved it
13. *Bronwyn:*		this has been restored and everything
14. *Pat:*		What's on there?
15. *Gary:*		ah Monty Python

Source: Slade and Norris 1986, cited in Hatch 1992, 32.

4. How do you indicate that you are unsure about the truthfulness, correctness, manner of presentation, or relevance of what you are saying? Give examples in at least one language that you know well.

5. Do you agree with Grice that human beings follow the CP and the four maxims in their interactions with others? Why or why not? Give evidence to support your opinion.

6. Provide an analysis of this bit of talk.
   A: where've you been?
   B: out
   A: where'd you go?
   B: somewhere

7. What are the limitations of Grice's CP and maxims? Can you think of others that were not included in this chapter? Give examples.

8. Complete the following task (adapted from Steinberg Du 1995) on your own. Be as natural as you can in your responses. Then code your answers in terms of Brown and Levinson's macro and substrategies of politeness. Finally, state whether or not you have violated any of Grice's principles in your responses. Note that it is important to do this task in the order in which you have been asked to complete it. This is not a test; it is a chance for you to practice applying what you have learned.

Discourse Completion Task

Information about you

Age _____ Sex _____ Birthplace_____

Mother tongue _____

Other languages you speak _____

Imagine yourself in the following situations and write down exactly what kind of reaction you would normally have (what you might say, or what you might do, including silence, etc.). If your reaction would depend on the person you are dealing with, whether male or female, older or younger, and so on please give specific explanations.

1. Your friend is visiting you at home, and you find her lingering around your favorite handicraft—a miniature bamboo boa—and repeatedly expressing her admiration: "It's so pretty, so real."
You would:

2. You and your next-door neighbors usually get along well, but recently their daughter is taking violin lessons at home in the evenings and you find yourself unable to do anything because of the noise.
You would:

3. You and your friend are in a department store. Something on the shelf catches your friend's eye, who exclaims: "My, I've been looking for this for a long time, I just have to buy one. I wish I had more money with me!"
You would:

4. You go to a movie with a friend, who keeps asking after you sit down: "Are you comfortable sitting there?"
You would:

5. Your friend asks to borrow some money and promises to return it as soon as possible. You don't want to lend the money, but you don't want to hurt your friend's feelings.
You would:

6. You and your professor are heading for the library together, but just before leaving his office, you see a big tear in his shirt.
You would:

7. Your classmate wrote a poem that he likes very much and wants to get published. After reading it, you think the poem has no chance to be published.
You would:

8. After lunch, you and a classmate are headed toward class. You notice that spinach is stuck in his or her teeth.
You would:

9. Your housemate always leaves messes in the areas of the house you share. You decide you have to point out that cleaning up is your housemate's duty.
You would:

10. You are talking with a classmate whose breath smells strongly of garlic. You happen to have a pack of chewing gum with you.
    You would:

Suggested Readings

Davis, S., ed. 1991. *Pragmatics: A reader.* New York: Oxford University Press.

Grice, H. P. 1975. Logic and conversation. In *Speech acts,* ed. P. Cole and J. L. Morgan. Vol. 3. of *Syntax and semantics.* New York: Academic Press.

Hyland, K. 1998. *Hedging in scientific research articles.* Amsterdam/Philadelphia: John Benjamins.

Levinson, S. C. 1983. *Pragmatics,* chap. 3. New York: Cambridge University Press.

Mey, J. L. 1993. *Pragmatics: An introduction,* chap. 4. Oxford: Blackwell.

Chapter 8
Sociolinguistic Approaches

Sociolinguistics is essentially the study of language in use, in particular variation in use depending on features of the context such as the status, age, and the relationship of the social actors. Moving from Grice's notion of speakers and listeners as rational individual actors, the two perspectives in chapter 8 focus on the socially influenced patterns in the enactment of talk. They are *preference organization* and *speech act theory*. The effect of social variables on the linguistic and discursive context is emphasized by the first, while their effect on the speech event is emphasized by the second.

Preference Organization

One issue that grew out of Gricean pragmatics is the nature of coherent discourse. Grice's CP and maxims provide reasons for a piece of language to be more than a string of random sentences. Human beings create discourse, that is, utterances that cohere, according to Grice, because people cooperate in communication. Coherence is the result of the speaker's making relevant contributions and of the hearer's seeking the inferences, utilizing overt markers (such as discourse markers) or imposing coherence even where it is only implied through the linguistic forms.

Preference organization, which rests on a presumption of coherence in discourse, draws its premises from conversation analysis (CA), described in chapter 1 as an approach to language analysis that focuses on conversational structure and is characterized by use of extended samples of naturally occurring talk. The main concept of CA concerns the fact that the nature of talk, despite the chaotic appearance of a transcribed sequence of an interaction, is structured; in other words, interactants produce predictable patterns. If human beings did not do so, talk would appear to be incoherent. *Preference organization* accounts for the fact that B's response to A's question, statement, or command is contextualized. Because a particular response is likely to whatever prompts it in a conversation, preference organization comprises a theory of pragmatic meaning. The coherence in discourse is another example of how the means to engage in communication are manipulated to facilitate success.

The first section introduces two of the main concepts of conversational analysis. Then, this introduction is followed by an explanation of preference organization. The third section focuses on the role of a variety of features of talk that are implicated in interpreting interactional meaning. Finally, the role of the constituent features of CA in second language learning and teaching is discussed.

Data-Driven Categories

The main premise of conversation analysis states that premature formalization is to be avoided. Rather than developing categories for analysis theoretically, detailed analysis of natural language data is to be carried out first to discover inductively categories and regularities of conversation, leading to generalizations about the nature of talk. In other words, the categories of analysis are data-driven. The goal of CA has been to use rigorous methods of analysis so as to arrive at generalizations about the structure of talk that cut across social and cultural groups.

The major problems addressed by CA have been (1) turn-taking, (2) overall organization of conversations, such as closings and openings, and (3) adjacency pairs. These three areas are regarded as "problems" in the sense that speakers and hearers have to know how to exchange turns at talk, how to open and close conversations, and how to make a response relevant to the previous speaker's contribution.

Turn-Taking

An early, seminal paper in the field of CA is the Sacks, Schegloff, and Jefferson (1978) article entitled "A Simplest Systematics for the Organization of Turn-Taking for Conversation." Their analysis of talk in interaction generated a list of facts that had to be accounted for:

1. Overwhelmingly, one party talks at a time.
2. A change of speaker recurs.
3. Transitions between turns with no gap are common.
4. The order of turns is not fixed, but varies.
5. The length of turns is not fixed, but varies.
6. The length of conversation is not specified in advance.
7. What parties say is not specified in advance.
8. Relative distribution of turns is not specified in advance.
9. The number of parties can vary.
10. Talk can be continuous or discontinuous.
11. Techniques to allocate turns are used.
12. Mechanisms exist for dealing with turn-taking errors or violations.

These facts, apparent upon observation of conversation, viewed as the most basic, prototypical form of social interaction, can be couched in the form of a metaphor of a market economy.

> In this market, there is a scarce commodity called the floor which can be defined as the right to speak. Having control of this scarce commodity at any time is called a turn. (Yule 1996a, 72–73)

From this basic frame evolves the features listed above, signaling how the competition for taking turns at holding the floor is handled. Because turn-taking is an example of social action, some form of local management must be present in the conventions that interactants tacitly agree to. Note that normally they do not discuss how all of this is managed; human beings learn how to engage in conversations through the socialization process of their own cultures and it is usually performed out of awareness. However, whenever another form of interaction presents itself, such as committee meetings, the individuals involved may negotiate a set of conventions to govern committee proceedings, including the organization of talk, for their meetings. Robert's Rules of Order and parliamentary procedures are examples of the conventions.

Of the items on the list from Sacks, Schegloff, and Jefferson 1978, turn-taking became the focus of the researchers attention, and a model was developed to account for the features they had observed about talk. This is a summary of the options open to the first speaker in their model; in the first option, the first speaker can control the type of utterance that comes next:

> The first speaker can select the next speaker by naming or alluding.
> The first speaker can constrain the next utterance but not select the next speaker.
> The first speaker can select neither the utterance nor the next speaker and leave others to self-select.

Essentially, the model claims that the next speaker in a conversation is either selected by the current speaker or is left to join the interaction without any signal from the current speaker. The advantage for the current speaker in designating the next speaker is that it allows the current speaker to have some control over the talk. The person selected by the current speaker has the exclusive right and even obligation to speak next. However, the current speaker may elect to stop talking, leaving the floor open to whomever wants to complete a turn at talk, relinquishing any control over the floor or over the talk itself.

A particular aspect of turn-taking that interested Sacks, Schegloff, and Jefferson was the question of how interactants know when a speaker has ended a turn at talk. Since it is generally the case that only one speaker talks at a time, how do coparticipants avoid bumping into each other on the floor? If the current speaker asks a question or addresses a particular listener by name, the copresent interactants can readily recognize the signal and then take a turn. However, when the current speaker makes no attempt to select the next speaker or if a listener wishes to attempt to take over the floor, listeners need to be able to predict a possible entry point. That point is called a transition relevant place (TRP). The TRP designates the moment of a possible change of turn.

It is necessary now to describe what the TRP might look like for participants. Both speaker and listener play a role. The listeners are constantly observing the speaker for cues that may signal the speaker is ready to relinquish the floor, while the speaker uses a combination of cues to signal the end of a turn. Several cues may be present:

Unfilled pauses
Turning one's head toward the listener
A drop in pitch or loudness
Relaxation of the foot or feet of the speaker
Audible inhalation
Drawling on the final syllable, and a general slowing down
Head nods, body posture
Eye contact
Intonation contour

In fact, almost never is just one cue present; rather, cues occur in clusters, which vary according to the situation. Obviously, telephone conversations cannot depend on nonverbal cues. Speaker and hearer engage in a dance, with constant mutual awareness and self-monitoring to carry out smooth turn-taking. As turn-taking is a primary form of social action, attention to the face needs of coparticipants is assumed.

Adjacency Pairs

Another very noticeable feature of natural language use observed by Sacks, Schegloff, and Jefferson is formulaic, two-part sequences such as this North American greeting that every learner of English studies:

A: hi, how are you?
B: fine, thank you, and you?

This is called an adjacency pair and consists of a first-pair part, that is, what A says, and a second-pair part, what B responds. The important point is that the first pair part constrains the second pair part. That is, certain responses are preferred. A transparent example is that a question in the first pair part usually requires an answer in the second pair part.

Further, the first pair part constrains the way in which the second pair part is interpreted. In the following example, because a yes/no question would predict a yes or a no answer, the second pair part is interpreted as a negative answer. In other words, because B's response is not expected, a conversational implicature is present as a result of the flout.

A: there is a good film on at the Duke's; it starts tonight
B: I've got a paper to finish by tomorrow

More analysis of talk-in-interaction, however, leads to the awareness that not all adjacency pairs occur in such a straightforward pattern. There can be embedding of pairs within pairs.

1. *A:* are you coming tonight?
2. *B:* can I bring a guest?
3. *A:* male or female?
4. *B:* what difference does that make?
5. *A:* an issue of balance
6. *B:* female
7. *A:* sure
8. *B:* I'll be there

The question posed in utterance 1 does not get answered until utterance 8. Adjacency pairs are embedded within the sequence: numbers 2 and 7, 3 and 6, and 4 and 5. These are called *insertion sequences*. Other speech acts are enacted in the same way. The following dialogue includes a request-response adjacency pair:

Jean:	could you mail this letter for me?	Request
Fred:	does it have a stamp on it?	Question
Jean:	yeah	Answer
Fred:	okay	Acceptance

(Yule 1996a, 78)

Many other types of adjacency pairs occur in natural conversational data. Whenever the expected adjacency pair pattern is not enacted, the violation is interpreted as meaningful. From a hesitation in acceptance of a request to outright silence in response to a greeting, all such behaviors are significant and regarded as conveying pragmatic meaning. In the next section, more detail on the concept of preference organization allows us to examine the expectations of this form of social action.

Preferred and Dispreferred Responses

Preference organization, a general characteristic of talk, develops the basic point of adjacency pairs. Identifiable two-part pairs occur in instances of talk; the first pair part constrains the second pair part, either in terms of the type of response or in the interpretation of the meaning of the second pair part. Pomerantz (1984) drew attention to the existence of preferred and dispreferred responses:

Preferred: *A:* could you put the light on?
              B: sure

Dispreferred: *A:* I'm getting fat
              B: [*silence*]

These examples demonstrate the tendency for the first pair part to elicit a second pair part that, from the point of view of social action and the need to attend to the face needs of conversational partners, is preferred by the speaker of the first pair part. In the preferred example above, A expects B to show cooperation by giving a preferred response of acceptance to the request. In the second example, the silent response of B is dispreferred and implies acceptance of A's comment. The accompanying table outlines the types of preferred and dispreferred responses for some commonly occurring speech acts.

	Request	Offer	Assessment
Preferred/ expected	Acceptance	Acceptance	Agreement
Dispreferred/ unexpected	Refusal	Refusal	Disagreement/ no answer

Agreement and disagreement are particularly interesting for studying the notion of preference organization and the question of face needs. Here is an example:

A: it's a beautiful day, isn't it?
B: yeah, it's just gorgeous

This adjacency pair is what Pomerantz (1984) calls an assessment, where A comments on the quality of the weather for the day, from her point of view, assuming that most conversational partners would agree without further discussion. In this instance, B responds with the preferred, agreement type of response in the second pair part. However, it is possible that a dispreferred response might be given; human agency is certainly possible.

B: well, yes, but I heard on the weather forecast this morning that it's going to change any day now

This is a dispreferred response, with the tell-tale "yes, but . . . " linguistic phrase, signaling initial agreement ("yes") and followed by a proposition expressing if not outright disagreement, then some hesitation in giving complete agreement.

In one type of first pair part a disagreement is actually the preferred response, and this is when the first pair part speaker comments negatively on him- or herself:

A: I'm so dumb, I don't even know it . . . [*laughter*]
B: no, you're not dumb

Unless they are close friends, B would be viewed as very impolite in agreeing with A.

Silence is ambiguous and can only be interpreted within the context of the adjacency pair. In the example given above,

A: I'm getting fat
B: [*silence*]

the silence is interpreted as agreement. In the following one, the contrary is true.

A: Isn't it dreary?
B: [*silence*]

B is communicating disagreement with A's comment about a movie they are watching.

Dispreferreds are often marked by delay in responding or other distinctive features: (1) delays, for example, in the form of pauses before delivery; (2) prefaces, such as "Oh, well" or token agreements ("yes, but . . . "), or appreciations before disagreements ("I very much appreciate . . . "); (3) accounts, that is, reasons for the dispreferred alternative; and (4) mitigated or indirect forms ("Well, I don't think I'll be able to come . . . " rather than "I have no intention of coming").

Preference organization is also noticeable in repair sequences, where self-initiated corrections are preferred to other-initiated corrections of a speaker's performance mistakes. In instances of everyday talk, the participants tend to correct their own slips of the tongue or lexical inaccuracies rather than allowing the listeners to do so. Moreover, it also offers a general explanation for prerequests, preinvitations, and prearrangements, where a possible face threat to the speaker is avoided by means of this strategy to prevent a dispreferred second pair part from being performed. Here is an example of a preinvitation or a prerequest:

A: are you very busy these days?
B: terribly

B's answer tells A that B is not going to be free to accept an invitation or carry out a request and, as a result, A may decide not to make the invitation or a request.

In sum, a general characteristic of conversation is preference organization. It accounts for the observed coherence in turn-taking, by accounting for the regularities and expectations that are embedded in and constrain talk. One manifestation of preference organization occurs in adjacency pairs, found in the presence of preferred and dispreferred responses. As with the flouting of the CP and the maxims or any violation on the part of the speaker to adhere to the presumption of relevance of a contribution, any breaking with the expectations of preferred responses is meaningful and can generate, if done with intention, implicatures. Moreover, preference organization is linked to face needs and politeness, as defined in chapter 6. With a compliment, for example, the preferred response in North America is acceptance, in other words, agreement with the assessment made by the speaker in the first pair part.

The next section elaborates on speech act theory and its limitations.

Speech Acts and Speech Events

The basic notion that human beings use language to act on the world, both to create obligations and new social relations as well as do such things as reassure, promise, and apologize, derives from insights of J. L. Austin, a philosopher of language. A collection of his lectures at Harvard University in 1955 was published in *How to Do Things with Words* in 1962. Austin contended that truth or falsehood and the logical relationships between words were inadequate to account for language use and that "the more we consider a statement not as a sentence (or proposition) but as an act of speech . . . the more we are studying the whole thing as an act" (1962, 20). From Austin's insights grew a perspective that is one of the well-recognized attempts to account for pragmatic meaning.

Speech Act Theory

At first, Austin argued that actions are performed via utterances only with verbs he called *performatives,* the prototype speech act. A performative is a verb or verbal phrase, typically formulaic, which explicitly indicates the act the speaker is actually performing as it is uttered.

> I christen you John Christopher.
> I bet you one million yen.
> I promise to meet you at 5 P.M. tomorrow.

The basic argument is that some utterances are not statements or questions, but rather actions. From this category of verbs, all used with the first-person singular pronoun and referring to present time only (present indicative active), Austin generalized the notion of performing actions with language, arguing that all utterances had the underlying performative structure:

I (hereby) Vp you (that) + utterance.

For example, "Clean up that mess!" can be rewritten as "I hereby order you to clean up that mess." The imperative sentence form with the utterance functioning as a command becomes an explicit performative speech act. Austin called his theory the *performative hypothesis.* However, soon Austin realized that there were serious limitations to this hypothesis.

First, the two versions of "clean up that mess" are not equivalent in meaning. The imperative form to make a command or order is direct; nevertheless, depending on the intonation contour and the voice quality, it can be used among friends and intimates and be considered friendly. However, the underlying performative structure brought to the surface is likely to be read as a very strong order, used only by someone who has recognized power over the addressees. Thus, the explicit performative and the indirect version do not carry the same implicatures.

Second, outside a list of formalized, explicit performative verbs *(bet, christen, promise),* and the grammatical criteria for person ("I") and tense (present), it is difficult to decide which verb is appropriate for a particular function in all instances. In the course of the argumentation in his book, Austin reaches the insight that, in fact, "stating" is also a form of "doing, " that is, performing an act, and, consequently, a special category of verbs is unnecessary, as all language use in a speech situation is performative.

Third, Austin recognized that analysis of individual speech acts may not account for all of the aspects of language use. He concluded that a more important consideration is "the total speech act in the total speech situation" (1962, 148) and that stating, betting, christening are only three of many speech acts and are not to be considered a privileged class (1962, 148–49).

Consequently, Austin shifted to a more inclusive classification of how language is used to carry out actions. He argued that there are three acts enacted simultaneously with each speech act:

Sentence
locutionary act — The literal, basic meaning of the proposition, the lexico-grammatical meaning that has truth value and sense; that is, the proposition or sentence describes a state of affairs and has determinate meaning.

Utterance
illocutionary act — The speech act or force showing the intention of the speaker; how the act is to be understood by the addressee

perlocutionary act — The effect on the addressee, unpredictable, possibly nonlinguistic

Some perlocutions are intended by the speaker; however, others are not, as they are unpredictable (for example, no one laughs at the joke the speaker thinks is hilarious) and the addressee can always refuse to recognize the intended meaning (a greeting may not be reciprocated). To the extent that the effect is nonlinguistic, pragmatics has tended to avoid discussion of the perlocutionary act. Note, nonetheless, that in this book the perlocutionary act can be included in the scope of analysis.

Recognition of the Intended Force

Austin realized that some speech acts can be enacted indirectly. That is, no verb in the utterance specifies which speech act is being performed. For example, "I'll see you later" could be a promise, a prediction, or comment about a future event, or perhaps a warning or reprimand. The most salient features to distinguish the speaker's intended meaning would be prosodic cues in this example.

When the force of the speech act is marked directly, an illocutionary force indicating device (IFID) is present, usually a performative verb that explicitly names the speech act ("I command/order you to see me later" → "I hereby Vp you that . . . "). Most speech acts, however, are enacted indirectly; that is, the illocutionary force is not signaled and the addressee has to work out the force by inference.

It was also recognized that the declarative, interrogative, and imperative sentence forms, and accompanying intonation contours commonly correlate with particular speech acts. This is the classical approach to account for the illocutionary force of an utterance (Clark 1996, 136).

You're going! (rise-fall)	assertion
You're going? (rise)	request for confirmation
Are you going? (rise)	asking for information

In the following examples of speech acts in English (from Clark 1996, 136), the relation between form and function is transparent:

Declarative form: assertions	I need to borrow your coat.
Imperative form: order	Please lend me your coat.
Yes/no interrogative: ask for information	Can you lend me your coat?
WH-interrogative: ask for information	When can you lend me your coat?
Exclamation: exclamation	You've lent me your coat!

However, within speech act theory, it is problematic to state just what the relationship is between indirect speech acts (ISAs), that is, the function, and the form of the utterance. While one sentence form tends to co-occur with a typical speech act, there is no necessary relationship between form and illocutionary force. An indirect speech act can be performed by a declarative to signal a request to close the window: "It's chilly in here." If the form-function relation were constant, then an interrogative would be used with a request in every case. "It's freezing outside!" is a direct assertion of a state of affairs; however, it can function as an indirect speech act of requesting the heat be turned on. In fact, the most frequent are ISAs. In chapter 6, possible reasons for this phenomenon of indirectness were discussed. The matching or mismatching of form-function is a matter of the speaker's choice, as is the encoding of illocutionary force.

In addition to sentence form, the IFIDs are often manifested in conventional devices, such as "please" with a request and "I'll . . . " for a promise or an offer. However, these are not adequate to achieve recognition on the part of the listener of the speaker's intended illocutionary force.

Taxonomy

One question often raised about speech acts is their number: one hundred? one thousand? ten thousand? While that question is all but impossible to answer, several scholars have proposed classification schemes of speech acts. Searle (1969), another language philosopher, developed a taxonomy of speech acts, grouping them according to common functional characteristics.

1. Directives — Asking, questioning, inquiring; that is, getting the hearer to do or not do something
2. Representatives — Asserting, concluding; that is, committing speaker to truth of expressed proposition
3. Commissives — Promising, threatening, offering; that is, committing to a course of action
4. Expressives — Thanking, apologizing, welcoming, congratulating; that is, expressing a psychological state
5. Declaratives — Declaring, firing from employment, ordering; that is, affecting the immediate environment

Although there are acknowledged problems with Searle's taxonomy, it continues to provide a base from which further research and analysis can take place.

Felicity Conditions

One recurring theme in this book is intention; the addressee has to recognize the speaker's intended meaning. This holds true for speech acts. Certain expected, contextual features must be present for the speech act to be recognized and for uptake to occur. These are called *conditions of appropriateness* or *felicity conditions.* For example, with the category of promises, the following felicity conditions are in operation (see Grundy 1995, 90):

1. The speaker must believe that what the speaker wants to promise to do is within his/her power to do.
2. The speaker has good reasons to believe what is promised will be of some benefit to the receiver.
3. The speaker must believe that what is promised will not happen anyway.

Note that this is only a partial list of the felicity conditions for promises. Felicity conditions may appear to be similar to presuppositions: they have to be present before or as the act is being performed. However, they differ in that, rather than just being part of what the speaker and the listener individually bring to the act of utterance, they involve aspects of both the speaker and listener. Further, they are not part of any assumed background knowledge. Although Austin stated the need for felicity conditions for performatives in another way, the basic point is that the circumstances and the social actors, the speaker and the hearer, must be such that the speech act will "go through." For example, one can only divorce a spouse by saying "I hereby divorce you" three times in countries whose laws allow this speech act to have legal consequences. In this particular example, the felicity conditions are codified in the laws of a country or in religious practices that have the force of law. The notion of felicity conditions is one approach to conceptualizing contextual features that affect how a speech act is interpreted. They, in effect, specify underlying norms of human communication. As all schoolchildren learn early in life, a promise is only a promise if certain conditions can be met, including the sincerity of the person doing the promising!

Limitations of Speech Act Theory

Austin's work helped move language analysis away from concern for truthfulness. Speech acts continue to constitute a main area of interest in pragmatics research, as will become apparent in the chapters on cross-cultural pragmatics and interlanguage pragmatics. Nevertheless, speech act theory faces particular limitations. First, because there is no one-to-one correspondence between the function or illocutionary force and the form of the verb or the sentence form, the classification of speech acts is indeterminate. With regard to illocutionary force, "Could you shut the door?" can be a request or an order. This is particularly problematic in nonconventional, indirect speech acts, where the illocutionary force may be difficult to assign. With "It must be time to go," only world knowledge or common ground enables the hearer to assign the force of "request" for someone to tell the speaker the time, and not as a statement of the state of affairs. Some speech acts may be deliberately ambiguous: "You will come, won't you?" One interpretation of this utterance produces the following reading: in the first clause, "you will come," an assertion is made, followed by a request for information, "won't you?" However, the actual force of this utterance derives from the tag form in utterance-final position; it camouflages the assertion. The speaker appears to want to put the addressee in a position where a "no" answer is unacceptable or at least dispreferred. A true request for information would allow options to the addressee.

Second, the analysis of speech acts does not facilitate understanding of how conversations proceed. The social context is often ignored in such analysis. Although it has been a valuable tool for examining the connection between function and linguistic forms, it typically only looks at single utterances, that is, particular instances of realization, without considering the adjacent sociolinguistic context or co-text.

Speech act theory has been expanded to include more than single utterances. Austin himself (1962), expressing doubts about assigning special status to "statements," wrote that "it is important to take the speech situation as a whole" (1962, 138), and concluded that "what we have to study is *not* the sentence but the issuing of an utterance in a speech situation" (1962, 139). However, he did not develop that line of thought. Now, a minimum context or situation for speech act analysis comes from the field of conversational analysis, which introduced the notion of adjacency pair.

A: would you mind giving my lecture for me?
B: I have one of my own in an hour

B is enacting an indirect refusal, dependent for interpretation on contextual features, in particular the notion of common ground. The indexicals in "one of my own" signals to a fellow academic that B has a lecture to give that s/he must prepare for and "in an hour" suggests that B needs that hour to get ready for the lecture.

Another example of expanding the context of analysis for speech acts introduces a discourse analytic perspective, where some schools of analysis of text, for example, the Birmingham group, examine the structure of text before the individual speech act. They seek to understand how speakers make choices about speech act realization in the context of ongoing, extended discourse. In particular, the group has focused on classroom discourse.

> P: Can we give in our grammar on um Wednesday?
> T: Can you give in your grammar on Wednesday? You have a lot of homework for tomorrow?
> Ps: Yes yes
> P: We have our last exercise.
> T: You have to do
> P: Our last exercise
> T: Oh, that's because you have been lazy and didn't do your work properly, that's why you have extra work to do right? So I'm sorry you have to do it otherwise]=
> Ps: [No
> T: = won't be able to finish marking your books to give you before the holidays
>
> (Tsui 1994, 90)

Tsui focused on requesting speech acts; she contrasted cases where a request allows for the addressee to have an option with others where the speaker does not give the addressee the option of saying no. In the preceding example, the pupils are making a genuine request and the teacher does not comply. The point here is that, without more text than the speech act itself, the analyst cannot assess the force of utterances, nor the perlocutionary effect on the addressee. In general, there has been more and more interest in empirical studies of natural language use where speech act analysis is combined as one tool with those of conversational analysis or ethnography of speaking in studies of cross-cultural discourse.

A third limitation derives from the fact that it is not possible in a nonarbitrary way to ascertain that an utterance is a single versus multifunctional act.

> Hey, Miguel, you passed your thesis defense! Asserting
> Congratulating
> Apologizing for any previous doubts

While recognizing that intonation and other prosodic features will usually enable the addressee to disambiguate the speaker's meaning, speech act theory itself cannot explain the multifunctionality of illocutionary acts.

Finally, speech act analysis cannot provide psycholinguistic evidence of how a particular set of linguistic elements comes to have a particular illocutionary force. The theory is based on surface level linguistic forms and says nothing about the psycholinguistic reality of the premises and concepts of the theory.

Speech Events and Activity Types

Once one concludes that speech act analysis is too limited and that the listener's recognition and uptake must be considered, then expansion of the text for analysis becomes the "normal" perspective to take. The step first to adjacency pairs and then beyond may be observed in the analysis of much longer passages or texts, particularly in the work of conversational analysts and those whose research comes out of an ethnographic approach to language study. Two possible analytic perspectives are the speech event and analysis of activity types. Both imply an expectation of coherence due to the frame provided by the speech event or activity type. The interactants in the speech event or activity presume that the talk within the frame will be situationally appropriate and coherent.

A speech event is a discourse structure larger than a collection of speech acts or adjacency pairs. Examples are making introductions or complaints and giving advice or compliments (Hatch 1992, 136–52).

The basic structure of one such speech event is compliment + acknowledgment (or acceptance) + bridge to other talk.

Compliment →	A: hey, that's a beautiful tie
Acknowledgment/ Acceptance →	B: thanks, I kinda like it . . . got it in Bangkok, you know, Thai silk . . .
	A: it's really lovely
Bridge →	B: so . . . where did you spend your Christmas holidays?

Note that not all people accept a compliment and may downgrade the compliment, saying, "Oh, it's just some old thing my mother gave me years ago." Direct denials are carried out with "Oh, it's nothing" or "It's not new." Another strategy is to shift the focus: "Oh, those chairs . . . they were on sale, a really cheap buy." A change of topic is another possibility.

Speech event analysis links individual speech acts within a larger textual unit; it is ethnographic in nature, as a complete speech event analysis would include descriptions of the setting and the participants, as well as the structure or schema of the event (Hatch 1992, 152). Hymes's (1972) SPEAKING mnemonic exemplifies the orientation of this type of analysis (definitions of the terms in this mnemonic follow):

S setting
P participants
E ends
A acts
K keys
I instrumentalities
N norms
G genre.

In the preceding mnemonic, Settings = where and when the speech event is taking place; Participants = the people involved; Ends = purposes or outcomes; Acts = sequences; Keys = the tone in which the event takes place, such as modality in grammatical forms; Instrumentalities = channels (oral, written, telegraphic, etc.) and forms of speech, that is, varieties or dialects; Norms = concepts such as Grice's CP and maxims, that is, norms of production and interpretation; Genres = lecture, poem, business letter, and so on.

A conventional, formal speech event, such as a wedding ceremony, would be a macro category within which micro categories, such as giving compliments or teasing the groom, are framed and acquire the local contextual interpretations.

In addition to speech events, another analytic perspective of extended texts, activity types, comes from Levinson (1992). Levinson drew the basic concept of embedding language use in human activities from Wittgenstein's (1958) "language games," exploring with empirical data the validity of Wittgenstein's original insight. Levinson states that the activity type, generally equivalent to a macro speech event, constitutes a culturally recognized activity within which language use is studied, although actions other than talk may occur during the activity as well. The focus in Levinson's elaboration is on allowable contributions, that is, who, what, and when coparticipants contribute to the interaction, and on the constraints of the setting; he sought to describe the structure of the activity and the style of language used. The following is a particularly vivid example of allowable contributions, a plaintiff testifying (Levinson 1992, 83).

1. *L:* . . . You have had sexual intercourse on a previous occasion haven't you?
2. *P:* Yes
3. *L:* On many previous occasions?
4. *P:* Not many
5. *L:* Several?
6. *P:* Yes
7. *L:* With several men?
8. *P:* No
9. *L:* Just one
10. *P:* Two
11. *L:* Two. And you are seventeen and a half?
12. *P:* Yes.

Concerning allowable contributions, it is clear that the trial lawyer asks the questions and the witness is expected to reply. It is also noticeable that the lawyer uses a negative tag question in line 1, which leads the witness to give the preferred response, that is, a positive answer. In line 9, no surface-level question is asked, but the lawyer's intonation is likely to make the word "just" prominent and to add a slight note of a rising tone at the end of the utterance, which implies some doubt or question in his or her mind. Finally, the confirmatory question in line 11 again implies that the addressee will be giving a positive response. Consequently, the evidence in this questioning in a trial supports Levinson's claim that the activity type will constrain and influence the allowable contributions by the participants.

Both speech events and activity types entail certain constraints on the participants and what counts as allowable, expected language. The constraints, in fact, comprise the underlying inferential schemata for interpretation of pragmatic meaning. If the listener shares the same knowledge of the activity event schema with the speaker, then the listener can recognize and understand the force of the speaker's speech acts. In the example above, the woman testifying in a rape trial may not know consciously what strategy the lawyer is using. However, she may realize upon reflection a sense of unease without being able to pinpoint the cause of her feelings.

As Clark (1996, 139) points out, speech acts can only be interpreted within the context of the social practices of a speech community. Some are formalized, such as those at wedding ceremonies or in arrests by police; others are not codified and remain informal, such as directives at a dentist's office or requests for advice via the e-mail system. Nevertheless, the basic point is that the joint activities of speaker and listener take place not in a vacuum but in the social world of which they are active, participating members.

Form-Function Problem: Case Study

As stated above, a major problem for speech act theory is the mismatch of form and function in utterances. In general, one of the unsolved problems of linguistic phenomenon is the relationship of the formal features of an utterance and the situation or context that leads to a particular interpretation of the function or illocutionary force of an utterance.

An example from a study of a Japanese verb pattern illustrates the misunderstanding that arises in confusing form with function. In structural analyses of Japanese and in textbooks, it is claimed that polite requests are commonly formed by using V + *-te kudasai* (Jorden with Noda 1987, pt. 1, 93–94). However, anecdotal evidence indicates that this form is not always interpreted as signaling politeness. If a person on a bicycle has run into a jogger and only utters a phrase with + *-te kudasai,* the addressee, who anticipated an apology, will not view it as a polite request.

Shiraishi (1997) carried out a functional analysis of empirical uses of this form in a variety of contexts. Her results indicated that V + *-te kudasai* is used for requests, orders, instructions, directions, offers, invitations, complaints, and encouragements. Further, it became clear that, in situations where a speech act of polite requesting would be the most likely to occur, the form was used only 2.9 percent of the time. Shiraishi concluded that V + *-te kudasai* is most frequently used

> when the speaker has the right to ask the hearer to do the act;
> when the imposition on the hearer is not heavy; and/or
> when the speaker has a higher rank than the hearer or the acts are beneficial to the hearer.

These felicity conditions were found for the V + *-te kudasai* form. However, an exception was found in emergency situations, where the form was used frequently. The form may function in the bicycle-jogger incident as a complaint, an order, or a direction to walk elsewhere. A functional analysis asks first what meaning the speaker is enacting in the context of utterance and assigns that meaning to the form; the form itself does not carry the label "request" in all instances of use.

Discussion Questions

1. What follows is Searle's description (Searle 1969, 66–67, cited in Levinson 1983, 240) of some of the felicity conditions for requests and warnings. Develop a similar list for the speech act of complaints, including the four conditions given in Searles's list.

Discuss the difficulties you encounter and the pros and cons of this approach to characterizing speech acts.

Conditions	Requests	Warnings
Propositional content	Future act A of H	Future event E
Preparatory condition	1. S believes H can do A. 2. It is not obvious that H will do A without being asked.	1. S thinks E will occur and is not in H's interest. 2. S thinks that it is not obvious to H that E will occur.
Sincerity condition	S wants H to do A.	S believes that E is not in H's best interest.
Essential condition	Counts as an attempt to get H to do A.	Counts as an undertaking that E is not in H's best interest.

2. Compare your schema for the act of complaint with others in your group. Are there any differences? If another member of your group knows another language well, are there, for example, special verbs for complaining? Are there significant differences in the act of complaint across cultures you know?

3. Construct at least one example for each of the following speech acts: request, disagreement, and warning in any languages that you know. Compare and contrast your example with those of others in the group or class.

4. The conventional forms for requesting in English are of the kind "Can you . . . ," "Could you . . . ," or "I would be much obliged if you . . . " How does one make a request in other languages you or your group members know?

5. What is the form-function problem? Do the following task (from Astley and Hawkins 1985, 4).

178 • An Introduction to Pragmatics

Get the message? (From Astley and Hawkins 1985. Reprinted with the permission of Cambridge University Press.)

Here are the spoken messages exchanged by one family as they got up and came down for breakfast:

1. Do you know what time it is?
2. I *am* getting up!
3. I can't find my socks!
4. Cornflakes please!
5. Ta dad!
6. Thank goodness it's Friday!
7. Have you seen my trainers?
8. No, why should I?
9. What do you mean, I haven't combed my hair?
10. Try taking the top off first!
11. Well done!
12. Bye mum!
13. Be careful!
14. Okay. Don't worry!
15. What a lousy day!
16. Somebody's left the door open!

Each of these speakers was trying to do something with words. Below is a list of things we do with language. Find an example of each in the family's spoken messages. Note which examples could have more than one function. Example: Asking for information: 1. Do you know what time it is?

   a. Asking (i) for information (asking a question)
               (ii) for something or asking someone to do something (making a request)
   b. Telling (giving information)

c. Refusing (to do or say something)
   d. Advising (warning or threatening or persuading or suggesting? What is the difference between these uses of language?)
   e. Ordering
   f. Promising
   g. Greeting
   h. Thanking
   i. Denying (saying something is not true or hasn't happened)
   j. Showing friendship
   k. Congratulating
   l. Saying how you feel

Text Analysis

What is the speech event in the following table? What can you state about the speech acts that occur?

> *E approaches counter. C looks up.*
> E: //Hi
> C: //Hi what k'n I do for yuh?
> E: I'm returning this "grolit." It doesn't work.
> C: Yeh? What's wrong with it?
> E: Don't know. I plugged it in and it just doesn't work. Not your fault / but
> C: //You buy it here? You got your receipt?
> E: Yeh. Here.
> C: Uhh okay. You wanna get a new one or you want your money back?
> E: No, I want another one (.2) that works.
> C: Yeh, okay, so go back and get another one and bring it up here and I'll write it up for you.
> E: Okay, thanks.
> C: Yeh.

Source: Hatch 1992, 144.

Suggested Readings

Austin, J. L. 1962. *How to do things with words.* Oxford: Clarendon Press.

Davis, S., ed. 1991. *Pragmatics: A reader.* New York: Oxford University Press.

Goffman, E. 1963. *Behavior in public places: Notes on the social organization of gatherings.* New York: Free Press.

Pomerantz, A. 1984. Agreeing and disagreeing with assessments: Some features of preferred/dispreferred turn shapes. In *Structures in social action,* edited by J. M. Atkinson and J. Heritage, 57–101. Cambridge: Cambridge University Press.

Searle, J. R. 1969. *Speech Acts: An essay in the philosophy of language.* Cambridge: Cambridge University Press.

Chapter 9
Cognitive Approaches

This chapter takes up cognitive, or psycholinguistic, approaches to pragmatic meaning. Attempts to understand the mental processes involved in human behavior are important for any theory about communication. The validity of a theory is dependent on getting the proper match between external behaviors and the internal processes. Whether one reads a chapter in a book about second language acquisition or an article from *Scientific American,* scholars discuss the "hardware"—the central nervous system, or the "software"—the information-processing systems of the human mind. Pragmatics is anchored in concerns about information processing. For example, it has been known since the 1980s that young children attend to incoming information that is new or salient in some way. Thus, the distinction between the given and the new described in chapter 5 has psycholinguistic reality.

In the quest for understanding how the human mind interprets linguistic messages, subfunctions of psycholinguistic processing need to be studied so that better theories can be built. For example, Brown and Yule (1983a, 225) claim that the mind must accomplish three tasks: (1) computing the communicative function of the utterance, (2) incorporating sociocultural knowledge, and (3) determining the inferences. The process of interpreting messages is conceptualized by such metaphors as bottom-up or top-down processing and, to represent background knowledge, frames, scripts, and schemata (see chapter 5).

Recently, two psycholinguistic perspectives on how human beings comprehend what is said beyond the literal linguistic cues have drawn attention. The first, relevance theory, has become well known since the initial work of Sperber and Wilson in the 1980s. The second, action theory, has not drawn as much attention; it attempts to account for both the cognitive and the social nature of coherence in conventional discourse, thus going beyond the more narrow framework of relevance theory. Both are worthy of consideration; both are theories, yet to be supported by empirical research using naturally occurring language in everyday environments.

Relevance Theory

Relevance theory, like Gricean pragmatics and speech act theory, aims at providing a comprehensive explanation of pragmatic meaning. Its originators, Sperber and Wilson (1986), argue that the ultimate goal is a general theory of communication, a strong claim that would link linguistics with cognitive psychology and other fields seeking a holistic theory of human communication. Their stance represents movement away from the sociological to an emphasis on, indeed a prioritizing of, the cognitive dimension of communication.

The theoretical position taken by Sperber and Wilson (1986) is that Grice's CP and the four maxims can be replaced by one "principle of relevance." Indeed, it can be argued that Grice's model comprises a general principle of relevance, as it is impossible to find instances where relevance is not invoked by the speaker. According to relevance theory (RT), relevance is a property of any utterance conveyed by a speaker. Specifically, the principle of relevance is based on the presumption that speakers at least attempt to have their contributions be optimally relevant. Every act of overt communication that is deliberate and involves intentions "has two aspects: on the one hand, it creates a presumption of adequate effect, while on the other it creates a presumption of minimally necessary effort" (Blakemore 1992, 36). That is to say, every utterance produces an expectation that the information in it will be relevant to the addressee, and the addressee thereby seeks the interpretation of the utterance that will generate the most salient "effect" or relevance, with the least amount of cognitive effort.

One distinct advantage of RT over Grice's theory of pragmatic meaning is derived from Sperber and Wilson's claim that "successful communication" does not require the interactants to share the principles of mutual cooperation manifested in the CP and the maxims. Rather, the requirement according to RT is that the successful communicator make his or her intended meaning transparent to the addressee. Sperber and Wilson state that "communicators do not 'follow' the principle of relevance; and they could not violate it even if they wanted to. The principle of relevance applies without exceptions" (1986, 162).

This chapter will explore in more detail some of the basic concepts of RT. Note that much of what follows comes from Blakemore's work *Understanding Utterances* (1992).

Relevance Theory: An Interface of Semantics and Pragmatics

RT proposes an inferential theory of utterance interpretation, located within the field of human psychology and drawing from both semantics and pragmatics. Utterance interpretation is dependent on linguistic forms and constructions; however, the linguistic or semantic properties of the constituents of an utterance can provide only a "blueprint" (Blakemore 1992, 43) for the full, contextually based interpretation. RT is a theory of utterance interpretation that can show how the hearer fleshes out the blueprint with contextual information to derive pragmatic meaning. According to Blakemore, "the hearer has to use the linguistic clue provided by the speaker in conjunction with contextual information. The semanticist's and pragmatist's jobs interact" (1992, 44). Thus, the linguistic forms, the contextual assumptions, and the presumption of relevance are regarded as the essential ingredients for utterance interpretation by RT.

The goal of RT to marry semantics and pragmatics is problematic for researchers who adhere to the more inclusive definition of pragmatics defined in chapter 1. That is, pragmatics includes both linguistic and nonlinguistic signals in the context of socioculturally constructed activities. The inclusive definition of pragmatics emphasizes the study of actual linguistic performance in the everyday world. This view contrasts with that of RT, which prioritizes analysis of the linguistic constituents and, moreover, maintains a distinction between linguistic and nonlinguistic knowledge. Emphasis on the linguistic forms locates the approach within the modular view of language. RT is consequently consistent with Chomsky's generative model of language, which uses reified, created sentences of the linguist for data.

The next section introduces some of the basic tenets of RT, leading the reader through the stages of argumentation that underlie this theory of what Sperber and Wilson called ostensive-inferential communication, where ostension refers to behavior that seeks to make manifest the intention to communicate something. Human intentional communication is ostensive behavior.

Basic Tenets

One basic tenet is that there are different degrees of inferencing; in other words, different hearers may interpret the same intended meaning of a speaker within a range that goes from approximating to being distant from the speaker's conveyed meaning. The implicatures of an utterance may not be processed by all of the addressees to the same level of understanding on the assumption that not all of the hearers have the same inferential capacity.

A related assumption concerns the fact that relevance is a matter of degree. Relevance theory claims a vital role for the presumption that speakers intend to communicate with "optimal relevance." Optimal relevance is defined in terms of cognitive effects; that is, an utterance is optimally relevant when the processing efforts are minimal for the listener.

The essential theorem of relevance theory is that to understand an utterance is to prove its relevance. Here is an example from Blakemore (1992, 58):

> *A:* Did you enjoy your holiday?
> *B:* The beaches were crowded and the hotel was full of bugs . . .
> [Implicature: B did not enjoy his holiday.]

Relevance theory attempts to account for the cognitive processing that leads A to arrive at B's implicature, first, by requiring that the background assumptions be made explicit. According to Sperber and Wilson (1986, 109), the implicature "is deductively calculated by the interaction of the literal meaning conveyed by the utterance and such background assumptions which are brought by the hearer" to clarify the role of the background assumptions. Turner (1995) states that, although Grice acknowledged the role of such background assumptions, he did not do more than mention them; he did not elaborate on what they are nor on the role they play. Second, relevance theory makes claims concerning the characteristics of the inference processes, a topic about which Grice said nothing (Turner 1995). Although most researchers today regard inferencing as a nondeductive process, either inductive or probabilistic, those who adhere to the premises of RT argue that deductive reasoning is central in the calculation of implied meaning.

A third basic tenet of RT is that the principle of relevance, their pragmatic principle, plays a role in recovering levels of meanings, which will be described below.

The next section draws on these basic tenets to illustrate the determination of implicatures according to relevance theory.

Determination of Implicatures

According to Gricean pragmatics, B's implicature in the example above is, as indicated, that he did not enjoy his holiday. To account for this pragmatic interpretation of B's utterance, contextual information (i.e., the crowded beaches and the bugs in the hotel) is brought in, as well as the presumption that B's reply is relevant to A's question. The pragmatic principle of the maxim of relation drives the interpretations by A and presumably the analyst as well.

RT, as a cognitive theory of pragmatic meaning, provides an analysis of the mental processes that take place to arrive at the implicature. Here is the preceding example, with the step before the implicature spelled out (Blakemore 1992, 58):

What Is Said
A: Did you enjoy your holiday?
B: The beaches were crowded and the hotel was full of bugs.

Mental Processing
Explicature: [The beaches at the resort where B stayed were crowded with people and the hotel was full of insects.]
Implicature: B did not enjoy his holiday.

Blakemore explains that the sentence in brackets is a "fleshing out" of B's utterance: it is called an *explicature*. An explicature includes such features as the assigning of reference (*the* beaches, *the* hotel) in addition to any disambiguation that may be needed ("bugs" does not mean listening devices hidden in the walls!). The explicature is derived from the meanings of the linguistic items of B's answer, yet also goes beyond them, providing a full semantic representation. In other words, the explicature spells out what A must understand before calculating the implicature. According to RT, this unconscious cognitive activity occurs in accordance with the principle of relevance. In sum, to the two stages of Grice's theory (the said and the implicated), this model adds an intermediate stage: (1) what is said, (2) explicature, (3) implicature.

Degrees of Meaning

In some cases a hearer fails to determine the constitutive features of an explicature. This may result in an inability to infer the implied meaning of the speaker.

> *A:* have you seen any of the new Jane Austen films?
> *B:* all a bit too much, don't you think?
> [Explicature: There have been too many of these commercialized versions of Austen films.]

The argument goes as follows: unless A can assign this background interpretation to B's utterance, A will not be able to recognize B's intended meaning, which is that he is disapproving of such films. He is being indirect, using the tag question to seek agreement from A. Now A may understand that B is disapproving for some reason—the intonation, perhaps facial expression—but may fail to fully comprehend the message. B may be less than enthusiastic for any number of reasons: the sheer volume of films, the storybook cinematography, the gap between Victorian values depicted in the films and those of today, or of the gap between the rich and the poor. And if A is a non-British anglophile, attending a formal reception while visiting the United Kingdom, A may be taken aback by B's comment, which may be processed as an overly negative comment about a well-known writer and a representative of British culture abroad!

In sum, owing to the speaker's judgment of the hearer's resources—contextual and background knowledge, cognitive abilities, and shared, common ground—the explicature required to recognize the implied meaning may not be fully fleshed out, resulting in degrees of understanding, even failure to understand, on the part of the interactant. It is of course possible for the hearer to recover the explicature fully or only partially and still arrive at an adequate understanding of an implicature of an utterance. For successful communication to occur, RT claims that, of the possible interpretations of any utterance, all of which are theoretically accessible to the interactants, one is so salient, that is, consistent with the principle of relevance, that all others are excluded. The question that must now be addressed involves the notion of accessibility and, more specifically, how a listener recognizes the most relevant representation of the speaker's meaning. A cognitive process must be enacted to achieve comprehension.

Accessibility

Accessibility is not a new term introduced by RT; it refers to "information that has been activated from a previously *semiactive* state" (Chafe 1994, 72). RT identifies three types of information in the cognitive processing of utterances: given, new, and accessible, with the last term designating information that was active earlier in a text or associated with some feature of the nonlinguistic environment (Chafe 1994, 86). It is as if the human mind holds in a semiactive mode information just used or soon to be needed, available for recall and use and thus made active at a particular point in the course of an interaction. The information is available or accessible, although not active. RT considers accessible information as the mutual cognitive environment of the interactants.

Accessing information from memory has costs, which Chafe calls the activation cost (1994, 72). For Blakemore, accessibility is measured in terms of yielding "a maximal contextual effect for a minimum cost in processing" (1992, 32).

As was mentioned previously, the principle of relevance seems to be the most basic, indeed the minimum requirement. For a text, spoken or written, to have coherence and to communicate meaning, the utterances and sentences must have connections, whether explicit (i.e., with discourse markers such as *and* or *because*) or implicit (provided by the human mind). In other words, utterances and sentences are supported by the presumption of relevance to each other, to the context, or to the hearer. Therapeutic discourse provides evidence that a lack of relevance in a client's utterance to a therapist may signal the presence of mental distress or illness (Labov and Fanshel 1977).

Just as there are different degrees of relevance, the hearer has varying access to the most relevant interpretation of an utterance. To establish the most relevant interpretation is to locate the most accessible one, which requires the least amount of cognitive effort: "a phenomenon is relevant to an individual to the extent that the effort required to process it is optimally small" (Sperber and Wilson 1986, 153). Indeed, research has shown that the more plausible and the more frequently used an assumption is, the more accessible it is for immediate recall. Hence, the effort to recall or activate the assumption is minimal.

Establishment of Relevance

The notion of degrees of relevance derives from the multiplicity of possible background assumptions within a context, or cognitive environment (Blakemore 1992, 28). Access to the context of utterance depends on such factors as memory, imagination, and observation of the physical environment. One among possible assumptions, along with the information in the proposition in the utterance, will lead the hearer to arrive at context-dependent conclusions, or what Sperber and Wilson call contextual implications: "Contextual assumptions combine with the context of utterance to yield the contextual implications needed to establish relevance" (Sperber and Wilson 1986, 18). The following example illustrates the process (Sperber and Wilson 1986, 16–17).

    A. *Flag-seller:* Would you like to buy a flag for the Royal National Lifeboat Institution?
    B. *Passer-by:* No thanks, I always spend my holidays with my sister in Birmingham.

The flag-seller assumes the passer-by has access to the following contextual assumptions—activated in the context of the utterance—for the passer-by to understand the implicature of the utterance (that the passer-by is not interested in purchasing a flag because she has no need for the services of a lifeboat).

1. Birmingham is inland.
2. The Royal National Lifeboat Institution is a charity.
3. Buying a flag is one way of subscribing to a charity.
4. Someone who spends his/her holidays inland has no need of the service of the Royal National Lifeboat Institution.
5. Someone who has no need of the services of a charity cannot be expected to subscribe to that charity.

The contextual implication is arrived at by combining the information in B's response with these assumptions: The speaker B cannot be expected to subscribe to the Royal National Lifeboat Institution. Thus, another way of defining optimal relevance is to describe it in terms of a proposition that has at least one contextual implication, that is, a context-dependent conclusion.

The establishment of relevance is related to deriving the contextual effects. A general pragmatic principle is that the context has an effect on the interpretation of an utterance. RT focuses on the effects that result from the interaction of new information from the utterance, and old information from existing assumptions. Sperber and Wilson are interested in "the deduction based on the union of new information $\{P\}$ and old information $\{C\}$," which they label "a contextualization of $\{P\}$ in $\{C\}$" (1986, 108). This contextualization of new information within old information gives rise to contextual effects; in other words, the process of contextualization results in some effect, which then influences utterance interpretation.

There are three types of contextual effects: (1) those that are actually the same as the contextual implications, (2) those that come from the strengthening of already existing assumptions; and (3) those that result from a weakening of already existing assumptions. These three categories describe the ways in which already existing assumptions and newly presented information are combined in the cognitive context. At least one contextual effect is regarded as a minimum necessary condition for relevance and has the function of making one particular contextualization of {P} within {C} worth processing.

On the basis of information processing theory, in general, human beings can form potentially any number of assumptions or presuppositions in the context of utterance, yet only some are activated. Sperber and Wilson claim that from the contextual assumptions comes a relevant contextual implication, which in turn leads to a contextual effect, all derived by inference. An utterance that achieves at least one adequate contextual effect and requires minimal cognitive effort can be presumed to be optimally relevant. Relevance then is established on the basis of a proposition having a contextual effect in a context of utterance (Blakemore 1992, 30). Moreover, speakers and hearers assume mutual efforts to achieve optimal relevance (Blakemore 1992, 36–37).

Turner (1995, 11) suggests that relevance be "defined as an equation of contextual effects over processing efforts," that is,

relevance = contextual effects / processing effort.

Contextual effects interact with processing effort, computed on the basis of linguistic complexity plus accessibility of the context plus the inferential effort required. Given both the contextual effects and the processing effort, the most relevant interpretation becomes accessible if it (1) provides a contextual effect that makes the hearer's efforts worthwhile and (2) the hearer does not have to exert extraordinary efforts. In other words, the payoff for the hearer, in terms of being able to understand the speaker's intended meaning, has to balance out the cost or cognitive efforts.

> To communicate is . . . to claim someone's attention, and hence to demand some expenditure of effort. People will not pay attention unless they expect to obtain information that is rich enough in contextual effects to be relevant to them. Hence, to communicate is to imply that the stimulus used automatically conveys a presumption of its own relevance. This fact we call the *principle of relevance*. (Wilson and Sperber 1992, 68)

The following diagram presents Sperber and Wilson's explanation of the nature of relevance and their characterization of the cognitive processes comprising the interpretation of implicatures.

Utterance
Explicature

contextual assumptions
contextual assumptions + propositional content
contextual implications
contextual effects
contextual effects + processing efforts
relevance

Implicatures

Bridging Reference

Clark (1977) introduced the concept of *bridging reference*.

1. John went for a walk.
2. The leaves on the trees in the park had already turned beautiful fall colors.

The claim is that, to assign reference to "the" in "the park," inferences have to be generated based on the hearer's knowledge or beliefs. There are no linguistic forms in the first sentence to which "the" can be referring. The bridging assumption, which the hearer creates, is that John went to a park where he commonly goes for a walk. According to Clark, the best bridge is that which is accessible and easily retrieved from memory, in other words, related to given rather than new information.

RT attempts a slightly different account. First of all, it is claimed that the hearer would have access to the hypothesis that John went for a walk in a park; at least people living in urban environments tend to do such things. Then, this hypothesis becomes an assumption related to another assumption, that is, that the leaves on the trees in the park are relevant to John's walk. According to Blakemore (1992, 76), the bridging assumption is an *implicated assumption*. It aids in assigning reference and facilitates the creation of the explicature: "this means that the hearer incorporates the mental representation made accessible by [the implicated assumption] into the propositional content of the utterance" (Blakemore 1992, 76).

The advantage of RT over Clark's analysis is the attention to the "accessibility of the context in which the proposition expressed by the speaker is relevant" and not only on the "accessibility of the referent" (Blakemore 1992, 77). That is to say, Clark focused on locating the referent, or more correctly, the entity to which the speaker is referring, claiming it could be found in the memory bank of the individual's concerned. RT, in addition, cites a role for the context, that is, of the bridging or implicated assumption. RT seeks to make transparent stages of inferential cognitive processing that have previously been left undeveloped.

Criticism of Relevance Theory

Relevance theory has critics as well as advocates. On the supportive side (see Mey 1993), RT does not attend to any notions of speaker–hearer communicative goals or of mutual, shared purposes in interactions. Rather, RT focuses exclusively on an instrumental definition of successful communication, defined as the coparticipants' recognition of the speaker's intention. The intention is "mutually manifest" for speaker and hearer: within the cognitive environment, the interactants presume and recognize relevance.

Mey (1993) identifies five limitations of RT. First, the requirement that an utterance be relevant is either obvious or trivial. The tautology that what is relevant is whatever is optimally relevant does not entice researchers who seek a deeper understanding of how speakers and hearers produce and understand the "extra" meaning. Second, RT is too encompassing; in other words, Sperber and Wilson try to account for too much, and thus the theory loses explanatory power.

Third, RT pays no attention to the sociocultural dimensions of language use. RT ignores any factors in the establishment of contextual effects and of relevance other than linguistic forms and supposed cognitive processes. This approach is contrary to much of recent work in linguistics and related fields that are prioritizing the interaction of linguistic, cognitive, and social aspects of language use (see, for example, Sweester 1990; Ochs, Schegloff, and Thompson 1996). In particular, in considering languages such as Japanese with complex systems of honorifics that index social status, age, and gender differences among interactants, it is difficult to contemplate a theory of pragmatic meaning, indeed of communication, that does not include sociocultural contextual features. As Coupland and Jaworski (1997, 235) state, relevance theory is not concerned with joint, communicative activities; rather, it describes an individualistic model of inferential cognitive processes.

Fourth, because the concepts and principles of RT cannot be tested, they cannot be disproved and therefore are unscientific.

Finally, Sperber and Wilson's theory describes what is essentially a computer metaphor for cognitive processing. Mey and Talbot (1989) and Talbot (1994) reject the construction of human beings as dependent entirely on the individual's cognitive environments to the exclusion of cultural and societal effects.

Action Theory

The next part of chapter 9 considers action theory, developed by Clark to incorporate both social and cognitive aspects in a theory of pragmatic meaning. Clark suggests that Grice's CP and maxims were only meant to be "rules of thumb" (1996, 146), and that researchers need to focus on the coordination of speakers and addresses. RT, in Clark's opinion, is taking pragmatics in the wrong direction, focusing on what is only one area of interest, the listener's comprehension of the speaker's meaning. RT's lack of attention to social and cultural considerations limits its appeal to those who regard human beings as inherently social actors.

Clark's approach (1996, 29) was introduced in chapter 1 as an example of a model of pragmatic meaning. Relevance theory, also within the cognitive or psycholinguistic paradigm, considers language use an individual process. The more socially oriented approaches, such as politeness theory, emphasize the sociolinguistic and sociocultural dimensions in language use to the exclusion of cognitive factors. Clark's theory represents his thinking and research about integrating both the individual and the social in explaining language use.

Basic Notions

In Clark's view, language use is a form of purposeful "joint action." This is more than the sum of two individuals using language to do things; rather, the interactants coordinate their actions, merging their cognitive processes and sociolinguistic production. Consequently, their joint actions combine individual cognitive processes in social action, a means to act in the world. Although language is used in a variety of settings, conversation as the basic, prototypical setting is the site of Clark's theory. It has the following features (Clark 1996, 9):

Copresence	Speaker and hearer are physically present.
Visibility	Speaker and hearer can see each other.
Audibility	Speaker and hearer are within channel linkage.
Instantaneity	Speaker and hearer receive each other's talk immediately.
Evanescence	The talk fades as soon as spoken.
Recordlessness	No record of the talk remains.
Simultaneity	Speaker and hearer simultaneously receive and produce talk.

How, given these prototypical features, do the participants coordinate their joint actions? The speaker and the listener interact with each other in a dynamic manner; a completed adjacency pair exemplifies this notion (see chapter 8). No only do they "take actions *with respect to each other,* but they *coordinate* these actions with each other" (Clark 1996, 11). This happens when the "two essential parts" of a joint action are present: (1) a signal by the speaker and (2) a recognition of the signal by the addressee. "Signals are deliberate actions" that can consist of an "utterance, gestures, facial expressions, eye gaze, and perhaps other actions" (Clark 1996, 13). The important point is that the signals have to be recognized as deliberate.

Signals that can be identified by the listener require a common ground. All theories of pragmatic meaning include this basic notion, whether labeled shared background knowledge or world knowledge or, as here, common ground. Interpreting the utterance "New York has gotten better over the last decade" is not possible unless the speaker and hearer share some knowledge about New York in recent years.

Action and Activity

Joint actions can consist of speech events, in which conversants "negotiate deals, gossip, get to know each other" (Clark 1996, 17). Clark also includes speech acts: requests, disagreements, compliments. The frame for the joint actions is a *joint activity*, a construct Clark adopts from Levinson's (1992) notion of activity type. An example is a sales transaction in a retail store, carried out by participants in recognizable roles with specific goals. The participants achieve their goals by coordinating their joint actions. Conventional procedures, such as selecting an item on sale and proceeding to the cashier, can be incorporated in joint actions, following the frame or script for purchasing items in a shop, the common ground shared by the participants.

In the developed world at least, a customer can do the weekly shopping in a supermarket without using spoken language. However, it is when the joint activity is achieved through joint actions involving language use that the action approach becomes particularly relevant. The next section will explore the coordination problem, that is, how the participants achieve their communication goals jointly.

Coordination Problem

The first point concerns the reasons the interactants coordinate their actions. Clark assumes that they do so to achieve their goals, which they realize is impossible unless they work together.

Participants engage in joint actions, that is, converse with each other, to coordinate joint activities such as planning a party. Coordination problems at the level of local joint actions are multiple, the primary one being "coordinating what speakers mean and what their addressees understand them to mean" (Clark 1996, 73). This microcoordination problem is worked out through language, the conventional signaling system par excellence, or through coordination devices such as gestures. The minimum criterion is joint salience: all participants must recognize the meaning of the signal, usually on the basis of common background knowledge. The following example (from Clark 1996, 31–32) illustrates coordination.

> [*Clark walks up to a counter and places two items next to the cash register. Stone is behind the counter marking off items on an inventory. Clark, looking at Stone, catches her eye.*]
> Stone: [*meeting Clark's eyes*] I'll be right there.
> Clark: Okay . . . These two things over here. [*Stone nods, takes the*

two items, examines the prices on them, and rings them up on the cash register.]

Stone: Twelve seventy-seven.

Clark: Twelve seventy-seven. [*Clark takes out his wallet, extracts a twenty-dollar bill, hands it to Stone, then rummages in his coin purse for coins.*] Let's see that's two pennies I've got two pennies. [*Clark hands Stone two pennies.*]

Stone: Yeah. [*Stone enters $20.02 in the register, which computes the change.*]

Stone: [*handing change to Clark*] Seven twenty-five is your change.

Clark: Right. [*Clark puts the money in his wallet while Stone puts the items and receipt in a bag. She hands the bag to Clark, they break eye contact, and he turns and walks away.*]

In providing this real-life example, Clark demonstrates the kind of joint activity he carries out with Stone through a series of joint actions, some of which are linguistic, some nonlinguistic, yet all important to the activity. Clark claims that there are levels of psycholinguistic processing, which he calls "action ladders" (1996, 389).

Speaker A's Actions	*Speaker B's Actions*
4. A is proposing joint project w to B	B is considering A's proposal of w
3. A is assigning that p to B	B is recognizing that p from A
2. A is presenting signal s to B	B is identifying signal s from A
1. A is executing behavior t to B	B is attending to behavior t from A

The action ladders describe the cognitive processing involved in coordinating joint actions. However, these ladders are not distinct, as presented here. At each level, the ladders must be linked and are mutually dependent to complete the joint action.

Social Dimensions

Social derives its meaning from the Latin *socius*, "partner" or "companion" (Clark 1996, 388). Clark thus joins other theorists of social action in pointing that "language is rarely used as a means in itself" (387). Participants carry out activities with others in roles defined by the social context, and language is a system of signals used to enact everyday joint activities. Clark's new contribution is his interpretation of the relation between language and joint activities: "Many phenomena have been treated as features of language use when they are really features of the joint activities in which the language is being used" (388). Three examples are cooperation, turn-taking, and closure. Cues are devices to aid listeners in the cooperative creation of a conversation by participants. Turn-taking is essential to cooperative talk as well (participants who dominate a meeting, for example, are accused of not allowing others to "take a turn"). Finally, closure, bringing a conversation to a recognizable end, is a basic ingredient of cooperative talk as well. These are all noticeable phenomena of talk; when they are violated or ignored, speakers are uncomfortable, misunderstandings arise.

Consequently, language adjusts to meet the functional needs of the participants to carry out joint activities (see LoCastro 1999). Features of language use—the length of clauses, the rhythmic placement of cues, and tag questions—develop out of the need to achieve joint activities.

This brief review of Clark's action theory provides a sketch of this sociocognitive model to account for human communication, specifically language use. Since pragmatics is defined as the study of language use, specifically of how language is employed to mean something to another, Clark's contribution is relevant to scholars interested in developing a theory of pragmatic meaning. Clearly, in the enactment of joint action, "extra" meaning that goes beyond the linguistic signals is created.

In addition, unlike other researchers in the field of pragmatics, Clark attaches equal importance to nonlinguistic methods of signaling. "Nods, smiles, gestures—these are all necessary to understanding ordinary *linguistic* communication" (1996, 392). It is in this context that Clark pushes for an extended definition of language; he distinguishes between *languages-s* and *language-u,* the latter being the extended meaning of language in use.

Applications to SLA

With regard to cognitive processing, human beings have two components, "hardware," or the central nervous system, and "software," or information-processing systems. Since pragmatics is concerned with information processing—production and comprehension—cognitive approaches to pragmatics study the constituents of the software, that is, systems that regulate attention, perception, memory, and production. Attention is a key factor. Relevance theory analyzes how a listener decides which in-coming signal is most "relevant" to understand a speaker's meaning. Clark likewise focuses on this aspect. General cognitive models of human functioning emphasize the role of selective attention. Tagging some information as important and other for rejection is necessary; otherwise, fatigue would cause the systems to shut down due to information overload. From an early age, children's information-processing systems selectively focus on what is novel, salient, or ostensive.

Selective attention works together with resource allocation. The resources of the human systems are limited and must be allocated as the task requires. For example, it is possible to go for a walk and continue to plan one's weekend. However, a difficult math or theoretical linguistic problem may require complete attention and all mental resources.

The ability to deal with a task that is cognitively challenging depends then on (1) the information available and (2) the resources available or processing capacity. Some processing is automatic, such as using a conventional conversational routine to answer a telephone call. The other form of processing, controlled processing, requires more individual, direct control over the resources. For example, a new foreign employee in a Japanese company in Tokyo quickly learned to use a formulaic routine for answering the telephone in the office:

A: Lingua Academy de gozaimasu [Language Academy.]
B: suzuki-bucho, irrashaimasu-ka? [is the manager, Mr. Suzuki, there?]
A: shosho o machi kudasai [hold on a minute, please]

However, if the telephone caller produced some talk more difficult to understand, A could only resort to uttering the final line to put the caller on hold. A did not have enough information or the processing capacity to respond quickly and efficiently. Processing capacity was overloaded due to low proficiency level in Japanese.

This example illustrates the situation second language learners find themselves in. Automatic processing can enable them to use conversational or formulaic routines to comprehend and to respond in predictable contexts. Greetings, conventional politeness routines, and direction asking will not task the resources of intermediate level of learners, although their response time may be slow and they may make minor errors. However, more elaborate syntactic patterns to enact politeness, for example, demand a greater allocation of resources and of selective attention as well as more use of controlled processing.

> Avec mes remerciements, veuillez agréer, monsieur, l'expression de mes sentiments distingués. [Please accept with my thanks, sir, the expression of my sincere sentiments.]

An even more difficult context for an NNS is avoiding either *tu* or *vous* until it becomes clear which form of address the NS uses.

Thus, cognitive approaches to pragmatic meaning have provided models that can inform second language researchers and educators. Each component, each step in information processing has to be examined, considering that L2 learners may not have the same background information base as the NS, information organized in their memories in the form of schemata and frames. Further, L2 learners will not have the same information processing capacity, neither automatic nor controlled, until they slowly acquire and learn more of the L2 and its sociocultural rules of speaking. Consequently, like young children and adults with illnesses such as aphasia or Alzheimer's, learners' pragmatic performance will be affected.

It is necessary to consider both relevance theory and action theory from the point of view of second language learning and teaching. Do these two models of human communication apply to interactions where a speaker uses a second language? It seems safe to assume then that, while the two theories aim to explain pragmatic meaning in general, neither Sperber and Wilson nor Clark is particularly concerned with foreign language learners. While the cognitive processes may be the same and social factors are still factored into the carrying out of joint activities, a second language perspective needs to consider where the differences arise. Now, a consideration of the model of a researcher within SLA is in order.

Bialystok's work (1993) on pragmatic competence development of children and adult second language learners is particularly helpful on language processing. Her psycholinguistic model focuses on the cognitive mechanisms involved in language learning and language use as well as the cognitive demands that functional language use requires of learners. "Language proficiency . . . is considered in terms of the *fit* between the processing abilities of the learner and the task demands imposed by a specific language use situation" (Bialystok 1993, 47).

Bialystok's model identifies two components, the analysis of knowledge and the control of the processing. The analysis of knowledge involves the building up of domains of knowledge, with mental representations that become available for use in comprehension and production. However, processing control is also needed and, in conversational situations, the domains of knowledge must be activated and available for use under real time pressures (see also Chafe 1994). Efficient language use requires that the participants not be distracted by unimportant information.

From an SLA perspective, learners may have problems at several levels. The domains of knowledge linked to the second language, such as knowledge of the code itself and sociocultural aspects, may be only partially built up. In addition, processing control may be weak, with less than the needed automaticity to respond fluently, especially due to the pressures of real time demands. Further, because the learner does not share with the native speaker or proficient speakers of the language the same common ground, the learner may be distracted by unimportant information in a conversation. Therefore, due to the cognitive demands of L2 learning and of L2 communication, the learner may not carry out the same steps that a L1 speaker would. The L2 learner is likely to be slower in comprehension and production and perhaps make errors, both of which can have a serious effect on the conversation.

Since pragmatic meaning is, according to Bialystok, a question of matching form with the social context, learners need to develop knowledge of the functional equivalents between their L1 and the L2 from which they can select the most appropriate formulaic routine to communicate the intended meaning. Both development of the representations and fluency in use take time. The explicatures are not processed quickly enough to maintain a conversation and the cues, even if only in the form of nonlinguistic ones, such as gestures, are not salient or transparent enough to disambiguate the pragmatic meaning quickly enough for the learners.

Thus, within the context of cognitive approaches to pragmatic meaning, the question is not whether the interactants are L1 or L2 speakers. The issue of pragmatic development revolves around (1) the building up of a common knowledge base, (2) accessing the mental representations quickly, and (3) developing automaticity with both. Inferencing is a universal cognitive activity. Learners' skill in inferencing in their L1 can be transferred. L2 learners are disadvantaged at least until they achieve higher levels of proficiency in the L2, when they can quickly use selective attention and allocate their resources for automatic and controlled processing.

Discussion Questions

1. Briefly, what does RT add to Grice's attempt to account for implicatures?

2. List some of the possible contextual assumptions and the likely contextual implication for the following:
   A: we will be meeting the others at No. 1 Green Street
   B: at No. 1 Green Street?
   A: yes
   B: at No. 1 Green Street? at No. 1 Green Street!

3. The following is an American joke about psychotherapists (Lakoff 1990, 75) Demonstrate that comprehending relevance is required to process the intended meaning.
   A: How many shrinks does it take to change a lightbulb?
   B: One, but it has to really *want* to change.

4. What is accessibility? What is its role in RT? Discuss how our existing assumptions, new information, and the principle of relevance apply to the following contrasting conversations (from Blakemore 1992, 35).
   A: What happened at work today?   A: What happened at work today?
   B: Oh, the usual.   B: I got fired.

5. In a group, choose a topic and write it on the board or on a large piece of paper so it can be seen by all the group participants. Then, have everyone write a sentence for the chosen topic. Put all of these on the board or on the paper and bring them together under the topic by establishing relevance. What kind of contextual resources would be needed to do this with success?

Text Analysis

Using the terminology and concepts introduced in this chapter, fully analyze the following dialogue (from Sperber and Wilson 1986, 145).

Mary: What I would like to eat tonight is an *osso-bucco*.
Peter: I had a long day. I'm tired.

Provide an analysis of the bridging in the following two examples:

1. I got on a bus yesterday and the driver was drunk.
2. The last of the allied prisoners of war have been flown to Saudi Arabia. There were thirty-five on board, including nine Britons (Blakemore 1992, 77).

Suggested Readings

Bialystok, E. 1983. Symbolic representation and attentional control. In *Interlanguage pragmatics,* ed. G. Kasper and S. Blum-Kulka. Oxford: Oxford University Press.

Blakemore, D. 1992. *Understanding utterances: An introduction to pragmatics.* Oxford: Blackwell.

Chafe, W. 1994. *Discourse, consciousness, and time: The flow and displacement of conscious experience in speaking and writing.* Chicago: University of Chicago Press.

Sweetser, E. E. 1990. *From etymology to pragmatics: Metaphorical and cultural aspects of semantic structures.* Cambridge: Cambridge University Press.

Synder, L. S., and Downey, D. C. 1983. Pragmatics and information processing. *Topics in Language Disorders,* December, 75–86.

Part 3

Pragmatics in the Real World

Because pragmatics engages the teacher and researcher in the everyday world of cross-cultural communication, teaching and learning languages, issues of empowerment in institutional settings, and more, we need to go beyond building theories to examine the role of pragmatics in larger issues. An awareness of pragmatics opens up even mundane encounters as sites for analysis of the ubiquitous presence of implied meaning. We can see how interactional discomfort can spiral out of control, leading to the reinforcement, perhaps creation of stereotypes and misunderstandings.

It is in that light that part 3 takes up a series of topics, all of which implicate the production and comprehension of implied meaning. In particular, connections between pragmatic concepts and theories and second language acquisition are drawn. The purpose is to demonstrate the importance of pragmatic analysis in contexts of higher orders of meaning, including but not limited to an examination of the linguistic forms per se. Empirical data from a variety of studies support the next six chapters. In addition, the concerns of teachers of second and foreign languages are addressed directly, particularly in the exercises at the end of each chapter.

Chapter 10
Behavior of Listeners

If pragmatics is defined as "meaning in interaction," then interactions are joint activities, involving *both* speakers and listeners. Chapters 1 and 9 summarized Clark's framework, in which speakers and listeners engage in actions within a joint activity, such as questioning in a trial, negotiations over the purchase of a car, or an informal chat. Inclusion of the listener balances the focus in the literature, which has centered on the interpretation of the speaker's intended meaning, neglecting the important role of the listener in the co-construction of the talk. As the speaker needs the cooperation of the listener to enact a joint action, the speaker necessarily orients the talk to signal, first the intention to act, and then to carry out the act so that the listener can interpret the speaker's meaning. The speaker designs the talk to meet the expectations of the audience, whether composed of one or many individuals. Consequently, an appreciation of the parameters of the listener's role is required to comprehend the reasons for the speaker's behavior. For example, if a speaker chooses to shift codes or styles, the listener must know what pragmatic meaning those strategies carry in the context of the utterance.

As if in a ballroom dance with the speaker, the listener contributes to the joint action. It is consequently necessary to understand what the functions of the listener are and what meanings are conveyed by the listener's behavior in the joint activity. Here are some of the questions this chapter addresses: who is the listener? What are the salient features of the role? What constitutes the listener's behavior? What kinds of pragmatic meanings does listening behavior signal?

This chapter looks then at the role of the listener in the co-construction of talk. Even though the convention is the singular form in discussing the "listener," it is generally preferable to assume there is more than one. The listener is an active participant, giving a variety of verbal and nonverbal signals to help the speaker monitor the progress of the talk; they tell the speaker if the intended meaning is being conveyed successfully. The listener's role, however, is more complex than simply providing a means to check on the success or failure of the communication of a speaker's meaning; the listener must recognize the specific signals of the speaker and show in turn understanding by responding with some cue to the speaker's contribution. In particular, this chapter examines what the listener does in two environments: (1) while the speaker is continuing a turn at talk, and (2) at the end of a speaker's turn. First of all, however, an overview of listeners' behavior is necessary.

Discourse Roles

During "talk-in-interaction" (Schegloff 1982), at least one listener must be involved. Speakership and listenership are created through interaction, each partner performing necessary discursive roles. Both roles are ascribed through the nature of the turn-taking system; while one participant speak, in most cases, the others are expected to listen.

Definition of Speaker's Role and Listener's Role

One reason for the relative lack of attention to the listener's role is the difficulty of defining it. The speaker's role is less problematic than the listener's, for the simple reason that there is vocal evidence. The speaker is the person who produces the utterance. Levinson (1983), however, discusses the question of authorship of a speaker's utterance; in other words, the speaker may be acting as a spokesperson for someone else and thus be reporting information. The fact that the speaker may not be the author of the information being transmitted can make interpretation of a speaker's meaning more difficult. Nevertheless, the discourse role of the speaker may, for most purposes, be simply the "ordinary speaker" (Levinson 1983, 72).

As for the listener, the term is used frequently in the literature without definition and seems to designate the person or persons who attend to a speaker's utterance. A definition of the listener includes the fact that the person performing that function is within channel linkage and can actually hear and receive what the speaker is saying; further, the listener shares the same language code well enough to be able to interpret the speaker's meaning. These are the minimum attributes. The listener is "B" of A's utterance and then becomes the speaker in the second-pair part:

A: would you mind turning that down . . . or using the headphones?
B: oh, don't you want to hear my new CD?

However, the term *listener* needs to be carefully analyzed to understand the differences in the ways in which listenership is constituted. The listener's discourse role can be broken down into three categories (Levinson 1983; Clark and Carlson 1982):

Addressee
Side participant
Overhearer

Although all three categories of participants are within channel linkage of the speaker, the roles are different. The addressee—there can be one or more—is the designated or ratified listener; this is the person to whom the speaker addresses the talk. The speaker designates the addressee by means of gaze, posture, direct second-person address, gesture, or a combination. In a similar way, a potential addressee can signal availability for talk through gaze, posture, and kinesics.

The side participants, who may or may not attend to the speaker's talk, are not directly addressed. Yet they have a role. On talk shows, a politician will speak directly to the interviewer and, at the same time, be speaking to all the side participants in the television or radio audience. The politician in this way is informing the public, accommodating to that audience in efforts to get votes. It may be argued that the speaker is in fact addressing the side participants and not the interviewer, who is a vehicle for the politician's real aims.

The overhearer, the third discourse role for the listener, is commonly not viewed by the speaker as participating in the talk. However, people engaging in conversations may suddenly lower their voices, whisper, or switch to another language so that a person cannot overhear what they are saying. This can be called "off-record" talk. Yet, in other cases, the coparticipants may speak so that the overhearers do indeed receive the message. This behavior indicates an awareness, albeit on a subconscious level, of the potential importance of the overhearer discourse role. What may appear to be off-record is actually intended to be "on-record" talk. Speakers may design their utterances for all possible listeners to achieve particular communicative ends.

The listener is thus a complex concept. Whether the coparticipants in a conversation are viewed as addressees, side participants, or overhearers by the speaker causes adjustments in the speaker's talk that can influence how the speaker's intended meaning is understood.

Complexity of the Listener's Role

First of all, the listener is not a passive participant in an interaction. Even when not holding the floor for a turn at talk, all participants play a role in the interaction. A Ping-Pong metaphor of communication conveys the image of a dyad, sending and receiving each other's talk, and then sending it back.

Sender → Transmitter → (via channel) → Receiver → Destination
or encoder   or decoder

However, this is an erroneous, dated model, as the listener does not receive the speaker's talk, as a player receives the Ping-Pong ball, but can control the success or failure of the talk. The listener reacts to the incoming talk and is free to create a response that may not meet the speaker's expectations. Human beings may choose to act on their world, enacting agency. For example, refusing to have eye contact with a speaker may bring about an abrupt end to a conversation (Goodwin 1981).

Second, there may be cross-cultural differences in the way speaker-listener roles are constituted in talk. Philips (1976) claims that Warm Springs Reservation Indians have a system of speaker-listener discourse roles that differs from that of white Anglo-Americans. In the Anglo-American system, the addressee or designated listener need only shift gaze and/or posture to cause the speaker to cease talking. Consequently, an addressee from a different cultural background who does not use direct gaze to signal listenership may be viewed by an Anglo-American speaker as unwilling to engage in talk, in general, to be unfriendly.

Warm Springs Indians make little distinction between the addressee and unratified listeners; the speaker gazes toward the participants without direct eye contact, and the failure of the listeners to look at the speaker will not cause the talk to stop. As Philips (1976) explains, the Warm Springs Indian speaker-listener relationship seems not to depend as much on gaze and on speaker designation of specific listeners as in Anglo-American discourse.

Third, the listener, like the speaker, has social attributes or indexicals: social status, age, and gender. The listener has rights and obligations associated with the role; generally, it is assumed the designated addressee will respond to the speaker's talk, cooperatively, and that the speaker will allow the addressee a turn at speaking. Moreover, as part of the context of the talk, the listener's social attributes need to be taken into consideration in interpretation of a speaker's meaning. For example, in speaking Japanese, the speaker must attend to the listener's age, social status, and gender, in selecting the proper verb forms in a conversational interaction. These features are grammaticalized in Japanese; that is, they are part of the morphosyntax of the language, and the speaker or writer must make choices between the indexicals in producing the language. Spanish and French also require such forms as exemplified in the choice of *tu/usted* or *tu/vous*. Here is an example from Spanish:

> Me dirijo a usted pidendole disculpas por este e-mail. [*usted*]
> Me dirijo a ti pidendote disculpas por este e-mail. [*tu*] [I would like to ask your forgiveness for this email message.]

A sudden change of social register, signaled by use of a plain verb form or a different address form, may be interpreted as the speaker's indicating a desire for a more friendly, intimate, relaxed relationship. Or it could signal rudeness; in 1978, striking students at Tokyo University used the plain verb forms to insult their professors, who had been accustomed to honorific forms.

With regard to social attributes, the question of equality must also be considered. It is not uncommon to find definitions of *conversation* that include the notion that the speaker and listener have equal rights and obligations to participate in the talk. Yet research in the field of language and power and in gender issues has shown that actual equality of speaking rights (and presumably listener rights) of participants in talk may rarely be possible, even in societies considered to be egalitarian. Speaking rights are more equal in a causal conversation than in a job interview, where the interviewer functions as a gatekeeper. In Anglo-American cultures, participants may dominate through interruptions of another's utterance, amount of talk, number of turns, and the kinds of speech acts (see Spender 1985, for example).

In cultures with a strongly hierarchical social structure, there may be little or no equality of the discourse roles. Listening is considered to be an appropriate role of participants in the relatively subordinate social role in a conversational interaction (Condon 1984). In Japanese married couples, the husband will speak Japanese with verbs in the plain form, as if the listener (the wife) were his social inferior, whereas the wife is expected to use forms signaling deference (Smith 1983). In television interview and news programs in Japan, typically a male speaker is asked questions to lead him to talk about the interview or news topic by a younger, female partner. In both examples, the female takes a subordinate, listener role, avoiding statements of her own opinions. Cultural norms and stereotypes can both be developed and reflected in the role the listener takes in interactions.

Clearly, speakership-listenership is co-constructed in the interaction, and how this is done differs interculturally. The listener's role cannot be reduced to that of a simple receiver of talk, as the speaker must take into consideration attributes of the listener. Reciprocally, the listener must be aware of the speaker's expectations, based on the speaker's sociocultural background, in order to interpret meaning. Listenership is done differently in different contexts.

Designation of the Listener

The preceding overview of the listener's role raises awareness of how misunderstandings may arise. The ways in which listenership is co-constituted and the importance attached to the social attributes of the listener may cause uncomfortable moments, worse, the development of stereotypes. Erickson and Schultz (1982) examined videotaped data of interviews between college counselors and students and found that African American students signaled listenership differently than did white students. The African American students did not use gaze in the way the white students did, and they were regarded by the counselors as uninterested and unmotivated. This study suggests that negative stereotypes can develop from subtle cues.

The way in which signaling of channel linkage of speaker-listener is done may differ in several ways. In some languages, according to Levinson (1983, 165), it is done through interactional behaviors, in others, through linguistic forms. In languages with honorifics, such as Japanese, particular attention must be paid to speaker, addressee, and third-person referent roles. Japanese culture emphasizes careful attention to others, which is reflected in language use influenced by the audience design of utterances.

There may also be linguistic forms to refer to the overhearer. In Japanese certain forms *(kana* vs. *kashira)* tell overhearers whether or not the speaker intends the listener to attend to the utterance. *Kana* (for example, *soo kana . . .* [I wonder about that]) signals to anyone in channel linkage that, though the speaker is talking to him- or herself, others may listen. *Kashira (kono kutsu de shite mo ii kashira?* [I wonder if it is okay to play in these shoes]) implies to any overhearer that the speaker is talking just to him- or herself. Thus, such pragmatic particles designate whether the listener is free to respond, as in the case of a secretary who overhears a boss's self-directed talk.

Such linguistic forms can be called response cries, or "outlouds" (Goffman 1981). An outloud is a phrase uttered to oneself: if I drop a knife in the kitchen when I am by myself, I may utter something such as "Oh, damn." When within channel linkage of others, a response cry or outloud may have other functions. For example, conversations with strangers while queuing for a bus may start when an overhearer responds to an outloud about the delays in the bus service or the incompetence of the local mayor.

The grammatical or linguistic forms that encode participant roles in some languages are easier to examine than the more interactional means to designate discourse roles. In the case of outlouds, Japanese provides grammatical forms *(kana* vs. *kashira)* to invite or deter listeners' responses. However, with English, it is in fact through use of interactional means that this is achieved: uttering "Whoops!" is not grammaticalized and thus does not necessarily signal a welcome or a deterrent cue to any listener. The presence of channel linkage may or may not sanction responses. Other interactional, nonlinguistic means to designate the ratified listener(s) include voice quality, gaze, restarting or full repetition of an utterance, and posture. It may be problematic for participants to understand what discourse role they are to assume. An addressee may, in fact, be designated as such, yet the speaker is indirectly communicating with a side participant. This possibility of ambiguity may be used for strategic ends to allow the speaker to escape from attribution of responsibility for talk that may be hurtful.

The Listener's Behavior

Thus, it is the speaker who generally assigns the roles of addressee, side participant, and overhearer by the audience design of utterances and body language. However, the listener can also affect an encounter through verbal and nonverbal cues. This perspective on the listener's role reinforces the need for an interactive model of talk, such as Clark proposes.

We need to be aware of cultural differences in listeners' behavior, which may include culture-specific features. Hall remarks, "I slowly learned that how one indicates that one is paying attention is different for each culture. . . . I ultimately learned that to look directly at a Navaho was to display anger" (1969, 379). Hall draws from his work examples of cultural differences in signaling listener's behavior and raises awareness of the possible misunderstandings that can result from ignoring the differences.

However, human physiology dictates some commonality across languages (Rosenfeld 1978). That is, the range of possibilities is limited, and, consequently, universal characteristics can be studied, such as the presence or absence of gaze. However, the commonalities should not prevent more in-depth analysis.

Case Study: Japanese *Aizuchi*

A case study of Japanese-American listener behavior will exemplify aspects of the listener's behavior in a specific cross-cultural context. The focus will be on what happens when the speaker is continuing a turn at talk with a copresent listener. It will then be possible to describe the ramifications of the cultural differences of these short responses made by the listeners as the speaker continues a turn at talk.

Constituents of Listeners' Behavior

A listener's behavior includes a range of short verbal and nonverbal cues, given by the listener in the course of interactions. Nonverbal cues include gaze, posture, gestures, nods of the head, eye movements, and vocalizations or "noises." Common examples of verbal responses in English are "yeah," "right," "uhuh," and "Oh, I see." Japanese has a greater variety of forms, which vary in formality and by age and gender of those conversing. For example, *hai* is the most common response in formal contexts, whereas *ee, un,* or *n* are typically used by both men and women in informal talk. Thus, listeners' cues index the social status of the interactants. *Uso* ("What a story!") or *usobakkari* ("What a big lie/liar!") are more likely to be used by young women. In both Japanese and English, verbal cues may include sentence completions (" . . . and difficult, right?"), short clarification questions *(Soo desu ka?),* and comments ("Incredible!").

These forms of behavior are particularly noticeable when one participant is taking a long turn at talk, perhaps telling a story, recounting how the day went, or giving instructions, and the listener indicates reception of the speaker's talk. Yngve (1970), a communication theory engineer, called the listener's responses "back channel cues." The speaker is using the "main" channel, while the listener or coparticipants signal to the speaker that they are within channel linkage by communicating in the "back" channel.

The Japanese language has a word for listeners' behavior: *aizuchi*. The existence of a folk term indicates greater sensitivity to this behavior in Japanese culture than among Anglo-Americans. The word originally meant "two swordsmiths hammering a blade in turn. . . . Two people talking and frequently exchanging response words is thus linked to the way two swordsmiths hammer on a blade" *Aizuchi* is also viewed as "chiming in with another's conversation" (Mizutani and Mizutani 1987, 18). Participants are expected to show active listenership so as not to interfere with speech; the cues are spoken softly, at the end of a phonemic phrase, and with dangling intonation.

Aizuchi or back channel cues can occur at possible speaker exchange points and at expected moments of a speaker's turn at talk. It is common for more than one cue to be used, for example, head nods along with vocalizations. Listeners' responses thus tend to form a multicue cluster at listening response relevant moments (LRRM: see Erickson and Schultz 1982, 25). It is this characteristic of the listener's behavior that the next sections explore. As a multicue subsystem, several cues may be used differently in different cultures, and uncomfortable moments, even misunderstandings, may arise due to different interpretations of a listener's meaning. The head nod may be salient in one culture, but not in another. In Japan, a gaze-avoidance culture, vocalizations to signal listener behavior may be more common than where eye contact is expected.

Importance of Listeners' Responses

In 1983 a defendant in the IBM-Hitachi-Mitsubishi case claimed that, contrary to the charges against him, he had not agreed that the FBI undercover agents should steal secret documents for him. His defense counselor argued that the defendant's use of "yeah" and "uh huh" was not to show agreement, but rather to indicate he was attending to what the agents were saying (LoCastro 1987). The defense arguments were based on the notion that Japanese differs from American English in the functions of *aizuchi*. The lawyer argued that listeners' responses differ interculturally and that the defendant, Mr. Ishida, was transferring Japanese meanings or functions of *aizuchi* to English. Thus, back channel cues were a crucial variable in this legal case.

Three areas of listeners' responses to be examined here are (1) where and how often cues occur in the stream of speech, (2) the functions of the listener's responses, and (3) the distinction between responses that tell the speaker to continue talking and those that indicate the listener wants a turn at talk. Presumably, smooth changes of speakers require different behavior by the listener within a turn than at the end.

Location and Frequency of Listeners' Responses

Research on the location of listeners' responses indicates that they tend to occur at the ends of phonemic clauses. Usually, prosodic, grammatical, and semantic cues co-occur. Listener cues tend to occur at that pause (the LRRM), or briefly before it, as if the listener were anticipating the end of the clause. The listener's responses aid the speaker in monitoring the interaction. From asynchronic responses by the listener, for example, the speaker may guess that the meaning of the talk is not being understood. Learning to speak Japanese includes learning to give responses when and where they are expected.

In addition to timing, the frequency of responses is important. Research shows that back channel cues occur more frequently in Japanese, as in the conversation in the accompanying table. The conversation appears to be an almost seamless piece, responses coming just at the end of the speaker's utterance with little perceptible pause. A videotape would show nods of the head with each listener cue.

The following conversation in American English involves three women (C does not participate in this part, functioning as a side participant).

> *A:* she talked to someone today who made her feel better that, oh he might be looking at six months to a year (+) in jail and (0.2) that would be a lot better than (+) she was thinking of seven years (+) Shawn would be grown up, going to college already or something
> *B:* laughter . . . [*simultaneous talk and laughter*]
> *A:* so now (0.2) it won't be that long (0.3) she hired this attorney today, so (+)
> *B:* is he expensive?
> *A:* umh (0.2) I don't know (+) I think they all are (+) but she didn't want to take her chances with a public attorney
> (LoCastro 1990b)

> *A:* Huransugo shika tsukatcha-ikenai dakara huransujin no sensei ga [You aren't supposed to speak anything but French so our French teacher]
>
> *B1:* Un un
> *B2:* [yeah, yeah]
>
> *A:* nihongo dekitemo burikko shite sa [although he understands Japanese, he pretends not to]
>
> *B3:* un [uh huh]
>
> *A:* Huransugo skika shaberanai de sa [and speaks only in French]
>
> *B4:* Un [hum]
>
> *A:* Yaro hito iru jan [There are such people, you know]
>
> *B5:*
> *B6:* } Un, Un, Un [Yeah, yeah, yeah]
> *B7:*

Source: Maynard 1989, 170–71.

The frequency of vocalized back channel cues is higher in the Japanese conversation than in the American. Research shows that the ratio is in general approximately three to one. In both Japanese and English, the listeners' responses come at the end of clauses.

The existence of the folk linguistic term *aizuchi* in Japanese does suggest greater attention to this behavior. Some researchers believe that the frequency of back channel cues in Japanese is a unique feature of interaction. Others suggest that the Japanese language structure facilitates a greater frequency of responses. The language structure may reflect the social value attached to cooperative listenership in Japanese cultural practices (LoCastro 1999), providing more opportunities for the listener to contribute to the talk.

Another impression is that women use *aizuchi* more frequently than men, particularly in interactions with men. Their socialized role is that of the listener, asking questions strategically to encourage the men to continue to talk. However, more study of situated language is required, as empirical data show no differences in frequency or timing of back channel use in conversations with all-female or all-male participants.

Functions of Listeners' Responses

There are two major categories of responses by listeners: those that occur during a speaker's turn at talk, and those that are short turns at talk. The first category is considered in this section.

Research has shown that listener behavior signals different degrees of *(a)* attentiveness, *(b)* understanding, and *(c)* agreement, as well as *(d)* a response functioning as a continuer (see Schegloff 1982). In this case, the listener signals that the speaker does not need to give up the floor. The listener opts out of a turn at talk, despite invitations to speak.

Are these four forms functionally equivalent? Are they signaled in the same way with the same cues, the context alone aiding in interpreting the listener's meaning? Research suggests that cues are indeed ambiguous. This is the basis for the defense counselor's claim that Ishida did not intend to indicate agreement. The defendant had signaled attentiveness, a particularly Japanese back-channel function, by saying "yeah," a close equivalent to the Japanese *hai*. If all four functions are signaled by the same ambiguous cues, only a videotape of prosodic features and facial expressions would demonstrate his meaning. But a correct interpretation might require still more information about the context of situation.

A second question concerns cultural differences. It is claimed that Japanese tend to use *aizuchi* more frequently than Americans to indicate attentiveness, transferring from practices in Japanese culture where the listener is expected to show vocal support, encouraging the speaker, often in tandem with the speaker's cues (e.g., use of interactional particles [*ne, nee, na*] to elicit responses). Americans apparently are more likely to expect listeners to signal agreement with the content of the speaker's talk, in keeping with a worldview that prioritizes the transfer of information in interactions (see Tannen 1986). Undoubtedly, listeners do not behave identically in all cultures, yet it is unwise to claim that a trait is unique without research into a variety of cultures. (Evidence of cultural variability in the regulation of talk can be found in Philips 1976 and Clancy et al. 1996).

Third, it is not intuitively satisfying to claim that within a language or culture all functions are signaled by the same cues, as smooth interactions require the participants correctly interpret each other's meanings. This may be an area where ambiguity is desirable. According to Moerman (1988), Thai villagers utter *khap* ("yes") in response to requests and directives from visiting police authorities. Such responses, however, do not indicate compliance with the directives. In any language, a speaker can say, "Yes, of course," smile, and walk away without doing what was asked. Continuers allow the listener to slip into fuzzy territory and deny responsibility for the content of the talk.

Some research shows differences among the four categories. For example, agreement signals may be more complex, with multiple head nods, coming slightly before the end of a speaker's utterance. Single cues may imply only attention, whereas multiple ones may suggest understanding or agreement. In the case study of *aizuchi* above, the data (LoCastro 1990b) suggest that the number of listener responses at one LRRM may indicate agreement.

In the following extract, an American male and a Japanese male are discussing a business problem. The American has a higher social status and is older. Others within channel linkage are another American and two Japanese, all males. The Japanese speaker transfers into English the typical pattern of *aizuchi*.

1. *A:* . . . submit it the application without it
2. *J:* un
3. *A:* and we can proceed with the interview process
4. *J:* un
5. *A:* and then ugh
6. *J:* un
7. *A:* add the TOEFL score later
8. *J:* un [*overlapped by perhaps three others present who give some listener responses as well*]
9. *A:* that's a good point to put in
10. *J:* un, un, un, un, un [*simultaneous with preceding line*]

The listener responses are in their typical location, at the end of a unit of talk. J's responses are turn-supportive, signaling that the speaker should continue. However, there are two things to notice about J's final set of responses. First, it is simultaneous with A's words. J may be giving back channel cues for the others present, for the overhearers. The multiple *aizuchi* in line 10 likely indicate strong agreement with A's suggestion that J wants others to recognize. Analysis of the full transcript, in addition to ethnographic knowledge of the situation and of the cultural context, enables one to assign this interpretation to J's behavior with some confidence.

The complexity of meaning in such a conversation, particularly in intercultural contexts, must be acknowledged. Each variable may have different weight in different dialogues. And we should remember that ambiguity may be a way participants avoid attribution of responsibility, even within one culture.

Listener Behavior and Turn-Taking

The second type of listener behavior is short responses in lieu of a turn at talk. It is not easy to differentiate listener cues that variously signal (1) a claim on a turn at talk, (2) a short response that is not a turn at talk, or (3) (through turn-internal cues) understanding, agreement, or channel linkage. Misfires may occur even when participants share the same first language and background knowledge.

All participants need to decide when a speaker has come to the end of a turn and wishes to cede the floor, and when the speaker is merely pausing before continuing. Duncan (1972, 1973) calls these "speaker-turn signals" and "speaker-state signals," respectively. Gaze and posture may be significant. In a similar way, the listener needs to indicate whether the speaker should continue, even if the speaker has signaled readiness to switch to the listener's role. This requirement is even stronger with regard to talk on the telephone, where visual cues are not possible.

Gumperz labels the speaker-listener cues "contextualization cues" (1982a), defined as "constellations of surface features," that is, features of linguistic forms that signal how an utterance is to be interpreted. Prosodic phenomena and listener cues are part of the constellation, and they can only be interpreted locally as part of the context of the interactive event. For example, an increase in the loudness or number of cues, or a change in the intonation contour, may signal pragmatic meanings.

Sociocultural Values in Listener Behavior

To sum up, the variables to consider on listener behavior are

1. The forms used to signal listenership: linguistic and nonlinguistic cues, noises, and so on
2. The means to designate listenership and how the ratified listener is cued
3. The roles of addressee, side participant, and overhearer
4. The extent to which speaker-listener cues are sensitive to audience design features, that is, social and other attributes of the coparticipants
5. The frequency of occurrence
6. The functions of cues
7. The sociocultural value attached to listenership

These seven variables are interdependent, separated here only for the purpose of analysis. It is the final, seventh category that provides the context within which all the actual linguistic and nonlinguistic behaviors are interpreted.

Active listenership is positively valued in a variety of cultures. Many movie theaters in the United States have signs asking members of the audience to refrain from making comments when watching a film. Some audience members may come from sociocultural backgrounds in which such behavior is acceptable.

One place where listener behavior is particularly noticeable is Japan, where group harmony and interpersonal relations are emphasized. This value may cause listeners to use more *aizuchi* to show willingness to cooperate in conversation and support for the speaker. The speaker must attend to the participants as well, using the correct honorifics and eliciting responses by employing the interactional particle *ne*.

Mother: Oimohori shitai **ne.** [(We) want to go dig up potatoes, don't we?]
Son: Uun [Uhun.]

(Cook 1990, 31)

The mother uses the particle to invite agreement from her son. Any violation of the expected behavior of speaker or listener can be seen to threaten the social order.

It is generally considered inappropriate to interrupt to ask for clarification in Japan. Using *aizuchi* as a continuer, the listener allows the speaker to continue holding the floor, expecting at some point to be able to have a turn at talk. Or the listener may decide to opt out of expressing opinions, for example, as doing so may be unacceptable, because of status differences among the participants, for example. A request for clarification may be regarded as confrontational in some cultures, especially when interactants differ in status.

Back channel cues may also express attentiveness without committing the coparticipants to agreement with, for example, the speaker's requests. Listener behavior can be a means to defer to higher-status persons, managing the conversation smoothly while concealing bad news or conflicting attitudes. Active listenership is attentive to the face needs of the conversational partners. The "general rapport rule" (Leech 1983, 141) may be more important than the transmission of ideas or information. Leech's suggestion is derived from Malinowski's notion of "phatic communion," defined as "a type of speech in which ties of union are created by mere exchange of words" (1974, 151). Participants seek a warm bath of positive attitudes and smooth interactions. Furthermore, with reference to the transmission of information, it is also possible that the "information" being transmitted differs from Anglo-American expectations: "information" can also refer to emotions, feelings, and attitudes. Stereotyping must be avoided, however. If Maslow is right (1970), human beings universally need to be acknowledged as worthy. Phatic communion is as common in the Anglo-American environment as it is elsewhere.

Applications to Language Teaching

Even when it is not conscious behavior, good listenership is part of pragmatic competence in any language. Because students may not recognize its importance, teachers are responsible for drawing their attention to features of listening, including frequency and timing, the variety of tokens used, and cultural expectations. One method is to show videos, with the sound turned off, of people interacting in two or three different languages. Exercises and discussion can focus on differences and commonalities. Once they are acquainted with the features and roles of listener cues, students can transfer their knowledge to other languages and cultural contexts. For further development, learners can practice using listener cues in role-plays, or find examples in films (which they might view in a language learning center). Transcribing part of a scene also focuses attention on nonverbal cues and vocalizations. Finally, teachers can ask students to note instances of listenership they observe outside the classroom. Fostering curiosity, so that learners take an ethnographic approach to their own pragmatic competence, helps them to become more autonomous about language learning (see Roberts et al. 2001).

Conclusion

Norms for listener behavior and interpretations differ from culture to culture. In intercultural encounters, these elements of talk can lead to uncomfortable moments. In E. M. Forster's *A Passage to India,* one of the main characters draws attention to the importance of "subtle"—that is to say, back channel—cues, and to the discomfort that can result from a mismatch of expectations and inferences between the British and Indian protagonists.

> Tangles like this still interrupted their intercourse. A pause in the wrong place, an intonation misunderstood, and a whole conversation gone awry. (1942, 238)

Discussion Questions

1. Why has the role of the listener been ignored in the research on conversational interaction? Does this reflect at least in part the sociocultural values of the researchers? Discuss other reasons.

2. It seems that in some cultures the listener participates very actively, for example, in public performances. What are some reasons

for these cultural differences? What values might active listenership reflect?

3. Try to become aware of what you do as a listener in different situations. Make notes of your behavior and be ready to discuss them with classmates.

4. How do students in second or foreign language classrooms show they are attending to the teacher? If you have been the teacher, have you noticed anything in listener behavior that has made you uncomfortable? Try to analyze the behavior and reasons for your discomfort.

Tasks

1. Listeners have a role in conversational interactions. Observe what happens when you, as the listener in a conversation where your partner is telling a story or explaining something, turn your gaze away. What does the speaker do? Try this if possible with speakers who come from different ethnic backgrounds. Is there any pattern in their behavior? Any differences?

2. Take a particular social event, for example, a wedding, a teacher's meeting, or a religious ceremony. Describe and analyze the discourse roles of the participants.

3. Place yourself in an overhearer discourse role, for example, at a party, at a family dinner, or in a teacher's room. Observe the nonverbal cues used by the participants that convey availability for talk. How do the participants indicate they do not want to enter into a conversation? How do they show they do?

4. Find out more about how gaze is used in interactions by speakers and listeners. If possible, videotape some interactions for short five-minute periods. Observe different situations. Interview people from different backgrounds. Find some information in a library. Then pool the information with classmates and give an oral presentation or write a short report.

5. Does your first language use linguistic forms to designate listenership? Or does it do so interactionally? With a partner, discuss how listenership is signaled in any languages or cultures you know. If possible, check your ideas with someone who grew up in that culture.

6. Do any of the languages you know have words, like Japanese *aizuchi,* for listener behavior? Try to collect some information about this by asking people and checking in a library.

7. What are common listener response cues in languages you know? In Czech and Slovak, one often hears *dobre* being used by the listener. These cues are especially noticeable during telephone conversations. Can you think of a reason to explain this?

8. Tape if possible a naturally occurring conversation. If that is not possible, tape a television or radio talk show. Then analyze the talk for listener responses, looking at frequency, location, and functions.

9. Discuss stereotypes about listener behavior. We sometimes make the comment "He just doesn't listen." What does this mean? Can you think of other expressions about listener behavior?

10. In a public performance situation, for example, at a concert, movie, or play, how does the audience behave? Does the audience sit quietly listening throughout? Or does it interact with the performers by making comments outloud?

11. Look up in a book of quotations some expressions about listening. Find in your first language idioms, proverbs, religious sayings about listenership. Then analyze them. Can you make any generalizations about the sociocultural values they reflect?

Suggested Readings

Cook, H. M. 1990. The sentence-final particle *ne* as a tool for cooperation in Japanese conversation. In *Japanese-Korean Linguistics,* ed. H. Hoji. Stanford, Calif.: Center for the Study of Language and Information.

Gumperz, J. J. 1982a. *Discourse strategies.* Cambridge: Cambridge University Press.

LoCastro, V. 1987. Aizuchi: A Japanese conversational routine. In *Discourse across cultures: Strategies in world English,* ed. L. E. Smith. New York: Prentice Hall International.

Roberts, C., M. Byram, A. Barro, S. Jordan, and B. Street. 2001. *Language learners as ethnographers.* Clevedon, U.K.: Multilingual Matters.

Schegloff, E. A. 1982. Discourse as an interactional achievement: Some uses of "uh huh" and other things that come between sentences. In *Georgetown University Roundtable on Languages and Linguistics, 1981: Analyzing discourse: Text and talk,* ed. D. Tannen. Washington, D.C.: Georgetown University Press.

Chapter 11
Cross-Cultural Pragmatics

Cross-cultural pragmatics (CCP) may be defined as the study of linguistic acts carried out by language users with different cultural backgrounds (Kasper and Blum-Kulka 1993). It can be divided into two subcategories: contrastive pragmatics (CP) and interlanguage pragmatics (ILP). With regard to contrastive pragmatics, researchers compare speech acts across cultures and languages to understand how the kinds of linguistic actions talkers engage in reflect their backgrounds. Interlanguage pragmatics, the study of the pragmatic development of second and foreign language learners, focuses on nonnative speakers' (NNS) use and acquisition of pragmatic competence of a second or foreign language. Contrastive pragmatics does not view the participants as learners, but rather as full members of the target language community, in the business world or as sojourners in another part of the world. CP is the focus of this chapter, while ILP is taken up in the following one.

The aim of CCP is to define the systematic relationships between the sociocultural contexts and the functions and structures of language in use. The main premise of this field of pragmatics is that language use reflects the underlying values, beliefs, cultural assumptions, and communication strategies of the users. A corollary then is that NNS language use will display some degree of cross-linguistic transfer for the mother tongue or other languages the speaker knows, not only linguistically but also at all levels of language use, including the enactment and comprehension of pragmatic meaning. While the cultural background of a speaker cannot be said to determine the use of a language, transfer does occur. The transfer will constrain such features of language use as speech act and speech event realization, the role of prosody in signaling meaning, and the preferred types of politeness strategies.

This chapter introduces two approaches to explaining problematic cross-cultural communication. Following these sections is a survey of work on cross-cultural speech acts, a field of research within CCP that has provided important insights into the communication of pragmatic meaning.

Values and Beliefs

What must be taken into consideration to account for cultural influences on language and related behavior? CCP investigates how social actions, which derive from the participants' underlying values and beliefs, indeed worldview, are translated into linguistic forms. From the time when both Sapir (1933) and Whorf (1941) wrote seminal works on the relationship of language, thought, and culture, this controversial area has been marked by disagreements in scholarly circles. To what extent does culture influence language and thought, leading to culturally constrained ways of speaking and writing?

Most researchers have adopted the view that culture does indeed have a role to play in language behavior. Specifically, it has been established that the speaker's intended meaning, mediated by linguistic symbols, may be interpreted or misinterpreted in cross-cultural contexts as the result of each interactant's own cultural norms of interpretation. That is, the linguistic social action of speakers of a particular language mirror the underlying worldview of the speakers; manifestations of the cultural models of thought are embedded in talk both in the micro features and at the macro level. The list of micro behaviors includes prosodic features, listener behavior, turn-taking, conversational routines, constituents of an activity type, conventional indirectness, nonverbal cues, and speech act realizations. With regard to macro-level concerns, differences in cross-cultural communication arise as well, in the context of comprehension, with attribution of illocutionary force, perception of politeness, violation of different maxims, and adherence to Grice's CP. As for production, problems are likely to become apparent with form/function mismatches, the transfer of sociopragmatic norms from the first-language culture, and topics that are taboo in a second language culture. Even in a second language one may adhere to the cultural norms of one's mother tongue so as to maintain ethnolinguistic identity. This list is not exhaustive, but suggests everyday features where culture influences the production and interpretation of meaning.

What we are discussing is not culture with a capital *C*, that is, the literature, music, and art of one speech community. Rather, it is culture as a reflection of the values and beliefs about the world, held by the members of a speech community, in effect, the substratum underlying all aspects of daily life. The largely unexamined values and beliefs influence perceptions, expectations, and assumptions about the role of language and communication in general and the interpretations of language use.

A useful heuristic is to view societies as multilayered. Some behaviors are manifest or overt; others are latent or covert. For example, an intonation contour that accompanies a phrase, interpretable only by examining latent meanings, such as how a particular society conceives male and female roles. The language use may signal that women are expected to use language differently than men.

Holmes (1992) reports on studies of standard and vernacular forms used by men and women in Sydney and Montreal. In general, women use more standard forms than men do. Moreover, research has shown that gender interacts with socioeconomic background. In all social classes, women use more standard forms than men do. Why is this pattern consistent across Western speech communities? Holmes mentions four explanations. First, women are more aware that how they speak signals their social class. Second, societies tend to expect women to speak "correctly" as upholders of societal values. Third, members of subordinate groups (women, minority group members) are polite to superiors. Finally, vernacular forms may have covert prestige for men in contrast to the overt prestige of the standard forms for women.

Some researchers (see, for example, the collection of Holland and Quinn 1987) have studied the language use of cultural groups to understand the values reflected in conceptual categories. A well-known work is that of G. Lakoff (1987), entitled *Women, Fire, and Dangerous Things*. Lakoff found that the Australian aboriginal language Dyirbal has a conceptual category, *balan,* that includes the items mentioned in the title of his book. In the Dyirbal model of the world, the items are grouped into the category of "dangerous."

It is informative as well to learn how some cultural groups enact their values through speech events and language use in the event.

In studies of a culture's worldview, analysis has focused on how a culture deals with authority, individualism versus interdependence, secular as opposed to sacred concerns, trust, spontaneity, and cooperation versus competitive interactions among participants. Thai people, for example, value dependence, restraint, hierarchy, and separation of private and public life (Mortlock 1986). Such studies have been helpful in providing a baseline against which comparisons can be made. For example, an awareness of the value attached to positive or solidarity politeness in North America, in contrast to the preference for negative or deference politeness in the United Kingdom (Scollon and Scollon 1983), provides insights into language use and other behavior in those two parts of the world. It must be kept in mind, nevertheless, that CCP is based on generalizations; no country of the world is homogeneous, and this fact must be acknowledged to guard against overgeneralizations, stereotyping, and discrimination.

This overview of potential sources of discomfort, even misunderstanding, in cross-cultural contacts illustrates the difficulties in interpretation of pragmatic meaning in general. What is left unsaid becomes considerably more complex in cross-cultural pragmatics, and the determination of what is meant from what is said a virtual quagmire, as the usual processes of interpretation and of production of pragmatic meaning must contend with influences from the interactants' first or other language cultures. The next section provides an explanation of two approaches to the analysis of the causes of miscommunication in cross-cultural contacts.

Pragmatic Failure

Failure to produce and to understand situationally appropriate language behavior is termed *pragmatic failure*. According to Thomas (1983), the inability to interpret intended meaning may be due to regional, ethnic, gender, and class differences within a community and across cultural boundaries. In other words, there are intracultural and intercultural differences. Culturally influenced patterns of language behavior not only result in production difficulties, but also comprehension problems, as listeners tend to interpret other's language use through the lens of their own worldview. Even within one culture, pragmatic norms differ from region to region. Tannen's work on New York conversational style (1984) indicates that the machine-gun questions of New Yorkers communicate positive, solidarity friendliness—a pragmatic norm—whereas midwesterners may regard the speaker as being overbearing, nosey, and aggressive.

Three categories of pragmatic failure have been identified (Erickson 1984). First, at the level of explicit, referential meanings, there can be inappropriate transfer of speech act realization strategies or of expressions from the L1 into the L2 that can be interpreted differently. This is termed *pragmalinguistic failure,* which is concerned with differences in the linguistic encoding of pragmatic meaning or force. This type is usually due to transfer from the first language and can be observed, for example, in the linguistic forms that are used to apologize, to enact politeness, and to hedge a request. One everyday context in which pragmalinguistic failure is observable concerns how to address waiters and waitresses in different types of restaurants throughout the world. In Mexico, *joven* (young person) is used; in Japan, in noodle shops, *onisan* or *onesan* (sister) is common. In the United States, clicking one's fingers or whistling would result in no service at all as most service personnel in restaurants would expect to hear, "Could you please bring me a glass of water?"

Second, *sociopragmatic failure* is misinterpretation at the level of implicit social meaning. The mismatches are due to different assessments of social aspects of the context, such as the social distance between the speaker and addressee(s). An example involves the assumption that calling a senior faculty member by his first name entitles the graduate student to telephone that person at his home late at night or during the weekend. This category involves both production and comprehension of linguistic forms where the awareness of sociocultural norms, such as social distance, degrees of imposition, and rights and obligations of speakers and listeners, is essential (Leech 1983, 10).

In fact, both categories involve underlying perceptions of sociocultural norms. In the example of ordering in restaurants, whether one can use a direct imperative form, call the waitress your sister, or use politeness markers relates to dimensions of power, social distance, and how service personnel are viewed in different cultures. Kasper has suggested that pragmalinguistic dimensions tend to be context or text-internal factors, whereas sociopragmatic issues tend to be context-external (1992, 209). The main point here is that these two categories are not dichotomous, that is, two separate classes of pragmatic failure; rather, they represent two ends of a scale or continuum. The linguistic enactment of politeness demands awareness of sociocultural norms. A response such as the following sentence from an e-mail message indicates that the writer has been socialized to address the professor with the formal *usted* according to the sociocultural practices of Mexican society: "Su respuesta me ha ayudado mucho, y le estoy muy agradecido" [Your answer has helped me very much, and I am very grateful to you].

Third, there can be misattribution or faulty assessment of other participants' intentions, competence, and background knowledge. In this case, the presuppositions underlying a speaker's meaning need to be unpacked. In the north of England, postal clerks, both male and female, may address their regular customers with "Morning, *luv,* what can I do for you?" Customers not used to the word "luv" may take offense, seeing the male clerk, in particular, as being sexist or too familiar with women. The effect of deviations of this sort from the target language community norms is often to attribute misunderstandings in cross-cultural contact environments to personality flaws (someone may be regarded as rude as the result of his or her personal communication style). Or the discomfort may be said to be due to ethnocultural origins, thereby stigmatizing or stereotyping all members of that ethnic group (see Tannen 1986). Grammatical errors made by a NNS may be forgiven, attributed to a low proficiency in the target language. However, pragmatic failure is less frequently explained away. Personal fault is attributed even to the native speaker of English who does not know the local city customs for ordering coffee to go in a New York deli!

Requesting Behavior

In one example of pragmalinguistic failure (White 1993), the speech act realization strategies of Japanese and English requesting behavior were found to cause discomfort, particularly because of the word "please" used to accompany requests in English. In the case of requests, the speaker wants the addressee to do something that will benefit the speaker.

> **Please** open the door for me. My hands are full.

A request is an FTA for the addressee, which typically causes the speaker to use a form of mitigation to do redressive action. Moreover, a request is not successful if the addressee is the beneficiary.

However, it is common for Japanese speakers of English to use the word "please" when they would use *dozo* in Japanese. *Dozo* is normally translated as "please," even though the two words are not functionally equivalent. *Dozo* can be used with speech acts of requesting, inviting, giving permission, and offering. In the case of invitations and offers, the speaker wants the addressee to do something that benefits the addressee; in other words, the addressee is the beneficiary. Consequently, a Japanese speaker of English may use "please" inappropriately with invitations and offers, essentially transferring from Japanese.

> Have a seat, please. [Dozo okake kudasai.]

Due to the transfer from the first-language realization strategies, the Japanese speaker causes a pragmalinguistic mismatch. One can argue that there is no serious misunderstanding in such a case. Nonetheless, the level of discomfort, which may result in the Japanese being perceived as not being appropriately aware of role and status differences, can result from the mismatch of "please" with the speech act of giving permission. The following speech act was enacted with an imperative form, transferred from the V+ *te-kudasai* pattern in Japanese, produced by a secretary to a non-Japanese superior.

> Please go back to your office now.

The implicature of the English speech act realization is that the superior is being treated as a subordinate, thus threatening his face needs to be acknowledged as the director of the program.

Job Interviews

Sociopragmatic failure can be observed in the context of job interviews in cross-cultural situations. Job interviews are a type of gatekeeping situation where the interviewees must answer questions and in general present themselves so as to meet the expectations of the interviewer. In the twenty-first century, with increasing globalization and therefore more contact between people who do not share the same backgrounds, values, or language, cross-cultural communication problems arise with increasing frequency in job interviews. In addition to actual language problems, the participants may not share the same expectations about the purpose of the interview. Roberts, Davies, and Jupp (1992, 42–48) claim, in particular, that the interviewees may not be able to "read between the lines" to correctly interpret the interviewer's hidden or covert meanings. The Anglo-American interview style, for example, requires candidates sell themselves, whereas an interviewee from a different sociocultural background may shy away from such self-presentation.

The conversation in the table that follows is from a job interview in London. N, the English interviewer, is talking with B, a bilingual Asian, probably from India or Pakistan, with near-native proficiency in English but a different view of the norms for an interview (Roberts, Davies, and Jupp 1992, 42–45). Particularly in line 9, N is in effect asking B to make some positive comments about his company, whereas N misinterprets his questions and appears to be self-serving. His value system is exposed, and his motivation for wanting the job seems to derive from personal desires and not because he would find the new company better in ways that would make him a desirable employee. B may have believed that he was responding in the manner in which he was expected to respond. "The candidate's honesty combined with rather different assumptions about how personal to be or how to present one's commitment and worth, set the interview off on the wrong footing" (Roberts, Davies, and Jupp 1992, 46).

In effect, the entire interview represents sociopragmatic failure. The individual lines or instances of language use contributed to the whole picture of B's not being aware of the covert expectations of the British interviewer. He could not interpret the pragmatic meaning of

> 1. *N:* Yes, and you've been there for how long?
> 2. *B:* Four years
> 3. *N:* Four years . . . Why do you actually want to leave? It's a nice steady job.
> 4. *B:* Well the thing is um you know it's better to change the jobs and get other jobs. I was very interested in working for L____ Transport. You know, right at the beginning so . . . Because I couldn't get the job I had to take the R____.
> 5. *N:* Uh huh. So did you actually apply to us before for a job?
> 6. *B:* I applied once very I . . . once when I came here you know a long time ago
> 7. *N:* And what happened then . . . at that stage?
> 8. *B:* Well um I failed the test [*chuckles*] . . .
> 9. *N:* For a guard and you failed the test at that stage. OK. And since then you've worked as a process operator. What do you think L____ Buses is going to offer you that R____ don't offer you?
> 10. *B:* Well, quite a lot of things, for example, like um . . . Christmas bonus.
> 11. *N:* Uh huh
> 12. *B:* So many things, holidays and all that. Well, we get holidays in R____, but you er . . . get more holidays than you get in R____ [*laughs*].

Source: Roberts et al. 1992, 42–45.

N's question in line 9 because he did not share a sociocultural background with N.

Conventional Usage and Interactive Dimensions

A second approach to studying cross-cultural communication mismatches is Richards and Sukwiwat's (1985, 129), who provide a taxonomy of "how culturally specific assumptions and strategies for conversation surface" in two macrocategories: (1) conventional usage in conversation and (2) interactional dimensions of conversation.

Conventional Usage in Conversation

The lack of match between form and function of a speech act realization strategy is a norm of human communication. Icebreakers, that is, a strategy to start up a conversation, exemplify mismatch of form and function. Asking someone for the time or commenting on the weather while waiting in the bus queue may function as a means to "break the ice" in a nonthreatening way to engage a copresent individual person in talk. Any kind of direct statement, such as "I'd like to talk with you while we are both waiting for the bus," would be face threatening.

However, mismatches are more likely to be apparent when interlocutors do not share the same sociocultural background (Richards and Sukwiwat 1985). Cross-linguistic influences can cause miscommunication in different ways. First, social situations may be viewed differently across cultures. A wedding carries different connotations in North America and in Indonesia. Some events may be culture-specific; a Buddhist ordination ceremony for a young man in Thailand has no counterpart in another part of the world. A corollary is that the linguistic and nonlinguistic behaviors vary and reflect the values and beliefs about the event as it is defined by the culture in which it is embedded. Richards and Sukwiwat suggest three categories of mismatches of conversational usage: (1) same situation: different routines; (2) same routine, different function; and (3) correct routine, wrong situation.

As for a conversational routine being regarded as different even though the situations are the same or similar, Richards and Sukwiwat cite compliments. Although acceptance of the compliment is the most appropriate response in English, a Thai hostess will deny or avoid any compliment on her clothing or cooking. What constitutes an apology varies cross-culturally; according to Olshtain and Cohen (1983), an apology may consist of one or more of five realizations: (1) an expression of apology, (2) an explanation for the behavior, (3) acknowledgment of responsibility, (4) an offer of repair, or (5) a promise not to repeat the same action.

1. I'm sorry; I apologize.
2. The bus broke down.
3. It was my fault; I didn't leave enough time to get back to my office.
4. I'll treat you to lunch.
5. I'll be more careful next time.

The second way in which a conversational routine can go wrong arises when the same routine may have different functions; this is particularly likely with translation in contrast with functional equivalents. *Please* and *dozo* are translation equivalents, but only functionally equivalent with speech acts of requesting. In Thai, the expression *maj pen raj* may be translated as "You're welcome," "Don't mention it," "It doesn't matter," or "Never mind." It is used as a response to show gratitude and to apologize. However, some of the translations in English result in pragmatic failure (Richards and Sukwiwat 1985, 132–33).

Boss: thanks a lot . . . that was a great help
Secretary: never mind [translating from Thai]

The secretary's response misfires, as in English "never mind" is not used to acknowledge thanks.

The third case in which the usage may be inappropriate is found when what is a linguistically correct routine may misfire owing to the context of situation. Richards and Sukwiwat (1985, 133) give the following examples, where B is a Thai speaker of English:

A: Would you like to see a movie?
B: Excuse me, but I'm not free.
A: Do you like the steak?
B: Without a doubt, it's excellent.

In both instances, B uses an infelicitous phrase. Speaker A may still understand what B wanted to say; however, B would not be viewed as a pragmatically competent user of English.

A second category in the taxonomy to account for misunderstandings due to cross-linguistic influence concerns the presence of different felicity conditions for a routine (Richards and Sukwiwat 1985, 133). As discussed in chapter 8, a speech act of baptizing a child can only be successful if the felicity condition holds, that the person carrying out the speech act is someone authorized to do it. In China, it is not appropriate for parents to praise their children, and parents do not accept praise from others. This traditional practice reflects a fear that particularly young children could easily be stolen. Drawing attention to one's children was dangerous; it was better to hide them from the evil eyes of ghosts and other malevolent spirits. Though this belief has disappeared in modern Chinese adults, the linguistic practice continues.

Still another category of the taxonomy comprises the problems that result from formulaic, idiomatic routines being decomposed or translated. All languages have gambits, discourse markers, and idiomatic expressions that can only be learned through repeated observation of their use in context. Richards and Sukwiwat (1985, 134) list several in English: "not on your life," "let's face it," "you bet!" and "mind you though." Sometimes the result can be amusing: many L2 French learners have used "Je suis plein" to say that they have had enough to eat when asked if they would like some more food, or were told to "help yourself." However, the functional meaning is not the direct translation, "I am full," but rather "I am pregnant."

Interactional Dimensions of Conversation

The second category of reasons for cross-cultural communication problems related to pragmatic meaning includes the interactional dimensions in conversation (Richards and Sukwiwat 1985, 134). In this case, the focus is very similar to that of studies of sociopragmatic failure. The focus is on the social dimensions of the speech event itself, not limiting the analysis to individual speech acts or conversational routines. Specifically, Richards and Sukwiwat examine cross-cultural differences in the marking of social distance, status, and power through language.

Because microphenomena such as lexis, morphemes, syntactic patterns, and prosodic features enact the local production of the social structure, they can vary greatly cross-linguistically. For example, suasion is expressed by such devices in English as the auxiliary verb *do:* "*Do* come and visit us." In Thai, suasion is signaled by word tone and the repetition of the main verb and the final particle: "maa jiam raw na, maa na" [Come visit us *na*. Come *na*]. Learners of Thai or English as foreign languages must learn that the linguistic means differ.

The choice of register for the particular situation may vary. Formal and informal styles can be signaled by lexis, morphosyntax, prosody, and nonverbal features (gaze, posture, eye contact). According to Richards and Sukwiwat (1985, 136) there are four speech levels in Thai: *(a)* royal, *(b)* deferential, *(c)* neutral, and *(d)* vulgar language. Each level has distinctive features using one or more of the linguistic and nonlinguistic resources of the language.

The extent to which power is communicated or made explicit has to be taken into consideration in cross-linguistic communicative situations. Generally, Americans consider their culture egalitarian and avoid displays of power through language, whereas other cultures are characterized by explicit marking of a hierarchical structure, with overt signaling of an individual's social status, occupation, and age. The use of *tu* to address household workers in such countries as Mexico is common practice; the nonreciprocal form of address enacts the status difference between the workers and the employers. Even within a country, local customs vary. It is still considered appropriate by some people, particularly those who are older or from the Southern parts, to address women unknown to them or who are in positions of authority as "ma'am." However, Northerners find the term offensive, as it is connected with the period when African Americans were expected to use it to address white females.

Further, the presentation of self in public and private domains may vary. Barnlund (1975) found clear differences between Japanese and American conceptions of acceptable topics of conversation, the amount of personal information shared, the number of persons with whom individuals interact, and the degree of spontaneous versus regulated occasions for talk.

Finally, the need to do face work is culturally influenced as face costs vary according to the cultural and socioeconomic backgrounds of the participants. Asking questions of clarification of a professor is common in university classrooms in North America; in Japan, however, students generally wait until the class is over to ask questions. Such questions may be regarded as FTAs, that is, expressions of criticism. In addition, the type of face to which a particular culture attaches value, *lien,* or *lien* and *mien-tsu,* results in language behavior that reflects which type is more highly valued. In Thailand, as more value is attached to age and accomplishments, the *mien-tsu* face gets priority, leading to linguistic forms showing attention to the face needs of older people with higher perceived social status.

All of these aspects included above are potentially sensitive to cross-cultural misunderstandings due to the interactants' perceptions, expectations, values, beliefs, and knowledge of the world, all of which are culturally influenced.

Speech Acts

One area of research that has contributed immensely to cross-cultural pragmatics is speech acts. Since the 1960s anecdotal descriptions have been replaced by empirical research on the transfer of speech acts from one cultural and linguistic background to another, and on second language acquisition, thus enabling learners and teachers to avoid stereotyping ("New Yorkers complain all the time") and to learn strategies to enact speech acts successfully.

Olshtain and Cohen (1983) in particular made major contributions to this important area during the 1980s, describing speech act sets recognized by native speakers. A speech act set includes the subacts performed with a speech act. In addition, they researched felicity conditions, purpose, and semantic prerequisites. For example, an apology requires that some violation of social norms has occurred for which the speaker (and hearer) believes an expression of regret is necessary. The precondition—behavior that warrants an apology—leads the speaker to seek to make amends, which is the goal or purpose of the apology. Olshtain and Cohen (1983) list five semantic formulas or strategies for the speech act set of apologizing (see the accompanying table). The importance of this work on speech acts sets derives from the careful description of the dimensions for individual speech acts. This knowledge enables learners and teachers to be aware of the complexities involved. At any point along the way of uttering a speech act, it can go awry if the speaker happens to come from a cultural background with different realization strategies

1. An expression of an apology	
a expression of regret	I'm sorry.
b an offer of apology	I apologize.
c a request for forgiveness	Excuse me.
2. A expression or account of the situation	The bus was late.
3. An acknowledgment of responsibility	
a accepting the blame	It's my fault.
b expressing self-deficiency	I wasn't thinking.
c recognizing the other person as deserving apology	You are right.
d expressing lack of intent	I didn't mean it.
4. An offer of repair	I'll pay for the broken vase.
5. A promise of forbearance	It won't happen again.

Source: Ellis 1994, 176.

or semantic formulaic renditions. Blum-Kulka's study (1983) of cultural preferences for conventional or nonconventional indirectness with requests, for example, showed that conventional indirectness is preferred and that although indirectness appears to be a universal, there are distinct cultural differences with the realization strategies.

Another invaluable contribution to cross-cultural speech acts is a comprehensive empirical study called the Cross-Cultural Speech Act Research Project (CCSARP) (Blum-Kulka, House, and Kasper 1989), which is based on data collected by a Discourse-Completion Test (DCT). The languages were French, Danish, German, Hebrew, and three varieties of English, from seven different countries. The study focused on requests and apologies, chosen in particular as they are face-threatening acts and normally require some redressive action; moreover, they both concern the speaker's attention to the hearer's face needs.

The choice of a DCT has been criticized on the grounds that self-report data is not reliable. Nevertheless, it was chosen as the most appropriate instrument to collect a large sample of speech acts while maintaining the same contexts. The test consists of a situation followed by an incomplete dialogue that the respondent is asked to complete. Here are two examples, the first designed to elicit a request, the second, an apology (Blum-Kulka, House, and Kasper 1989, 14):

At the university
Ann missed a lecture yesterday and would like to borrow Judith's notes.

Ann: _____

Judith: Sure, but let me have them back before the lecture next week.

At the college teacher's office
A student has borrowed a book from her teacher, which she promised to return today. When meeting her teacher, however, she realized that she forgot to bring it along.

Teacher: Miriam, I hope you brought the book I lent you.

Miriam: _____

Teacher: OK, but please remember it next week.

The researchers provide a coding manual (Blum-Kulka, House, and Kasper 1989, 273–94). In the informants' responses to the DCT questionnaire, the first step is identifying the part to be analyzed. In the following example from the CCSARP (275), the basic coding procedures are visible:

John, get me a beer, please. I'm terribly thirsty.

The actual request is called the *head act:* Get me a beer. In addition, there are *alerters* and *supportive moves*. In the example, "John" is an alerter. Alerters are opening moves, such as a term of address or an attention getter *(Excuse me, Oye, ano).* Supportive moves are external to the request and can mitigate or maximize the speech act. "I'm terribly thirsty," by giving a reason or explanation, mitigates the request. However, if someone says, "Stop bothering me or I'll call the police," the second clause aggravates the request. It is external syntactically to the request and is information not necessary for the request to be understood. The coding manual can be used successfully for the analysis of speech acts and other forms of naturalistic data (see LoCastro 1997a).

Since the 1980s, cross-cultural speech act studies have included the following: apologies, refusals, rejections, compliments, complaints, requests, expression of gratitude, disagreement, chastisement, giving embarrassing information, and correction. The various studies have addressed a variety of issues in the enactment of speech acts: variation in levels of directness, gender differences, degrees of pragmatic transfer from the L1, differences between perception and production of pragmatic meaning, research instruments to collect natural data, status differences, conversational routines, perlocutionary effects, and mitigation to redress FTAs.

Speech Act Realization in Particular Cultures

According to Blum-Kulka (1983), linguistic, sociocultural, and pragmatic knowledge is necessary for comprehension of a speech act. Searle (1969) and others have made claims of universality of the rules for speech act interpretation and performance, although the manifestations of a speech act may vary across languages. Blum-Kulka cites an example from Labov and Fanshel (1977), who describe preconditions for requests: "the hearer must believe that the speaker believes there is a need for action and the request, that the hearer has the ability and obligation to carry it out and that the speaker has the right to tell the hearer to do so." However, Blum-Kulka contends that these pragmatic preconditions are universal only at a very general level. With indirect speech acts, such as indirect requests, the realization strategies are more complex. Specifically, Blum-Kulka explains that in Hebrew, a request always involves asking the addressees if they can perform the request:

Child: Can you fix the needle?
Adult: I'm busy.
Child: I just wanted to know if you can fix it.

In Hebrew, the linguistic realization would include the extra dimension that cannot be rendered in English. Therefore, the illocutionary force differs, as well as the social appropriateness of the speech act. A direct questioning of the addressee's capacity to carry out the request is normative in Hebrew, according to Blum-Kulka, while a more indirect realization strategy, such as with a tag question, is more appropriate in American English.

Cultural Norms and Speech Acts

Every culture has characteristic speech acts that reflect its norms and values. Scholars such as Wierzbicka (1991) have attempted to develop a form of semantic analysis to facilitate cross-cultural comparisons at a macro conceptual level to avoid culture- and language-specific labels. Wierzbicka wants to avoid viewing other cultures through frameworks created solely by Anglo-American researchers working with English. She has developed a shorthand manner to describe the semantic structure for speech acts that she claims enables the researcher to distinguish cultural differences. The accompanying table gives an example for the verb *ask* in English and Walmatjari, an Aboriginal language spoken in Western Australia (Wierzbicka 1991, 159); this analysis is based on the researcher's interpretation of the logic of the verb, using self-generated sentences.

Ask	Japirlyung
(a) I say: I want you to do something good for me (X)	(a) I say: I want you to do something good for me (X)
(b) I say this because I want you to do it.	(b) I say it because I want you to do it.
(c) I think: you don't have to do it	(c) I think: you have to do good things for me
	(c') I think you know: everyone has to do good things for some other people (because of the way we are related)
(d) I don't know if you will do it	(d) I think: you will do it because of this

Source: Wierzbicka 1991, 159.

Comparing the verb *ask* in English with the comparable verb in Walmatjari, Wierzbicka argues that the two verbs cover different semantic territories. Specifically, the Aboriginal language domain reflects the values attached to kinship rights and obligations; the request speech act (see point c′) indicates that due to the kinship base of the society, the request will not be refused, as it might be in English.

Another attempt to examine how speech acts mirror specific values of a culture can be found in work on compliments (Manes 1983; Manes and Wolfson 1981). In the United States, compliments have the function of establishing or reinforcing solidarity between the interactants. Consequently, if an individual wants to be complimented, the person must do things worthy of compliments. American English compliments show an emphasis on similarity and conformity to societal values in taste or appearance, or in the quality of something produced through skill or effort, such as a handmade quilt. A study of compliments in an Asian culture would undoubtedly produce data indicating that, generally speaking, compliments are denigrated or ignored (see Hatch 1992).

Apologies have been of particular interest (Blum-Kulka, House, and Kasper 1989; Fraser 1981), particularly in the context of comparing the speech act realization in Anglo-American and Asian cultures, specifically in Japan (see Coulmas 1981a). This particular speech act is a good example of how pragmatics can go beyond individual instances where the local interpretation of the act may cause miscommunication between the coparticipants. Apologies, in the case of Japan, Germany, and other countries involved in wars as aggressors, may involve payment of large sums of money to citizens injured, killed, or involved in sex slavery. Therefore, it is of major consequence which of the possible dimensions of an apology are recognized as legitimate for an apology to be successful by a particular culture. In addition, the status of the speaker of an apology is of great concern to all concerned.

Applications to Language Teaching

There have undoubtedly been more cross-cultural studies of pragmatic ability than any other area of pragmatics, particularly from the perspective of L2 learners or speakers. Further, most of the studies have been on L2 use, in particular NNSs' perceptions of speech act force, levels of politeness, and the role of contextual variables in choosing realization strategies and linguistic forms, among other factors (see Kasper and Rose 1999). Questions regarding development of pragmatic competence have been less frequently addressed (see, however, LoCastro 2001; Salisbury and Bardovi-Harlig 2000). Developmental studies have looked at the effect of instruction in particular. LoCastro (2001) observed that inadequate materials and teachers untrained in the field of pragmatics may hamper the learners' development. Salisbury (2000) found that the ability to use modality, lexical and grammatical forms, is sensitive to a developmental sequence. Consequently, despite instruction and exposure to the use of modality by NSs, the learners' movement from lexical forms ("maybe" or "I think" to express uncertainty) appears to follow a developmental sequence that overrides instruction.

It is, therefore, difficult for L2 teachers to intervene. For certain, they can attempt to seek and to use materials that have been developed by writers knowledgeable about pragmatics and aware of its importance. Further, they can themselves increase their knowledge in the field. From this base, instruction can be developed. Despite the developmental sequences, raising awareness is always useful, ensuring exposure to such notions as that politeness is carried out differently depending on the culture. Then, as learners progress through the linguistic developmental sequences, they have a base from which to produce pragmatically appropriate utterances. Without this awareness, their attempts to learn the linguistic forms may be for naught. They need to know the reasons, first, for using the variety of forms of modality and those for expressing other pragmatic meanings.

Discussion Questions

1. Discuss with group members your experiences of communication problems caused by participants' cultural backgrounds. Use what you learned in this chapter to analyze these events.

2. Name two or three values and beliefs you have about the contemporary world that differ from those of your parents' generation. How would you handle a heated discussion with participants from different generations?

3. Is pragmatic failure a problem in the daily world of intercultural communication? Support your opinion with evidence. Then consider the effect of miscommunication, especially if it occurs with some frequency.

4. Discuss job or other interviews you have experienced where the outcome was successful and then others that were unsuccessful. Can you explain the reasons and differences?

5. Generate examples for the categories of the Richards and Sukwiwat taxonomy.

6. Select a speech act and study it. Collect naturally occurring data and then compare and contrast your findings with classmates. Consider the variables connected with speech acts that were discussed in the chapter.

Tasks

1. Decide what cultural values are embedded in the following letter. Document your analysis with evidence from the letter, specifically citing the language used. Then assess in what ways the letter might result in a cross-cultural misunderstandings between the sender and the receiver.

> Universidad de las Americas-Puebla
> Vicerrectoría Administrativa
> Departamento de Seguridad
>
> Asunto: Violación al Reglamento de la Zona Residencial UDLA-P, a 22 de Noviembre del 2000
>
> Dra. X
> Residente Casa YY, Conjunto "A:
> Zona Residencial
> Campus Universitario
>
> En relación los hechos ocurridos el Jueves 9 de Noviembre del año en curso, en los que el perro pro-

priedad de la Dra. Z, residente de la casa B, conjunto C, mató a su gatita de tres meses, me permito comunicarle que respecto al contienido del Reglamento de la Zona Residencial, el termino "mascotas" se aplica a todo tipe de animales, incluyendo a los gatos.

Por lo anterior, se debe asumir la responsabilidad correspondiente al permitir que la gatita estuviera suelta o no encerrada en la casa de su proprietaria.

En espera de su comprensión y apoyo, quedo de usted.

Atentamente
El Jefe del Departamento de Seguridad

[With regard to the event that occurred on Thursday, November 9, of the current year, during which the dog belonging to Dr. Z, resident of House B, killed your cat of three months. Permit me to remind you that, with regard to the Rules for the Residential Zone, the term "pets" refers to all types of animals, including cats.

Consequently, you are asked to assume responsibility for having allowed your cat to be outside without a leash or for not being kept in your house.

I look forward to your understanding and support.

Yours truly,
Head of campus security]

2. The duration of the speaker exchange point in talk—the brief silence or switching pause that occurs before the listener starts talking—varies by culture. Scollon and Scollon (1983) carried out a study in northern Alaska with Athabaskans, a local indigenous people, who, when they interacted in English with non-Athabaskans, could not get a word in edgewise. In the Scollons' study, the response latency, or pause, exceeded 1.5 seconds in conversations between Athabaskans; a shorter pause, less than one

second, was the norm with English speakers. Both groups transferred their practices when conversing in English with each other. Consequently, the Athabaskans felt that they were never given an opportunity, as the English speakers failed to wait long enough for the Athabaskans to speak.

The question now is whether this pattern of pause length can be found in other cultures. The accompanying table presents statistics from a study of Japanese and American television interviews. There were three interviews: the first with all participants speaking in American English; the second with the participants speaking in Japanese; and the third conducted in English, with one participant speaking his first language, English, and the second speaking his second language, English.

For the first two rows, the speakers were using their first languages, English and Japanese, respectively. The third row lists the data when the American speaker was followed by the Japanese, the fourth row the reverse order. (Note that for rows 3 and 4, the language used was English.) In the interview between two Americans, for example, twenty-nine pauses were measured, lasting from a minimum of 38 milliseconds to a maximum of 1,550 milliseconds. The mean was 635 milliseconds.

Type	Minimum (ms.)	Maximum (ms.)	n	Mean (ms.)	SD
American, American	38	1,550	29	635	496
Japanese, Japanese	32	582	28	280	158
American, Japanese	83	2,930	20	869	783
Japanese, American	62	1,036	18	373	314

Source: LoCastro 1990b, 232.

Discuss the data and come to some conclusion about the pattern of switching pauses. Generate a list of explanations related to cross-cultural pragmatics for the observed behavior.

Suggested Readings

Blum-Kulka, S. 1983. Interpreting and performing speech acts in a second language: A cross cultural study of Hebrew and English. In *Sociolinguistics and language acquisition,* ed. N. Wolfson and E. Judd. Rowley, Mass.: Newbury House.

Blum-Kulka, S., J. House, and G. Kasper, eds. 1989. *Cross-cultural pragmatics: Requests and apologies.* Norwood, N.J.: Ablex.

Cohen, A. D. 1996. Speech acts. In *Sociolinguistics and language teaching,* ed. S. L. McKay and N. H. Hornberger. Cambridge: Cambridge University Press.

Holland, D., and N. Quinn, eds. 1987. *Cultural models in language and thought.* Cambridge: Cambridge University Press.

Lakoff, G. 1987. *Women, fire, and dangerous things: What categories reveal about the mind.* Chicago: University of Chicago Press.

Olshtain, E., and A. D. Cohen. 1983. Apology: A speech act set. In *Sociolinguistics and language acquisition,* ed. N. Wolfson and E. Judd. Rowley, Mass.: Newbury House.

Wierzbicka, A. 1991. *Cross-cultural pragmatics: The semantics of human interaction.* Berlin: de Gruyter.

Chapter 12
Interlanguage Pragmatics

Chapter 11 focused on cross-cultural pragmatics, that is, the transfer from the realization strategies and worldview of a speaker's first language, into interactions in the speaker's second or foreign language. The question addressed was the possible effect of the transfer on communication, both comprehension and production. This effect is commonly considered a barrier, but positive pragmatic transfer does occur and paves the way for more successful cross-cultural communication. Greetings, for example, exist in all cultures; however, how they are realized is culture-specific. Note that negative transfer does not necessarily lead to pragmatic failure. In general, transfer need not lead to miscommunication (Kasper 1992).

In this chapter, interference from the L1 is again an issue. In this case, the focus is on learners of the L2: the types of errors and their causes, and pragmatic development. It must be kept in mind that the ability to comprehend pragmatic meaning may be affected by the L1 norms of interpretation. Furthermore, although all research shows some evidence of transfer in cross-cultural and interlanguage communication, it is not yet clearly understood. The psycholinguistic basis of transfer in pragmatics has not been fully established. The same kinds of errors may be studied from a cross-cultural perspective; the focus, however, is different within the Interlanguage pragmatics (ILP) approach, where the concern is on helping learners' progress through the developmental stages. Teachers, in particular, need to understand the domain of ILP to modify their teaching practices to facilitate pragmatic development.

The development of the field of second language acquisition (SLA) since the late 1960s has reflected the dominance of the structuralist and Chomskyan paradigms in linguistics. This has translated into an almost exclusive interest in studying usage, that is, the language learner's ability to employ the linguistic resources—phonological, lexical, and grammatical systems—according to the norms of the second language (Ellis 1994). Recently, however, more attention is being given to use, in other words, how learners understand and convey pragmatic meaning and achieve successful communication in their second language. Further, the focus has shifted from an emphasis on single sentences to an appreciation of language in the form of discourse or text, from utterances to academic essays. Since the early 1990s, in particular, the acquisition of pragmatic ability has found a place in SLA research.

This chapter first of all explains the aims of interlanguage pragmatics (ILP) and provide definitions of key terms. Then it considers possible causes of learners' difficulties in using and comprehending pragmatic meaning in a second language. In a third part, attention is given to pragmatic development; how can learners best be helped in classrooms to become more successful communicators in their second or foreign language?

Key Concepts in Interlanguage Pragmatics

Interlanguage pragmatics has been defined as "the study of nonnative speakers' use and acquisition of linguistic action patterns in a second language" (Kasper and Blum-Kulka 1993, 3). It is a second-generation, interdisciplinary field that draws on studies in SLA and pragmatics, both of which are interdisciplinary (Kasper and Blum-Kulka 1993, 3). The term *interlanguage* refers to an important construct within SLA first proposed by Selinker (1972) to explain the developing system of learners that is neither that of their L1 nor that of the L2. It is an intermediate, unstable and transient linguistic system that, according to the theory, continues to develop over time as the learners strive to attain nativelike proficiency. Blum-Kulka and Kasper's definition notes that the main focus of ILP has been on "linguistic action," in other words, speech acts and their enactment by learners. Indeed, the literature in ILP has been dominated by speech act realization studies. Nevertheless, increasingly attention has been directed toward a discourse perspective, which engages the researcher in the analysis of texts of natural language data to study such areas as conversational topics (Zuengler 1993), nonnative speaker responses in tutorials (see below), and the achievement of successful communication despite relatively low proficiency levels in the L2 (Aston 1993).

Specifically, ILP seeks to understand and explain what gets in the way of a learner's comprehending and producing pragmatic meaning. Much of the research has involved English, although recently that has begun to change. Studies have centered on such features as the following (Kasper and Blum-Kulka 1993, 4–7):

Attribution of illocutionary force
Perception of politeness and of indirectness
The role of linguistic form versus contextual information
The impact of the L1 background and of stereotypes of L2 language behavior
The processing of conventional and conversational implicatures
The perception of such sociopragmatic features as social status and weight of imposition

The research has demonstrated that the cognitive ability to infer implied or pragmatic meaning is not an issue, as it is a basic processing skill that can be transferred from L1 language contexts. The goal of ILP, by means of microanalysis of local instances of the enactment of social action, is to zero in on the factors that contribute to less than successful comprehension of pragmatic meaning.

Comprehension, needless to say, precedes production. Native speakers of Spanish cannot correctly produce a /b/ and not a /v/ in English, for example, unless they can first hear the differences between the two phonemes. In the same way, production of social action and the enactment of pragmatic meaning by learners to achieve their strategic, communicative goals is predicated on comprehension of the particular ways in which implied meanings are conveyed in a specific second or foreign language. For example, a learner of Japanese who needs to make some requests for information and help at a ward office of the city government in Japan will successfully and smoothly achieve that goal by having the knowledge that a negatively worded request is preferred to a positively worded request in Japanese:

> Pamfuletto o itadakemasen ka? [Don't you have a brochure I can have?]

In Mexican Spanish, use of the imperfect with *querer* with requests is preferred:

> Hola, quería unos billetes para ir a la Canarías. [Hello, I'd like some tickets to go to the Canaries.]
> (Chodorowska-Pilch 2000, 34)

Such requests pragmatically imply greater politeness.

ILP, then, is concerned with identifying the obstacles to learners' situationally appropriate production of pragmatic meaning. According to Kasper and Blum-Kulka (1993, 7), the main reasons for difficulty in enacting their pragmatic knowledge derives from either their "restricted L2 linguistic knowledge, or difficulty in assessing it smoothly." That is to say, learners, first of all, may have low proficiency in the L2 or may not be able to retrieve from their memories the linguistic forms and routines needed, automatically, with little delay. Still other possible factors are

> Transfer from the L1, or other languages the learner may know
> The influence of possible stages in interlanguage development
> Lack of adequate exposure to the second or foreign language use
> Inadequate or uninformed teaching
> A strong ethnolinguistic identity factor, precluding adoption of L2 pragmatic and cultural norms
> Motivation

These may continue to influence the pragmatic competence of even very fluent speakers of a second or foreign language. These six potential causes of pragmatic failure in learners' enactment of implied meaning are addressed in the next sections. Before turning to consideration of these six areas individually, a definition of pragmatic competence is in order.

Pragmatic Competence

The idea of competence derives originally from Chomsky's distinction between linguistic competence and performance. With competence defined as the mental representation of linguistic rules, which form the innate, internal grammar of the speaker-hearer, performance is the use of this grammar in both the comprehension and production of language. In 1972, Hymes, however, introduced the notion of communicative competence, which, he claimed, includes not only rules for correct language behavior, but also knowledge that enables speakers to use language to achieve their communicative goals. That is to say, Hymes's inclusive, functional definition of native speakers' competence in their L1 includes both linguistic and pragmatic knowledge.

Applied linguists built on Hymes's contribution; Canale and Swain (1980), Canale (1983), and Bachman (1989) have all attempted to specify in detail the components of communicative competence. Bachman's (1989) model (see chapter 1) explicitly lists pragmatic competence as a constituent, itself subdivided into sociolinguistic and illocutionary competence. The first, sociolinguistic component refers to "knowledge of the sociolinguistic conventions which govern appropriate language use in a particular culture and in varying situations in that culture" (1989, 252). The illocutionary force constituent comprises the knowledge of how speech acts or language functions are enacted in a particular culture.

Bachman's model has received its share of criticism; further thought is needed to develop a better model. However, the real source of controversy concerns the validity of including pragmatic competence within the category of competence. Despite Ellis's (1994) definition of pragmatic competence as being a form of "knowledge" and "therefore distinct from actual performance" just as linguistic knowledge is, SLA researchers who adhere to the formal linguistic, universal grammar approach to language analysis tend to reject the inclusion of pragmatics as a constituent component of the abstract, innate knowledge of language with which every child is born. Chomsky does recognize "pragmatic competence," which he defines as "a system of rules and principles" that determines how the grammar of a language "can effectively be put to use" (1980, 224). Hymes's notion of sociolinguistic competence, a constituent of communicative competence, is, however, much broader and inherently social, demonstrating the particularly social dimension of pragmatic competence (Taylor 1988) as the term is used within the field of pragmatics.

In the view of universal grammar scholars, pragmatics, associated with language use, cannot constitute part of the abstract grammar of the speaker-hearer. According to Taylor (1988), Hymes's represents a change in the meaning of the word *competence*. A full consideration of the most appropriate location of pragmatic competence is beyond the scope of this book (see Taylor 1988), but the lack of agreement is to be noted, with the controversy attributable to different research paradigms and views on the composition of language knowledge. This book adopts the view that pragmatic competence comprises a constituent of the knowledge base that underlies the ability to use language in situationally appropriate ways. In other words, pragmatic ability is part of the innate competence that is observed in actual performance, just as knowledge of linguistic rules is.

Pragmatic Transfer

An important distinguishing aspect of transfer in ILP needs to be emphasized. Chapter 11 dealt with cross-cultural pragmatics, comprising an implicit comparison of L1 and L2 pragmatic differences. This chapter presents a third dimension, the interlanguage of the learners. Following Kasper (1992, 207), ILP considers the L1, L2, and the developing, unstable language system of the learner, all three of which contribute to the learner's pragmatic knowledge, in addition to input from universal pragmatic knowledge. Analysis of performance data suggests insights into the composition of pragmatic knowledge. It must be constantly kept in mind that, as with attribution of errors in learner language in general, it is very difficult to state with certainty the source of a pragmatic error, as it is with grammatical error (see Dulay, Burt, and Krashen 1982, for example). Indeed, there is likely to be more than one factor.

Influence from the learner's first language and cultural background can have both positive and negative effects on performance in the second language. Positive transfer has not received the attention that the results of negative transfer have had, undoubtedly due to the fact that successful communication tends to go unnoticed and therefore unstudied. Moreover, there are difficulties in attributing positive transfer to the L1;

it may derive from a more general, universal pragmatic knowledge. Kasper and Schmidt (1996) report some pragmatic universals, such as the use of indirectness to convey pragmatic intent and the ability to vary linguistic action according to the context of utterance (Blum-Kulka 1991). Others are principles of conversational organization and attention to contextual factors, such as social power and social distance. Repetition with rising intonation is an example of a strategy of universal pragmatic transfer (Mori 1996, 56).

Teacher: so current education?
Student: current?
Teacher: current world is happening now, current education should be changed

Such repetition to ask for further information about a word occurs in L1 and L2 data.

As for positive transfer, where a linguistic form or routine or a communication strategy is used as part of a learner's IL with success, one example is question formation in such languages as Japanese and French. Unlike English, both French and Japanese can form interrogatives with morphemes:

French: **Est-ce-que** tu as bien mangé?
Japanese: Yoku tabemashita-**ka?**

In the case of French, the phrase must be put at the head of the utterance, with the reverse being the case for Japanese. Learners of French or Japanese whose L1 also uses such morphemes soon realize that these interrogative markers can be utilized any time they want to ask a question. This instance of positive transfer from their L1 gives the NNS of French or Japanese a constantly needed communicative strategy.

The literature on negative transfer is extensive (see Kasper 1992) and the same pragmalinguistic-sociopragmatic continuum has been used to explain the kinds of pragmatic failure experienced by learners. At the sociopragmatic end of the continuum, much of the research has examined the ability to assess the context of utterance in order to select the appropriate level of politeness to employ in enacting FTAs. Here is an example from Japanese-English learner language.

M: (1) You are leader . . . (2) discussion is what effects should be changed to make college life more successful, (3) so we must discuss about what should be changed.

(LoCastro 1996)

In the context of a group discussion, this student wanted to refocus the group on the task they had been asked to do. However, from the point of view of pragmatic norms in English in this context, the learner's comments were much too direct. "You are leader" is heavy criticism of the leader for not performing that role properly. The second utterance, citing a general rule, could be regarded as too direct in a situation where all the coparticipants are peers. The learner had not assessed the social context well enough to enact a more appropriate level of directness/indirectness.

The actual selection of the linguistic realization, such as cues to signal the illocutionary force, mitigation, and hedging, fall into the pragmalinguistic domain (Kasper 1992; Kasper and Blum-Kulka 1993). However, it is not only the linguistic action, but also communicative strategies, such as the frequent use of apologies in a Japanese learner's English interlanguage, that affect communicative success. Another example is questions in speech events. LoCastro (1990b), Green (1989), and Beebe and Takahashi (1989) all document the repetition of questions by Japanese in English to express disagreement. In the following instance, A is the director of an educational program, and he is conferring with two Japanese men who are staff of the cooperating Japanese organization in Tokyo; they are planning a graduation party for the first group to complete the program in Japan.

1. *A:* the reception we'd cover . . . uhm . . . yeah
2. *J2:* reception, no alcohol?
3. *A:* well . . . beer
4. *J2:* [*laughter*]
5. *J1:* [*laughter*] oh really?
6. *A:* not hard beer . . . right

(LoCastro 1990b)

This short segment of a much longer sequence illustrates the use of questions by both J1 and J2 to lead A to a decision about the reception, with the implied meaning that they are uncomfortable about A's view of what a reception should be, including what kind of beverages to serve. The pragmatic meaning is further conveyed by the laughter seen in lines 4 and 5. This indirect strategy is transferred from the L1 into the speaker's IL; it reflects the preference in Japan for avoidance of explicit, direct signals of disagreement in the L1 culture. However, due to the mismatch of this Japanese pragmatic norm with that of more direct signals of disagreement in (American) English, conversational partners may not comprehend the pragmatic meaning behind the questions.

Developmental Question

The second source of possible reasons for pragmatic failure derives from the notion of developmental stages in the learner's progress toward L2 pragmatic norms. The interlanguage construct itself, ignoring for a moment the question of pragmatic competence, is based on a developmental model. Morpheme acquisition studies (Clark and Clark 1977, 345, cited in Ellis 1994) demonstrated the existence of stages of increasing syntactic complexity through which a learner must pass to reach higher levels of proficiency in the L2. In addition, studies of first-language acquisition outline stages of development with regard to the acquisition of negative structures, question formation, and relative clauses. Researchers such as Pienemann, Johnston, and Brindley (1988) and Doughty (1991) claim on the basis of their work on second language learners that the developmental sequences are very similar to those of children acquiring the same language as their L1. Furthermore, the stages are similar across learners from different L1 backgrounds (Lightbown and Spada 1999), thus demonstrating that transfer may not be as strong an influence in early interlanguage development as are developmental sequences.

The existence of stages of interlanguage syntactic development supports predictions that stages are likely also to be present for pragmatic norms. Although Kasper and Schmidt (1996) state that so far no order of acquisition for ILP has been described, such as has been done for morphosyntax, Tanaka (1997a, 1997b) has found some evidence for an acquisition order in the acquisition of point of view and passive voice in Japanese as a second or foreign language.

While acknowledging that the research cited above to support the hypothesis of developmental stages has been mostly on linguistic behavior and not pragmatic competence, it is possible to argue that learners must reach a minimum level of L2 proficiency and knowledge to comprehend and produce appropriate pragmatic meaning in a language. Bialystok (1993, 47) attempts a theoretical account, comparing child and adult acquisition of "the social uses of language." Kasper and Schmidt (1996, 158) claim that pragmatic competence is "an area of communicative competence which is closely tied to cognitive ability and social experience" in any language, L1 or others.

Blum-Kulka (1991) describes three phrases of pragmatic competence development in learner language: (1) reliance on situational cues to interpret the illocutionary force and on simplification of strategies to produce pragmatically appropriate speech; (2) differentiation of alternative realizations and evidence of transfer from the L1; and (3) approximation of NS pragmatic norms, but continued display of transfer of "deep" cultural elements. Siegal (1994) and LoCastro (1998) claim, for example, that Anglo-American women find it difficult to learn the social appropriateness rules for female language in Japanese; the movement toward non-sexist language has influenced attitudes in the United States and Britain to the extent that language use that overtly seeks to maintain male-female roles is intolerable. Another example of a subsystem of English frequently employed to convey pragmatic meanings, modality seems to require a high level of proficiency for correct usage to be achieved. Kasper (1984) shows that modality reduction occurs in situations where the learners seem to be focusing on the propositional content of their utterances and not on such linguistic forms as modal verbs and adverbs, commonly used to show hesitation and possibility in English. In other words, automatic control in the use of modality to convey expected levels of politeness is not available to learners. Whether the explanation of this phenomenon is due to communicative pressure to respond or to a developmental stage, due to modality being a more cognitively demanding subsystem in the L2, remains to be addressed in actual empirical studies.

Exposure to Pragmatic Norms

One major question with reference to pragmatic competence development concerns the context of foreign language education: can the knowledge of pragmatic norms and the ability to utilize that knowledge in actual everyday production be developed in a foreign language setting with little or no exposure to the L2 language community? Bouton (1994, 157) studied the extent to which NNSs can use implicature in the L2 "with little or no instruction." Although conversational implicature seems to be a universal feature of human communication, Bouton (1994) found that approximately one-fifth (21 percent) of the time, reasonably proficient NNSs of English could not interpret implicatures in the same way as the NSs of American English. Bouton carried out a longitudinal study of two groups of international students at an American university, testing their ability to interpret implicatures at three times: on arrival in the United States, after eighteen months, and then after fifty-four months of residence. After eighteen months, the international students still had problems understanding implicatures involved in such instances as flouts of the relevance maxim. Here is an example from Bouton's questionnaire (1994, 163):

> Relevance Maxim: Bill and Peter have been good friends since they were children. They roomed together in college and traveled Europe together after graduation. Now friends have told Bill that they saw Peter dancing with Bill's wife while Bill was away.
> *Bill:* Peter knows how to be a really good friend.
> Which of the following best says what Bill means?
> (a) Peter is not acting the way a good friend should.
> (b) Peter and Bill's wife are becoming really good friends while Bill is away.
> (c) Peter is a good friend and so Bill can trust him.
> (d) Nothing should be allowed to interfere with their friendship.

Only half of the NNSs indicated (a) was the best choice, in comparison to 84 percent of the NSs. When the same task was set earlier, that is, on arrival, only 33 percent of the NNSs chose (a). Most of the NNSs chose (c) on both occasions, a response that indicates transfer from their different L1 sociocultural norms about marriage and friendship.

However, in general, after fifty-four months of residence, the NNSs had become proficient in interpreting the implicatures. This suggests that a long period of exposure to the L2 community is necessary. Hinkel (1996) found that, although residence in the L2 community enabled her informants to comprehend the implicatures, they did not necessarily produce with fluency the speech acts she studied.

The same phenomenon of the importance of residence in the target language community can be observed in the use of the indirect passive and perspective-taking in Japanese by students of the language residing in Japan in comparison with those studying the language in their L1 communities. Tanaka's longitudinal study demonstrates that some structures of Japanese, such as the giving and receiving verbs—*te-kureru* and *te-morau*—are only acquired during residence in Japan and that the ability to use them successfully disappears once her informants returned to their home environment. These verbs are sensitive to pragmatic variables such as the status of the person doing the giving and the receiving.

Inadequate or Uninformed Teaching

As more attention has been directed toward pragmatics in general within the context of SLA research in the last decade, the question of whether pragmatic competence can be taught has come to be of major interest in ILP. Conferences in the 1990s witnessed plenary speakers (Kasper 1997) and numerous presentations addressing this question, although it must be admitted the number of studies remains small. Both the effect of instruction in SLA and in foreign language acquisition (FLA) contexts and the kind of instruction (e.g., different teaching methods, explicit versus implicit teaching, deductive, inductive, versus zero instruction) have been examined (see Rose and Kasper 2001). The results are so varied as to make a summary problematic. One general pattern, however, is that some attention to pragmatic features is necessary for learning to take place (Schmidt 1993), whether the environment is a naturalistic or instructed setting. This statement is supported by the results of L1 pragmatic development studies that show that caregivers actively teach children rules of politeness and other situationally appropriate behavior (Schmidt 1993).

As was mentioned previously, exposure to the L2 community is necessary to acquire the pragmatic norms of that language in use (Bouton 1994; Tanaka 1997b); however, the development is slow (Bouton 1994). It can be argued that language educators must engage in the explicit instruction of pragmatic norms of the target language, raising learners' awareness and facilitating their noticing how implied meanings are conveyed. It is not possible to depend on adequate L2 exposure for the majority of learners in foreign language classrooms throughout the world for the rich input that is needed.

An unfortunate aspect of pragmatic instruction has been that teachers in their classrooms have attempted, usually on a case-by-case approach, to inform learners about situationally appropriate language use, often depending on teaching materials that are less than adequate. Despite efforts since the early 1970s in the teaching of language use (see, for example, Wilkins 1976 and van Ek 1975), textbooks and other teaching materials have been based on intuitions of native speakers and not on empirical studies of pragmatic norms and strategies for the signaling of pragmatic meaning. A couple of examples illustrate the type of input provided for classroom learners.

Abdullah: Gosh, you look great, Beverly! Have you lost weight?
Beverly: That's nice of you to notice—I've lost about 10 pounds, but I still need to lose another 5 or 6.

(Wall 1987, 191)

This is not the way people talk. Even in the United States, men do not compliment women unless they are close friends; in particular, comments on weight are usually inappropriate. Further, his name indicates that the man is probably a Muslim, and it is highly unlikely that a Muslim male would compliment a woman in such a way. Such contrived examples are less useful than talk that might actually occur.

Another example comes from a senior high school English textbook from Japan.

He hurried to San Francisco and went to a tailor. He showed the tailor his roll of canvas. "**I want you to** make a pair of pants out of this material," he said. "**Can you do that?**" "Yes, of course, " said the tailor. "And your name?" "Strauss. Levi Strauss." (See LoCastro 1997b)

Notes in the teacher's manual provide translations of *may/can/could/might,* with no comment about the use of modals to make requests. The phrase "I want you to . . . " is frequently used by Japanese learners to make requests instead of shifting to more polite forms, such as "I'd like to ask you to . . . " or "Could you please . . . " The example reinforces this tendency to transfer inappropriate patterns taught to learners.

A worldwide survey of textbooks would generate numerous examples of inadequate materials, which put teachers and learners at a disadvantage in pragmatic development, particularly in FLA settings. Researchers such as McCarthy and Carter (1994) have made efforts for more than a decade to raise awareness among language educators of the need to base materials and teaching practices on natural language data.

Loyalty to the First-Language Culture

Inadequate attempts to enact L2 pragmatic norms by learners may not indicate low pragmatic knowledge or fossilization of IL development. Rather, nonnative speakers may wish to maintain their L1 cultural identity. Researchers interested in intergroup relations have contributed to SLA research to account for the fact that accommodation and convergence to the pragmatic norms of the L2 may be regarded by learners as undesirable for a number of reasons, reflecting individual choices or societal pressures. One account of this phenomenon is called the ethnolinguistic identity model; the construct claims that less fluent second language proficiency may occur in speakers of the language who experience some threat to their ethnic identity due to societal and intergroup conditions (Taylor, Meynard, and Rheault 1977).

Although the ethnolinguistic identity model has been employed to explain primarily situations of interethnic contact, such as that found in Quebec, Germany, and Belgium, the same model can raise awareness that sociocultural influences may retard the development of native-speaker-like pragmatic norms of any learner of a second language. Members of speech communities that feel under threat are less likely to accommodate to the pragmatic norms of the second or foreign culture. Nonnative speakers may seek to maintain their ethnolinguistic identity owing to pressures from their L1 community, fearing disintegration in the face of hegemonic moves on the part of a dominant culture, such as that of English as the international language of communication. In addition, there is anecdotal evidence that maintaining a foreign "accent," whether phonological or pragmatic, allows the speaker to avoid heavy sanctions for pragmatic failure by being identified as a nonnative speaker. In the case of immigrants, maintenance of some features of their L1 identity may reflect deep conflicts regarding the uprooting and migration they experienced. Although complete convergence to the L2 norms is virtually unattainable if the acquisition or learning of the L2 began after the critical period at puberty, nonnative speakers may in any case seek consciously or subconsciously to distance themselves from the second or foreign language community for ideological and personal reasons.

Some examples of ethnolinguistic identity maintenance are (1) code switching, (2) maintenance of sociolinguistic markers in speech, such as "He don't know nothing" in the talk of Spanish speakers of English in American cities, and (3) unwillingness to use humbling, honorific forms by NNSs of Japanese whose L1 culture values more egalitarian language use.

Motivation

Closely associated with loyalty to the L1 culture is the issue of attitudes and motivation and the extent to which they play a role in ILP. Research on all forms of learning indicates that positive attitudes and high levels of motivation, along with aptitude, are significant in promoting learning (see Kasper and Schmidt 1996). It seems reasonable to predict that the same generalization would hold for ILP development and, in particular, the ability to use the pragmatic norms of the learned language.

The early studies of Gardner (1985) on second language motivation resulted in identification of what is called integrative motivation. Learners who desire to become members of the target language community had positive attitudes toward both the speakers and the language itself and were more likely to achieve high proficiency. It can be assumed that integrative motivation would correlate with rapid, successful pragmatic development. Other types of motivation have been suggested; however, none of the studies explicitly addresses the correlation of motivation, attitudes, and pragmatic development (Kasper and Schmidt 1996).

Another perspective on motivation can be found in some recent studies within the context of language socialization in the L2 community. Norton Peirce (1995) suggests that the notion of "investment" rather than motivation may be useful in analyzing the attitudes of immigrant women in the United States and Canada toward adopting the pragmatic norms for interactions in the new home environment. Siegal (1994) also prioritizes the social-affective dimensions in assessing pragmatic development, in this case, of American women acquiring Japanese in Japan.

As with most studies on attitudes and motivation, it seems intuitively correct to assume a strong correlation between positive attitudes and integrative motivation and language proficiency. The research has, nevertheless, not demonstrated that connection to lead to clear, confident conclusions (see LoCastro 2001). Much remains to be done, particularly with regard to pragmatic competence development.

Pragmatic Competence Development

What features cause even a fluent speaker of a second or foreign language to be viewed as "foreign"? Phonological cues and lack of total control over the prescriptive rules of grammar of the language are among the causes. Social appropriateness norms are influenced by transfer of the social norms of the first language (Blum-Kulka 1983). In addition, the linguistic realization strategies and procedures may be enacted differently, causing an unintended shift in illocutionary force. Studies of speech act realization by native and nonnative speakers of a language that violate the expectations would provide a firm foundation for cross-cultural communication. To make the matter even more complicated, we also need to take into consideration the role of other languages that a trilingual person may know. In this context, it is not only the language, but also the culture of the country in which the language is used. So called third-culture people can shift, for example, the degree of directness and indirectness in making requests according to the particular culture in which they happen to be functioning; their first-language culture may have become influenced due to residence abroad over a number of years.

Language learners feel a need to overcome these problems and become more pragmatically aware and capable in the context of language classrooms. It behooves teachers, materials designers, and evaluation and testing experts to understand better the question of pragmatic competence development. McCarthy and Carter (1994) emphasize the need for research on naturally occurring language to inform the work of materials and test writers. Native speakers' pragmatic norms are difficult to assess, however, because of sociolinguistic variation, the paucity of information available on adult development of pragmatic competence, and the difficulty of deciding among different norms (American? British? RP? Lower middle class?). As there are now more nonnative speakers of English in the world, for example, than native speakers, it is legitimate to question the wisdom of setting one particular variety as the standard for all speakers. Research of the sort just mentioned is indispensable, and yet Bouton's study, summarized above, indicates that more than exposure is necessary. Direct teaching, drawing learners' attention to linguistic forms and their functions in conveying pragmatic meaning, must become integrated into learning environments.

Can pragmatic competence be taught? Because it is "a type of knowledge that learners possess, develop, acquire, use or lose," Kasper argues that instruction can only hope to "arrange learning opportunities" so that competence can develop (1997). Some aspects of pragmatic knowledge are universal, but learners may not use the knowledge they possess. Moreover, advanced learners of an L2 may still have problems negotiating indirect responses and the corresponding implicature in an adjacency pair such as the following:

> *Sue:* How was your dinner last night?
> *Anne:* Well, the food was nicely presented.
>
> (Kasper 1997)

Consequently, Kasper argues, direct teaching has a role in helping learners overcome problems in comprehension and production (which speech act? which linguistic realization strategy?).

Once we acknowledge that direct teaching is necessary, how is it to be done? Tateyama et al. (1997) analyzed the value of explicit and implicit instruction in an exploratory, data-based study. They conclude that with a college student population explicit instruction is more effective; specifically, explicit awareness raising about language and communication in general is very important in comparison with instruction that just focuses on exposing learners to the L2 in communicative practice activities. Their study showed, furthermore, that communication practice in the form of role-plays and elicited conversations can be vital.

One possible approach to the actual classroom teaching of pragmatic ability is films. Rose (1993, 1994, 1997) has been developing corpuses of films in which instances of a particular speech act can be found (1996). For example, using Manes and Wolfson's (1981) corpus of compliment strategies in English, Rose has added a film corpus of compliments and an analysis of the common syntactic realizations (1997, 127, 143–44). To utilize films for instructional purposes in a language classroom, Rose suggests the following type of lesson for requests:

> Teach about the levels of directness with requests.
> View video clips, label the requests according to the levels of directness, and discuss the reasons the requests were made in a particular way.
> Discuss the importance of the social context.

Other activities that learners may engage in to promote their pragmatic ability are

> Study the scripts of films or plays
> Perform a play
> Work with critical incidences of miscommunication between members of different cultural groups
> Do ethnographic, natural observation outside the classroom
> Interview native informants

By means of direct, interventionist teaching such as exemplified above, awareness is developed and problems of understanding and producing pragmatic meaning are discussed. These lessons can be followed up with role-plays, which can be videotaped and then critiqued.

The less interventionist approach common to communicative language teaching, particularly in foreign language teaching environments, does not provide enough of the right kind of input for learners who do seek to become pragmatically proficient in the L2. Many are aware of the disadvantages of missing the pragmatic implicatures, and unpleasant or uncomfortable experiences can be demotivating.

Studies of Interlanguage Communication

This section presents two studies of Japanese students who faced situations in which their pragmatic competence in English was inadequate. They had demonstrated sufficient competence (say on a TOEFL or the Cambridge First Certificate) to be enrolled in content or writing courses; in other words, they were not in class to learn English. They were functioning in situations where the discussion concerned content.

The first study (Mori 1996) examined tutorials in which Japanese first-year university students discussed their essays in one-on-one conferences with teachers who were native speakers of English. The focus was on students' strategies to (1) signal nonunderstanding, (2) confirm information, or (3) request clarification. The talk between the teachers and learners was audiotaped and analyzed for the linguistic and nonlinguistic cues. The analysis highlighted how the learners enacted the three types of action in the context of the writing tutorial in the L2.

1. *S:* em I . . . my topic is m . . . recent education should change . . . should change
2. *T:* current, you mean education the way it is now? the way people are educated now in Japan should be changed?
3. *S:* yes
4. *T:* so current education
5. *S:* current?
6. *T:* current . . . world is happening now current education should be
7. *S:* oh, I see . . . changed the (method of) current education should be changed okay

(Mori 1996, 73)

The teacher assumed that the student was making a clarification request in line 5 by repeating the word "current" using rising intonation, implying that the word was unfamiliar. However, it is possible that the student was doing a confirmation check, that is, trying to make sure she had heard the word correctly. If this was the student's intent, then there was pragmatic failure in conveying her intended meaning. Here is another example:

1. *T:* all right so what are your important words in this sentence?
2. *S:* m . . . important?
3. *T:* Noriko, that's a question, in this sentence what are the important words? what are the key words?
4. *S:* ah!
5. *S:* key words a (*jaa*) democracy and critical mind
6. *T:* yeah yeah okay

(Mori 1996, 74)

In this case, the student's repetition of the word "important" in line 2 was also ambiguous for the teacher in that it may have been a confirmation check, which is the interpretation of the teacher, as seen in line 3, or an indication of nonunderstanding of what the teacher meant by "important words."

Another instance of ambiguity regarding the pragmatic meaning conveyed by the learner is as follows:

1. *T:* descriptive words? are talking about descriptive words?
2. *S:* description? no em . . .
3. *T:* detail? to give more detail?
4. *S:* detail? no
5. *T:* is that what you mean? Hirono? is that what you mean words that that give lots of detail?
6. *S:* ah, yes
7. *T:* ok, but show me . . .

(Mori 1996, 88)

In this exchange, the student seems to have given up attempting to convey her own intended meaning and just accepted the teacher's interpretation. However, because the student's response in line 6 is ambiguous in propositional content and in intonation, the teacher asks the student in line 7 to show in her essay what her concern is. The learner was apparently unable to pose questions to the teacher or to comprehend the pragmatic norms for a writing tutorial with a NS teacher.

Hiraga and Turner (1995, 1996a, 1996b; Turner and Hiraga 1996) have studied interactions of Japanese students in fine arts tutorials with professors in British academic settings. They have been interested in the differing perceptions of face in British and Japanese academic conferences and the related sociopragmatic failure on the part of Japanese students to elaborate when a British professor gives an elaboration-cueing prompt.

British tutor: What kind of music do you like best?
Japanese student: Minimalism
British tutor: I wonder what it is about minimalism that you like so much?
BT: em . . . this has a feeling . . . of em, er, techniques of Nihonga
JS: ah [*after a pause, the tutor went on to elaborate*]
(Turner and Hiraga 1996, 132)

These and other examples demonstrate a mismatch owing to the Japanese students' nonunderstanding of the implied meaning of the tutor's questions. The British tutor attempts to get the student to explain. The student, however, fails to do so; this possibly is due to the student's assumptions about what constitutes a pragmatically appropriate response in this type of interaction. The student and the teacher have different perceptions about expected language behavior in this setting.

In sum, had the learners been taught communication strategies for appropriate language use and been given opportunities to practice in social contexts, the discomfort that both teachers and learners experienced in these tutorials would have been lessened.

Conclusion

Interlanguage pragmatics is the field within pragmatics that is most relevant to L2 teachers. A well-developed knowledge of ILP can be invaluable for the teacher who wishes to make informed decisions on classroom practices, materials, preparation of exercises and tasks, and the use of multimedia such as videos to raise learners' awareness and support role-plays and simulations. Issues brought up in this chapter prepare teachers for what they are likely to confront and suggest the need to treat the learners with understanding and sensitivity. Imposition of

L2 norms may be counterproductive. Rather, the teacher must attempt to raise awareness, inform, instruct, and then let the learners make their own decisions as to how "nativelike" they become.

Discussion Questions

1. What is interlanguage pragmatics? What is included in analysis of language carried out from this perspective?

2. What is pragmatic transfer? Is it always negative? Give examples.

3. What kinds of problems does ILP address? What are the categories of analysis?

4. Discuss with classmates some reasons learners do not always adapt to the L2 pragmatic norms. Review what you learned in this chapter and then add examples drawing on your own experiences.

5. Discuss the differences between cross-cultural and interlanguage instances of miscommunication. Which type is more likely to cause problems of communication?

6. Generate instances of conversational implicature where misunderstanding occurred. Draw on your own experiences. If you were a teacher, how would you help your learners handle such problems of communication?

Text Analysis

1. Here are two examples of talk between a British tutor and British students. Compare and contrast them. Which one do you think the tutor is likely to give a high mark to? What are the reasons for your choice? (Hiraga and Turner 1996b).

    Tutor: Have you visited any art galleries recently?

    Student A: Yes, I went to see the X exhibition at the Y gallery. I'd seen a previous exhibition of her work about three years ago . . . and I wanted to see how it had changed. . . . It seems to have become more architectural. . . . The objects are much larger in scale, less like furniture and more to do with architectural space . . . , relating to the whole body being able to walk round, under, or through them. . . . It's quite an unexpected turn in her work to take . . . , much less predictable than it used to be, much richer than the previous formula.

Student B: Yes, I went to see the X exhibition at the Y gallery. It was very impressive. . . . The gallery also featured the Z as a special display of the month. . . . As I didn't have enough time . . . to go to both, I just saw the X, because it was what Prof. A recommended in class. . . . I would certainly like to go back there in one of the mornings next week when the gallery is relatively empty.

2. Now, provide a cross-cultural/interlanguage pragmatic analysis of this fine-arts tutorial with a British tutor and a Japanese art student. Justify every point you make by citing examples from the data (Hiraga and Turner 1996b, 102–3).

BT: Which is the best one?
JS: Mm, I can't say that because—
BT: Which is the worst one? . . . Are there any that are not here because they were no good?
JS: Just . . . these . . . [meaning "I have only done these"]
BT: They're not all of the same value.
JS: Yeah?
BT: Understand? . . . Mm, if we were to say, I'm going to ask you to choose four . . .
JS: Mm-m
BT: And I'm going to put eight of them on the fire. And save four . . . Which four would we keep?
JS: I cannot choose.
BT: Yes, you can. You must.
JS: Why do you know, why do you want to know that? Because . . .

BT: Because it will tell me something.
JS: Mm. It's a universe, they're part of the universe. I like to show . . . eh, construction—
BT: . . . But, but if you say, "because I made it, it therefore is OK—"
JS: Mm-m.
BT: You will never develop any . . . critique.

Suggested Readings

Bouton, L. F. 1994. Conversational implicature in a second language: Learned slowly when not deliberately taught. *Journal of Pragmatics* 22:157–67.

Kasper, G. 1989. Variation in interlanguage speech act realisation. In *Variation in second language acquisition,* ed. S. Gass, C. Madden, D. Preston, and L. Selinker. Clevedon, U.K.: Multilingual Matters.

———. 1995. Interlanguage pragmatics. In *Handbook of pragmatics,* ed. J. Verschueren, J. O. Ostman, and J. Blommaert. Amsterdam: John Benjamins.

———. 1997. Can pragmatic competence be taught? <http://www.lll.hawaii.edu/NFLRC/Network/N.>

Kasper, G., and S. Blum-Kulka, eds. 1993. *Interlanguage pragmatics.* Oxford: Oxford University Press.

Rose, K. 1993. Sociolinguistic consciousness-raising through video. *Language Teacher* 17, no. 10: 7–8.

———. 1994. Pragmatic consciousness-raising in an EFL context. *Pragmatics and Language Learning,* monograph series, 5:52–63.

Tateyama, Y., G. Kasper, L. P. Mui, H. M. Tay, and O. O. Thananart. 1997. Explicit and implicit teaching of pragmatic routines. *Pragmatics and Language Learning,* monograph series, 8:163–72.

Chapter 13
Politeness Revisited

Chapter 6 presented Brown and Levinson's theory of linguistic politeness, face, and indirectness, and introduced the universal value in interactions of the face needs of participants. However, several researchers, influenced by sociocultural beliefs and practices outside Anglo-American traditions, have challenged Brown and Levinson's theory on the basis of cross-cultural variations in the interpretation of linguistic politeness. Researchers have also pointed out that politeness comprises nonlinguistic forms and is enacted in written discourse as well.

Yet another reason for revisiting politeness is its importance in L2 teaching and learning. Second language learners experience great difficulty in acquiring formulaic routines so that they can present themselves in situationally appropriate ways. Most learners seek to be polite in the L2 or to be impolite, when necessary, in appropriate ways. In this chapter politeness gets a closer look from the point of view of L2 learners. The following sections discuss cross-cultural challenges to politeness theory, politeness in writing, and nonlinguistic forms of behavior that signal attention to the face needs of the interactional partners. First, however, a brief review of face and politeness is offered.

Review of Face and Politeness

Put simply, politeness has to do with the addressee's expectations that the speaker will engage in situationally appropriate behavior. That is, the addressee judges whether an action has been enacted as it should according to the relevant sociocultural norms. An example is the expectation in English that "please" accompany requests. Concern for the manner in which the force of a speech act is conveyed reflects mutual attention to the face needs of interactional partners. Each person in an interaction seeks to preserve his or her own face while showing consideration for the needs of conversational partners. Ignoring face needs can lead to misinterpretation of the speaker's communicative intent. The speaker is viewed as rude, aggressive, or overly friendly; cultural stereotypes may be created or reinforced. In other words, the intended implicatures may not be read as polite by the interactional partners in cross-linguistic situations.

Fraser (1990) provides an overview of the four main approaches to politeness among researchers. As most writers do not explicitly define "politeness," it is a difficult concept to discuss. The first perspective is the social-norm view, which is based on norms, sometimes described at length in etiquette manuals, held by a society about ways of talking, behaving, and even thinking. In this view, politeness correlates with formality. The second perspective, the conversational-maxim view, has developed out of Grice's Cooperative Principle and maxims. They function as constraints on language behavior; flouting them signals speakers' intentions through conversational implicatures. A rational analysis would cause the hearer to arrive at the conversational implicature that a speaker, making a request indirectly, was doing so to avoid offense, thus, to be polite.

The third view is face-saving, derived from Brown and Levinson's model of politeness, which is itself based on Grice (1975) and Goffman's (1967) notion of face. The underlying concept is that politeness strategies—negative and positive—are used to soften the potential face threat to the hearer, speaker, or both, of certain acts occurring in interactions (see chapter 6). The final and fourth perspective is called the conversational contract view. The main point that distinguishes this approach from the others is that the rights and obligations of speaker and hearer are negotiated anew for each interaction, based on a variety of factors such as a history of previous encounters, participants' perceptions of status, power, and roles, and other features of the context of situation. Fraser (1990, 233) states that "being polite constitutes operating with . . . the (usually tacit) understanding of our current conversational contract (CC) at every turn."

This latter view reflects Boyle's (2000) claim that preference organization (see chapter 8) can only be understood in a particular context;

in other words, what is a preferred response in one case may not be so in another. It is similar with regard to politeness, according to Fraser. While acknowledging the important role of conventions, assigning a polite interpretation to some example of linguistic behavior may depend very much on contextually negotiated factors.

The next section examines the possibility that, despite Brown and Levinson's claim that their theory is universal, there may be cross-cultural differences in the purposes and interpretation of politeness phenomena.

Cross-Cultural Challenges

The feature of Brown and Levinson's theory of politeness that provokes most criticism involves their view that speakers and hearers can make decisions about politeness as individuals, and not as members of a family, social class, company, or age cohort. Researchers who prioritize membership rather than the individual claim that people from collectivist backgrounds are always aware of their relative social position. Moreover, their choice of situationally appropriate language signals their social position.

Matsumoto attacks the concept of negative face, understood as the individual's desire to be unimpeded in his or her actions, using the Japanese culture as a counterexample.

> The concept of individual territory is not indigenous to Japanese. . . . What is of paramount concern to a Japanese is not his/her own territory, but the position in relation to others in the group and his/her acceptance by those others. Loss of face is associated with the perception of others that one has not comprehended and acknowledged the structure and hierarchy of the group. The Japanese concepts of face, then, are qualitatively different from those defined as universals by Brown and Levinson. (Matsumoto 1988, 405)

Also challenging Brown and Levinson from a cross-cultural perspective is Gu (1990, 241–42), who assesses negative face in Chinese society:

Offering, inviting, and promising in Chinese, under ordinary circumstances, will not be considered as threatening [the addressee's] negative face, i.e. impeding [the addressee's] freedom. . . . The Chinese negative face is not threatened in [these cases]. Rather, it is threatened when what self has done is likely to incur ill fame or reputation.

Further, some scholars argue that Brown and Levinson's model of factors affecting linguistic choices is simplistic; relative power, social distance, and weight or rank of imposition, as composite categories, do not capture all possible variables. Social distance, for example, may include familiarity and positive or negative attitudes toward each other. Consequently, an insult in one context may be a compliment among close friends.

A: what did you do to your hair?!!
B: oh, just experimenting—wanted to see if dyeing my hair would make me look younger

This example demonstrates the multifunctionality of utterances (is A complimenting, making fun of, or just being friendly?) in general and of the difficulty of assigning one meaning.

Other factors that must be considered are the presence of an audience and social status and hierarchical factors in a culture (Turner 1996). If a third coparticipant or overhearer is present, a speaker's intention may be to use politeness so as to increase any positive value attached to the speaker by the third person, that is, to be regarded in as positive a light as possible rather than to attend to the face needs of the perceived addressee. It is also possible to argue that, in the case of relatively static social structures or hierarchies, such as the caste system in India, politeness used by members of lower castes toward members of the higher caste is a fossilized enactment of the social structure, reflecting their disenfranchised status. It is interesting to note that linguistic politeness tends to be denigrated in societies undergoing revolutionary transformations of the social structure, as in *comrade* as a form of address in Communist countries.

Another criticism of Brown and Levinson has to do with the absence from their model of politeness strategies of means to maintain social equilibrium. Gu comments that politeness can be the glue of predictable normalcy:

> Politeness is not just instrumental. It is also normative. . . . A society, to be sure, consists of individuals, but it is more than a total sum of its individual constituents. Politeness is a phenomenon belonging to the level of society, which endorses its normative constraints on each individual. (1990, 241–42)

Thus, Brown and Levinson's means-ends reasoning, where individuals are regarded as rational evaluators of the costs and benefits of a particular linguistic action to achieve their strategic goals, projects a view of human behavior as "qualitatively different" from that of other cultures, according to Matsumoto (1988, 405). Although the need for mutual face consideration is universal, cross-cultural differences force a reassessment of all current approaches to politeness.

The Universal Basis of Politeness

Goffman's (1963) studied how a society seeks to maintain normalcy out of fear of chaos, an avoidance of uncertainty and of anyone or anything that might lead to instability. This universal sense of danger is reflected in both linguistic and nonlinguistic avoidance behavior. Politeness in Japanese illustrates the connection. Niyekawa (1991) explains that the *keigo* or honorific system is based on two dimensions. First of all, when a speaker must decide on the appropriate level of speech, s/he considers whether the addressee is a member of the same group. The in-group is labeled *uchi* (literally "house"), and out-group members are called *soto* ("outside"). If the coparticipant is *uchi,* then the second dimension, namely hierarchy, is the basis for interaction. If not, then hierarchy is not invoked and either nonpolite or minimal polite language is used reciprocally. The following list reflects several aspects of politeness in Japanese.

> Group membership as a determining factor
> Provision for acknowledgment of familiarity, affect

Recognition of the need to be most concerned about the face needs of others one is most likely to have dealings with

Avoidance of all but impersonal contact with people outside one's group

Use of politeness as a normative constraint on social behavior and societal structures.

Use of language to reflect societal structures and to proactively create them

Social interactions with others are viewed as inherently problematic, and the system of politeness has developed to handle this basic human concern. It can be argued that individual cultures make salient one or more of the universal characteristics listed above. Thus, while there are commonalities across cultures, politeness systems may differ from one another.

The next section continues to highlight cross-cultural differences in the enactment of politeness, specifically with regard to written texts.

Politeness in Writing

Another area that raises awareness of cross-cultural differences is strategies in writing. Forms of politeness in business letters are common knowledge, but all forms and styles of writing involve attention to the face needs of the reader. An interest in academic essay or expository writing has developed over the last two decades as a result of the increasing number of L2 learners who have left their countries to pursue undergraduate and graduate education, typically in North America, the United Kingdom, and Australia. What at first seemed an easy task, to provide study skills courses for this student population, soon led to the realization that empirical studies were needed to understand what academic writing is from a cross-cultural perspective. Some recent studies have focused on politeness. A writer of a scientific research article in any language does not state claims or counterclaims directly. FTAs are an issue in this context as well.

How does an extended written text present information in accord with norms of politeness? Commonly there are two styles of information structuring or flow: inductive and deductive. With the inductive style, the supporting arguments or reasons come first, followed by the main point; in the deductive style the main point is introduced at the beginning before stating reasons or supporting evidence. A number of researchers claim that the deductive pattern is preferred by writers influenced by Western rhetorical practices, while the inductive or delayed introduction of the main topic is more likely to be used by Asians. Consider the following two letters (the first one is from Kirkpatrick 1991 [189] and has been edited).

Miss ___,
How are you? . . . I heard Radio Australia's Cantonese programs. I really liked them! *Because* I, the lover of Cantonese and Cantonese songs . . . Now I listen to your program every day and my Cantonese has greatly improved. . . . [I] feel great affection for Radio Australia. . . . I shall always remember that at 11800 kilohertz, I have a good friend. . . . Here, I want for my good friend . . . a Li Keqin song. . . . *Also* heartfelt wishes for happiness to all listeners of Radio Australia! In addition, I would like to ask for a program schedule for Radio Australia's Cantonese programs. . . .
Wishing you happiness at work,
Loyal Listener ___

Dear ___ School:
I would like to congratulate you on your ninetieth anniversary of your fine school's existence. I know that you have been a great help to the many Americans in Japan.
I would like to wish you many continued years of excellence in education. Please let me know if my staff or I can ever be of any assistance to your fine school.
Sincerely

The first letter, written in the L2 of a Chinese young adult, demonstrates the inductive style, in that the main point, a request for the program schedule, is delayed to the end. The writer of the second one states in the first sentence the reason for the letter, exemplifying the deductive style. The text of the letter indicates the author was most likely an American using his or her L1.

A study of the inductive and deductive patterns used by Chinese students demonstrates factors that affect the choice of style. Scollon and Scollon (1995) note that Chinese university students tend to use the deductive pattern in two contexts: *(a)* when they interact with their peers and *(b)* in transactional contexts, such as when purchasing something or using a taxi, thus in service or "outside" encounters. These situations contrast with "inside" contact situations that require more sensitivity to interpersonal dimensions, such as with people at one's place of work with whom one expects to have an ongoing relationship (see Wolfson 1986 on "bulge" theory). Scollon and Scollon further claim that Confucian influences on student-teacher relations are still present in contemporary Hong Kong and China. Consequently, a student, low in the university hierarchy, is not in a position to introduce a topic, entailing the inductive pattern in writing essays. In other words, the student is expected to acknowledge social positions, humbling him- or herself and showing restraint through discursive mitigation in the form of introducing a topic only after providing reasons and evidence.

Western use of the inductive pattern provides further support for the claim that delayed introduction of the topic is a form of negative politeness. The inductive structure can be found in instances where a Westerner is hesitant to broach a difficult topic such as borrowing a large sum of money or giving embarrassing information (Scollon and Scollon 1995). Topic introduction is delayed to buy time to feel out the mood or opinions of the others.

Rather than attribute the inductive and deductive rhetorical strategies to cultural differences per se, it is more appropriate to consider them first as reflecting assessment of *(a)* the particular situation, *(b)* the relationship between the participants, and *(c)* the sensitivity of the topic. Second, the preference of a specific culture for signaling social position and concern for face needs is taken into consideration. Note that this decision making is applied to both spoken and written discourse; the two styles have been conventionalized in written texts. The deductive rhetorical strategy, for example, has been preferred in the Western tradition, implying an absence of an explicit, hierarchical differential between the writer and the presumed audience, as the following features demonstrate; this excerpt comes from a textbook on English as an L2 academic writing.

1. The thesis statement that contains the main point of the essay is stated at the beginning, often in the first sentence/paragraph.
2. Each section has the main point at the beginning.
3. Each paragraph has a topic sentence, usually the first one.

The increase in the use of nuclear power should be stopped. Nuclear power stations are extremely dangerous. In 1979 a station in the USA went out of control and thousands had to leave their homes. The waste from nuclear power stations can be dangerous to man for thousands of years. Nuclear stations are unnecessary. The demand for electricity in the West is increasing very slowly and can be met by existing stations. If extra power is needed, it should be provided by wind or tidal power stations. They are safe and there is no danger of pollution. For these reasons all work on nuclear power stations must be halted immediately. (Glendinning and Mantell 1983, 103)

These rhetorical conventions have developed over time to signal attention to the mutual face needs of the writer and the reader. Politeness analysis illustrates that what might be regarded solely as historical remnants of styles of writing are rather features that work together to accommodate the writer's desire to be well received while making points the writer wishes to communicate, and the reader's to avoid unpleasant behavior and to be regarded as worthy of consideration.

Nonlinguistic Politeness

With the views of researchers such as Matsumoto and Gu in mind, one can argue that politeness may signal position in a hierarchy or a group and have normative aims. Opening up the definition of politeness leads to an acknowledgment that it is also appropriate to examine the role of nonlinguistic behaviors as signals that intend to communicate mutual attention to face needs, often co-occurring with language. "Linguistic" politeness refers to the forms themselves, functioning as signals of attention to the face needs of the speaker and of the conversational partners. For example, the following sentences will have different effects on the addressee:

> I want you to write a recommendation letter for me.
> I'd like to ask you to write a recommendation letter for me.

While the first one communicates the speaker's intention directly, the second is characterized by a modal, "I would like . . . ," which mitigates the force of the FTA for the addressee. It would thus be the preferred enactment of the speech act of requesting to a professor or in general to anyone who is the position of writing a reference letter for a student.

Nonlinguistic politeness transcends specific, formal items and conveys politeness at a more general level of communicative purposes. A speaker is concerned with the addressee's needs and feelings, but also seeks to maintain his or her own face needs by communicating an identity of cooperativeness, considerateness, and, importantly, social desirability.

Nonlinguistic politeness, it has been argued, is not within the purview of linguistic inquiry. Yet at the folk linguistic level, the average member of the public in any part of the world is very much aware of politeness or what is called etiquette, with regard to such behaviors as using a fork and knife, blowing one's nose in public, or showing a willingness to engage in conversation at a party.

Two further reasons can be cited in favor of this broader view of politeness phenomena. Researchers in communication forcefully claim that the nonverbal features are more important than the verbal in most instances of interactions (Birdwhistell 1965). Further, cross-cultural considerations need to be addressed; there may be various historical and societal forces that have resulted in Western researchers factoring out nonlinguistic politeness. Other parts of the contemporary world, as shall be demonstrated in the examples below, may attend more to the implied, pragmatic meanings conveyed by social actors through nonverbal means. From a research point of view, the language used in giving a gift may appear to be the most salient feature, and it is that part of the joint activity which is easily tape recorded, transcribed, and analyzed. However, from an ethnographic perspective, gift giving in Japan, Thailand,

and Indonesia involves as well body movements, the giver versus the receiver as beneficiary, and the wrapping or lack of wrapping of the gift itself, all of which enter into the assessment of politeness. The next section examines some examples from a variety of cultures.

Greetings

A greeting may be no more than a word or phrase uttered to an acquaintance or upon meeting a person for the first time. However, greetings may be much more elaborate; at formal events in Japan, the higher status individual will do the *aisatsu,* a greeting that may continue for several minutes followed by short speeches by guests before a toast, a *kampai,* all part of the "greeting" before the formal party or event can start. In sub-Saharan Africa, a greeting may involve many nonlinguistic features.

> You cannot walk past people who are eating without wishing them "good appetite." That would be very rude. And they will immediately invite you to eat with them. Twenty times a week, I go through this ritual, with colleagues taking their midday meal . . . or with Old Brother's farm workers at the gate. Sometimes I am hailed by Old Brother himself, taking a late breakfast in the shade of a mango tree. In the case of Old Brother, who is a very dominant person and head of our "Family," it is impossible to refuse. So I walk across to the mango tree, and take a seat for two minutes. While I sip tea, I listen to his advice. . . . Having fulfilled my obligations of politeness, I then ask permission to "take to the road." (Lacville 1991, 19)

Were the author of this account to omit this ceremonious greeting, sociocultural norms would be violated; his position as a respected person would be jeopardized.

High-Pitched Voices

A high-pitched voice, accompanied by a fixed, stylized smile, conventionalized hand movements, an erect posture, and situationally appropriate clothing and hairstyle are all part of polite behaviors for women in Japan. This sociolinguistic phenomenon is easily observed in department stores and other business enterprises in Tokyo, and recent studies support this anecdotal evidence: "If you're being courteous, your voice naturally rises" (Kristoff 1995). In some circumstances, female singers of popular songs and female newsreaders are following a trend toward lower voices. In informal settings, women's natural voices are used. Nevertheless, in offices, stores, and restaurants, the high-pitched voice is still considered a marker of politeness.

Indebtedness

As a cultural practice, acknowledging indebtedness can constitute a positive politeness strategy (Fujikawa 1997). The intended meaning of this behavior goes beyond the pragmatic meaning of the linguistic forms employed. It enacts a higher order of politeness by conveying attention to position in the social hierarchy as well as enactment of the normative function. The following is an example of a conversational routine regularly enacted in social contexts in Japan (e.g., when a wife, by chance, meets the addressee, a colleague of her husband, on campus; this greeting also is used at formal receptions).

> Shujin o doozo yoroshiku oneigaishimasu. [I ask you to please take care of my husband; literally, "My husband please take care."]

In this instance a wife wishes to convey concern for her family by identifying herself with her family, and it is that "group" that she wishes will benefit from the relationship with the addressee, not just her husband (Fujikawa 1997). In humbling herself before the addressee, she is engaging in deferential behavior. By doing so, she preserves her own face, as ignoring her lower social status would be regarded as arrogant. However, as a request, the speech act is an imposition on the addressee, who, as a result of having a higher social position, is expected to take care of people of lower rank. Rather than a burden, this responsibility is welcomed; only due to high social status can an individual acquire this "imposition." Consequently, the deference of the wife appeals to the positive face of the addressee and is thus a positive politeness strategy (Fujikawa 1997).

Principle of Greater Effort

Hudson (1996) suggests that such utterances as "We *do* apologize for the late arrival of this train," in train stations in Britain are motivated by politeness. Brown and Levinson (1987, 93–94) indicate that extra effort by a speaker is more polite. The emphatic stress, even in contexts where no explicit comparison is being conveyed by the speaker (e.g., "I *do* have a hard copy . . . "), is something "extra," presumably to attend to the face needs of the addressee. This grammaticalization of stress works on such words as the verb *to be,* auxiliary verbs and prepositions in English. A main verb cannot take this marking.

> Our first topic *is* the crisis in X.
> Now we *go* to a newsmaker interview with X.

The first can be heard on newscasts, while the second is anomalous (Hudson 1996). Of the following two possible sentences, a bank manager would likely write sentence 1, not sentence 2.

1. I am writing to inform you that your account is overdrawn.
2. Your account is overdrawn.

The first sentence requires greater effort to produce than the second. The same principle can be seen in the Japanese politeness system, as longer utterances are correlated with greater politeness. Here are some examples of requests from the Japanese data (Hill et al. 1986, 355).

Least polite	aru	[A pen.]
	kaeiteii	[Let me borrow a pen.]
	kaeitemoraemasenka	[Do you mind if . . .]
Most polite	okarisitemoyoroshiidesyooka	[Would it be possible . . .]

There is a direct correlation between length of utterance and the level of politeness. The same correlation may not be found in all sociolinguistic contexts.

Nonverbal Elements in Routines in Indonesia

Margaret Dufon (1999) has been studying nonverbal behaviors that are considered to implicate politeness, from an ethnographic, insider perspective of Indonesian cultural practices. Her data—journal entries, group discussions, and interviews—come from accounts of American and Japanese learners of Bahasa Indonesian during yearlong home stays in Indonesia and her own participant observation periods of residence. From the data can be drawn descriptions regarding the following themes: (1) gift giving, (2) accompanying the guest, (3) touring the house, (4) using the right hand, and (5) greeting. There are linguistic elements accompanying nonverbal behaviors.

For example, gifts are to be given in specific circumstances, such as when arriving for a stay at someone's house, or when returning from a trip, in particular abroad. Related issues are whether or not the gift itself is wrapped or unwrapped, opened in front of the giver, and commented on by the receiver. As for the meaning of the gift, it is viewed as an expression of appreciation by the giver, thus focusing on the person giving the gift, not the receiver.

The five thematic areas listed above all involve social rules of politeness in Indonesian culture. In each case, pragmatic meanings are conveyed, all motivated by giving face to interactional participants. Furthermore, the social actor is seen as concerned about being viewed as an acceptable member of the society, even if sacrifice is involved.

As meaning is "at the heart of all communicative acts" (Clark 1996, 125), all signals used to communicate meaning require attention. Many signals are linguistic—for example, a verbalized greeting—but many are not: the waving of a hand can also be a greeting.

> It isn't signals that are linguistic or non-linguistic. . . . Most signals are composite signals. . . . Some might conclude that the nonlinguistic methods are crude, unsystematic, ad hoc, and marginal, and deserve to be relegated to the periphery of language use. . . . On the contrary, the nonlinguistic methods are subtle, highly systematic, and not at all ad hoc. . . . Ignoring nonlinguistic methods has distorted people's picture of language use, and it is important to put that picture right. (Clark 1996, 156)

Clark's approach includes pragmatic meaning, where the "signal" may be the giving of a gift, how the gift is received, and the giver's or the receiver's needs have priority.

Conclusion

The enactment of politeness according to the norms of an individual's L1 sociocultural values is both acquired and learned. It is acquired, out of awareness, during the socialization process in the context of the family, school, and other institutions of the society over a period of two decades. It is also learned: parents, teachers, and other adults may actually instruct children and adolescents about what to say or do in which circumstances. Etiquette books and seminars teach how to be "polite" both linguistically and nonlinguistically (see Cameron 1995).

The same process has to take place for L2 learners. However, the process cannot be the same, particularly in a foreign language learning environment. Most L2 learners in the world do not have a target language community in which to become socialized into the L2 politeness system. Moreover, their teachers, even if a NS of the L2, are not always well prepared to enter into the nitty-gritty of linguistic politeness (see chapter 15). The complexity can be overwhelming. However, awareness on the part of the teachers is the starting point in giving learners some ground on which to build further their L2 pragmatic competence.

Discussion Questions

1. Generate and discuss examples of nonlinguistic politeness from different cultural groups that you know about.

2. Find examples in the letters to the editor in a local newspaper and discuss to what extent the writers use linguistic politeness. Also discuss the information structures in the letters.

3. Rearrange the following in order of politeness. Start with the least polite. Be prepared to explain the reasons for the order you chose.

Pass me the salsa.
Could you please pass me the salsa?
Can you pass the salsa? I need it.
Please pass me the salsa.
Are you finished with the salsa?

4. Some children are making too much noise at a birthday party. One mother tries twice to get her son to be quieter. She calls him "Ben." Then a third time, she says: "Benjamin, please!" Is she being polite the third time? Discuss.

5. Collect some examples of linguistic politeness from segments of a video. Compare and contrast, for example, the talk of young people with the talk of older people, or the talk in formal and informal contexts. Research has shown a developmental sequence in politeness. Most young people do not begin to use formal language correctly until their late teens. Do you find any evidence of this? Discuss.

6. This time, view a film from another culture and select a segment that demonstrates a different view of politeness from what you are accustomed to with your family, friends, colleagues from work, or classmates.

Text Analysis

In a well-known study, Fiksdal (1988) studied rapport-building and rapport-maintaining strategies as forms of linguistic politeness. Such forms of politeness are included in Brown and Levinson's model. In the interview data Fiksdal collected, a foreign student advisor was interacting with both native and nonnative English speakers who were foreign students at an American university.

Study the examples below (from Fiksdal 1988, 8–9) and underline the rapport strategies. Suggest as detailed an analysis as you can of the purpose of the strategies you observe.

Example 1
1. *S:* . . . and they then started on the tack that I was—
2. because I was staying with my girlfriend I'd been
3. living in the country
4. *A:* right right
5. *S:* but it went *that* way and . . .

Example 2
1. *A:* he went home for Christmas and when you're talking
2. to a student *that* age about getting a bachelor's degree
3. in something as y'know as common as phys ed you
4. don't think about what—telling them what to say at
5. a—at a visa office

Example 3
1. *A:* simply say that you—you know that you have a chance
2. to take a job in Panama. doesn't make any difference
3. to them
4. *S:* yeah
5. *A:* um and that you're coming back through you're gonna
6. complete the visit you didn't get a chance to
7. complete before
8. *S:* ok (silent laugh)
9. *A:* y'know you can make up almost any story

Suggested Readings

Boyle, R. 2000. Whatever happened to preference organization? *Journal of Pragmatics* 32:583–604.

Fiksdal, S. 1988. Verbal and nonverbal strategies of rapport in cross-cultural interviews. *Linguistics and Education* 1:3–17.

Fraser, B. 1990. Perspectives on politeness. *Journal of Pragmatics* 14:219–36.

Gu, Y. 1990. Politeness phenomena in Modern Chinese. *Journal of Pragmatics* 14:237–57.

Matsumoto, Y. 1988. Reexamination of the universality of face: Politeness phenomena in Japanese. *Journal of Pragmatics* 12:403–26.

Wolfson, N. 1986. Research methodology and the question of validity. *TESOL Quarterly* 20, no. 4: 689–99.

Chapter 14
Learner Subjectivity

The notion of learner subjectivity is grounded in language socialization theory (Schieffelin and Ochs 1986). It has become an important topic within pragmatics, particularly with regard to ILP development, as it has explanatory value concerning L2 learners' acquisition in a sociocultural context. Further, it introduces the important dimensions of learners' beliefs, values, and identity construction and how those factors influence pragmatic development.

Socialization, a concept from sociology, is the process through which children learn how to be members of their family, society, and culture. The social interactions in which they participate are the environments where they internalize and perform the behaviors common to the older members of their society. Children's cognitive, social, and linguistic development occurs in their sociocultural environment. However, children are not passive participants; they may in fact socialize adults in their family into living with teenagers or the use of electronic media, for example (Schieffelin and Ochs 1986).

In particular, language socialization, an important factor in children's cognitive development, means "both socialization through language and socialization in the use of language" (Schieffelin and Ochs 1986, 2). In other words, children learn about their sociocultural context through language-mediated interactions. At the same time, children learn how to use language to mean, to carry out social action, and to articulate their own social identity. Language is both the tool for conveying sociocultural content and the medium for signaling attitudes, politeness, their own worldview (Schieffelin and Ochs 1986).

This theoretical framework can be adopted to study the language development of second or foreign language learners. Since carrying out social action in an L2 involves the ability to comprehend and produce pragmatic meaning, the learner ideally needs to undergo language socialization for the L2 community. It is through target language interactions that the learner acquires comprehensible input, not only grammatical and lexical, but also input on how to enact speech acts, carry out redressive action, and show deference, all successfully for the L2 target community. In the process, the learners create an identity for themselves in the L2.

The language socialization perspective, which focuses on first-language development, often in non-Western contexts (see the Schieffelin and Ochs 1986, collection), dovetails with the work of Vygotsky and of other Soviet developmental psychologists. The two strands of thought emphasize the role of language as the most important tool for cognitive and social development of children. The Vygotskian perspective (Vygotsky 1962) has been introduced into the domain of SLA, labeled "sociocultural theory," by in particular Lantolf and his colleagues (Lantolf 1994, 2000; Lantolf and Appel 1994). The next section surveys some of the basic notions of sociocultural theory; the overview of Vygotsky's work draws on the work of Moll (1990) and Mitchell and Myles (1998). Then this chapter focuses on one aspect, that is, how learners create and enact their social identities in the L2.

Vygotsky

Although Vygotsky lived from 1896 to 1934 in Russia—one of the three influential members, with Luria and Leontiev, of the Soviet sociohistorical school of psychology—his work did not receive due attention in the U.S. educational system or second language acquisition research until the 1980s. As more and more of his writings became available in English, the importance of Vygotsky's work, anchored in cognitive psychology, to education evolved, especially with teachers and specialists involved with children who were blind, deaf, or otherwise in difficult circumstances. In particular, Vygotsky's emphasis on the social context of thinking and learning struck a cord with scholars engaged in the theoretical support for educational change. An educational system is, after all, the primary locus of socialization (after the family) in any sociocultural system. If it can be understood how new forms of thinking facilitate the development of an individual's potential within the social context of a school, then perhaps new approaches to fostering literacy, achievement, and equity are possible.

Vygotsky's theories and concepts also intrigued colleagues in the West as his approach was inherently "critical." He questioned what were the "received" views within psychology during the 1920s and 1930s and worked to develop a more "holistic" view of human cognitive development.

What is perhaps the most central concept of Vygotsky's thinking plays an important role in sociocultural theory and SLA. The concept is the "zone of proximal development" (ZPD). It is defined by Vygotsky as

> the difference between the child's developmental level as determined by independent problem solving and the higher level of potential development as determined through problem solving under adult guidance or in collaboration with more capable peers. (1978, 85, cited in Mitchell and Myles 1998, 146)

In other words, it is not so much a physical space as it is an opportunity for learners to develop cognitively beyond their current level of ability. The ZPD is based on the assumption that, for whatever problem the learners confront, they already have the basic potential to solve it. It is within their ZPD; however, they need to be "pushed" to realize it through the interaction with the teacher and peers. The learners have to create new tools, new thinking processes, to accomplish a task; this change is a socially mediated activity.

Vygotsky and SLA

Vygotsky's concept of ZPD finds an echo in SLA research, specifically Krashen's (1982) notion of i + 1, that is, input plus one. Krashen has argued that progress in L2 development occurs in the context of comprehensive input (the "i"), that is, one stage (the "1") beyond that which the learners can currently handle. This theory has been influential in SLA; it is not known, however, to what extent it has been successfully applied to classroom teaching of foreign languages.

Mitchell and Myles (1998) elaborate on one example from general educational literature (Mercer 1996) of how Vygotsky's concept of ZPD could be implemented in classrooms. In the process of supportive dialogue known as scaffolding, the teacher typically co-constructs with the learners an instructional dialogue. In the course of this joint creation, the teacher embeds in the discourse the key information or steps, leading the learners to "solve the problem," whether it be a math or linguistic problem. The peers have a role to play in the social environment; they can also help with directing an individual learner's attention to a key point and correcting mistakes.

Scaffolding performs the following functions (Wood, Bruner, and Ross 1976, cited by Mitchell and Myles 1998, 147):

1. Recruiting interest in the task
2. Simplifying the task
3. Maintaining pursuit of the goal
4. Marking critical features and discrepancies between what has been produced and the ideal solution
5. Controlling frustration during problem solving
6. Demonstrating an idealized version of the act to be performed

This summary of the role of scaffolding illustrates well the value of this interactive tool that teachers in all disciplines can use to push development within the ZPD.

Scaffolding has become a concept with direct relevance to SLA, as suggested above. The SLA literature reviews studies of the role of foreigner talk in providing comprehensible input for learners so that their knowledge of syntactic, lexical, and pragmatic aspects of the L2 improves. Particularly researchers interested in pragmatic development find Vygotsky's concepts (whether stated explicitly or not) of value because of his attention to both the social and the cognitive dimensions of human learning.

Kanagy (1999) studied the language socialization of children enrolled in a Japanese immersion kindergarten in the United States. She was interested in how the children acquire L2 interactional skills. Videotaped classroom interactions of teacher and students were analyzed qualitatively. Daily classroom routines of greetings, attendance taking, and personal

1.	T:	shusseki o torimasu, hai. ja shi [We will take attendance. Okay, shh.]
2.	T:	hai, te wa ohirza, tatte [Okay, hand in your lap, stand up.]
3.	S:	tatte [Stand up.]
4.	S:	tatte [Stand up.]
5.	T:	tatte kudasai, ne, ne, hai, ja ki o tsuke [Stand up, Okay? Okay? Okay? at attention.]
6.	T:	kakato o tsukete yo, kakato o, kakato o tsukete [Put your heels together, your heels, put your heels together.]
7.	T:	a, TY, oshiri wa te, buru ni tsukemasen. [Oh, TY, don't put your behind against the table.]
8.	T:	hai, koo ne, koo, ko ne, koo [Okay, like this, okay, like this, like this, Okay, like this.]
9.	T:	oshiri wa te, buru ni tsukenai, ne, tsukenai, ne [Don't put your behind against the table, okay, not against, okay.]
10.	T:	hai, ja moo ikkai, mite yo, kotchi o mite yo. [Okay, look at me again, look this way.]

Source: Kanagy 1999, 1472.
Note: TY = identified student.

introductions demonstrated the target verbal and nonverbal behaviors, modeled and critiqued by the teacher. Scaffolding was a key feature of the teacher-student discourse (Kanagy 1999, 1472). The accompanying table is an example of a morning greeting. It is clear that the teacher not only reviews the language component of this daily routine, but also socializes the students into the body posture that is expected to accompany the linguistic message of greeting in schools in Japan. The teacher is carrying out the six functions of scaffolding listed above.

Sociocultural Context

All human activity occurs within a sociocultural context where the roles of the individuals, the social others, and the cultural context are crucial in cognitive functioning and in the maturation of an individual from child to adult. It has been argued that the Vygotskian approach to cognitive development can be applied to explain pragmatic competence development of children, assuming that first-language pragmatic norms are acquired and practiced by children in the context of the caregivers and the sociocultural milieu of their primary socialization. Pragmatic norms constitute one component of their cognitive development.

Chapter 14 adopts the same theory to address the issue of second or foreign language pragmatic development. Rogoff's (1990, 19) statement that "communication involves bridging between two views of a situation with some modifications in the perspectives of each participant" applies even more clearly in cross-cultural interactions where divergent perspectives are likely. Some SLA studies have begun to focus on the learner, in particular, on the learner's self-identity creation as seen in the presentation of the self in activities and social practices in the second language cultural context. The assumption is that the speaker's identity is implicated in the enactment of pragmatic meaning.

Recent discussions particularly within the social constructionist or sociocultural approaches to self and language (Siegal 1996; Norton Peirce 1995, 2000; Wertsch 1991) illustrate the complex issue of learner subjectivity, pragmatic norms, and standards for assessing pragmatic competence development. A related area of second language acquisition and foreign language acquisition (SLA/FLA) research concerns the role of attitudes and motivation in promoting language proficiency. Although much of the work on attitudes and motivation (see, for example, Gardner and Lambert 1972) has focused on target language proficiency in terms of grammatical accuracy, nativelike pronunciation, and unexamined target language cultural norms, more recently, with the models of Canale (1983) and Bachman (1989), inspired by Hymes's (1972) construct of sociolinguistic competence, SLA researchers are interested in pragmatic competence, an important component of recent definitions of successful language learning/acquisition. Specifically, questions arise with regard to the components of attitude and motivation and learners' willingness to adopt NS standards for pragmatic action in their creation of a social identity for themselves in the target language.

There is a need to explore correlations between attitudes and motivation in language learning and pragmatic competence development. Whether one adopts Gardner's socioeducational model of integrative/

instrumental motivation (1985) or H. D. Brown's extrinsic/intrinsic dichotomy (1990), the learners' social identity, that is, the construction of the self in the target language, is implicated. Do the learners want to integrate into the target language community, thereby accepting those norms? Or do they resist and contest the reconstruction of the self that the integrative motive implies? If so, does such resistance, overt or covert, introduce a stumbling block to their ability to adjust to, or even adopt the interaction patterns and social action norms of the target language community?

Learner social identity and the role of attitudes and motivation in the acquisition of L2 pragmatic norms are examined in the next sections. This overview serves to introduce the reader to an increasingly important area of SLA (see *TESOL Quarterly* 1997).

Second Language Self-Identity

The traditional view of language learning sees the learner as memorizing and absorbing the second or foreign language until a minimum, threshold level of proficiency is achieved in phonology, morphology, syntax, and vocabulary. Then, miraculously, the individual is deemed to be capable of using the language, potentially in any and all situations. A more informed view has recognized the need for practice in using the language in meaningful ways, preferably in an environment composed of target language speakers where, over time, the learners will "pick up" the sociolinguistic and pragmatic norms of the L2, simply through exposure in an input-rich environment. However, even this more informed view ignores a number of other factors that require attention (Siegal 1996):

Individual factors:	Learner's position in the L2 societal context
	Consciousness of the aims of language learning and language use
	Consciousness of the self in general
Societal factors:	Face concerns
	Power relations
	Male/female roles, age
	Discrimination

These factors, by no means an exhaustive listing of individual and societal categories, constrain the acquisition and learning of a second or foreign language, particularly in a target language community. Over the past decade, a variety of scholars in SLA have attempted to incorporate these concepts and thinking into a more inclusive theory of second language acquisition. A movement away from a purely linguistic interest in language learning has taken place, and Norton Peirce has drawn attention to this shift in the research paradigm in SLA through her work in language socialization.

Norton Peirce (1995) summarized the contributions from a number of poststructural and postmodern educational theories, in particular Weedon's (1987) conception of subjectivity. According to Weedon, Western philosophy depicts the individual—the subject—as having a fixed, unique, and integrated personality or self. Poststructuralism, in contrast, sees the individual as having a decentered identity composed of multiple selves. McNamara (1997, 564) lists familial, professional, class, gender, sexuality, and age identities, among others. The term *subjectivity* is employed by Norton Pierce to denote this second conception of social identity. She adopts Weedon's claims that there are three characteristics of subjectivity: "the multiple nature of the subject; subjectivity as a site of struggle; and subjectivity as changing over time" (cited in Norton Peirce 1995, 15). On this view, there is no one "true self." Rather, contradictions are normal, with the contradictory selves played out in the variety of "social sites" in which individuals act and interact with others on a daily basis. (The notion of multiple selves has been present in Asian psychology for some time: see, for example, Rosenberger 1992.) Further, individuals have agency; in other words, they are not passive, but can contest a particular way in which they have been positioned in a social site, seeking to create a new social position for themselves. Such activity results in changing the social identity and "opens up subjectivity to change" (Weedon 1987, 33, cited in Norton Peirce 1995, 16).

The learner subjectivity perspective accounts for the active, self-aware participation of the second or foreign language learners who seek to develop a self, one of their selves, in the L2. Once we abandon the notion that there is one unique self, an "essential subjectivity" (Weedon 1987, 33, cited in Norton Peirce 1995, 33), a route opens to the acceptance of change, of the presence of multiple selves within one individual.

L2 learners, rather than spongelike beings with regard to the L2 and its pragmatic norms, may actually struggle against imposition of those norms. Their refusal of accommodation and positive convergence toward the L2 pragmatic norms is complex and multifaceted, as they seek to create their own social identity through the language.

Presentation of Self

In addition to the construct of multiple subjectivities, other concepts need to be taken into consideration regarding social identity. The learner does not operate within a vacuum, free to act, as if unencumbered: the individual interacts with others with a complex of societal factors. For example, an individual cannot escape from the fact that one's self-identity may not correlate with the identity assigned by the out-group or receiving group. The presentation of self, that is, one's social identity, is influenced by the socially constructed position of second or foreign language learners in a given society or culture. According to Siegal (1996), who carried out a case study of an American white woman learning Japanese in the target language community, the position of women in Japanese society played an important role in what interactions she could participate in, how she was expected to use language, and generally how she was viewed. In particular, the learner experienced difficulties from (1) the pressure to use situationally appropriate language despite her beginning proficiency and (2) her efforts to avoid loss of face for herself and others in the encounters, which required acknowledging the hierarchy of groups within which she interacted (i.e., professionally at the university where she taught, for example).

Consequently, constructing a social identity in a new language requires socialization into the given culture in addition to improvement in language proficiency. The socialization is complex and dynamic, implicating subjectivity, that is, cognitive, social, and emotional aspects that are, in the best of all possible worlds, shared by all the individuals or subjects concerned, that is, the learners and members of the receiving group. It is obvious that shared intersubjectivity is problematic in cross-cultural contact situations and in second and foreign language learners. The learner's presentation of self in actual encounters in the L2 has to be constantly negotiated intertextually, through language use, conversational structure, and other features, with the sociocultural pragmatic norms of the L2 in place. Efforts on the part of the L2 learners are influenced by their attitudes and level of motivation vis-à-vis the target language, the target language speakers, and the target language culture.

Investment

Most of the work on attitudes and motivation until recently has been carried out in second language acquisition environments (that is, an ESL rather than an EFL environment) from a social psychology perspective, assessing the correlation of positive attitudes and high motivation with a variety of societal and psychological factors. Two classic studies by Gardner and Lambert (1972) and Gardner (1985) established the notions of integrative and instrumental orientations. Integrative attitudes and motivation are said to facilitate successful language learning due to the learner's having a strong desire to become a member of the target language culture. An instrumental orientation is characteristic of learners who have utilitarian purposes, related to employment, economic interests, and short-term study and training experiences in the L2 environment. However, although the research has continued to support in general Gardner's socio-educational model, studies done, in particular, in foreign language contexts have indicated that some revision of the model is needed to account for factors not yet addressed in Gardner's approach. Though a recent publication by Gardner, Tremblay, and Masgoret (1997) indicates greater attention to societal factors, the theory is weaker for not considering intergroup relations. Clearly, the relations between an immigrant group, such as Mexicans, and the receiving population, such as the white, nonimmigrant populations along the U.S.-Mexican border, cause tensions for all concerned and do not facilitate integration of the two groups.

Consequently, there has been a search for a more inclusive model to explain attitudes and motivation and successful language learning, one that attends to the foreign language environment and, according to Norton Peirce (1995, 17), the "relation of power, identity, and language learning." Drawing on several sources, including Bourdieu (1977), Norton Peirce contends that the notion of investment is preferable to Gardner and Lambert's model for explaining the motivation of L2 learners.

> If learners invest in a second language, they do so with the understanding that they will acquire a wider range of symbolic and material resources. . . . Learners will expect or hope to have a good return on that investment—a return that will give them access to hitherto unattainable resources. (1995, 17)

In other words, learners will invest themselves in studying another language if they believe they can achieve something by doing so, which is personally of value to them, as they define it. Investment implies effort and psychological and emotional involvement in learning the L2. Specifically, Norton Peirce sees the investment as including the potential for learners to change and adapt who they are, their self-identity, in the constantly changing contemporary world; "an investment in the target language is also an investment in a learner's own self identity" (Norton Peirce 1995, 18).

The notions of investment and of social identity have explanatory power with regard to learners who do not successfully acquire an L2 as well. Despite high levels of motivation and positive attitudes toward the L2 itself and the L2 culture, learners may experience discomfort and hesitate to speak in particular with NSs with whom they have "a particular symbolic or material investment" (Norton Peirce 1995, 19). This behavior is observed in immigrants to a country whose future lives involve economic factors (getting jobs, finding a place to live and paying the rent, etc.) and symbolic issues, such as acceptance as a member of the society. So much is at stake in adapting to the new environment that the resulting anxiety may be a strongly demotivating factor. Further, for any language learner, experiences with discrimination, marginalization, and inequitable social practices may result in learners' refusal to accommodate to the L2 sociolinguistic and pragmatic norms. Considering the impact of all these factors, it becomes clear that the learner's investment in acquisition of the L2 creates the potential for the enactment of a new, full, rich social identity in the second or foreign language. Gardner and Lambert's construct of integrative and instrumental orientations does not capture the deeper level of the acknowledgment on the part of many L2 learners that, not only can they not achieve NS proficiency levels in the L2 due to the critical age constraint, but also they may not want to, preferring to live with the contradictions arising from the enactment of their multiple selves. Nor can theory account for the fluent English-speaking child, born and raised in an English-speaking country, who refuses to use the language in the beginning-level, required English class in his/her home country, such as in Mexico or Japan.

The next section considers the issue of pragmatic norms. The notion of norms does not just include correct and appropriate language use; it involves the expectations of the NSs of the second or foreign language with regard to the language behavior of the learner.

Pragmatic Norms

McGroarty (1996, 22) explains that there are both descriptive norms, statements about how most speakers generally use a particular language, and prescriptive norms, statements about rules for use of a language in all settings. Descriptive norms include acceptance of variation, while prescriptive norms promote one standard language, published in grammars and dictionaries. According to Cameron (1995), linguists claim their field of research comprises description only of language phenomena, which contrasts with the views of members of the public who are more concerned with prescriptive statements about appropriate language and language use.

Pragmatic norms are implicated in this discussion. Linguists may regard *norm* as a neutral term, reflecting the statistical probability that one linguistic form will appear in a specific linguistic environment rather than another. McGroarty (1996) notes, however, that members of the public include a positive evaluation. That is, an L2 speaker whose use of the language is pragmatically appropriate is more positively regarded than a speaker who is pragmatically inappropriate. In the best of all possible worlds, variation in the realization of pragmatic norms would be not only be tolerated, but be viewed as "normal." However, it must be acknowledged that, in most societies, maintenance of the standard language and adherence to local pragmatic norms of interactions is part of the dominant ideology. Although this ideological position is largely an unexamined view, considered to be common sense, even if it is brought to awareness, second or foreign language learners are in a disadvantaged position. Many NNSs come to share the view as well and engage in great efforts to achieve NS accuracy and fluency, refusing to take classes taught by nonnative speakers. Others do not do so for a variety of ideological and psychological reasons.

Further, particularly with regard to English as a language of international communication, the question of "whose" pragmatic norms must be raised. The world Englishes movement (see Kachru and Nelson 1996; Brutt-Griffler 2002), which has attracted considerable attention over the last decade, explicitly problematizes any possibility of maintaining one set of pragmatic norms for speakers of English, a language used daily by more NNS than NSs. Critical pedagogy scholars (see Giroux 1992) suggest that this issue of norms is bound up with much wider concerns of hegemony and dominance of one group over another (see Chick 1996).

Enactment of Learner Subjectivity

This final section of the chapter presents two examples of learners of English in New York City and in Tokyo to exemplify learner subjectivity. A final example comes from a magazine published bilingually in Spanish and English in New York City. In the first case, a Chinese woman writes about her life and her identity as an immigrant to the United States (Blot and Berman Sher 1978, 29–30).

> I was born and raised in Hong Kong. For the past six years I've been living in the United States. I work as a salesgirl in a large department store. Right now I'm going through a difficult period of my life which is hard for me to talk about. A few months ago I went to Hong Kong for a visit. It was the first time I'd gone back there since coming to the United States. . . . I really got a shock when I arrived. Hong Kong was not the same city I left six years ago. . . . The shock from the physical changes in the city was nothing compared to the confusion and hurt I soon began to feel in my parents' home. I began to feel that something was wrong. I noticed that my family, especially my mother, would sometimes glance at me in a strange way when I was speaking. . . . I decided to talk to my mother. She asked me, "Have you forgotten your Chinese way?" I asked her what she meant. She said, "You've forgotten the place of a woman in a Chinese home. You talk when you should remain silent. You speak on matters that are of concern only to the men. You speak openly of your inner feelings and desires. That's not the

way of a Chinese woman. We keep our thoughts and feelings to ourselves." As my mother spoke, I realized what had happened to me. Americans, including American women, are much freer in expressing their thoughts and feelings. . . . Now I feel homeless. I don't feel like an American. Americans haven't accepted me.

Lee Fong's story is undoubtedly not unique. Many people have lost one identity and not yet created a new one in their country of adoption. An important issue from the point of view of pragmatic ability is how the woman's belief that she still had a home in Hong Kong affected her language development. Further, seeing herself as still anchored in the Far East may have had a negative impact on her job and her schoolwork. Her motivation to improve her language proficiency and learn the rules of pragmatic appropriateness may not have been strong. Yet her identity as a woman had changed, albeit outside of awareness. She had begun to use language, to ask questions, and to state opinions that were more American and less Chinese, according to her mother.

The second example concerns Japanese university students' use of English as the target language to carry out classroom tasks. Data were collected of first-year students engaged in group discussions in English of a reading homework assignment. They had been given a worksheet with questions that asked them to review what they had read and then discuss the content of the reading, giving their own views and opinions. Within the context of this activity, that is, a classroom group discussion, the learners constructed their particular version of this speech event in an English class in a Japanese university. The spoken discourse of the learners was analyzed for recurring themes. What emerged from the data were eight such themes, which express what the learners believed they were doing or should be doing in the group discussion. Each of the eight examples below from the learners' discussion is preceded by the theme that the segment of discussion exemplifies (LoCastro 1996).

1. This is a group interaction: we have to do this together and agree on our answer.
   T: does anybody agree? he's honest
   A: he's honest
   T: or a liar?

    H: maybe honest
    T: maybe honest
    A: maybe honest because villagers give him food or something to eat
    T: where?
    A: so they they trust him like him.
    T: ok, now let's go to another question
2. This is a classroom task: follow the teacher's directions (i.e., please record your discussion).
    T: gesture, no gesture say something
3. We are learners of English: use the language correctly and practice using English.
    A: what is "calling"
    T: Akiyo-san . . .
    A: occupation by nature
    H: how do you think, *Ryohei-san?*
4. We have a worksheet with questions to be answered.
    K: but the question is who is he
    T: who is he? at first, who is he, shaman, ok
5. You have to be the group leader when it's your turn: elicit talk from the other group members.
    K: another opinion, is there another opinion, Y, how about your opinion?
6. We are having a discussion: disagree sometimes, but keep the discussion going.
    T: no no no you say something different from me, please go ahead
7. We must have the discussion in English: that is, don't use Japanese.
    N: surprise *ja nai*
    H: I was not surprised
    N: disappointed
    H: rather uh so *ne* rather
8. But we can use Japanese sometimes (we're Japanese and this is Japan).
    K: and fine finally what adjectives would you use to describe him? adjectives from the text so, I think, *adjectives adjectives* is in Japanese *keioshi?*

In these themes can be observed both the influence of the particular activity type on the student's language behavior and their presentation of themselves as members of a group with a task to carry out for their English teacher. Their Japanese selves, nevertheless, are present in the tendency to avoid elaboration in responses; in "I think" transferred from the phrase—*to omou,* which in Japanese functions as a form of mitigation in opinion-giving contexts; in checking with other group members as to agreement with a point of view before moving on to the next question; and in the conflict between avoidance of Japanese and code switching into Japanese. These themes and the examples presented do not exhaust the richness of the data with regard to the enactment of their social identities as learners of English as a foreign language.

Objections may be raised that the learners had no choice but to be their Japanese selves, due to their proficiency level. However, this point of view cannot be sustained, as a full analysis of the data would demonstrate more fully the extent to which the learners reenact features of lessons from primary school mother tongue classes (LoCastro and Netsu 1997). The extent of the cross-linguistic transfer suggests that, rather than simply strategic or utilitarian measures until L2 pragmatic norms for group discussions can be acquired, learner identities were creatively constructed to achieve group goals for the task.

The final example introduces a popular, mass circulation magazine for women, called *Latina,* which has been published bilingually in Spanish and English since 1996. The following comes from an ad for the magazine's website (*Latina* 2000, 133).

> Latina.com
>
> Entérate . . .
>
> Get a sneak peek at the next issue of Latina. See celebrity photos from our exclusive library. Preview música latina.
>
> Comunícate . . .
>
> Get in touch with the magazine staff. . . . Chat con tu gente about issues of interest to our community.
>
> Prepárate . . .
>
> Research job opportunities through our career center. Meet fellow Latinos with similar interests.

This representative passage is interesting from the point of view of social identity, in this case, of a minority group in the United States. English is used more than Spanish, but Spanish words are left untranslated. Within the three passages, key words are in Spanish: *música latina, con tu gente,* and *Latinos.* Further, the content creates a sense of solidarity with other Latinos: "chat *con tu gente* ["with your people"] about issues of interest to our community"; "meet fellow Latinos with similar interests" regarding employment and careers. *Latina* is actively creating an identity of modern, bilingual, urban Spanish-speaking people through its articles, advertisements, and website. The image is one that includes code switching as a normal form of language use.

Applications to Language Learning

The role of power and bias based on gender can affect the opportunities of students in language classrooms and thus the development of an identity in the L2. Just as in the real world of business and affairs, men, women, or members of minority groups find that they cannot achieve their professional or personal goals due to, for example, power of interviewers in gatekeeping situations. SLA researchers have successfully argued that progress in language learning develops in the context of meaningful use of the target language in interactions in and outside classrooms, with native and other nonnative speakers of the language. Learners need to be able to ask clarification questions, seek confirmation, and ask for information, that is, use the language to negotiate meaning and obtain comprehensive input. It follows from this perspective that all the learners in a classroom should have equal access to opportunities to engage with the target language. This assumption, however, may not in fact be part of the reality of all classrooms. Teachers may not, first of all, have been exposed to the SLA research results. Second, due to a variety of factors, they may use the power they possess as teachers in an institution to manipulate the learning environment in ways that are not advantageous to all of the learners.

Gass and Varonis carried out several studies during the 1980s to assess how gender and minority group membership influenced progress in language proficiency. Specifically, Gass and Varonis (1986) studied sex differences in NNS-NNS interactions. They had ESL learners, all of whom had Japanese as their L1, tape thirty conversations in ten dyads. The data analysis considered (1) negotiation of meaning, (2) topics, (3) shows of dominance, and (4) interpersonal phenomena. Gass and Varonis found that the frequency of efforts to negotiate meaning was influenced by whether the coparticipants were the same sex or not. However, there was also an effect for discourse role. In other words, both male and female informants tended to take on different roles—as initiators of negotiation or topics, or obtainers of comprehensible input—depending on whether they were in same-sex or mixed-sex dyads. Therefore, along with differences related to gender, discourse roles also influence the rate of language development.

Access to opportunities for pragmatic development in the classroom vary according to a number of factors, including the learners' personality, levels of motivation, and learning strategies. However, the Gass and Varonis study suggests that gender cannot be discounted. Even if the intentions are good—one teacher explained she called on the boys more frequently in her junior high school language class, as they were more disruptive if she didn't—the girls would be disadvantaged (see also Carrasco 1979). In addition to gender, other studies have demonstrated that similar instances of unequal treatment result from ethnic and racial prejudices (Shea 1994), stereotyping, perceptions of competence, conversational style, and ideological biases.

Teachers must become aware of their own patterns of behavior in the classroom context to avoid skewing the opportunities for pragmatic development. McGroarty (1996) cites a series of studies that found teachers scaffolded and, in general, managed the classroom discourse in ways that were more supportive of the white children than the black children. Chapter 15 takes up this topic again.

Discussion Questions

1. If you know a second or foreign language, how do you feel about adopting the ways of speaking of that L2 community? Would you rather maintain your own L1 pragmatic norms? Why? Why not?

2. Some people feel that speaking another language and adopting its pragmatic norms is a chance to experience a different side of themselves. It can be liberating, in their view. How do you feel about this idea?

3. Forms of address often involve the identity of the person being addressed. For example, some individuals prefer first names, while others can feel insulted by their use. What are your attitudes and those of your classmates about first versus family names (with title, such as *Mr., Ms., or Dr.*)? What can first-name forms of address signal? Why might some people feel offended?

4. Here are three excerpts from writings by individuals who have had to learn another language. Discuss your reactions in light of what you have read in this chapter about learner subjectivity and your own experiences.

> In English, my name means hope. In Spanish, it means too many letters. It means sadness, it means waiting. It is like the number nine. A muddy color. It is the Mexican records my father plays on Sunday mornings when he is shaving, songs like sobbing.
>
> It was my great-grandmother's name and now it is mine. She was a horse woman too, born like me in the Chinese year of the horse—which is supposed to be bad luck if you're born female—but I think this is a Chinese lie because the Chinese, like the Mexicans, don't like their women strong . . .
>
> At school they say my name funny as if the syllables were made out of tin and hurt the roof of your mouth. But in Spanish my name is made out of a softer something, like silver, not quite as thick as sister's name—Magdalena—which is uglier than mine. Magdalena who at least can come home and become Nenny. But I am always Esperanza.
>
> I would like to baptize myself under a new name, a name more like the real me, the one nobody sees. Esperanza as Lisandra or Martiza or Zeze the X. Yes. Something like Zeze the X will do.
>
> Sandra Cisneros, *The House on Mango Street* (1984)

She lacked not the vocabulary but the inflection which might request or admonish without causing offense. Her voice, so expressive and alive in her native Cantonese, became shrill, peremptory, and strangely lifeless in its level pitching when she spoke English. She would have sounded hostile and nervous; a cross between a petulant child and a nagging old shrew, neither of which descriptions adequately fitted the mature and outward-going young woman who was Lily Chen.

Timothy Mo, *Soursweet* (1982)

The words I learn now don't stand for things in the same unquestioned way they did in my native tongue. "River" in Polish was a vital sound, energized with the essence of riverhood, of my rivers, of my being immersed in rivers. "River" in English is cold—a word without an aura. It has no accumulated associations for me, and it does not give off the radiating haze of connotation. It does not evoke.

Eva Hoffman, *Lost in Translation: A Life in a New Language* (1989)

Text Analysis

Provide an analysis of the following excerpts from an English L2 textbook published in Japan. How might learners using these materials react? Elaborate.

A: Say, do you know any really foxy chicks?
B: I know a few. Why?
A: I'd like to meet one. How about it?
B: Well, I think that could be arranged.

A: You're the best looking thing I've seen today.
B: Why, uh, thank you.
A: If you'll have just one drink with me, you'll make me a very happy man.
B: Well, maybe just one.

A: Is it proper to ask if a girl is married?
B: If the time and place are right.
A: Are you married?
B: Why do you ask?
A: Because you're too beautiful to be single and alone.

(Gilbert, cited in Sakuma 1996)

Suggested Readings

Kanagy, R. 1999. Interactional routines as a mechanism for L2 acquisition and socialization in an immersion context. *Journal of Pragmatics* 31:1467–92.

Lantolf, J. P., ed. 1994. Special issue "Sociocultural theory and second language learning." *Modern Language Journal* 78, no. 4.

———, ed. 2000. *Sociocultural Theory and second language learning.* Oxford: Oxford University Press.

Lantolf, J. P., and G. Appel. 1994. *Vygotskian Approaches to second language research.* Norwood, N.J.: Ablex.

Moll, L. C., ed. 1990. *Vygotsky and education: Instructional Implications and applications of sociohistorical psychology.* Cambridge: Cambridge University Press.

Schieffelin, B. B., and E. Ochs, eds. 1996. *Language socialization across cultures.* Cambridge: Cambridge University Press.

TESOL Quarterly. 1997. Special issue "Language and Identity," vol. 31, no. 3.

Chapter 15
Pragmatics in the Classroom

This final chapter provides an opportunity to consider the development of pragmatic ability in the language classroom. Attention to the classroom and related institutional environments flows naturally from two rationales. First, as this introduction to pragmatics includes an SLA focus, it is only proper to turn to pragmatic meaning in the formal learning context, undoubtedly the most important environment for the development of communicative competence. Both teachers and teachers in training are likely to be interested in expanding their knowledge in this area.

Second, in raising awareness of the classroom environment, the content of previous chapters will be brought to bear on understanding the development of pragmatic ability of L2 learners. In a classroom all the areas of pragmatics are potential problems for L2 learners and members of minority groups who have limited proficiency in the dominant language of the community.

Specifically, this chapter concentrates on learners and their achievement in a second or foreign language. The learner is viewed "as a motivated human being, whose existential experience, world view, and intentions all influence classroom behavior" (Gillette 1994, 196). One dimension of learners' goals in studying an L2 is what Ellis labels "impression management," that is, the ability of L2 learners to "create social meanings favorable to themselves" (1994, 160). The focus is on interactions in which students' resources are implemented in establishing their identity as L2 learners and users. Yet the learners are not free to pursue their goals as individuals. The classroom is a prototypical unequal encounter, unequal for two reasons. First, students lack the teacher's knowledge of the L2. Second, the teacher is given power by the institution to evaluate students' language competence and thereby influence their future careers. The inequality is particularly poignant if the teacher is a native speaker of the target language or if some students in the class are from the dominant L1 background.

This chapter looks into problems that arise when the goals of the learners themselves, or the goals the community has for them, are not achieved. Community is here broadly defined, as it may be a physical space, as in a town in Canada, or a discourse community, as in the international business or academic environment in which the participants work or study. After surveying classroom research on instructed learning related to pragmatic development, dimensions of the formal learning context that can influence learners' development are considered, specifically what input learners are exposed to and what opportunities to practice they are given. Then three studies of the context of learning are presented. A study on pragmatic competence in teacher-student advisement sessions illustrates just how learners fare in a nonclassroom educational context. The aim here is to raise awareness of second language teachers and teachers in training of their role in assisting learners—L2 students and others, such as graduate students in a variety of disciplines—to develop their communicative competence. Pragmatic ability is one of the important components in successful communication. Even in our first language, to present ourselves as we wish requires comprehending and producing pragmatic meanings in a variety of contexts, ranging from a simple speech act requesting the salt to processing irony and comprehending joking. The two final studies look at learners successfully achieving their goals and a case of a teacher's becoming more aware of her own classroom behavior.

Research on Pragmatic Development and the Classroom

Classroom research on interaction patterns is probably as old as the teaching profession itself, starting with the first teacher who asked, "What can I do to help the students learn more?" "Is there something in my way of organizing the class that influences how well the students succeed?" Probably the first published evidence of teachers' adjusting their practices to foster learning is found in Plato. The Socratic method, which involves the creation of a dialogue among the teacher and students, with the teacher playing the devil's advocate in asking difficult, probing questions, exemplifies one teacher's solution to the age-old problem of getting students to think!

Second language classroom discourse dates back to the 1980s in North America. During that decade, several books and edited volumes appeared, although the first comprehensive review (Chaudron) was published in 1988. It must be kept in mind, nevertheless, that research on classrooms in general predated the SLA-oriented studies. For example, scaffolding was originally described by Bruner, a cognitive psychologist interested in learning, in 1978, and Barnes produced his influential book on small groups and language learning in content subjects in 1976. It is important for SLA professionals to keep in mind that the field of education, in particular, educational psychology and teacher development, has contributed immensely to our knowledge of classroom discourse and learning (see, for example, Cazden 1988).

The extensive research since the 1980s on L2 classroom discourse has come out of two traditions. Quantitative studies are commonly based on pre- and post-test instruments to measure progress over a period of time, comparing an experimental with a control group. The qualitative approach uses discourse-analytic, process designs to examine teacher-student interaction patterns. One early book on teacher talk is that of Sinclair and Brazil (1982), which introduces a coding scheme for teacher-student discourse and elaborates on the role of prosodic features, such as intonation and stress patterns, in interpreting pragmatic meanings. However, few studies until recently have explained the processes (social, cognitive, and interactional) that foster pragmatic development.

Chaudron (1988) surveys the phases the classroom-centered studies went through. The initial stage focused on the quantity of teacher's talk and the frequency of modifications in the teacher's input, called "teacher talk." Two principal concerns were that an excessive rate of speech and syntactic complexity could impede students' progress. Chaudron points out (1988, 163), however, that "there is only an inkling of a relationship between comprehensibility or frequency and learners' progress."

As awareness of the need for a more interventionist approach grew, research shifted to form and explicit instruction in grammar. Studies found that explicit talk about grammar produced slightly better results. However, evidence of "the precise extent of effect of formal instruction" was still lacking (Chaudron 1988, 166).

The third stage of SLA research focused on learners' behavior—their production, negotiating behaviors in the classroom (initiation, for example), and their learning strategies. Findings did not indicate strong effects for teaching or learner behavior, particularly not with regard to the quality of production. There was no correlation between quantity and quality of the learners' production. Chaudron suggests, however, that the results may reflect inadequate research.

In the next stage, research concerned pragmatic abilities such as the appropriateness of input, in particular, the language learners used to negotiate meaning in interactions. The studies looked at the language addressed to the learners, including the teacher's use of the L1 or only the L2 in bilingual classrooms, the questions used to elicit talk, and the teacher's feedback. The results suggest the need for future research to assess which variable is most likely to affect students' progress (see Lightbown and Spada 1999).

Studies continue on learning outcomes, particularly with regard to development of pragmatic competence. K. E. Johnson's *Understanding Communication in Second Language Classrooms* (1995) is a useful recent contribution. The author uses data from classrooms to examine the moment-by-moment behaviors in teacher-student interactions. Lightbown and Spada (1999) have also surveyed studies of classroom learning and the effects of group work, NNS-NNS interactions, proficiency levels, recasts, and communicative practice on learners' development. Despite the lack of confident answers, the studies do elaborate on some of the variables in the classroom that influence second or foreign language pragmatic development.

Input. What Students Are Exposed To

Teachers

Ever since Krashen (1982) first proposed the notion of comprehensible input, second language teachers and teachers in training have been aware of the importance of providing appropriate, adequate, and rich input to foster learners' pragmatic development. One main source of input is teachers themselves. They provide content, such as the basic rules of politeness, the need to be aware of social markers, and what to say to whom in which contexts. At the same time, they model the appropriate formulaic expressions and explain the differences in the variety of linguistic forms that can be used. The assumption is that the teacher knows the L2 code well and has studied pragmatics. In other words, the teacher has knowledge of social appropriateness through language use and can act as an informed model for learners.

Without experience in the target language culture, the teacher may lack such knowledge. It has been argued that teachers without extensive experience in different areas of employment outside the classroom may not be competent to teaching social rules of speaking. Teachers of English for specific purposes, for example, for business negotiations, may feel at a loss that they are not competent to teach a course in an area that requires knowledge of the subject and experience with negotiations in the business world.

Materials

A second source of input in the learning environment is the materials: textbooks, dictionaries, videos, multimedia, and tests. Unfortunately, the materials may misrepresent the target language culture and its practices. All too often they are not based on naturally occurring language. Consequently, the rules of speaking or politeness norms may be distorted. Stereotypes may be reinforced or created, for example, about the level of directness used by Americans (LoCastro 1997b; N. Tanaka 1988; Robinson 1992). The following example of artificial talk comes from a textbook used in junior high school English classes in Japan:

> *Student:* For my generation, life is so difficult.
> *Teacher:* Huh? Why?
> *Student:* It's so difficult to be original. Lindbergh crossed the Atlantic. Others have climbed Mount Everest and gone to the moon. What's new?
> *Teacher:* How about a cure for cancer? Could you find one?

Student: **Who, me? You must be kidding.** But I'd like to be in the famous *Book of Records.*

(Cited in LoCastro 1997b, 252)

Perhaps this conversation could take place, but most native speakers English would consider the student's response in boldface inappropriate. Certainly it would not be typical of talk between teacher and student and thus is arguably inappropriate in a textbook for the teaching of the English language.

Avoiding inaccurate representations of pragmatic knowledge and practices, materials should also be accessible to learners. Accessibility means that the lessons and practice sessions are connected to their daily lives in and out of the classroom. Just as language at the appropriate level is required to teach science to adolescents—not the language of academic publications such as *Nature*—so must the various discourse levels of adolescents, young adults, and older adults be recognized by teachers (Brown and Yule (1983b). Language tests should use examples or passages that are accessible to the test takers. The English language part of a Japanese university entrance examination supplies the following example of what not to do (see LoCastro 1990a, 351).

Boy: How about coming out with me tomorrow night? We can go somewhere for something to eat together.
Girl: Well, actually, as it happens, *I am a little short of cash just at the moment.*
Boy: Oh, don't worry about that. Of course, *I'll take care of the expenses.*
Girl: Well, it's not only that. As a matter of fact, I don't eat supper because I want to lose some weight.
Boy: Oh, I can't believe that. *It seems to me that you've got a great figure.* But anyway, let's skip eating; er, how about going roller skating together?
Girl: Oh, that's impossible. *I haven't a clue about skating* and, anyway, I don't have any skates.
Boy: It's easy, you can get some there. And I'll be happy to show you how.

Girl: Well, maybe. But—oh, I've just remembered: I'm going out with one of my school friends that evening.

Boy: Oh, heck. Why don't you ask her if she can't come another day?

Girl: Yes, but, actually, she's leaving for home the day after, and *I shan't see* her again for months, so really I can't let her down on her last day.

Boy: Yes, I see. Well, there's always another day. I'll be free on Friday. *And I had thought about taking in a ball game.* What do you say?

Girl: Mmm, I've got a sociology quiz on Saturday, so I've just got to stay home on Friday and study.

Boy: Me, too, but I'm not going to *stick at home* studying just for some crummy old test.

Girl: *What a pity!* I do like intellectual boys. Bye-bye.

While there is much to be objected to in this dialogue (including the sexism of mentioning the "girl's" figure), the main point here is its dated language. It is a mixture of British and American conversational routines that does not fit the speakers, who are adolescents, or perhaps university students. The italicized portions are the most salient instances of the sort of language that would more commonly come from the parents of adolescents.

Other Learners

A third source of input in the classroom is what learners bring, their sociocultural backgrounds and corresponding expectations. According to Gillette (1994), learners' goals for learning an L2 are primarily a function of the social environment in which they grew up, their experiences with the world at large, and the value they attach to becoming a proficient user. A correlation between a positive level of motivation for learning an L2 and the willingness to develop pragmatic ability in it seems likely, although it has not been corroborated by research (but see LoCastro 2000a). Consequently, teachers should not ignore learners' motivation and their personal histories.

In addition to goals, learners also bring sociocultural expectations, embedded in the worldview they absorbed during the socialization process with their parents and community. As seen in chapter 11, the speech acts, indirectness, and redressive action in the L2 are influenced by transfer from the L1. However, learners' social history has still wider effects. Much has been done to raise the awareness of teachers about the existence of different expectations, learning and cognitive styles, discourse patterns, and communication styles in classrooms with a heterogeneous group of students (see early studies by Labov [1972] and others into the disadvantages that African American children experience, and, more recently, research on Latino students in the same contexts [Heath 1978; Moll 1981; Moll and Gonzalez 1994]). The same approach needs to be taken with learners of any target language. Their first-language patterns and expectations will have a strong influence on their behaviors in the language classroom. Consequently, teaching the linguistic forms and realization strategies to signal such pragmatic meaning as mitigation or hesitancy may be easier with explicit discussion of the differences.

Teachers might assume that working in groups in the classroom is unproblematic for learners from collectivist cultures (Japan, Korea, China), but Carlson and Nelson (1994) show that such learners can be less than enthusiastic about writing groups in an ESL classroom. The researchers identified three cross-cultural issues. First, learners from Japan and China felt that the writing groups benefited individuals, functioning differently from groups in collectivist cultures that helped everyone. Second, such learners tended to value group harmony too much to give critical reviews of a peer's essay. Third, they were likely to divide their writing group into an in-group (those from the same culture) and an out-group. Out-group participants were sometimes treated with hostility and competitive behavior. These three tendencies interact to create a challenge for teachers who want to use writing groups in ESL, perhaps also EFL, classrooms.

Organizing Opportunities to Practice in the Classroom

What the teacher does to organize learning opportunities using the materials chosen is the next aspect of the classroom environment to consider. SLA research has demonstrated that practicing what the learners have been taught facilitates learning and fluency in all areas of language, including pragmatic ability. "Writing to learn," talking, and practice improve long-term memory and readiness to use what has been taken in intellectually, whether it be linguistic content, a communication strategy, or a conversational routine.

The following is an example of the kind of everyday talk for which communicative practice can help the learner make the connections necessary to interpret pragmatic, not literal, meaning. Sam telephones Miguel in the morning, and Miguel's mother answers:

Sam: Quiero hablar con Miguel. [I'd like to speak with Miguel.]
Mother: No se encuentra. [He's not home.]

The literal translation of the mother's utterance is "He cannot be found." If Sam has just started learning Spanish, he may wonder why they are searching for Miguel. Is he missing? If Sam has had the appropriate pragmatic practice, however, he will understand that the mother's formulaic expression means he is not at home. And the more telephone calls Sam makes to Mexican families, the more he will hear the phrase used in the same context: "Lo siento, pero no se encuentra" ["I'm sorry, but s/he is not here right now."]

According to Ellis, mismatches of contextualization cues result in learners not being able to present themselves as competent partners in interactions with native speakers or more proficient, nativelike speakers of the L2. This problem of "impression management" derives from the learners' not sharing the same cues, or misinterpreting the cues. There is a pedagogical solution: until the learners can achieve higher levels of proficiency in the L2, they can use strategic communication strategies (Kasper and Kellerman 1997). Perhaps even emphasizing their foreignness can cue their conversational partners that indeed they may not be able to give the kind of impression they wish to create.

Interaction Patterns

Concerning opportunities to practice, organization of the classroom is important. Too often the teacher asks all the questions and the learners respond, sometimes in monosyllables. A classroom that encourages responses resembling testimony on a witness stand is counterproductive. The learners need to be able to answer all types of questions—either/or questions, why questions, and confirmation, clarification, and information questions—so as to obtain more comprehensible information about language and content. In addition, they need to be able to speak at length on a topic, write essays, journals, and business letters, and, in general, practice both structure and content in extended texts, not simply isolated sentences. If teachers do not vary the interaction patterns to enable the learners to use the L2 as they would have to use it outside the classroom, the learners are disadvantaged. Furthermore, researchers such as Lightbown and Spada (1999) have found that learners' errors fossilize when they are exposed to L2 language input in classrooms where they and the teacher share the same L1. In the same way, pragmatic ability will not develop beyond a threshold level unless the learners are pushed in a variety of ways, one of them being using the language in functionally different ways. While a NNS teacher may be hampered in some ways, an informed teacher can foster pragmatic development through films, interactive CD-ROM programs, and guests who are native speakers.

Kasper suggests that classroom organization is important because it controls the potential patterns of communication. Although modern educational practices devalue the teacher-fronted classroom, Porter (1986) and Lightbown and Spada (1999) have found that NNS-NNS interactions tend not to provide the model for socially appropriate language use that a teacher-directed activity can. In addition, Poole (1992) observed that teachers can provide the needed sociocultural information implicitly through teacher-student interaction. Kanagy (1999) demonstrated this in the teacher-learner interactions in the Japanese language immersion kindergarten classroom. Although it may be true that the typical I-R-F (initiation, response, feedback) pattern of teacher-student discourse is not always the most efficient means to supply pragmatic input, what may be needed is not favoring one form of classroom organization over others, but rather a creative, eclectic approach with a variety of organizational modes.

A starting point is for teachers to become aware of what they do in the classroom through peer and self-observation (audio or videotaping classes) and analysis of the discourse. According to Heath (1978), teacher talk in classrooms is characterized by three features. First, teachers usually regard themselves as caregivers and their talk reflects that self-image, creating a kind of register or style. For example, teachers tend to use "will" instead of the more normative "going to" to indicate intention. Even L2 learners interpret such language as an example of "talking down" to them. Second, Heath states that the discourse of teachers reflects their authority to decide who talks, whose topic is taken up, and who holds for floor for how long. Students learn to follow the contextualization cues and modify their behavior, reinforcing the teacher's authoritative role. Finally, the talk of teachers depicts them as "arbiters of good citizenship and order" (Heath 1978, 11). A sentence such as "We'll have to get our work done" communicates the idea of the teacher as controller of the classroom. "We" clearly does not refer to the teacher's getting some work done.

A teacher's correction of errors in oral or written work, prescriptive views of language (always use *were* and not *was* with *If I were you*), or unwillingness to allow for variability communicates to the learners that the teacher's will is to be respected. While there are reasons for the teacher's role as the authority in the classroom (e.g., to maintain discipline), the teacher should be aware of the disadvantages of a rigid, one-pattern organization of interactions.

Teacher-Student Talk

Classroom-based studies of pragmatic competence development illustrate the limitations of typical classroom practices. Hall (1995) studied the role that teachers play in foreign language classrooms in fostering development by structuring language practice activities. Research has shown that teachers are instrumental in fostering language development in two ways (Hall 1995, 38):

1. The communicative plans and goals and linguistic resources that teachers make available
2. The extended opportunities learners are given to work with these plans, goals, and resources with more expert communicators.

In foreign language classrooms, which have no target language community outside, teachers play an especially important role in exposing learners to communicative practices. According to Hall (1995, 38), that role is manifested in the framework of interactive practices, that is, the discursive structures and other linguistic resources teachers construct. The teacher models participation and is the organizer of opportunities to practice these structures and practices.

In general, there is too little empirical research on the actual linguistic resources, interactive practices, and language development of the learners that presumably results from interactive practice. One example of such features is Hall's of a first-year Spanish class in a high school in the United States, where she took a sociocultural perspective on the development of pragmatic competence. Specifically, she set out to examine topic development and management that the teacher and students discursively constructed in interactive environments. Although teachers know what is needed, that is, more practice to develop interactive competence, Hall's study showed that the interactive practices are not typical of those outside the classroom in the world at large. The practice Hall studied was labeled "practicing speaking" by the cooperating teacher. The goal was to develop the learners' ability to engage in "natural conversation" in Spanish (Hall 1995, 43). The rhetorical structure observed is the I-R-F pattern: the teacher initiates, the students respond, and the teacher gives feedback. This is a typical discursive structure found in classroom talk that essentially limits learners' involvement linguistically and socially. Learners' ability to engage in more complex forms of talk in the L2 is compromised. The pragmatic skills of "inferencing, anticipating, and building upon presuppositions in the creation of topically complex thought" (Hall 1995, 54) are not practiced or scaffolded by the teacher. The accompanying example illustrates the teacher's pattern of asking a question of one student, repeating the response, and then asking the same question of another student. The teacher is attempting to introduce the topic of "music" and to provide needed vocabulary by using a process labeled "lexical chaining." However, there seems to be no other reason for the lexical chaining, as no general topic or goal has been articulated. Thus, in line 11 Rafael expresses his frustrations by asking what the teacher intends to accomplish by this repetition of utterances.

1.	T:	es música no música no
2.	Julio:	no
3.	T:	es música es música es música
4.		ahora señor te gusta te gusta la música
5.	Julio:	no me gusta
6.	T:	no me gusta
7.	Julio:	no me gusta
8.	T:	no me gusta la múscia te gusta la música
9.		no me gusta la música te gusta la música
10.	Ss:	I do sí sí yeah sí
11.	Rafael:	aw man where you goin'
12.	T:	sí me gusta la música te gusta la música
13.	Andrea:	sí

Source: Hall 1995, 44.

Hall suggests that features of talk associated with the development of pragmatic competence were compromised in the foreign language classroom she studied. Further research is needed on what is provided, what value it has, and what could be done to establish a more conducive interactive environment.

Groups

Barnes's (1976) study of group work demonstrated that learners used more language and in different ways when they worked in groups. For example, they asked for clarification and confirmation; they made structuring moves as group leaders. They also used more exploratory language and took more risks with the language and with articulating their own thinking. The advantages of group work are by now common knowledge in the field of language teaching, and learners working in groups can be found in classrooms all over the world, in particular when the communicative language teaching approach is used.

However, there are limitations to group work:

1. The learners may not use the target language. Many teachers have learners work in pairs or groups without considering that

research on the value of group work assumes that the target language is used most of the time.

2. Their development may not be activated; without a teacher or a learner with higher skills, the zone of proximal development may be compromised. There may be no scaffolding, reconceptualization, or restatement, all salient features of the language work that teachers can provide (Cazden 1988, 110–18).

3. There is no teacher to focus attention on important language or content, give feedback, or provide language help the learners require at the moment (see Tudge 1990).

Teachers need to match learning goals, organization of the learners, and task demands. Group work is not a panacea for developing communicative competence, nor is it necessarily useful as a learning mode for all learners (see Carlson and Nelson above).

Topic Control

Research that has shown that NNSs can contribute as equal participants in controlling the topic of interactions. Woken and Swales (1989) point out that many studies have had as informants NNSs who were either ESL students or graduate students in applied linguistic or TEFL programs in United States universities where they were not likely to have high institutional status. Consequently, Woken and Swales (1989, 212) investigated NS-NNS conversations where the NNS informants

1. Were experienced though flawed speakers of English
2. Had greater content expertise than the NSs
3. Had higher authority as international teaching assistants

The results demonstrated that the NNS spoke more and engaged in more rhetorical inquiries, directions, and corrections. The greater expertise and higher authority apparently enabled them to feel confident enough to carry out those functions. In so doing, they used their L2 in ways they would not have, had they been in an interaction where they were dominated by the NSs.

Zuengler (1989) also examined performance variation in NS-NNS interactions. She hypothesized that, as long as the NNS' proficiency in the L2 is adequate, knowledge of the discourse domain or topic influences the role of the NNS in an interaction—that is, whether the NS dominate the conversation. Analyzing the discourse produced by NNS informants organized in dyads, Zuengler looked for correlations between topic and participation in conversations with graduate students who did not know each other. None were enrolled in ESL classes. One topic of the audio-recorded conversations—food—was outside their majors, while the other was related to their major, engineering. Analysis of the quantity of talk and interruptions indicated that the NNS were not dominated in either case by the NSs. Further evidence in the data suggests that variation in conversational involvement is a function of greater relative knowledge of the topic or discourse domain by either NNSs or NSs.

Thus, studies by Woken and Swales and by Zuengler point to the role of the teacher in setting up group or dyad activities that take these actors into consideration. Despite the fact that the topics were not typical of those found in most language classrooms, efforts could be made to construct group activities that would enable the learners to feel more successful in their use of the L2. For example, learners can choose the topics for group discussions. Oral activities can be based on previous listening, reading, and writing tasks, all designed to help the learners develop familiarity with the vocabulary and content of a particular topic first.

Three Studies of Formal Learning Contexts

Speech Acts and Status-Preserving Strategies: Advisement Sessions

Certainly one educational setting where native and nonnative speakers of the language of the university have their pragmatic competence tested is in academic advising sessions. Even with highly proficient nonnative speakers, the ability to negotiate an advisement interview is dependent on appropriate speech acts and communication strategies. Both types of language use implicate impression management, and graduate students in particular seek to be well regarded by their professors.

Bardovi-Harlig and Hartford (1990, 1993) carried out a study of advising sessions with faculty members and native and nonnative graduate students at a midwestern university to determine, first, which speech acts and strategies were used by professors and students and, second, the extent to which the nonnative speakers' pragmatic ability improved over the course of a semester. Their findings bring to light some important dimensions of this type of institutional discourse.

Faculty members have higher status than students, but graduate students at U.S. universities are expected to demonstrate independent thinking (Kress and Fowler 1979) by arriving for the session with some institutional knowledge and suggestions about the courses they want to take for the coming semester. Thus, the dilemma for the student is to acknowledge the faculty member's status while, at the same time, signal initiative; this requires careful use of appropriate or "congruent" speech acts (i.e., those that enact the expected role of both participants) and status-preserving linguistic (form) and nonlinguistic (e.g., timing) strategies. In the following dialogue a native speaker speaks with an adviser (Bardovi-Harlig and Hartford 1990, 488, example 11):

S: Now, for the uh, I think when I talked to you oh a year ago or so, um, I had, I was asking about electives.
A: mhm
S: And, if I understand it correctly, they have to be electives that are not used for, in another degree.
A: Right
S: Now, my first year while Mongol language courses cannot be used for the Master's degree in Mongol,
A: mhm
S: it can apply for the PhD.
A: I don't think that's a problem.
S: Oh, it's not a problem? Otherwise, I's thinking I, you know, could I just use it that, uh, here, and then, you know, not plan on using it over there.

The student uses downgraders to mitigate the suggestion made in the last turn of the example: past tense, showing tentativeness ("I was thinking"), a downtoner ("think"), and a cajoler ("you know"). As a result, the teacher agrees with the student-initiated suggestion.

Another example, from a nonnative speaker whose L1 is Spanish, illustrates a less-than-successful enactment of pragmatic meaning for the context (Bardovi-Harlig and Hartford 1990, 484, example 9):

A: Do you know what you want to do?
S: More or less.
A: Let's hear it [*pause*] You've done 530, 31, 34, so you probably want to do 542, I bet you . . .
S: Yes, that's phonological.
A: Yes, phonology.

In this case, the nonnative speaker is viewed as delaying the suggestion in the second turn, thus, not demonstrating, with more appropriate timing, independence and knowledge as a graduate student at the university. It is quite likely that the student was transferring behavior that would be pragmatically congruent in the L1 environment.

Bardovi-Harlig and Hartford (1993) continued their study of academic pragmatic competence over a semester to learn whether the graduate students improved their ability to employ appropriate speech acts and strategies. Those findings indicated that they did improve with regard to speech act behavior, where faculty members apparently processed the intended force of the acts (for example, a request would be interrupted as such, although the form might not be in standard U.S. English). However, the nonnative speakers were still having difficulties with the strategies to soften the force (mitigation) of the acts, and they tended to use aggravators more frequently than students who were native speakers. Bardovi-Harlig and Hartford (1993) claim that the results strongly point to a lack of classroom input and feedback on appropriate language use in advising sessions. That is, the students might know they should make a suggestion or a request, but lacked information about how to perform the acts linguistically.

The Bardovi-Harlig and Hartford study (1990, 1993) shows that careful, grounded analysis of classroom and other institutional data provides rich information for teachers who work with nonnative speakers and minority students in any speech community. Not only general pragmatic competence in the target language, but also context-specific behaviors are at stake. The study leads educators to consider the greater need for explicit teaching and exposure to linguistic and nonlinguistic input for learners to expand their pragmatic competence in the L2 or dominant language.

Successful Construction of Second Language Identities

This section discusses one example of how learners were able to develop their pragmatic ability and construct a successful identity for themselves in their L2. It involves graduate students in a TESL program and their efforts to overcome problems in giving oral academic presentations to become members of the discourse community of their targeted profession.

Morita (2000) studied one classroom event, the oral academic presentation (OAP) and the processes that the students in a graduate TESL program in Canada went through in becoming socialized to perform such speech events. In particular, she examined how the NNS students learned to produce a good OAP through discourse socialization processes. An ethnographic approach was used, and the data collection consisted of classroom observations, video recording and transcriptions, interviews with teachers and students, questionnaires, and relevant documents from courses. Students were required to present an academic article from course readings and lead the class discussion. Difficulties arose, however, because the teachers expected the presenter to avoid "regurgitating" content. Rather, they were expected to provide their own analysis and critique, what Ohta (1991) labeled "epistemic stance." Epistemic stance "is an important aspect of language socialization because novices must learn how to display their knowledge (or lack thereof) in a way that demonstrates their competence as members of the social group" (Ochs cited in Morita 2000, 289). In carrying out this function, the presenters were expected to trigger a discussion that would engage all the members of the seminar. In so doing, the presenter would attempt to act as the "expert" on the article and related content areas. The "performance was socially and collaboratively constructed" (Morita 2000, 292).

For NNS graduate students, the OAP was problematic (as it was for at least some of the NSs, although for different reasons). Morita states that there were three reasons the NNSs ($N = 6$) in her study had problems with the OAPs: linguistic, sociocultural, and psychological. The linguistic reasons included the NNSs' concern about their own proficiency in English. Difficulties in the classroom arose primarily because of their lack of communication skills in that context, rather than conflict between Canadian and their home countries' expectations about classroom behavior. They had problems getting a turn in discussions, for example, which caused them to feel uncomfortable. Another source of insecurity was their perceived lack of training in critical thinking and other intellectual skills. The psychological difficulties grew out of their lack of confidence, often the result of the linguistic and sociocultural gaps and pressures that they experienced.

To address the insecurities experienced by both NNS and NS students, teachers modeled OAPs to provide a norm for the activity, thereby communicating their expectations regarding the activity. The six NNSs in Morita's study developed a variety of strategies to overcome their perceived limitations: (1) rehearse the OAP, (2) prepare clear handouts and outlines, (3) prepare careful notes in English for themselves, (4) choose an article on a topic for which they already had some expertise, and (5) use audiovisual aids skillfully.

Morita's study informs not only the teachers of language, but also teachers of international students in academic programs. So that the graduate students in her study could learn to perform OAPs successfully, the teachers focused on the speech event as a socially co-constructed example of academic discourse. To view this type of oral language use as a problem of individual students would have missed the extent to which this activity and others comprise part of the acculturation into the academic discourse community. From a language socialization perspective, the students need to be guided to participate and to become proficient members of the social group of their community.

Learning More about One's Classroom

To help learners develop their pragmatic competence and more successfully communicate their intentions, views, and identities, teachers need to get to know their learners' strengths, competencies, and weaknesses.

Learners come to language learning with different cognitive and interactional styles that affect group work, cooperation and competition, asking for help from the teacher, and giving help to their classmates.

A study of how one teacher became more aware of the learners in her classroom is that of Carrasco (1979), who reports on a Spanish-speaking child named Lupita who joined a bilingual kindergarten classroom in the United States. This study used the teacher's objectives, classroom observation of the child, knowledge of Lupita's background, and her test scores in determining not only the child's competence, but also the interaction between the teacher and student (Carrasco 1979, 2). Carrasco used "ethnographic monitoring" (Hymes 1972), in this case to study the teacher-student and student-student interactions. By videotaping and observing Lupita in activities with the teacher and in small groups, and by listening to the account of a teacher's aide, who was Chicano like Lupita, Carrasco discovered that the teacher rarely called on Lupita to participate in class, having assumed she would have to repeat kindergarten rather than moving up to first grade. However, in small-group tasks, Lupita could be observed teaching others, in fact, acting as a leader and teacher with her peers. Once the teacher was made a aware of her own behavior and of Lupita's behavior, she modified her interaction with the child and used different teaching strategies. She became more and more aware of what the child could do in the different modes of learning in the classroom environment.

It was only through having another set of eyes observing and videotaping what was happening in the classroom that the teacher discovered to what extent this girl was learning and interacting in helpful ways with her classmates. Luckily for Lupita, the teacher acted on the new information and by changing her behavior was able to foster the girl's development.

Teachers also need to learn about the cultural and social backgrounds of the learners in their classroom. Different interactional styles, for example, influence not only the learners' progress in developing their communicative competence, but also the teacher's perceptions. Erickson and Schultz (1982) studied academic counseling interviews and used an ethnographic microanalysis approach (Erickson 1996) to analyze the videotaped data they collected. The informants were white or African American. The findings indicated that the different interactional patterns, even among white Americans from different ethnic backgrounds, resulted in reactions that were prejudicial toward the student who had come for counseling. The counselors were more helpful, it seems, with counselees with whom they had something in common, such as race, ethnicity, or gender. This example illustrates dramatically the effects of teachers' being unaware of their own behaviors and attitudes, which can have detrimental effects on the learners in their classrooms, both psychologically and in everyday outcomes (McGroarty 1996; Johnson 1995).

Conclusion

This chapter has reviewed some of the major dimensions of the classroom learning environment that can influence learners' pragmatic competence development. Perhaps the main goal is to raise awareness in the readers of this book—primarily second language teachers and teachers in training—particularly with regard to their becoming better observers of what goes on in classrooms. As Carrasco did, teachers need to carry out ethnographic monitoring to discover the depth and richness of learning and to uncover aspects that may hinder the learners' full development.

Teachers have most of the responsibility in the classroom for fostering the development of learners' L2 pragmatic ability. By expanding their own competence to examine L2 interactive discourse and to use appropriate frameworks (for example, sociocultural theory: see Lantolf 2000), educators can better understand how learners acquire L2 pragmatic competence through interaction. A recent book by Roberts et al. (2001) outlines rationales for training language learners who spend a year abroad as part of a degree program to become "ethnographers." An ideal training program for all L2 teachers would require that they have considerable experience themselves first as language learners, preferably abroad, and be required to carry out small ethnographic research projects. We need greater understanding of the complexity of language learning and teaching.

Discussion Questions

1. Reflect on times when you did not make the kind of impression you wanted to make in a second or foreign language you

know. What were the factors that caused you to experience discomfort?

2. Give an example of how you would use the Socratic method in teaching a second or foreign language.

3. In the following example of teacher-learner discourse, what is happening? How useful is such talk to the learner's development of competence?
    S: ah um . . . how many papers can . . . mm . . . should I . . . write?
    T: you mean how many drafts should you write?
    S: yeah

    (Mori 1996, 60)

4. Give an example of how you would teach a lesson on social appropriateness in a second or foreign language. Choose a situation, decide what the rules of social appropriateness would be, and develop a lesson plan.

5. Find examples in materials you use for teaching that misrepresent social variables and language use in a second or foreign language.

6. Generate examples of where your L1 influences your pragmatic competence when you are using another language.

7. In the following dialogue, learners did not take the opportunity to practice using the L2. Why didn't they? What could the teacher do differently in the interaction pattern so as to enable the learners to do so?
    T: okay, what have we been looking at in the past unit? What were you reading yesterday?
    S: ((. . .))
    T: So what have we been looking at in this unit?
    S: ((. . .))
    T: What?
    S: ((. . .))
    T: okay, remember? Time clauses? What tense? Past?
    S: Present

> T: Present time clauses. What are the ((. . .)) time phrases that we have been looking at? What are they?
> S: ((. . .))
> T: ((. . .)) match the two clauses with what? What do we do?
> S: um
> T: Put the clauses together. Before one, right?
> S: After
> T: After, what?
>
> (Benson 2000, 86)

8. What communication strategies could a learner who lacks fluency use to interact in the L2? Select some typical situations and describe the strategies.

9. How do you feel about working in groups? Elaborate and discuss with some classmates.

10. Isolate a problem you have with your L2, such as the one Morita describes in her study. Make a proposal as to how to deal with it.

11. "It is sometimes necessary to become conscious of the forms of social behavior in order to bring about a more serviceable adaptation to changed conditions" (Sapir 1951, cited in Cazden 1988). Do you agree or disagree with the point of view expressed? Explain.

Tasks

1. Videotape a language lesson, transcribe a ten-minute segment, and analyze it. Look for examples of the aspects discussed in this chapter.

2. The accompanying table presents segments from a lesson on English as a foreign language at a Mexican university taught by an NS of English. Study carefully the kinds of questions the teacher is asking.

1.	*Student:*	Arrangement?
2.	*Teacher:*	What are the arrangements?
3.	*S:*	(. . .) [*Silence*]
4.	*T:*	Check or review all the arrangements. The marriage license To get married, need a special license, a special paper
5.	*S:*	*Acta?*
6.	*T:*	Well, this is in the United States, isn't it the same in Mexico?
7.	*S:*	Like church? Or like the government?
8.	*T:*	The government. The license is something civil. You do, no?
9.	*Ss:*	No.
10.	*T:*	Yes, okay, so let's listen to this exercise, let's hear the instructions [*plays tape instructions*]
11.	*T:*	Okay, so you're going to match first match January What would be the action January?
12.	*S:*	Talk to the
13.	*T:*	Talk to the minister, okay? [*Plays the taped exercise*]
14.	*T:*	Okay, what happens in February?
15.	*Ss:*	Reception
16.	*S:*	Restaurant
17.	*T:*	The reception. Okay, a place for the reception Where? Where can you have a reception?
18.	*S:*	(. . .) [*Silence*]
19.	*T:*	What? So where? They mentioned two, a restaurant. They said it could be a restaurant or a hall. What would be a hall?
20.	*Ss:*	*Salon*
21.	*T:*	Uh huh, like a big room special for parties, that would be a hall For a reception that's February. Let's listen for March [*plays tape*]
22.	*T:*	In March, what?
23.	*S:*	Choose a gown
24.	*T:*	The wedding gown, the special dress [*plays tape*]
25.	*T:*	For April?
26.	*Ss:*	Wedding ring

Source: Benson 2000, 60–61.

Some of the questions are "real," that is, the teacher does not already know the answer. Some form a strategy the teacher uses to go over the content of the lesson. Are both present in this lesson? Which type is more like the kinds of questions found in the real world? What effect might the different questions have with regard to the learners' pragmatic development?

Suggested Readings

Barnes, D. 1976. *From communication to curriculum.* Middlesex, U.K.: Penguin.

Carrasco, R. L. 1979. Expanded awareness of student performance: A case study of applied ethnographic monitoring in a bilingual classroom. In *Culture and the bilingual classroom: Studies in classroom ethnography,* ed. H. T. Trueba, G. P. Guthrie, and K. H-P. Au. Rowley, Mass.: Newbury House.

Cazden, C. B. 1988. *Classroom discourse: The language of teaching and learning.* Portsmouth, N.H.: Heinemann.

Gillette, B. 1994. The role of learner goals in L2 success. In *Vygotskyan approaches to second language research,* ed. J. P. Lantolf and G. Appel. Norwood, N.J.: Ablex,

Hall, J. K. 1995. "Aw, man, where you goin'?": Classroom interaction and the development of L2 interactional competence. *Issues in Applied Linguistics* 6, no. 2: 37–62.

Johnson, K. E. 1995. *Understanding communication in second language classrooms.* Cambridge: Cambridge University Press.

Lightbown, P., and N. Spada. 1999. *How languages are learned.* Rev. ed. Oxford: Oxford University Press.

Moll, L. C. 1981. The microethnographic study of bilingual schooling. In *Ethnoperspectives on bilingual education research: Bilingual education technology,* ed. R. V. Padilla. Ypsilanti, Mich.: Eastern Michigan University Press.

Moll, L. C., and N. Gonzalez. 1994. Lessons from research with language minority children. *Journal of Reading Behavior* 26, no. 4: 439–56.

Morita, N. 2000. Discourse socialization through oral classroom activities in a TESOL graduate program. *TESOL Quarterly* 34, no. 2: 279–310.

Norton Peirce, B. 2000. *Identity and language learning: Gender, ethnicity, and educational change.* Harlow, England: Pearson.

Vygotsky, L. S. 1962. *Thought and language.* Cambridge: MIT Press.

References

Abou, Selim. 1978. *Liban deracine: Immigres dans l'aitre Amerique.* Paris: Librarie Plon.

Astley, Helen, and Eric Hawkins. 1985. *Using language.* Cambridge: Cambridge University Press.

Aston, Guy. 1993. Notes on the interlanguage of comity. In *Interlanguage pragmatics,* edited by Gabriele Kasper and Shoshana Blum-Kulka, 224–50. Oxford: Oxford University Press.

Austin, J. L. 1962. *How to do things with words.* Oxford: Clarendon Press.

Bachman, Lyle F. 1989. The development and use of criterion-referenced tests of language program evaluation. In *The second language curriculum,* edited by R. K. Johnson, 242–58. Cambridge: Cambridge University Press.

Bardovi-Harlig, Kathleen, and Beverly S. Hartford. 1990. Congruence in native and nonnative conversations: Status balance in an academic advising sessions. *Language Learning* 40, no. 4: 467–501.

———. 1993. Learning the rules of academic talk. *Studies in Second Language Acquisition* 15:279–304.

Barnes, D. 1976. *From communication to curriculum.* Middlesex, U.K.: Penguin.

Barnlund, Dean C. 1975. *Public and private self in Japan and the United States: Communicative styles of two cultures.* Tokyo: Simul Press.

Beebe, Leslie, and Tomoko Takahashi. 1989. Do you have a bag? Social status and patterned variation in second language acquisition. In *Variation in second language acquisition: Discourse and pragmatics,* edited by Susan Gass, Carolyn Madden, Dennis Preston, and Larry Selinker, 103–25. Clevedon, U.K.: Multilingual Matters.

Benson, Timothy J. 2000. A study of target language use in the upper-beginning EFL university classroom. Unpublished thesis, Universidad de las Americas–Puebla.

Bialystok, Ellen. 1993. Symbolic representation and attentional control in pragmatic competence. In *Interlanguage pragmatics,* edited by Gabriele Kasper and Shoshana Blum-Kulka, 43–58. Oxford: Oxford University Press.

Birdwhistell, R. L. 1965. Communication without words. Typescript.

Blakemore, Diane. 1992. *Understanding utterances: An introduction to pragmatics.* Oxford: Blackwell.

Bloor, Thomas, and Meriel Bloor. 1995. *The functional analysis of English: A Hallidayan approach.* London: Edward Arnold.

Blot, D., and P. Berman Sher. 1978. *Getting into it . . . an unfinished book.* New York: Language Innovations.

Blum-Kulka, Shoshana. 1983. Interpreting and performing speech acts in a second language: A cross cultural study of Hebrew and English. In *Sociolinguistics and language acquisition,* edited by Nessa Wolfson and Elliot Judd, 36–55. Rowley, Mass.: Newbury House.

———. 1987. Indirectness and politeness in requests: Same or different. *Journal of Pragmatics* 11:131–46.

———. 1989. Playing it safe: The role of conventionality in indirectness. In *Cross-cultural pragmatics: Requests and apologies,* edited by Shoshana Blum-Kulka, Juliane House, and Gabriele Kasper, 37–70. Norwood, N.J.: Ablex.

———. 1991. Interlanguage pragmatics: The case of requests. In *Foreign/second language pedagogy research,* edited by R. Phillipson, Eric Kellerman, Larry Selinker, Michael Sharwood-Smith, and Merril Swain, 255–72. Clevedon, U.K.: Multilingual Matters.

Blum-Kulka, Shoshana, Juliane House, and Gabriele Kasper, eds. 1989. *Cross-cultural pragmatics: Requests and apologies.* Norwood, N.J.: Ablex.

Boden, Deirdre, and Don H. Zimmerman, eds. 1991. *Talk and social structure: Studies in ethnomethodology and conversation analysis.* Cambridge: Polity Press.

Bourdieu, Pierre. 1977. The economics of linguistic exchanges. *Social Science Information* 16, no. 6: 645–68.

Bouton, Lawrence. 1994. Conversational implicature in a second language: Learned slowly when not deliberately taught. *Journal of Pragmatics* 22:157–67.

Boyle, Ronald. 2000. Whatever happened to preference organization? *Journal of Pragmatics* 32:583–604.

Bradford, Barbara. 1988. *Intonation in context.* Cambridge: Cambridge University Press.

Brazil, David. 1985. *The communicative value of intonation in English.* Birmingham: University of Birmingham.

Brown, Gillian. 1995. *Speakers, listeners, and communication: Explorations in discourse analysis.* Cambridge: Cambridge University Press.

Brown, Gillian, and George Yule. 1983a. *Discourse analysis.* Cambridge: Cambridge University Press.

———. 1983b. *Teaching the spoken language: An approach based on the analysis of conversational English.* Cambridge: Cambridge University Press.

Brown, H. Douglas. 1990. M&Ms for language classroom? Another look at motivation. In *Georgetown University Round Table on Languages and Linguistics,* edited by James E. Alatis, 383–93. Washington, D.C.: Georgetown University Press.

Brown, Penelope, and C. Fraser. 1979. Speech as markers of situation. In *Social markers in speech,* edited by K. Scherer and H. Giles, 33–62. Cambridge: Cambridge University Press.

Brown, Penelope, and Stephen C. Levinson. 1987. *Politeness: Some universals in language usage.* Cambridge: Cambridge University Press.

Bruner, Jerome. 1978. The role of dialogue in language acquisition. In *The child's conception of language,* edited by A. Sinclair, R. Javella, and W. Levelt, 241–56. New York: Springer-Verlag.

Brutt-Griffler, Janina. 2002. *World English: A study of its development.* Clevedon, U.K.: Multilingual Matters.

Cameron, Deborah. 1995. *Verbal hygiene.* London: Routledge.

Cameron, Deborah, Fiona McAlinden, and Kathy O'Leary. 1988. Lakoff in context: The social and linguistic functions of tag questions. In *Women in their speech communities,* edited by Jennifer Coates and Deborah Cameron, 74–93. London: Longman.

Canale, Michael. 1983. From communicative competence to communicative language pedagogy. In *Language and communication,* edited by Jack C. Richards and Richard W. Schmidt, 2–28. London: Longman.

Canale, Michael, and Merril Swain. 1980. Theoretical bases of communicative approaches to second language teaching and testing. *Applied Linguistics* 1, no. 1: 1–47.

Carlson, Joan G., and Gayle L. Nelson. 1994. Writing groups: Cross-cultural issues. *Journal of Second Language Writing* 3, no. 1: 17–30.

Carrasco, Robert L. 1979. Expanded awareness of student performance: A case study of applied ethnographic monitoring in a bilingual classroom. In *Culture and the bilingual classroom: Studies in classroom ethnography,* edited by H. T. Trueba, G. P. Guthrie, and K. H-P. Au, 153–77. Rowley, Mass.: Newbury House.

Carter, Ronald, and Michael McCarthy. 1997, *Exploring spoken English.* Cambridge: Cambridge University Press.

Cazden, Courtney B. 1988. *Classroom discourse: The language of teaching and learning.* Portsmouth, N.H.: Heinemann, 1988.

Chafe, Wallace. 1976. Givenness, contrastiveness, definiteness, subjects, topics, and point of view. In *Subject and topic,* edited by Charles N. Li. New York: Academic Press.

———. 1994. *Discourse, consciousness, and time: The flow and displacement of conscious experience in speaking and writing.* Chicago: University of Chicago Press.

Chaudron, Craig. 1988. *Second language classrooms: Research on teaching and learning.* Cambridge: Cambridge University Press.

Chick, J. Keith. 1996. Intercultural communication. In *Sociolinguistics and language teaching,* edited by Sandra Lee McKay and Nancy H. Hornberger, 329–48. Cambridge: Cambridge University Press.

Chodorowska-Pilch, M. 2000. The imperfect of politeness in Spanish. *Southwest Journal of Linguistics* 19, no. 1: 29–44.

Chomsky, Noam. 1980. *Rules and representations.* New York: Columbia University Press.

Cicourel, Aaron V. 1980. Three models of discourse analysis: The role of social structure. *Discourse Processes* 3:101–32.

Cisneros, Sandra. 1984. *The house on Mango Street.* New York: Vintage.

Clancy, Patricia M., Sandra A. Thompson, Ryoko Suzuki, and Hongyin Tao. 1996. The conversational use of reactive tokens in English, Japanese, and Mandarin. *Journal of Pragmatics* 26:355–87.

Clark, Herbert H. 1977. Bridging. In *Thinking: Readings in cognitive science,* edited by P. Johnson-Laird and P. Watson, 411–20. Cambridge: Cambridge University Press.

———. 1996. *Using language.* Cambridge: Cambridge University Press.

Clark, Herbert H., and T.B. Carlson. 1982. Hearers and speech acts. *Language* 58:332–73.

Clark, Herbert H., and Eva V. Clark. 1977. *Psychology and language: An introduction to psycholinguistics.* New York: Harcourt Brace Jovanovich.

Coates, Jennifer. 1996. *Women talk.* Oxford: Blackwell.

Coates, Jennifer, and Deborah Cameron, eds. 1988. *Women in their speech communities.* London: Longman.

Cohen, Andrew D. 1996. Speech acts. In *Sociolinguistics and language teaching,* edited by Sandra L. McKay and Nancy H. Hornberger, 383–420. Cambridge: Cambridge University Press.

Condon, Jack. 1984. *With respect to the Japanese.* Tokyo: Yohan.

Cook, Guy. 1989. *Discourse.* Oxford: Oxford University Press.

Cook, Haruko Minegishi. 1990. The sentence-final particle *ne* as a tool for cooperation in Japanese conversation. In *Japanese-Korean Linguistics,* edited by H. Hoji, 29–44. Stanford, Calif.: Center for the Study of Language and Information.

———. 1997. Situational meaning of the Japanese social deixis: The mixed use of the *masu* and plain forms. Typescript.

Coulmas, Florien. 1981a. Poison to your soul: Thanks and apologies. In *Conversational routines,* edited by Florien Coulmas, 69–91. The Hague: Mouton.

———, ed. 1981b. *Conversational routines.* The Hague: Mouton.

Coulon, Alain. 1995. *Ethnomethodology.* Thousand Oaks, Calif.: Sage.

Coupland, Nikolas, and Adam Jaworski. 1997. Relevance, accommodation, and conversation: Modeling the social dimension of communication. *Multilingua* 16, nos. 2–3: 233–58.

Crystal, David. 1985. *A Dictionary of linguistics and phonetics.* 2d ed. Oxford: Blackwell.

Davis, Steven, ed. 1991. *Pragmatics: A reader.* New York: Oxford University Press.

Doughty, Cathy. 1991. Second language instruction does make a difference: Evidence from an empirical study on SL relativization. *Studies in Second Language Acquisition* 13:431–69.

Dufon, Margaret. 1999. The acquisition of linguistics politeness in Indonesian as a second language by sojourners in naturalistic interactions. Unpublished Ph.D. thesis, University of Hawaii-Manoa.

Dulay, Heidi, Marina Burt, and Stephen Krashen. 1982. *Language two.* New York: Oxford University Press.

Duncan, Stanley D. 1972. Some signals and rules for taking speaking turns in conversation. *Journal of Personality and Social Psychology* 23:283–92.

———. 1973. Toward a grammar of dyadic conversations. *Semiotica* 9:29–47.

Duranti, Alessandro. 1994. *From grammar to politics: Linguistic anthropology in a Western Samoan village.* Berkeley and Los Angeles: University of California Press.

Duranti, Alessandro, and Charles Goodwin, eds. 1992. *Rethinking context.* Cambridge: Cambridge University Press.

Eggins, Suzanne. 1994. *An introduction to systemic functional linguistics.* London: Pinter.

Ellis, Rod. 1994. *The study of second language acquisition.* Oxford: Oxford University Press.

Erickson, Frederick. 1984. Rhetoric, anecdote, and rhapsody: Coherence strategies in a conversation among black American adolescents. In *Coherence in spoken and written discourse,* edited by Deborah Tannen, 81–154. Norwood, N.J.: Ablex.

———. 1996. Ethnographic microanalysis. In *Sociolinguistics and language teaching,* edited by Sandra L. Mackay and Nancy H. Hornberger, 283–306. Cambridge: Cambridge University Press.

Erickson, Frederick, and J. Schultz. 1982. *The counselor as gatekeeper: Social interaction in interviews.* New York: Academic Press.

Fairclough, Norman. 1989. *Language and power.* London: Longman.

———. 1992. *Discourse and social change.* Cambridge: Polity Press.

Ferrara, Alessandro. 1985. Pragmatics. *Handbook of discourse analysis,* 2:137–57. London: Academic Press.

Fiksdal, Susan. 1988. Verbal and nonverbal strategies of rapport in cross-cultural interviews. *Linguistics and Education* 1:3–17.

Finegan, Edward. 1994. *Language, its structure and use.* 2d ed. New York: Harcourt Brace.

Foucault, Michel. 1981. *History of sexuality.* Vol. 1. Harmondsworth: Penguin.

Forster, E. M. 1942. *A passage to India.* Harmondsworth, U.K.: Penguin.

Fraser, Bruce. 1981. On apologizing. In *Conversational routines,* edited by Florien Coulmas, 259–71. The Hague: Mouton.

———. 1990. Perspectives on politeness. *Journal of Pragmatics* 14:219–36.

———. 1996. Pragmatic markers. *Pragmatics* 6, no. 2: 167–90.

Fujikawa, Yoshiko. 1997. Unpublished paper for course on pragmatics, International Christian University.

Garfinkel, Harold. 1984. *Studies in ethnomethodology.* Cambridge: Polity Press.

Gardner, R. C. 1985. *Social psychology and second language learning: The role of attitude and motivation.* London: Edward Arnold.

Gardner, R. C., and W. Lambert. 1972. *Attitudes and motivation in second language learning.* Rowley, Mass.: Newbury House.

Gardner, R. C., Paul F. Tremblay, and Anne-Marie Masgoret. 1997. Towards a full model of second language learning: An empirical investigation. *Modern Language Journal* 81, no. 3: 344–62.

Garrido, Ismael. 2001. The use of politeness strategies in Mexican Spanish in university contexts. Unpublished M.A. thesis, Universidad de las Americas–Puebla.

Gass, Susan M., and J. Neu, eds. 1996. *Speech acts across cultures.* Berlin: Mouton de Gruyter.

Gass, Susan M., Carolyn Madden, Dennis Preston, and Larry Selinker, eds. 1989. *Variation in second language acquisition: Discourse and pragmatics.* Clevedon, U.K.: Multilingual Matters.

Gass, Susan M., and Evangeline Marlos Varonis. 1986. Sex differences in non native speaker–non native speaker interactions. In *Talking to learn: Conversation in second language acquisition,* edited by Richard R. Day, 327–51. Rowley, Mass.: Newbury House.

Gillette, Barbara. 1994. The role of learner goals in L2 success. In *Vygotskyan approaches to second language research,* edited by James P. Lantolf, 195–213. Norwood, N.J.: Ablex.

Giroux, Henri. 1992. *Border crossings: Cultural workers and the politics of education.* New York: Routledge.

Glendinning, Eric, and Helen Mantell. 1983. *Write ideas: An intermediate course in writing skills.* London: Longman.

Goffman, Erving. 1963. *Behavior in public places: Notes on the social organization of gatherings.* New York: Free Press.

———. 1967. *Interaction ritual: Essays on face-to-face behavior.* New York: Pantheon Books.

———. 1981. *Forms of talk.* Philadelphia: University of Pennsylvania Press.

Goodwin, Charles. 1981. Restarts, pauses, and the achievement of a state of mutual gaze at turn-beginning. In *Conversational organization: Interaction between speakers and hearers,* edited by Charles Goodwin, 272–302. New York: Academic Press.

Green, Georgia M. 1989. *Pragmatics and natural language understanding.* Mahwah, N.J.: Lawrence Erlbaum.

———. 1996. *Pragmatics and natural language understanding.* 2d ed. Mahwah, N.J.: Lawrence Erlbaum.

Greene, Judith. 1986. *Language understanding: A cognitive approach.* Milton Keynes, U.K.: Open University Press.

Grice, H. P. 1967. Logic and conversation. Unpublished manuscript from the William James Lectures. Harvard University.

———. 1975. Logic and conversation. In *Speech acts,* vol. 3 of *Syntax and semantics,* edited by P. Cole and J. L. Morgan, 41–58. New York: Academic Press.

Grundy, Peter. 1995. *Doing pragmatics.* London: Edward Arnold.

Gu, Yueguo. 1990. Politeness phenomena in modern Chinese. *Journal of Pragmatics* 14:237–57.

Gumperz, John J. 1982a. *Discourse strategies.* Cambridge: Cambridge University Press.

———, ed. 1982b. *Language and social identity.* Cambridge: Cambridge University Press.

Gumperz, John J., and Stephen Levinson, eds. 1996. *Rethinking linguistic relativity.* Cambridge: Cambridge University Press.

Hall, Edward T. 1969. Listener behavior: Some cultural differences. *Phi Delta Kappan* 50, no. 7: 379–80.

Hall, Joan Kelly. 1995. "Aw, man, where you goin'?": Classroom interaction and the development of L2 interactional competence. *Issues in Applied Linguistics* 6, no. 2: 37–62.

Halliday, M. A. K. 1967. *Intonation and grammar in British English.* The Hague: Mouton.

———. 1978. *Language as a social semiotic: The social interpretation of language and meaning.* London: Edward Arnold.

———. 1985. *An introduction to functional grammar.* London: Edward Arnold.

———. 1994. *An introduction to functional grammar.* 2d ed. London: Edward Arnold.

Hamilton, Edith, and Huntington Cairns, eds. 1961. *The collected dialogues of Plato.* Princeton, N.J.: Princeton University Press.

Hasan, Ruqaiya. 1985. The structure of a text. In *Language, context, and text: Aspects of language in a social-semiotic perspective,* edited by M. A. K. Halliday and Ruqaiya Hasan, 52–121. Oxford: Oxford University Press.

Hatch, Evelyn. 1992. *Discourse and language education.* Cambridge: Cambridge University Press.

Heath, Shirley Brice. 1978. *Teacher talk: Language in the classroom.* Washington, D.C.: Center for Applied Linguistics.

Hill, Beverly, Sachiko Ide, Shoko Ikuta, Akiko Kawasaki, and Tsunao Ogino. 1986. Universals of linguistic politeness: Quantitative evidence from Japanese and American English. *Journal of Pragmatics* 10:347–71.

Hinkel, Eli. 1994. Pragmatics of interaction: Expressing thanks in a second language. *Applied Language Learning* 5, no. 1: 73–91.

———. 1996. When in Rome: Evaluations of L2 pragmalinguistic behaviors. *Journal of Pragmatics* 26:51–70.

Hiraga, Masako K., and Joan M. Turner. 1995. What to say next? The sociopragmatic problem of elaboration for Japanese students of English in academic contexts. *JACET Bulletin* 10:13–30.

———. 1996a. Differing perspectives of face in British and Japanese academic settings. *Language Sciences* 18, nos. 3–4: 605–27.

———. 1996b. Pragmatic difficulties in academic discourse: A case of Japanese students in English. *Journal of the University of the Air* 14:91–109.

Ho, D. Y. F. 1976. On the concept of face. *American Journal of Sociology* 81, no. 4: 867–84.

Hoffman, Eva. 1989. *Lost in translation: A life in a new language.* New York: Penguin.

Holland, Dorothy, and Naomi Quinn, eds. 1987. *Cultural models in language and thought.* Cambridge: Cambridge University Press.

Holmes, Janet. 1992. *An introduction to sociolinguistics.* London: Longman.

Hudson, Richard. 1996. "Emphasis." *Linguist List,* January, <http://www.emich.edu/~linguist/issues/indices/Jan1996.html>, 7.143.

Hyland, Ken. 1998. *Hedging in scientific research articles.* Amsterdam/Philadelphia: John Benjamins.

Hymes, Dell. 1972. "SPEAKING." In *Directions in sociolinguistics: The ethnography of communication,* edited by John J. Gumperz and Dell Hymes. Oxford: Blackwell.

———. 1996. *Ethnography, linguistics, narrative inequality: Toward an understanding of voice.* London: Taylor and Francis.

Japanese mannerism is key point in IBN case. 1983. *Japan Times,* January 29, 2.

Johnson, Donna M., Yvonna Roepcke, and Kuniyoshi Kataoka. 1997. Constructing social groups in discourse. In *Pragmatics and Language Learning,* monograph series, vol. 8, 37–53. Urbana: Division of English as an International Language, University of Illinois.

Johnson, Karen E. 1995. *Understanding communication in second language classrooms.* Cambridge: Cambridge University Press.

Johnson, Robert Keith. 1989. *The second language curriculum.* Cambridge: Cambridge University Press.

Jorden, Eleanor Harz, with Mari Noda. 1987. *Japanese: The spoken language.* 3 parts. New Haven: Yale University Press.

Kachru, Braj B., and Cecil L. Nelson. 1996. World Englishes. In *Sociolinguistics and language teaching,* edited by Sandra Lee McKay and Nancy H. Hornberger, 71–102. Cambridge: Cambridge University Press.

Kanagy, Ruth. 1999. Interactional routines as a mechanism for L2 acquisition and socialization in an immersion context. *Journal of Pragmatics* 31:1467–92.

Kasher, Asa. 1994. Pragmatics, cognitive. In *The encyclopedia of language and linguistics,* edited by J. R. Asher, 6:3278–79. Oxford: Pergamon Press.

Kasper, Gabriele. 1984. Pragmatic competence in learner-native speaker discourse. *Language Learning* 34:1–20.

———. 1989. Variation in interlanguage speech act realisation. In *Variation in second language acquisition: Discourse and pragmatics,* edited by Susan Gass, Carolyn Madden, Dennis Preston, and Larry Selinker, 37–58. Clevedon, U.K.: Multilingual Matters.

———. 1992. Pragmatic transfer. *Second Language Research* 8, no. 3: 203–31.

———. 1995a. Interlanguage Pragmatics. In *Handbook of pragmatics,* edited by J. Verschueren, J. O. Ostman, and J. Blommaert, 1–17. Amsterdam: John Benjamins.

———, ed. 1995b. *Pragmatics of Chinese as native and target language.* Honolulu: University of Hawaii Press.

———. 1997. Can pragmatics be taught? TESOL '97 Plenary, Orlando, Florida, March 14, 1997. Second Language Teaching and Curriculum Center, NFLRC Net Work no. 6. <http://www.lll.hawaii.edu/NFLRC/Network/N.>

———. 1999. Learning pragmatics in the L2 classroom. Plenary at the Tenth International Conference on Pragmatics and Language Learning, University of Illinois, April.

Kasper, Gabriele, and Shoshana Blum-Kulka. 1993. Interlanguage pragmatics: An introduction. In *Interlanguage pragmatics,* edited by Gabriele Kasper and Shoshana Blum-Kulka, 3–20. Oxford: Oxford University Press.

Kasper, Gabriele, and Eric Kellerman, eds. 1997. *Communication strategies: Psycholinguistic and sociolinguistic perspectives.* London: Longman.

Kasper, Gabriele, and Ken Rose. 1999. Pragmatics and SLA. *Annual Review of Applied Linguistics.* 19:81–104.

Kasper, Gabriele, and Richard W. Schmidt. 1996. Developmental issues in interlanguage pragmatics. *Studies in Second Language Acquisition* 18:149–69.

Kirkpatrick, Andy. 1991. Information sequencing in Mandarin letters of request. *Anthropological Linguistics* 33, no. 2: 184–203.

Krashen, Stephen. 1982. *Principles and practice in second language learning.* Oxford: Pergamon Press.

Kress, Gunther, and Roger Fowler. 1979. Interviews. In *Language and control,* edited by Roger Fowler, Robert Hodge, Gunther Kress, and Tony Trew. London: Routledge and Kegan Paul.

Kristoff, Nicholas D. 1995. Land of rising voices. *Asahi Evening News,* December 14, pp. 1, 4.

Labov, William. 1972. *Sociolinguistic patterns.* Philadelphia: University of Pennsylvania Press.

Labov, William, and D. Fanshel. 1977. *Therapeutic discourse: Psychotherapy as conversation.* New York: Academic Press.

Lacville, Robert. 1991. When in Africa. . . . *Guardian Weekly,* November 7, p. 19.

Lakoff, George. 1987. *Women, fire, and dangerous things: What categories reveal about the mind.* Chicago: University of Chicago Press.

Lakoff, Robin Tolmach. 1971. Language in context. *Language* 48:907–27.

———. 1990. *Talking power: The politics of language.* New York: Basic Books.

Lantolf, James P., ed. 1994. Special issue, Sociocultural theory and second language learning. *Modern Language Journal* 78, no. 4.

———, ed. 2000. *Sociocultural theory and second language learning.* Oxford: Oxford University Press.

Lantolf, James P., and Gabriela Appel. 1994. *Vygotskian approaches to second language research.* Norwood, N.J.: Ablex.

Latina. 2000. Vol. 5, no. 1.

Leech, Geoffrey N. 1983. *Principles of pragmatics.* London: Longman.

Lemke, Jay L. 1985. *Using language in the classroom.* Oxford: Oxford University Press.

Levinson, Stephen C. 1983. *Pragmatics.* Cambridge: Cambridge University Press.

———. 1992. Activity types and language. In *Talk at work: Interaction in institutional settings,* edited by P. Drew and J. Heritage, 66–100. Cambridge: Cambridge University Press.

Li, C., and S. Thompson. 1976. Subject and topic: A new typology of language. In *Subject and topic,* edited by Charles Li. New York: Academic Press.

Li-Shih, Y. 1988. *Conversational politeness and foreign language teaching.* Taipei: Crane.

Lightbown, Patsy, and Nina Spada. 1999. *How languages are learned.* Rev. ed. Oxford: Oxford University Press.

LoCastro, Virginia. 1987. Aizuchi: A Japanese conversational routine. In *Discourse across cultures,* edited by Larry E. Smith, 101–13. New York: Prentice-Hall International.

———. 1990a. The English in Japanese university entrance examinations: A sociocultural analysis. *World Englishes* 9, no. 3: 343–54.

———. 1990b. Intercultural pragmatics: A Japanese-American case study. Ph.D. diss., Lancaster University.

———. 1996. Learner interactions in classroom tasks. Paper presented at the Eleventh World Congress of Applied Linguistics, Jyväskylä, Finland, August 4–9.

———. 1997a. Pedagogical intervention and pragmatic competence development. *Applied Language Learning* 8, no. 1: 75–109.

———. 1997b. Politeness and pragmatic competence in foreign language education. *Language Teaching Research* 1, no. 3: 239–67.

———. 1998. Learner subjectivity and pragmatic competence development. Paper presented at PacSLRF Conference '98, March 26–29, Tokyo. ERIC Document no. 420 201.

———. 1999. A sociocultural functional approach to fragmentation in Japanese. *Multilingua* 18, no. 4: 369–89.

———. 2000a. Evidence of accommodation to L2 pragmatic norms in peer review tasks of Japanese learners of English. *JALT Journal* 22, no. 2: 245–70.

———. 2000b. Unpublished data.

———. 2001. Individual differences in second language acquisition: Attitudes, learner subjectivity, and L2 pragmatic norms. *System* 29, no. 1: 69–89.

LoCastro, Virginia, and Machiko Netsu. 1997. Point of view and opinion giving in discussion tasks. Paper presented at the American Association for Applied Linguistics Conference, March 8–11, Orlando, Fla.

Lock, Graham. 1996. *Functional English grammar: An introduction for second language teachers.* Cambridge: Cambridge University Press.

Loveday, Leo J. 1981. Pitch, politeness, and sexual role. *Language and Speech* 24: 71–89.

Malinowski, Bronislaw. 1923. The problem of meaning in primitive languages. Supplement to C. K. Ogden and I. A. Richards, *The Meaning of meaning.* London: Kegan Paul.

Manes, Joan. 1983. Compliments: A mirror of cultural values. In *Sociolinguistics and language acquisition,* edited by Nessa Wolfson and Elliot Judd, 96–102. Rowley, Mass.: Newbury House.

Manes, Joan, and Nessa Wolfson. 1981. The compliment formula. In *Conversational routines,* edited by Florien Coulmas, F., 115–32. The Hague: Mouton.

Maslow, A. H. 1970. *Motivation and personality.* 2d ed. New York: Harper and Row.

Matsumoto, Yoshiko. 1988. Reexamination of the universality of face: Politeness phenomena in Japanese. *Journal of Pragmatics* 12:403–26.

Maynard, Senko. 1989. *Japanese conversation: Self-contextualization through structure and interactional management.* Norwood, N.J.: Ablex.

———. 1990. *An introduction to Japanese grammar and communication strategies.* Tokyo: Japan Times.

McCarthy, Michael. 1991. *Discourse analysis for language teachers.* Cambridge: Cambridge University Press.

McCarthy, Michael, and Ronald Carter. 1994. *Language as discourse: Perspectives for language teaching.* London: Longman.

McGroarty, Mary. 1996. Language attitudes, motivation, and standards. In *Sociolinguistics and language teaching,* edited by Sandra Lee McKay and Nancy H. Hornberger, 3–46. Cambridge: Cambridge University Press.

McNamara, Thomas. 1997. What do we mean by social identity? Competing frameworks, competing discourse. *TESOL Quarterly* 31:561–67.

Mercer, N. 1996. Language and the guided construction of knowledge. In *Language in education,* edited by G. Blue and Rosamond Mitchell, 28–40. Clevedon, U.K.: BAAL/Multilingual Matters.

Mey, Jacob L. 1993. *Pragmatics: An introduction.* Oxford: Blackwell.

———. 1994. Pragmatics. In *The Encyclopedia of language and linguistics,* edited by Ronald E. Asher, 3260–78. Oxford: Pergamon.

Mey, Jacob L., and Mary Talbot. 1989. Computation and the soul. *Semiotica* 72, nos. 3–4: 291–339.

Miller, Roy. 1967. *The Japanese language.* Chicago: University of Chicago Press.

Mitchell, Rosamond, and Florence Myles. 1998. *Second language learning theories.* London: Arnold.

Mitchell-Keenan, Claudia. 1972. Signifying, loud-talking, and marking. In *Rappin' and stylin' out: Communication in urban Black America,* edited by Thomas Kochman, 315–35. Urbana: University of Illinois Press.

Mizutani, Osamu, and Mizutani, Nobuko. 1987. *How to be polite in Japanese.* Tokyo: Japan Times.

Mo, Timothy. 1982. *Soursweet.* London: Abacus.

Moerman, Michael. 1988. *Talking cultures: Ethnography and conversation analysis.* Philadelphia: University of Pennsylvania Press.

Moll, Luis C. 1981. The microethnographic study of bilingual schooling. In *Ethnoperspectives on bilingual education research: Bilingual education technology,* edited by R. V. Padilla, 430–44. Ypsilanti: Eastern Michigan University Press.

———, ed. 1990. *Vygotsky and education: Instructional implications and applications of sociohistorical psychology.* Cambridge: Cambridge University Press.

Moll, Luis C., and N. Gonzalez. 1994. Lessons from research with language minority children. *Journal of Reading Behavior* 26, no. 4: 439–56.

Morgan, Marcyliena. 1996. Conversational signifying: Grammar and indirectness among African American women. In *Interaction and grammar,* edited by Elinor Ochs, Emanuel A. Schegloff, and Sandra A. Thompson, 405–34. Cambridge: Cambridge University Press.

Mori, Michiyo. 1996. Conversational Analysis of Writing Conferences between English-speaking Teachers and Japanese EFL Students. Master's thesis, International Christian University.

Morita, Naoko. 2000. Discourse socialization through oral classroom activities in a TESL graduate program. *TESOL Quarterly* 34, no. 2: 279–310.

Morris, C. W. 1938. "Foundations of the theory of signs." In *International encyclopedia of unified science,* vol. 2, bk. 1, edited by O. Neuratin, R. Carnap, and C. W. Morris, 77–138. Chicago: University of Chicago Press.

Mortlock, Elizabeth. 1986. *At home in Thailand: A guide for Americans living with Thai families.* Bangkok: United States Information Service.

Niyekawa, Agnes M. 1991. *Minimum essential politeness: A guide to the Japanese honorific language.* Tokyo: Kodansha.

Norton Peirce, Bonny. 1995. Social identity, investment, and language learning. *TESOL Quarterly* 29, no. 1: 9–32.

———. 2000. *Identity and language learning: Gender, ethnicity, and educational change.* Harlow, U.K.: Pearson Education.

Ochs, Elinor. 1979. Transcription as theory. In *Developmental pragmatics,* edited by E. Ochs and B. B. Schieffelin, 43–72. New York: Academic Press.

———. 1992. Indexing gender. In *Rethinking context,* edited by Alessandro Duranti and Charles Goodwin, 335–58. Cambridge: Cambridge University Press.

Ochs, Elinor, Emmanuel Schegloff, and Sandra A. Thompson, eds. 1996. *Interaction and grammar.* Cambridge: Cambridge University Press.

Ochs, Elinor, and Bambi Schieffelin, eds. 1979. *Developmental pragmatics.* New York: Academic Press.

Ohta, Amy Snyder. 1991. Evidentiality and politeness in Japanese. *Issues in Applied Linguistics* 2:211–38.

———. 1997. The development of pragmatic competence in learner-learner classroom interaction. In *Pragmatics and Language Learning,* edited by Larry F. Bouton, monograph series, vol. 8, 223–42. Urbana: Division of English as an International Language, University of Illinois.

Olshtain, Elite, and Andrew Cohen. 1983. Apology: A speech act set. In *Sociolinguistics and language acquisition,* edited by Nessa Wolfson and Elliot Judd, 18–35. Rowley, Mass.: Newbury House.

Partridge, Eric. 1958. *Origins: An etymological dictionary of modern English.* London: Routledge.

Philips, Susan U. 1976. Some sources of cultural variability in the regulation of talk. *Language in Society* 5:81–95.

Pienemann, M., M. Johnston, and G. Brindley. 1988. Constructing an acquisition-based procedure for assessing second language acquisition. *Studies in Second Language Acquisition* 10:217–43.

Pomerantz, Anita. 1984. Agreeing and disagreeing with assessments: Some features of preferred/dispreferred turn shapes. In *Structures in social action: Studies in conversation analysis,* edited by J. M. Atkinson and J. Heritage, 57–101. Cambridge: Cambridge University Press.

Poole, D. 1992. Language socialization in the second language classroom. *Language Learning* 42:593–616.

Porter, Patricia. 1986. How learners talk to each other: Input and interaction in task-centered discussions. In *Talking to learn: Conversation in second language acquisition,* edited by Richard Day, 200–224. Rowley, Mass: Newbury House.

Power, R. J. D., and M. F. Dal Martello. 1986. Some criticisms of Sacks, Schegloff, and Jefferson on turn-taking. *Semiotica* 58, nos. 1–2: 29–40.

Richards, Jack C., John Platt, and Heidi Platt. 1992. *Dictionary of language teaching and applied linguistics.* 2d ed. London: Longman.

Richards, Jack C., and Richard W. Schmidt, eds. 1983. *Language and communication.* London: Longman.

Richards, Jack C., and Mayuri Sukwiwat. 1985. Cross-cultural aspects of conversational competence. In *The context of language teaching,* edited by Jack C. Richards, 129–43. London: Longman.

Roberts, Celia, Michael Byram, Ana Barro, S. Jordan, and Brian Street. 2001. *Language learners as ethnographers.* Clevedon, U.K.: Multilingual Matters.

Roberts, Celia, Evelyn Davies, and Tom Jupp. 1992. *Language and discrimination.* London: Longman.

Robinson, M. A. 1992. Introspective methodology in interlanguage pragmatics research. In pragmatics of Japanese as a native and foreign language, edited by Gabriele Kasper, 27–82. Technical Report no. 3, University of Hawaii at Manoa, Second Language Teaching and Curriculum Center.

Rogoff, Barbara. 1990. *Apprenticeship in thinking: Cognitive development in social context.* Oxford: Oxford University Press.

Rose, Kenneth R. 1993. Sociolinguistic consciousness-raising through video. *Language Teacher* 17, no. 10: 7–8.

———. 1994. Pragmatic consciousness-raising in an EFL context. *Pragmatics and Language Learning,* monograph series, vol. 5, 52–63.. Urbana: Division of English as an International Language, University of Illinois.

———. 1996. Pragmatics in the classroom: Theoretical concerns and practical possibilities. Paper presented at the Tenth International Conference on Pragmatics and Language Learning, March, University of Illinois.

———. 1997. Film in interlanguage pragmatics research. In *Perspectives: Working Papers,* 111–44. Hong Kong: City University of Hong Kong.

Rose, Kenneth R., and Gabriele Kasper, eds. 2001. *Pragmatics in language teaching.* Cambridge: Cambridge University Press.

Rosenberger, Nancy R., ed. 1992. *Japanese sense of self.* Cambridge: Cambridge University Press.

Rosenfeld, H. M. 1978. Conversational control functions of nonverbal behavior. In *Nonverbal behavior and communication,* edited by A. W. Siegman and S. Feldstein, 291–328. Hillsdale, N.J.: Lawrence Erlbaum.

Sacks, Herbert, Emmanuel Schegloff, and Gail Jefferson. 1978. A simplest systematics for the organization of turn-taking in conversation. In *Studies in the organization of conversational interaction,* edited by J. Schenkein, 7–55. New York: Academic Press.

Sakuma, Julianne. 1996. An analysis of conversational English. Typescript.

Salisbury, T. 2000. The acquisitional grammaticalization of unreal conditionals and modality in L2 English: A longitudinal perspective. Unpublished Ph.D. diss., Indiana University, Bloomington.

Salisbury, T., and K. Bardovi-Harlig. 2000. Oppositional talk and the acquisition of modality in L2 English. In *Social and cognitive factors in second language acquisition: Selected proceedings of the 1999 Second Language Research Forum,* edited by B. Swierzbin, R. Morris, M. E. Anderson, C. A. Klee, and E. Tarone, 57–76. Somerville, MA: Cascadilla Press.

Sapir, Edward. 1933. Language. In *Encyclopedia of the Social Sciences,* 155–69.

———. 1951. The unconscious patterning of behavior in society. In *Selected writings of Edward Sapir,* edited by P. P. Giglioli. Harmondsworth: Penguin.

Saito, Hidetoshi, and Masako Beecken, 1997. An approach to instruction of pragmatic aspects: Implications of pragmatic transfer by American learners of Japanese. *Modern Language Journal* 81, no. 3: 363–77.

Sasaki, Michiko. 1995. Unpublished data, National Language Research Institute, Tokyo.

Saville-Troike, Muriel. 1982. *The Ethnography of communication: An introduction.* Oxford: Basil Blackwell.

Schegloff, E. A. 1982. Discourse as an interactional achievement. In *Analyzing discourse: Text and talk,* edited by Deborah Tannen, 71–93. Washington, D.C.: Georgetown University Press.

Schieffelin, Bambi B. 1990. Epilogue to "Some sources of cultural variability in the regulation of talk." In *Cultural communication and interactional contact,* edited by Donald Carbaugh, 345–47. Hillsdale, N.J.: Lawrence Erlbaum.

Schieffelin, Bambi B., and Elinor Ochs, eds. 1986. *Language socialization across cultures.* Cambridge: Cambridge University Press.

Schiffrin, Deborah. 1994. *Approaches to discourse.* Oxford: Basil Blackwell.

Schmidt, Richard W. 1993. Consciousness, learning, and interlanguage pragmatics. In *Interlanguage pragmatics,* edited by Gabriele Kasper and Shoshana Blum-Kulka, 21–42. Oxford: Oxford University Press.

Schmidt, Richard W., and Jack C. Richards. 1980. Speech acts and second language teaching. *Applied Linguistics* 1, no. 2: 129–57.

Scollon, Ron, and Suzanne Wong Scollon. 1983. Face in interethnic communication. In *Language and communication,* edited by Jack C. Richards and Richard W. Schmidt, 156–90. London: Longman.

———. 1995. *Intercultural communication.* Oxford: Blackwell.

Searle, John R. 1969. *Speech acts: An essay in the philosophy of language.* Cambridge: Cambridge University Press.

Selinker, Larry. 1972. Interlanguage. *International Review of Applied Linguistics* 10: 209–31.

Shea, David P. 1994. Perspective and production: Structuring conversational participation across cultural borders. *Pragmatics,* 4, no. 3: 357–90.

Shiraishi, Tomoyo. 1997. Pragmatics of Requests in Japanese: A Look at V + *te-kudasai*. Senior thesis, International Christian University.

Siegal, Meryl. 1994. Looking East: Identity construction and white women learning Japanese. Ph.D. diss., University of California at Berkeley.

———. 1996. The role of learner subjectivity in second language sociolinguistic competency: Western women learning Japanese. *Applied Linguistics* 17, no. 3: 356–82.

Sinclair, John, and David Brazil. 1982. *Teacher talk*. Oxford: Oxford University Press.

Slade, D., and L. Norris, 1986. Teaching casual conversation: Topics, strategies, and interactional skills. Adelaide, Australia: National Curriculum Resource Center.

Smith, Robert J. 1983. *Japanese society: Tradition, self, and the social order*. Cambridge: Cambridge University Press.

Spender, Dale. 1985. *Man made language*. London: Routledge and Kegan Paul.

Sperber, Dan, and Deirdre Wilson. 1986. *Relevance: Communication and cognition*. Oxford: Basil Blackwell.

———. 1997. Remarks on relevance theory and the social sciences. *Multilingua* 16, nos. 2–3: 134–52.

Steinberg Du, Jinwen. 1995. Performance of face-threatening acts in Chinese: Complaining, giving bad news, and disagreeing. In *Pragmatics of Chinese as native and target language*, edited by Gabriele Kasper, 167–206. Honolulu: University of Hawaii at Manoa Press.

Stilwell Peccei, Jean. 1999. *Pragmatics*. London: Routledge.

Stubbs, Michael. 1983. *Discourse analysis: The sociolinguistic analysis of natural language*. Oxford: Basil Blackwell.

Sweetser, Eve E. 1990. *From etymology to pragmatics: Metaphorical and cultural aspects of semantic structures*. Cambridge: Cambridge University Press.

Talbot, Mary M. 1994. Relevance. In *The encyclopedia of language and linguistics*, edited by J. R. Asher, 6:3524–27. Oxford: Pergamon Press.

Tanaka, Mari. 1997a. The acquisition of indirect-passive in Japanese as a foreign/second language. Paper presented at the Tenth Biennial Conference of the Japanese Studies Association of Australia, Japanese Studies Centre, Monash University, Melbourne, July 6–10.

———. 1997b. *The acquisition of point of view and voice in Japanese as a foreign/second language: The influence of the linguistic and non-linguistic environment*. Document no. 08680323. Tokyo: Ministry of Education..

Tanaka, Noriko. 1988. Politeness: Some problems for Japanese speakers of English. *JALT Journal* 9:81–102.

Tannen, Deborah. 1981. Talking New York: It's not what you say, it's the way that you say it. *New York,* March 30, 30–33.

———. 1984. *Conversational style: Analyzing talk among friends.* Norwood, N.J.: Ablex.

———. 1986. *That's not what I meant.* New York: Ballantine.

———, ed. 1993a. *Framing in discourse.* New York: Oxford University Press.

———, ed. 1993b. *Gender and conversational interaction.* New York: Oxford University Press.

Tateyama, Yumiko, Gabriele Kasper, Lara P. Mui, Hui-Mian Tay, and Ong-on Thananart. 1997. Explicit and implicit teaching of pragmatic routines. In *Pragmatics and Language Learning,* edited by Larry F. Bouton, monograph series, vol. 8, 163–78. Urbana: Division of English as an International Language, University of Illinois.

Taylor, D. M., R. Meynard, and E. Rheault. 1977. Threat to ethnic identity and second-language learning. In *Language, ethnicity, and intergroup relations,* edited by Howard Giles, 99–118. London: Academic Press.

Taylor, David S. 1988. The meaning and use of the term "competence" in linguistics and applied linguistics. *Applied Linguistics* 9, no. 2: 148–68.

TESOL Quarterly. 1997. Special Issue, Language and identity. Vol. 31, no. 3.

Thomas, Jenny. 1983. Cross-cultural pragmatic failure. *Applied Linguistics* 4, no. 2: 91–112.

———. 1995. *Meaning in interaction: An introduction to pragmatics.* London: Longman.

———. 1997. Pragmatics and English language teaching. Typescript.

Thomason, W. Ray, and Robert Hopper. 1992. Pauses, transition relevance, and speaker change. *Human Communication Research* 18, no. 3: 429–44.

Tsui, Amy. 1994. *English conversation.* Oxford: Oxford University Press.

Tudge, Jonathan. 1990. Vygotsky, the zone of proximal development, and peer collaboration: Implications for classroom practice. In *Vygotsky and education: Instructional implications and applications of sociohistorical psychology,* edited by Luis C. Moll, 155–72. Cambridge: Cambridge University Press.

Turner, Joan M., and Masako K. Hiraga. 1996. Elaborating elaboration in academic tutorials: Changing cultural assumptions. In *Change and language,* edited by Hywel Coleman and Lynn Cameron, 131–40. Clevedon, U.K.: Multilingual Matters.

Turner, Ken. 1995. The principal principles of pragmatic inference: Cooperation. Typescript.

———. 1996. The principal principles of pragmatic inference: Politeness. *Language Teaching* 29:1–13.

van Ek, Jan. 1975. *The threshold level.* Strasbourg: Council of Europe, and Oxford: Pergamon Press.

Vygotsky, L. S. 1962. *Thought and language.* Edited by Eugenia Hanfmann and Gertrude Vakar. Cambridge: MIT Press.

———. 1978. *Mind in society.* Cambridge, Mass: Harvard University Press.

Wall, Allie Patricia. 1987. *Say it naturally: Verbal strategies for authentic communication.* Orlando, Fla.: Harcourt Brace.

Watanabe, Suwako. 1993. Cultural differences in framing: American and Japanese group discussions. In *Framing in discourse,* edited by Deborah Tannen, 176–290. New York: Oxford University Press.

Weedon, C. 1987. Feminist practice and poststructuralist theory. London: Blackwell.

Weizman, Elda. 1989. Requestive hints. In *Cross-cultural pragmatics: Requests and apologies,* edited by Shoshana Blum-Kulka, Juliane House, and Gabriele Kasper, 71–95. Norwood, N.J.: Ablex.

Weizman, Elda, and Shoshana Blum-Kulka. 1996. Misunderstandings in news interviews. Paper presented at Eleventh World Congress of Applied Linguistics, Jyväskylä, Finland, August 4–9.

Wertsch, J. 1991. *Voices of the mind: A sociocultural approach to mediated action.* Cambridge: Harvard University Press.

White, Ron. 1993. Saying please: Pragmalinguistic failure in English interaction. *English Language Teaching Journal* 47, no. 3: 193–202.

Whorf, B. L. 1941. The relation of habitual thought and behavior to language. In *Language, culture, and personality: Essays in memory of Edward Sapir,* edited by L. Spier. Menasha, Wis.: Sapir Memorial Publication Fund, 75–93.

Widdowson, Henry G. 1978. *Teaching language as communication.* Oxford: Oxford University Press.

Wierzbicka, Anna. 1991. *Cross-cultural pragmatics: The semantics of human interaction.* Berlin: de Gruyter.

Wilkins, David. 1976. *Notional syllabuses. A taxonomy and its relevance to foreign language curriculum development.* Oxford: Oxford University Press.

Wilson, Deirdre, and Dan Sperber. 1986. *Pragmatics: An overview.* Centre for Language and Communication Studies Occasional Paper No. 16, Trinity College, Dublin.

———. 1992. On verbal irony. *Lingua* 87:53–76.

Wittgenstein, Ludwig. 1958. *Philosophical investigations.* Oxford: Blackwell.

Woken, Miles, and John Swales. 1989. Expertise and authority in native–non-native conversations: The need for a variable account. In *Variation in second language acquisition: Discourse and pragmatics,* edited by Susan Gass, Carolyn

Madden, Dennis Preston, and Larry Selinker, 211–27. Clevedon, U.K.: Multilingual Matters.

Wolfson, Nessa. 1986. Research methodology and the question of validity. *TESOL Quarterly* 20, no. 4: 689–99.

Wolfson, Nessa, and Elliot Judd, eds. 1983. *Sociolinguistics and language acquisition.* Rowley, Mass.: Newbury House.

Wood, D., Jerome Bruner, and G. Ross. 1976. The role of tutoring in problem solving. *Journal of Child Psychology and Psychiatry* 17:89–100.

Yngve, V. 1970. On getting a word in edgewise. In *Papers from the Sixth Regional Meeting, the Chicago Linguistic Society,* 567–77. Chicago: Chicago Linguistic Society.

Young, Linda Wailing. 1982. Inscrutability revisited. In *Language and social identity,* edited by John J. Gumperz, 72–84. Cambridge: Cambridge University Press.

Yule, George. 1996a. *Pragmatics.* Oxford: Oxford University Press.

———. 1996b. *The Study of language.* 2d ed. Cambridge: Cambridge University Press.

———. 1997. *Referential communication Tasks.* Mahwah, N.J.: Lawrence Erlbaum.

Zuengler, Jane. 1989. The influence of the listener in L2 speech. In *Variation in second language acquisition: Discourse and pragmatics,* edited by Susan Gass, Carolyn Madden, Dennis Preston, and Larry Selinker, 245–79. Clevedon, U.K.: Multilingual Matters.

Zuengler, Jane. 1993. Explaining NNS interactional behavior: The effect of conversational topic. In *Interlanguage pragmatics,* edited by Gabriele Kasper and Shoshana Blum-Kulka, 184–95. Oxford: Oxford University Press.

Index

Abou, Selim, 27
academic presentations, oral (OAP), 329–30
academic writing, 279, 281–82
accessibility, 187–88
action theory: coordination problems, 195–96; joint action, 49–50, 193–94; joint activity, 50–51, 195; signals in, 194; SLA, role in, 199; social dimensions of, 196–97
activation cost, 187
activity types, 13, 174–75
addressee, defined, 207
adjacency pairs, 159–64
advisement sessions, 326–29
aizuchi, 213–14, 216–17, 218–19, 220–21
ambiguity, 45–46
anaphora, 44
apologies, 235–36, 239–40, 244
Appel, Gabriela, 292
artificial intelligence (AI), 22–23, 90
Aston, Guy, 252
Austin, J. L., 164–66, 169, 170

Bachman, Lyle F., ix, 254, 296
Bardovi-Harlig, Kathleen, 245, 327–29
Barnes, D., 314, 324
Barnlund, Dean C., 238
Beebe, Leslie, 257
Beecken, Masako, 125
Bialystok, Ellen, 200, 259
biographies and histories, 38, 54–55
Birdwhistell, R. L., 283

Blakemore, Diane, 182, 184, 185–86, 187, 188, 190, 191, 192
Bloor, Meriel, 97
Bloor, Thomas, 97
Blot, D., 303–4
Blum-Kulka, Shoshana, 3, 7, 119, 123–24, 125, 148, 149, 226, 240, 241, 242, 244, 251, 252, 253, 256, 257, 259, 265
Bourdieu, Pierre, 300
Bouton, Lawrence, 259, 261
Boyle, Ronald, 275–76
Bradford, Barbara, 99
Brazil, David, 98, 99, 314
bridging reference, 191–92
Brindley, G., 258
Brown, Gillian, 22, 44, 62, 63, 91, 92, 93, 94, 95, 97, 317
Brown, H. Douglas, 297
Brown, Penelope, 14, 111, 113, 114, 117, 123, 124, 274, 275–78, 286
Bruner, Jerome, 294, 314
Brutt-Griffler, Janina, 303
bulge theory, 54–55, 281
Burt, Marina, 255

CA (conversational analysis). *See* conversational analysis (CA)
Cameron, Deborah, 75, 288, 302
Canale, Michael, 254, 296
Carlson, Joan G., 319, 325
Carlson, T. B., 207
Carrasco, Robert L., 308, 331
Carter, Ronald, 263, 266

cataphora, 44
Cazden, Courtney B., 314, 325
CCP (cross-cultural pragmatics). *See* cross-cultural pragmatics (CCP)
CCSARP (Cross-Cultural Speech Act Research Project), 240–42
Chafe, Wallace, 99, 187, 200
Chaudron, Craig, 314, 315
Chick, J. Keith, 303
Chodorowska-Pilch, M., 52, 253
Chomsky, Noam, 250, 254
Cicourel, Aaron V., 37–39, 53, 54, 55
Clancy, Patricia M., 217
Clark, Eva V., 258
Clark, Herbert H., 3, 5, 7, 8, 49, 50, 109, 167, 175, 191–92, 193–97, 207, 258, 287–88
classroom practice, 312–36; acquaintance with learners, 330–32; advisement sessions, 326–29; ethnographic monitoring, 331–32; group work, 319, 324–25; impression management, 312; inequality in, 312–13; initiation, feedback, response (IRF), 321, 323; interaction patterns, 320–22; interactive practice (teacher-student talk), 322–24; learning opportunities, importance of, 319–20; lexical chaining, 323–24; materials, 262–63, 316–18; oral academic presentations (OAP), 329–30; other learners, 318–19; research on, 313–15; second language identities, 329–30; teachers, NNS vs. NS, 302–3, 321, 325–26; teachers, quality of, 315–16; teacher talk, 314, 321–22; topic control, 325–26
closure, in action theory, 197
code model of communication, 49
cognitive psychology: in action theory (*see* action theory); in defining pragmatics, 9–10; of indirect speech, 120–21; metaphors for memory, 91–93; relation to pragmatics, 22–23; in relevance theory (*see* relevance theory [RT]); role in SLA, 197–201
Cohen, Andrew D., 73, 235, 239

communicative competence, viii, 254
communicative language teaching, viii
compliments, 116, 125, 147–48, 173, 235, 244
conditions of appropriateness, 168–69
Condon, Jack, 210
constraints: as characteristic of pragmatics, 29, 30; social relationships as, 109–10, 116; on speech events and activity types, 175
context: centrality of, 6–7, 8–9, 11–14, 19; contextualization cues, 26; co-text, as linguistic context, 14; defined, 14; and establishment of relevance, 188–90; interactional, 47–51; and meaning, 41, 42–43, 47–51; non-linguistic, 14; and preference organization, 156 (*see also* preference organization); and presupposition, 82–83; of situation, 12; of speech acts, 170–71, 175
contrastive pragmatics, 226–49; CCSARP, 240–42; conventional usage, 235–37; defined, 226; faulty assessment, 231; interactional dimensions, 237–39; job interviews, 233–34; pragmalinguistic failure, 230, 231, 232; pragmatic failure, 229–34, 253; requesting behavior, 231–32, 242–43; and SLA teaching, 244–45; sociopragmatic failure, 230, 231, 233–34; and speech acts, 239–44. *See also* cross-cultural pragmatics (CCP); interlanguage pragmatics (ILP)
conventional language: and CCP, 235–37; vs. conversational implicatures, 51–53; implicatures and CP, 138–39; indirect, 119; and interactional context, 49; vs. nonconventional, 4; presequences, 49; presupposition in, 82
conversational analysis (CA): adjacency pairs, 159–64; data-driven categories, 156; insertion sequences, 160; in preference organization, 155–56, 161–64; relation to pragmatics, 23;

transition relevant place (TRP), 158–59; turn-taking, 156–59. *See also* speech act theory
Cook, Haruko Minegishi, 71–72, 220
cooperation, in action theory, 197
Cooperative Principle (CP): vs. action theory, 193; conventional implicatures, 138–39; conversational implicatures, 139–40, 143–44; and indirectness, 137; limitations of, 146–50; the maxims (*see* maxims, Grice's); and politeness, 275; the pope question, 143; vs. RT, 182–83, 184–85; sentential connectors, 137–38
co-text, 14, 38
Coulmas, Florien, 244
Coulon, Alain, 12, 62, 74
Coupland, Nikolas, 193
CP (Cooperative Principle). *See* Cooperative Principle (CP)
critical discourse analysis, 24–25
cross-cultural differences: and CP, 148–50; in indirectness, 125–28; in listening, 220–21 (*see also* listeners, behavior of); in politeness (*see* politeness, cultural variation in); in speaker-listener roles, 208–9, 212. *See also* second language acquisition (SLA)
cross-cultural pragmatics (CCP): contrastive pragmatics (*see* contrastive pragmatics); defined, 226; difficulty of, 229; interlanguage pragmatics (*see* interlanguage pragmatics [ILP]); values and beliefs, 227–29
Cross-Cultural Speech Act Research Project (CCSARP), 240–42
Crystal, David, 7

data-driven categories, 156
Davies, Evelyn, 233–34
deductive/inductive styles, 279–82
deictic markers. *See* indexicality
discourse, defined, 31, 40
discourse analysis, 23–25. *See also* conversational analysis (CA)

Discourse-Completion Test (DCT), 240–41
dispreferred responses. *See* preference organization
Doughty, Cathy, 258
Dufon, Margaret, 287
Dulay, Heidi, 255
Duncan, Stanley D., 219
Duranti, Alessandro, 8–9, 12, 13

economy of effort, 38–39, 81, 190
Eggins, Suzanne, 95–96
Ellis, Rod, 251, 254, 258, 312, 320
endophoric reference, 44–45
Englishes, world, 303
entailment, 78–79
Erickson, Frederick, 211, 230, 331
ethnographic monitoring, 331–32
ethnography of speaking, 25
ethnolinguistic identity model, 263–64. *See also* identity in SLA
ethnomethodology, 27
ethnopragmatics, 8–9
etiquette, 112, 275, 283. *See also* politeness
exophoric reference, 43–44
explicatures, 185–86
eye contact, 208–9, 212

face: acquired vs. ascribed, 111; and CCP, 238–39; Clark's model, 109; compliments, 116 (*see also* compliments); defined, 110–11; distance, 116, 117; face needs, 112–13, 275; face-threatening acts (FTA), 112–18, 232, 238; imposition, 116–17; nicknames, 109–10; and politeness, 111–12; politeness strategies, positive and negative, 114–18; positive and negative face, concept of, 113–14, 276–77; power, 116, 117; on-record/off-record, 114, 115; redressive action, 114–15; thanking, 116–17. *See also* indirectness; politeness
Fairclough, Norman, 24, 124
Fanshel, D., 188, 242

felicity conditions, 168–69
Ferrara, Alessandro, 5–6
films, 267
Finegan, Edward, 98
force, 47
formal linguistics, 10–11, 16
form-function problems, 175–76
Fowler, Roger, 327
frames, 25–26, 92
Fraser, Bruce, 244, 275
Fraser, C., 14
FTA (face-threatening act), 112–18, 232, 238
Fujikawa, Yoshiko, 285
functional linguistics, 10–11

Gardner, R. C., 264, 296, 300, 301
Garfinkel, Harold, 27, 74
Gass, Susan M., 307–8
gender differences, 228, 307–8
genre studies, 40
Gillette, Barbara, 312, 318
Giroux, Henri, 303
given/new dichotomy, 98, 100, 187. *See also* prosody
Glendinning, Eric, 282
Goffman, Erving, 25–26, 211, 275, 278
Gonzalez, N., 319
Goodwin, Charles, 12, 13, 208
Green, Georgia M., 17–18, 62, 257
Greene, Judith, 91
greetings, nonlinguistic, 284
Grice, H. P., 126, 135–50, 275
group work, 319, 324–25
Grundy, Peter, 78, 84–85, 136, 169
Gu, Yueguo, 276–77, 278
Gumperz, John J., 26–27, 219

Hall, Edward T., 212
Hall, Joan Kelly, 322–24
Halliday, M. A. K., 10, 16, 95, 98, 99
Hartford, Beverly S., 327–29
Hasan, Ruqaiya, 10
Hatch, Evelyn, 54, 72, 172, 173, 244
Heath, Shirley Brice, 319, 321–22
hedges, 144–46
Hill, Beverly, 286

Hinkel, Eli, 117, 259–61
Hiraga, Masako K., 269–70
Ho, D. Y. F., 111
Holland, Dorothy, 228
Holmes, Janet, 70, 228
House, Juliane, 7, 240, 241, 244
Hudson, Richard, 286
Hymes, Dell, 9, 25, 173, 254, 255, 296, 331

IBM-Hitachi-Mitsubishi trial, 214
identity in SLA, 263–64, 297–99, 303–7, 329–30
illocutionary force indicating device (IFID), 166–68
ILP (interlanguage pragmatics). *See* interlanguage pragmatics (ILP)
implicated assumption, 191
implicatures: conventional, and CP, 138–39; conventional vs. conversational, 51–53; conversational, and CP, 139–40, 143–44; conversational, in indirect speech, 119–20; defined, 4; and presupposition, 85; in RT, 185–86
impression management, 312
indebtedness, 285
indexicality, 61–77; defined, 61–62; deixis, defined, 63–64; discourse deixis, 72–73; indeterminacy of, 62; indexical, defined, 61, 62; and listeners, behavior of, 209–10; person deixis, 64–66; proximal terms, 64; reported speech, 73–74; shared knowledge, importance of, 63; social deixis, 68–72; spatial deixis, 66; tag questions, 74–75; temporal deixis, 66–68
indirectness: baited, 126; conventional language, 119; conversational implicature, 119–20; and CP, 137; indirectness strategies, 119–20; indirect speech act, defined, 119; intentionality, 120; intercultural differences in, 125–28; pointed, 126; and politeness, 118–22, 124; purposes of, 122–25; risks and costs, 120–21; scale of, 121–22; signifying, 126–28. *See also* face; politeness

Index • 361

inductive/deductive styles, 279–82
inferencing: entailment, 78–79; in pragmatic meaning, 4, 10; presupposition (*see* presupposition); in RT, 184–85
information, Grice's focus on, 146–48
information structure, 90–107; frames, 92; intonation, 98–100; linearizaton, 94, 95; mental models, 93, 94; metaphors for memory, 91–93; phonemic clauses, 99; prosody, 98; scenarios, 92–93; schemata, 93; scripts, 92; staging, 95–98; thematizing, 97–98; topic-comment vs. theme/rheme, 100–102
initiation, feedback, response (IRF), 321, 323
insertion sequences, 160
integrative motivation, 264
intention: felicity conditions, 168–69; Grice's model (*see* Cooperative Principle [CP]); illocutionary force indicating device (IFID), 166–68; importance of, 19–20; and indirectness, 120; and meaning, 46. *See also* meaning
interactional context, 47–51
interaction patterns, 320–22
interactive practice (teacher-student talk), 322–24
interlanguage pragmatics (ILP), 250–73; developmental stages of, 258–59; exposure to norms, 259–61; Japanese students, studies of, 268–70; key concepts in, 251–53; and learner subjectivity, 291; loyalty to L1 culture, 263–64; motivation, 264–65; pragmatic competence, defined, 254–55; pragmatic competence, development of, 265–67; pragmatic failure, potential causes of, 253; pragmatic transfer, L1 to L2, 255–58; teaching, quality of, 261–63. *See also* contrastive pragmatics; cross-cultural pragmatics (CCP)
intonation, 38, 41, 84, 98–100
IRF (initiation, feedback, response), 321, 323

Jaworski, Adam, 193
Jefferson, Gail, 23, 156–57, 158, 159
job interviews, 233–34
Johnson, Karen E., 315, 332
Johnston, M., 258
Jorden, Eleanor Harz, 176
Jupp, Tom, 233–34

Kachru, Braj B., 303
Kanagy, Ruth, 294–95, 321
Kasher, Asa, 22
Kasper, Gabriele, 3, 7, 226, 231, 240, 241, 244, 245, 250, 251, 252, 253, 255, 256, 257, 258, 259, 261, 264, 266, 320, 321
Kellerman, Eric, 320
Kirkpatrick, Andy, 280
Krashen, Stephen, 255, 293, 315
Kress, Gunther, 327
Kristoff, Nicholas D., 285

Labov, William, 21, 188, 242, 319
Lacville, Robert, 284
Lakoff, George, 228
Lakoff, Robin Tolmach, 65, 85, 150
Lambert, W., 296, 300, 301
language data, 30–31
language in use, 12. *See also* action theory; social action
Lantolf, James P., 292, 332
Latina (magazine), 306–7
learner subjectivity, 291–308; attitudes and motivation, role of, 296–97; enactment of, 303–7; investment, 300–302; pragmatic norms, defining, 302–3; presentation of self, 299–300; scaffolding, 294; self-identity in SLA, 297–99; and SLA teaching, 307–8; sociocultural context, importance of, 295–97; subjectivity, defined, 298; Vygotsky on, 292–95; zone of proximal development, 293–94
Leech, Geoffrey N., 15, 147, 221, 230
Levinson, Stephen C., 13, 53, 69, 72, 79, 83, 111, 113, 114, 117, 123, 124, 174, 195, 206, 207, 211, 274, 275–78, 286

lexical chaining, 323–24
Li, C., 100
Lightbown, Patsy, 258, 315, 321
linearizaton, 94, 95
linear processing model, 15–16
linguistic action/act, 3
linguistic anthropology, 13
linguistic politeness, 112. *See also* politeness
listeners, behavior of, 205–25; *aizuchi*, 213–14, 216–17, 218–19, 220–21; and cultural differences, 208–9, 212; designation of the listener, 210–12; listener's role, complexity of, 208–10; listener's role, defined, 206–8; LRRM (listening response relevant moment), 214, 215; outlouds, 211–12; Ping-Pong metaphor, 208; responses, frequency of, 215–17; responses, functions of, 217–19; responses, importance of, 214–15; responses, location of, 215; and SLA teaching, 221–22; and social attributes, 209–10; sociocultural values in, 220–21; turn-taking, 219; verbal/nonverbal cues, 213–14
LoCastro, Virginia, 9, 14, 24, 41, 43, 44, 65, 197, 214, 215, 216, 218, 242, 245, 257, 259, 262, 265, 306, 316, 317, 318
locutionary, illocutionary, and perlocutionary acts, defined, 166
logical consequence, 78–79
loyalty to L1 culture, 263–64. *See also* identity in SLA
LRRM (listening response relevant moment), 214, 215

Malinowski, Bronislaw, 12, 221
Manes, Joan, 244, 267
Mantell, Helen, 282
Masgoret, Anne-Marie, 300
Maslow, A. H., 221
materials, classroom, 262–63, 316–18
Matsumoto, Yoshiko, 276, 278
maxims, Grice's: and cultural differences, 148–50; defined, 140–42; flouting, 142–44, 146, 148; hedging, 144–46

Maynard, Senko, 70, 216
McAlinden, Fiona, 75
McCarthy, Michael, 6, 23, 74, 263, 266
McGroarty, Mary, 302, 308, 332
McNamara, Thomas, 298
meaning, 36–60; ambiguity, 45–46; biographies and histories, 38, 54–55; Cicourel's framework for analysis, 37–39; and context, 41, 42–43; co-text, 38; economy of effort, 38–39; force, 47; Grice's concept of, 136; hearer's recognition and uptake, 48, 49–50; intentionality, 46; interactional context, 47–51; in joint action and activity, 49–51 (*see also* action theory); linguistic and paralinguistic features, 38, 41; micro- vs. macrophenomena, 38; pragmatic, 51–53; product approach, 49; reference, 42–45; rights and obligations, 38, 53–54; sense, 40; sentences, 39, 40; sociocultural knowledge, 38, 55–56; the speaker's, 48; utterances, 40, 41. *See also* intention
mental models, 93, 94
Mercer, N., 294
metaphors for memory, 91–93
Mey, Jacob L., 18, 22, 61, 83, 192, 193
Meynard, R., 263
mianzi, 111
Miller, Roy, 147
Mitchell, Rosamond, 292, 293, 294
Mitchell-Keenan, Claudia, 126
Mizutani, Nobuko, 214
Mizutani, Osamu, 214
Moerman, Michael, 218
Moll, Luis C., 292, 319
Morgan, Marcyliena, 126
Mori, Michiyo, 36, 256, 268–69
Morita, Naoko, 329, 330
Morris, Charles W., 5, 15
Mortlock, Elizabeth, 229
motivation, 264–65
Myles, Florence, 292, 293, 294

naturally occurring vs. written language, 30–31
Nelson, Cecil L., 303

Nelson, Gayle L., 319, 325
Netsu, Machiko, 306
nicknames, 109–10
Niyekawa, Agnes M., 278
Noda, Mari, 176
nonlinguistic context, 14
nonlinguistic politeness, 282–88. *See also* politeness, cultural variation in
nonlinguistic signals, in defining pragmatics, 7–8
Norton Peirce, Bonny, 264–65, 296, 298, 300–301
Nwoye, 25

OAP (oral academic presentations), 329–30
Ochs, Elinor, 13, 14, 74, 192, 291, 292, 329
Ohta, Amy Snyder, 329
O'Leary, Kathy, 75
Olshtain, Elite, 235, 239
outlouds, 211–12
overhearers, 207–8, 211

Parsons, Talcott, 12
Partridge, Eric, 8
performative hypothesis, 165. *See also* speech act theory
performative verbs, 164–65
person deixis, 64–66
Philips, Susan U., 208–9, 217
phonemic clauses, 99
phonology, 6, 15
Pienemann, M., 258
Ping-Pong metaphor, 208
Platt, Heidi, 39
Platt, John, 39
politeness: defined, 111–12, 274–75; and form-function problems, 176; and indirectness, 118–22; positive and negative strategies, 114–18; and pragmatic transfer, 256–57. *See also* face; indirectness
politeness, cultural variation in, 274–90; criticism of Brown and Levinson, 276–78; greetings, 284; high-pitched voices, 284–85; indebtedness, 285; nonlinguistic, importance of, 282–84; nonverbal behaviors, 287–88; principle of greater effort, 286; universal basis of politeness, 278–79; in writing, 279–82
Pomerantz, Anita, 161, 162
Poole, D., 321
the pope question, 143
Porter, Patricia, 321
pragmalinguistic failure, 230, 231, 232
pragmatic failure, 229–34, 253
pragmatics, defining, 3–15; characteristics of, 23–25, 29, 30; cognition, role of, 9–10; context, centrality of, 6–7, 8–9, 11–14; defined inclusively, 15; ethnopragmatics, 8–9; functional vs. formal linguistics, 10–11; implicatures, 4; inferencing, 4; language data used, 30–31; as linguistic, 5–6; and nonlinguistic signals, 7–8; origins of, 5; as social action, 3–4; usage and use, 31–32
pragmatics and related fields, 20–30; cognitive psychology and AI, 22–23, 90–93; conversational analysis (*see* conversational analysis [CA]); discourse analysis, 23–25; ethnography of speaking, 25; ethnomethodology, 27; interactional sociolinguistics, 25–27; role of pragmatics in, 29–30; sociolinguistics, 20–21
pragmatics in the field of linguistics, 15–20; formal linguistics, limitations of, 16; linear processing model, 15–16; semantics, 17–20; semiotics, 15
preference organization, 155–56, 161–64, 275–76. *See also* conversational analysis (CA); speech act theory
presequences, 49
presupposition, 79–86; conventional, 82; defined, 79–80; flouted, 84; and implicatures, 85; pragmatic, 82–83, and pragmatic meaning, 85–86; processing of, 81; and prosody, 84–85; shared knowledge in, 83–84; unstated, economy of, 81
principle of greater effort, 286
product approach, 49

prosody, 38, 41, 84–85, 98
psycholinguistic approaches. *See* cognitive psychology

Quinn, Naomi, 228

Reagan, Ronald, 65, 150
recognition and uptake, 48, 49–50
redressive action, 114–15
reference, 42–45, 61. *See also* indexicality
relevance theory (RT), 10, 22, 182–93; accessibility, 187–88; vs. action theory, 193; activation cost, 187; basic tenets of, 184–85; bridging reference, 191–92; contextual effects, 189–90; contextual implications, 188–90; criticism of, 192–93; defined, 182, 190; degrees of meaning, 186–87; establishment of relevance, 188–90; explicatures, 185–86; vs. Grice's theory, 182–83, 184–85; implicated assumption, 191; implicatures, determining, 185–86; and semantics, 182; and SLA, 199
repair sequences, 163
requesting behavior, 231–32, 242–43
Rheault, E., 263
Richards, Jack C., 39, 234–39
rights and obligations, 38, 53–54
Roberts, Celia, 222, 233–34, 332
Robinson, M. A., 316
Rogoff, Barbara, 296
Rose, Kenneth R., 245, 261, 267
Rosenberger, Nancy R., 298
Rosenfeld, H. M., 212
Ross, G., 294
RT (relevance theory). *See* relevance theory (RT)

Sacks, Herbert, 23, 156–57, 158, 159
Saito, Hidetoshi, 125
Salisbury, T., 245
Sapir, Edward, 227
Sasaki, Michiko, 108, 141
Saville-Troike, Muriel, 25
scaffolding, 294
scenarios, 92–93

Schegloff, Emmanuel A., 23, 156–57, 158, 159, 192, 206, 217
schemata, 93
Schieffelin, Bambi B., 14, 291, 292
Schiffrin, Deborah, 10, 25, 26
Schmidt, Richard W., 256, 258, 259, 261, 264
Schultz, J., 211, 331
Scollon, Ron, 229, 281
Scollon, Suzanne Wong, 229, 281
scripts, 92
Searle, John R., 168, 242
second language acquisition (SLA): analysis of knowledge, 200; classroom practice (*see* classroom practice); and cognitive theories, 197–201; and indirect speech, 120, 125–26; and listeners' behavior, 221–22; and meaning, 36–37; and politeness (*see* politeness, cultural variation in); and pragmatic meaning, theories of, 132–33; processing control, 200; scaffolding, 294; and socialization theory (*see* learner subjectivity); teaching trends in, viii–ix, 250–51; and Vygotsky, 293–95. *See also* cross-cultural pragmatics (CCP)
Selinker, Larry, 251
semantics, 6, 15, 17–20, 40, 182
semiotics, 15
sense, 40
sentences, 39
sentential connectors, 138–40
shared knowledge, importance of, 63, 83–84
Shea, David P., 308
Sher, P. Berman, 303–4
Shiraishi, Tomoyo, 176
side participant, defined, 207
Siegal, Meryl, 259, 265, 296, 297, 299
signals, 7–8, 194
signifying, 126–28
Sinclair, John, 314
SLA. *See* second language acquisition (SLA)
Smith, Robert J., 210
social action, 3–4, 8, 11–14, 196–97. *See also* action theory
socialization, 291–92

sociocultural dimensions: constraints on, 109–10, 116; of context, 14; of high-order predicates, 38, 55–56; in listenership, 220–21; in RT, 192–93. *See also* cross-cultural differences; cross-cultural pragmatics (CCP)
sociolinguistics, 20–21, 25–27. *See also* preference organization; speech act theory
sociopragmatic failure, 230, 231, 233–34
Spada, Nina, 258, 315, 321
speaker's meaning, 48
speaker's role, defined, 206
SPEAKING mnemonic, 173–74
speech acts, classification of, 168
speech act sets, and CCP, 239–44
speech act theory, 164–76; felicity conditions, 168–69; form-function problems, 175–76; intended force, recognition of, 166–68; limitations of, 169–72; locutionary, illocutionary, and perlocutionary acts, defined, 166; performative hypothesis, 165; speech event analysis, 172–74; taxonomy, 168. *See also* conversational analysis (CA)
speech events: analysis of, 172–74; defined, 25, 172; in ethnography, 25
Spender, Dale, 210
Sperber, Dan, 10, 22, 182, 184, 188–89, 190–91
spoken vs. written language, 30–31
staging, 95–98
stress, 38, 41, 84–85
structures of expectation, 93
Stubbs, Michael, 79
Sukwiwat, Mayuri, 234–39
Swain, Merril, 254
Swales, John, 325, 326
Sweester, Eve E., 192
syntax, 6, 15

tag questions, 74–75
Takahashi, Tomoko, 257
Talbot, Mary M., 22, 193
Tanaka, Mari, 258, 261
Tanaka, Noriko, 316

Tannen, Deborah, 55, 217, 230, 231
Tateyama, Yumiko, 266–67
taxonomy, 168
Taylor, D. M., 263
Taylor, David S., 255
teachers, SLA. *See* classroom practice
text, defined, 31, 40
textbooks, SLA, 262–63, 316–18
text linguistics, 40
thanking, 116–17
thematizing, 97–98
theory of action, 12. *See also* action theory
Thomas, Jenny, 6–7, 40, 41, 45, 47, 120, 123, 229
Thompson, Sandra A., 100, 192
topic-comment vs. theme/rheme structure, 100–102
transactional information, 146–48
transition relevant place (TRP), 158–59
Tremblay, Paul F., 300
truth-conditional semantics, 17–18
Tsui, Amy, 171
Tudge, Jonathan, 325
Turner, Joan M., 269–70, 277
Turner, Ken, 184–85, 190
turn-taking, 23, 156–59, 197, 219

usage, defined, 31
use, defined, 31–32
utterances, defined, 40, 41

van Ek, Jan, 262
Varonis, Evangeline Marlos, 307–8
voice, high-pitched, 284–85
Vygotsky, L. S., 292–95

Wall, Allie Patricia, 262
Watanabe, Suwako, 9
Weedon, C., 298
Weizman, Elda, 123, 148, 149
Wertsch, J., 296
White, Ron, 231–32
Whorf, B. L., 227
Widdowson, Henry G., 31
Wierzbicka, Anna, 243–44
Wilkins, David, 262

Wilson, Deirdre, 10, 22, 182, 184, 188–89, 190–91
Wittgenstein, Ludwig, 13, 174
Woken, Miles, 325, 326
Wolfson, Nessa, 54, 244, 267, 281
Wood, D., 294
world Englishes, 303
writing, politeness in, 279–82
written vs. spoken language, 30–31

Yngve, V., 213
Young, Linda Wailing, 100, 101
Yule, George, 22, 44, 61, 91, 92, 94, 95, 97, 112, 157, 160, 317

zero anaphora, 44–45
zone of proximal development, 293–94
Zuengler, Jane, 252, 326